PENGUIN BOOKS

BLACKADDER

Richard Curtis wrote the Blackadders, *The Vicar of Dibley*, *Mr Bean* and bits of *Not the Nine O'Clock News*, amongst other things. He's been to a lot of weddings.

Ben Elton has written *The Young Ones*, the Blackadders, *The Man from Auntie* and *The Thin Blue Line*, amongst other things. He used to own a shiny suit.

Rowan Atkinson has appeared in *Not the Nine O'Clock News*, *Mr Bean*, the complete *Blackadder* series and *The Thin Blue Line*, amongst other things. His performance in the first series, *The Black Adder*, won him the coveted BAFTA Award for Worst Haircut.

John Lloyd produced *Not the Nine O'Clock News*, the Blackadders and *Spitting Image*, amongst other things. He's got very nice eyelashes.

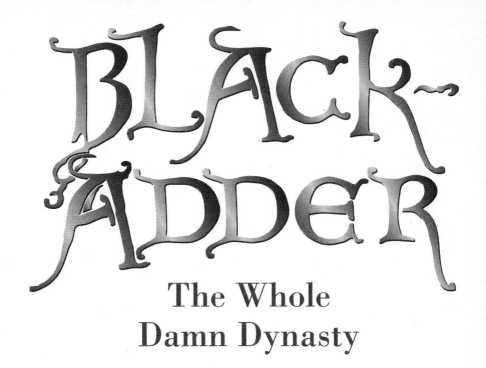

BLACK-ADDER

The Whole Damn Dynasty

PENGUIN BOOKS

PENGUIN BOOKS

Published by the Penguin Group
Penguin Books Ltd, 27 Wrights Lane, London W8 5TZ, England
Penguin Putnam Inc., 375 Hudson Street, New York, New York 10014, USA
Penguin Books Australia Ltd, Ringwood, Victoria, Australia
Penguin Books Canada Ltd, 10 Alcorn Avenue, Toronto, Ontario, Canada M4V 3B2
Penguin Books (NZ) Ltd, Private Bag 102902, NSMC, Auckland, New Zealand

Penguin Books Ltd, Registered Offices: Harmondsworth, Middlesex, England

This collection first published by Michael Joseph 1998
Published in Penguin Books 1999
5 7 9 10 8 6 4

THE SCRIPTS

XIII
THE BLACK ADDER

117
BLACKADDER II

233
$\mathcal{B}$LACKADDER THE $\mathcal{T}$HIRD

346
$\mathcal{B}$LACKADDER GOES $\mathcal{F}$ORTH

～ THE OTHER BITS ～

LIST OF ILLUSTRATIONS

The Blackadder Chronicles

PART ONE:

FROM THE DAWN OF HISTORY TO 1484

The history of these sceptred isles earlier than about 1800 BC is lost in the mists of time. What we do know is that, from earliest times, though Britain was relatively new, it was called 'Ancient', probably in an effort to encourage tourism.

In those days, the country was joined to Continental Europe by a land-bridge and it was probably by this route that Early Man arrived, around 800 BC. So British history began, and with it the dastardly chronicle of the Blackadder dynasty, agreed by all historians to be the vilest dynasty these British Isles have ever known – all historians that is, except Professor G. R. Blackadder, who describes the Blackadders as the 'nicest, sweetest, kindest, most like-a-bunch-of-little-kittens-in-a-basket type family of all time'.

The first recorded Blackadder was probably a Druid named Edmun. He worked as an overseer on the construction of Stonehenge, a job he apparently hated: a fragment of inscribed runes remains in which Edmun complains that 'five hundred ton pieces of granite hauled from North Wales are simply the wrong materials from which to construct a genuinely child-friendly slide-and-swing combination'. In order to do the work, he supervised a gang of motley labourers, headed by a certain fellow known as Bad Reek, on account of the noxious gases that escaped from his every orifice. Barely human as we would understand it, this stunted, unshaven thing was named by archaeologists as Homo non-erectus and his race nearly died out for two very obvious reasons.

In 54 BC the Romans arrived and Queen Boudicea of the Iceni saw the writing on the wall. 'The Queen is an Obvious Dyke' it read. The blame for this graffiti quite unfairly fell on the heroic figure of Blaccadda, who was summarily exiled.

The Romans brought with them death and destruction, but also decent plumbing and a wholly new concept called hygiene – something with which the Baldricks were to struggle in vain for the next two thousand years. Blaccadda, however, took to Roman rule like a duck to Chinese pancakes. He saw little future in the Ancient Britons, a race who laboured under the fatal misconception that painting themselves blue would in itself be enough to defeat organized troops. Swiftly donning a toga, he and his descendants integrated invisibly into Roman society, especially enjoying the part where it collapsed into anarchy, corruption and sexual decadence.

The Romans departed in AD 410, in such a hurry that they left both their Lions and their Christians behind. These continued gamely putting on shows – though with ever-dwindling attendances. Interest briefly rose when the billing was altered to Lions and Baldricks, but soon fell away again when the

Lions refused point blank to share a dressing-room at the arena with their opponents, still less put them in their mouths.

Soon it was time for the Dark Ages, a terrible time of darkness and filth and vile, putrid ignorance into which the Baldricks blended perfectly. The country was engulfed by wave after wave of Nordic invaders, Vikings whose entire ethos was based on getting drunk, fighting, having it off, and eating slightly unmanageable open sandwiches. Always angry on account of their permanent hangovers, these were truly the hard men of history, who made their cloaks out of live sheep and nailed cow horns directly on to their heads to impress the girls. It was a culture in which courage was valued above all things, and so (perhaps surprisingly) we hear little of the Blackadder family during this period.

The next recorded Blackadder does not appear until 1066, when the French invaded, cunningly calling themselves the Normans so they could sneak through Customs. The Duc D'Blackadder, we read, was ennobled by William the Conqueror for his helpful suggestion of compiling the Domesday Book so that the Normans would know exactly what to steal. The book's entry relating to Castle Blackadder reads: 'Absolutely Nothing Here'.

And so the British struggled on into the Middle Ages. For a while, this was a time of courtly love when it was possible to get laid simply by owning a pair of stripy tights and a lute. However, with the accession to the throne of Richard the Lionheart, the trumpets of war were sounded once again – much to the dismay of Blackadder the Chickenheart. The king's policy, backed not only by the Church, but by many of the kingdom's leading lunatics, arsonists and murderers, was that Christian principles would be best served by having a series of enormous battles in the desert with some people that they had never met. We hear little of any of the family in the long history of these foreign expeditions, until the exploits of Sir Edmund de Blackadder, leader of the disastrous 42nd Crusade. Undertaken over the August Bank Holiday weekend of 1972, this ended in ignominious defeat when the broadsword in his attaché case set off the bleeper at Tel Aviv airport.

The Crusades were swiftly followed by the Hundred Years War, known in Blackadder circles as the Hundred Years Hide, when the entire family spent the whole century in a large cupboard under some stairs in Northumberland. Coming up briefly to stretch their legs in November 1340, they noticed the Wars of the Roses going on, suddenly remembered they'd forgotten something and went back inside to look for it. When they emerged again, they quickly established themselves as distinguished horticulturalists, noted for having invented the world's first greenhouse. This ensured that they were never short of the right rose in their buttonholes when one army or other hove into view.

However, they couldn't avoid the fighting for ever. We join the first dramatized section of the Blackadder saga in the year 1484, on the eve of a great battle that would change the history of these islands for all time . . .

The
Black Adder

A Most Bloody and Most Gripping Historical Tale
by Richard Curtis and Rowan Atkinson

THE FORETELLING
From out of the swirling mists of the Dark Ages comes a lone horseman cursed from youth by a deformed haircut and sporting a particularly evil pair of tights.

BORN TO BE KING
Treachery, murder and Morris-dancing break out in all their full horror when an orange-faced stranger arrives at court.

THE ARCHBISHOP
The landscape is littered with dead Archbishops of Canterbury. Edmund's cunning plan is to get his deadliest rival appointed to the vacancy. It fails.

THE QUEEN OF SPAIN'S BEARD
The king's international treachery gives the hideous Edmund a chance to press his clammy body against one of Europe's most eligible princesses.

WITCHSMELLER PURSUIVANT
The king is a bit under the weather with the Black Death. Witchcraft is diagnosed by the Black Adder and only one man can root it out.

THE BLACK SEAL
In a final gesture of defiance, Edmund rides forth to seek out the Seven Most Evil Men in the land and return with them to seize the throne.

The Cast

Edmund, Duke of Edinburgh ....Rowan Atkinson
Richard, Duke of York (and later King Richard IV)...........Brian Blessed
The Queen ....Elspet Gray
Harry, Prince of Wales ....Robert East
Percy, Duke of Northumberland ....Tim McInnerny
Baldrick...Tony Robinson
Richard III ....Peter Cook
Henry VII...Peter Benson
Goneril ....Kathleen St John
Regan..Barbara Miller
Cordelia...Gretchen Franklin
McAngus, Duke of Argyll..Alex Norton
Jumping Jew of Jerusalem ....Angus Deayton
Celia, Countess of Cheltenham ....Joolia Cappleman
Sir Dominique Prique of Stratford ....Martin Clarke
2nd Wooferoonie ....Martin Soan
3rd Wooferoonie ....Malcolm Hardee
Messenger...David Nunn
Herbert, Archbishop of Canterbury................................Paul McDowell
Godfrey, Archbishop of Canterbury................................Arthur Hewlett
William, Bishop of London ....Arthur Hewlett
Mother Superior ....Joyce Grant
Sister Sara..Carolyn Colquohoun
Duke of Winchester ....Russel Enoch
Sir Justin de Boinod...Bill Wallis
Sir George de Boeuf ....David Delve
Lord Graveney ....Leslie Sands
Infanta María Escalosa of Spain....................................Miriam Margolyes
Don Speekingleesh, an Interpreter.................................Jim Broadbent
Mrs Applebottom...Jane Freeman
Revd Lloyd ....John Rapley
Mr Applebottom..Howard Lew Lewis
Lord Chiswick ....Stephen Tate
1st Messenger ....Kenn Wells
2nd Messenger ....Richard Mitchley
3rd & 4th Messengers ....David Nunn
Archbishop ....Willoughby Goddard
Princess Leia of Hungary ....Natasha King
Lady on Ramparts..Harriet Keevil
The Witchsmeller Pursuivant ....Frank Finlay

Lindsey, a Lord..Richard Murdoch
Broxtable, a Lord..Valentine Dyall
Tablett, a Lord ....Peter Schofield
Soft, a Guard ....Stephen Frost
Anon, a Guard...Mark Arden
Daft Red, a Peasant...Perry Benson
Dim Cain...Bert Parnaby
Dumb Abel ....Roy Evans
Dopey Jack ....Forbes Collins
Officer, an Officer ....Patrick Duncan
Jane Firkettle...Barbara Miller
Piers, a Yeoman ....Howard Lew Lewis
Mrs Field, a Goodwife ....Sarah Thomas
Mrs Tyler ....Louise Gold
Stuntman ....Gareth Milne
Murdered Lord ....John Carlisle
Trusting Father..Forbes Collins
Person of Unrestricted Growth ....Des Webb
Retired Morris Dancer..John Barrard
Mad Gerald...Himself
Pigeon Vendor ....Perry Benson
Friar Bellow...Paul Brooke
Jack Large...Big Mick
Three-Fingered Pete ....Roger Sloman
Guy of Glastonbury ....Patrick Malahide
Sir Wilfred Death ....John Hallam
The Hawk...Patrick Allen
Sean, the Irish Bastard ....Ron Cook

Prince Edmund trying to decide how to kill his barber

the Foretelling

History has known many great liars.

Copernicus. Goebbels. St Ralph the Liar. But there have been none quite so vile as the Tudor king, Henry VII.

It was he who rewrote history to portray his predecessor Richard III as a deformed maniac, who killed his nephews in the Tower.

But the truth is that Richard was a kind and thoughtful man who cherished his young wards, in particular Richard, Duke of York, who grew into a big strong boy.

Henry also claimed he won the Battle of Bosworth Field, and killed Richard III.

Again, the truth is very different. For it was Richard, Duke of York, who became king after Bosworth Field and reigned for thirteen glorious years.

As for who really killed Richard III and how the defeated Henry Tudor escaped with his life, all is revealed in this, the first chapter of a history never before told: the History of . . . the Black Adder.

SCENE ONE: THE GREAT HALL

The eve of the Battle of Bosworth Field, 21 August 1485.

A vast room with bare stone walls and a flagstone floor. Light filters down from the windows set high up. A couple of rich tapestries hang. Very sparse on decoration: a few candelabras are lit.

Various nobles and lords are gathered for a great feast. Richard III is addressing an enthusiastic gathering of lords. On his left sits Richard, Duke of York, a huge man with an enormous beard, who will soon be king, and his son, Prince Harry.

Richard, Duke of York
Silence. Silence for the king.

Richard III
Now is the summer of our sweet content made overcast winter by these Tudor clouds.
And I, that am not shaped for blackfac'd war . . .

Lords
Shame.

Richard III
I that am rudely cast and want true
majesty . . .

Lords
Never!

Richard III
Am forced to fight to keep sweet England
free.
I pray to heaven we fare well.
And all who fight us, go to hell!

Lords
Hurray! Hurray! Hurray!

Edmund
Hurray! Absolutely, hurray!

*Edmund is the Duke of York's second son,
a scoundrel with a stupid haircut. He sits
miles away at the far end of the table. His
over-enthusiasm leaves an embarrassed
silence, before a general heartiness is
resumed.*

Richard III
Who is that?

Richard, Duke of York
I know not, my lord. I'll ask my son.
Harry! Who is that?

Prince Harry
It is your other son, my lord.

Richard, Duke of York
It is my other son, my lord.

Richard III
Fights he with us on the morrow?

Richard, Duke of York
(*To Prince Harry*) What's his name?

Prince Harry
(*Quietly*) Edmund.

Richard, Duke of York
Edna! Fight you with us on the morrow?

Edmund
Oh, goodness no; I'll be fighting with the
enemy. Ha! Ha! Ha!

*He sits down. No one else laughs. They
never do.*

Richard III
You're not putting him anywhere near me,
are you?

Richard, Duke of York
No, Uncle. He will be somewhere with the
rabble.

Richard III
Oh. Arrow fodder?

Richard, Duke of York
Precisely.

*Richard III smiles and waves at Edmund.
Then says under his breath . . .*

Richard III
What a little turd!

*Edmund waves back enthusiastically, and
addresses the very foolish fellow beside
him, Lord Percy.*

Edmund
Hah. Percy, you see how the king picked
me out for a special greeting?

*Percy is the closest thing to a friend that
Edmund has.*

Percy
No, my lord?

*Baldrick interposes his head between
them. He's short, scruffy and, unexpectedly, quite clever.*

Baldrick
I saw it, my lord.

Edmund
Ah. And what is your name, little fellow?

Baldrick
My name is Baldrick, my lord.

Edmund
Well then, I shall call you 'Baldrick'.

Baldrick
And I shall call you my lord, my lord.

Edmund
I like the cut of your jib, young feller-me-
lad. How'd you like to be my squire at the
battle tomorrow?

*Baldrick goes down on one knee, deeply
honoured.*

Percy
It will be a great day tomorrow for we nobles.

He shoots a superior look at Baldrick.

Edmund
Well, not if we lose, Percy. If we lose, I'll be chopped to pieces. My arm'll end up in Essex, my torso in Norfolk and my genitalia stuck up a tree somewhere in Rutland.

Baldrick
No, my lord. With you at the helm, we cannot lose!

Percy
Well, we *could* if we wanted to.

Edmund
No, we won't, Percy, and I shall prove to all that I am a man.

Percy
But you are a man, my lord.

Edmund
But how shall it be proved, Percy?

Percy
Well, they could look up that tree in Rutland!

Edmund thumps Percy on the head.

Ow! Not in front of the staff, my lord.

Edmund
It shall be proved by my enemies rushing to the water closet in terror.

Baldrick
Hurrah!

Percy
Hurrah!

Edmund
So come, a toast! (*They all perk up*) Let all men who go to don armour tomorrow remember to go before they don armour tomorrow.

Percy and Baldrick
Hurray!

They clink glasses, a terrible trio, bonded for all time.

Edmund
Ha! Already I can hear the sound of battle ringing in my ears!

SCENE TWO: THE COUNTRYSIDE

On the brow of the hill over Bosworth Field, the three proud leaders – Richard III, the Duke of York and Prince Harry – deliver their battle orations to their loudly cheering troops. The sky behind their noble figures bristles with flags, spears and excitement.

Richard III
Once more unto the breach, dear friends, once more.
Consign their parts most private to a Rutland tree . . .

Richard, Duke of York
Let blood, blood, blood be your motto. Slit their gizzards!

Prince Harry
Now, I'm afraid there's going to have to be a certain amount of violence, but at least we know it's in a good cause, don't we?

Richard III
And gentlemen in London now abed
Shall think themselves accursed they were not here.
And hold their manhoods cheap while others speak.
Who fought with us 'pon Ralph the Liar's day!

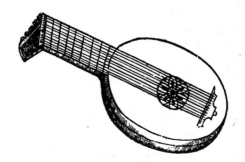

A huge cry resounds across the countryside.

SCENE THREE: EDMUND'S TOWER ROOM

Edmund's bedroom is quite a pleasant, light room in one of the castle towers. Edmund is fast asleep in his heavily tapestried, four-poster bed, snoring interestingly. Baldrick is fast asleep on the floor next to Edmund's bed. There is a knock at the door. The queen enters in a very merry mood.

Queen
(*Gaily*) Edmund? Edmund!

Edmund
(*Waking up*) Mmmh! Mother – what do you want?

Queen
Did you want to go to the battle this morning?

Edmund uncovers a sundial by his bed.

Edmund
Oh, my God. It's eleven o'clock!

He leaps up. Let's face it, he has overslept on a rather big day.

SCENE FOUR: A FIELD NEAR BOSWORTH FIELD

Edmund and Baldrick are galloping along on the horizon.

Baldrick
My lord, where is the battle, my lord?

Edmund
Somewhere called, oh, Bosworth Field.

They ride off.

Baldrick
Ah.

The horses neigh. They ride back going the opposite way.

Edmund
Damn! The first decent battle since I

reached puberty.

SCENE FIVE: NEAR THE BROW OF A HILL

Edmund and Baldrick ride on.

Baldrick
Here we are, my lord.

Edmund
Hurray! Onward, Baldrick, to glory!

At the top of the hill the noise of battle suddenly hits them, and Edmund's face goes white at what he sees. A real battle.

Yes. I'm not so sure we're needed you know, Baldrick. I mean . . . everything seems to be going very well, doesn't it? Everyone's fighting: clearly having the time of their lives. Some people over there aren't fighting. They're just lying down . . .

Baldrick
They're dead, my lord.

Edmund
Yes. Um. Damn, I knew I'd forgotten something. Would you excuse me a moment, Baldrick?

SCENE SIX: FURTHER ALONG THE BROW OF THE HILL

Out of the view of Edmund and Baldrick, Richard III emerges for a moment from the smoke of battle; unhorsed Richard, Duke of York, rides up to greet him. It is a massively hearty scene.

Richard, Duke of York
My lord, you have lost your steed: take mine!

Richard III
No, no: I have won the battle, I have saved the kingdom. I think I can find myself a horse!

Richard, Duke of York
Most true, most noble lord! I'll see you back at the castle.

Richard III
So be it.

He gathers himself together and strides gleefully on, in the merriest of moods.

A horse! A horse! My kingdom for a horse!

Then he spies Edmund's horse tied up before him. There is a shuffling in the bushes nearby and the odd metal limb showing. Edmund is relieving himself.

Ah! Horsie.

Edmund emerges in armour from behind a tree just as the king starts to untie the horse.

A neigh alerts Edmund to what's going on. He turns and unsheathes his sword.

Edmund
Oi! That's my horse!

Edmund scuttles over and cuts the king's head off with one simple, short slice.

There! That'll teach you. You won't be doing that again now, will you?

He moves confidently and picks up the head. As he picks up the head, the visor snaps open. Richard III's face is inside. Edmund snaps the visor down in horror.

Oh, my God: it's Great Uncle Richard. Aaaaaaah!

Baldrick
What is it, my lord?

Edmund throws him the head.

Oh, my God, it's Richard III. What are you going to do?

*The solution strikes Edmund.
He takes the head and tries desperately to jam it back onto Richard III . . .*

Edmund
Well, obviously . . . Come on, come on!

He manages to balance it for one, hopeful moment.

There we go . . . Now . . . wait!

But it is no good. He and Baldrick take a leg each and start to drag the body off. Baldrick has a bright idea.

Baldrick
My lord! That hut, over there!

They exit, dragging the body.

~

SCENE SEVEN: A WOODCUTTER'S HUT

Edmund
Come on, hurry up – pull. Pull! Come on, Baldrick. Pull your weight.

Edmund and Baldrick enter. Edmund carrying the king's shoes, Baldrick dragging the body by the feet.

Baldrick
Phewww.

A moment's pause.

Edmund
Where's the head?

Baldrick
I thought you had it.

Edmund
Baldrick, I can't be expected to carry everything.

*There are noises outside, Edmund and
Baldrick are terrified. Percy enters.*

Percy, you brainless son of a prostitute.
Where've you been?

Percy is very pleased with himself.

Percy
I've just proved that I'm a man. Look
what I've found.

He holds up the head.

Edmund
Oh, thank God. Put it down, Percy, and
let's get out of here.

Percy
No, I found it, it's mine!

Edmund
What do you mean, it's yours?

Percy
I'm going to use it as proof that I have
killed a nobleman.

Edmund
Which nobleman?

Percy checks under the visor.

Percy
Errmm . . . (*Proudly*) Well, it's the king
actually.

*Then he realizes that's not a good thing.
He throws the helmet with the head in
it to Edmund. Edmund throws the helmet
to Baldrick. Baldrick throws the helmet
in a barrel and they all head for the
door. Baldrick opens it and Henry Tudor
falls in. Their vile enemy. Not that they
recognize him.*

Henry VII
Lost. Lost. All is lost.

Edmund
What?

Henry VII
We must flee; flee!

Edmund
Oh, my God: quick.

Henry VII grabs his leg as Edmund is

making for the door.

Henry VII
Take me with you.

Edmund
Get your hands off!

Henry VII
If you leave me alone here, I will die.

Edmund
If you don't leave me alone, I'll kill you
myself.

Henry VII
I'll give you money!

*The door slams. They are gone. He shouts
after them . . .*

Ten thousand sovereigns.

*Percy's head appears back round the
door. He's interested.*

~

SCENE EIGHT: THE GREAT HALL

*The queen is standing in an alcove.
Edmund and Baldrick run in.*

Edmund
Mother!

Queen
Edmund dear, how did it go?

*Baldrick rushes to the arches at the other
end of the hall.*

Edmund
Within seconds, Henry Tudor will be here
at our gates.

Queen
Oh, Edmund, I'm not ready. I haven't
had a bath or anything.

Edmund
Mother, Henry is our *enemy*. When his
men get here they'll brutally ravish you
and every woman in the castle.

Queen
I shan't bother to change then.

Baldrick
My lord.

Edmund
What do you want?

Baldrick
Listen!

They hear the sound, ba-ba-ba-bum ba-ba-ba-bum, of distant drums. Edmund rushes to the window.

Edmund
Oh, my God, they're here already. Run for your lives! Run for the hills!

Baldrick
No, my lord, they are coming from the hills!

Edmund runs ineffectually back and forth.

Edmund
Run away from the hills! If you see hills, run the other way!

Percy
But they're flying the banners of our King Richard.

Edmund
That's impossible – he's dead, isn't he!

Queen
King Richard, dead?

Edmund is slightly caught out.

Edmund
Ah, yes. God knows how!

Queen
Oh, dear. That's really upset the tulip cart.

Edmund
Those flags are obviously just a cunning trick to deceive us into staying.

Percy
But, but, but . . .

The tramp of the army is getting closer.

Baldrick
I'm not so sure it's a cunning trick.

Edmund
Well, no, it's not a particularly cunning trick because we've seen through it . . .

Edmund locks the door.

But obviously they thought it was cunning when they thought it up.

Baldrick
I'm not so sure they did think it up.

Edmund
Oh, you think someone else thought it up and they borrowed it for the occasion?

Percy
My lord?

Baldrick
No, I'm not sure it's a trick at all.

Percy
I think we should go.

The tramping is now very close.

Edmund
You don't think riding up to a castle under someone else's banners is a trick?

There is a loud crash on the door.

Argh!

Percy
It's only your father.

Edmund rushes out and locks the door behind him. Baldrick tries to follow, and hides behind a tapestry. Percy dithers around the queen. There is another crash, the door falls down and Richard, Duke of York, enters with various lords.

Richard, Duke of York
Who locked that bloody door?

Queen
Oh, Richard, it's you.

Richard, Duke of York
Who did you expect it to be, woman?

Queen
Well, I thought it would be Henry Tulip.

Richard, Duke of York
Henry Tulip? Have you lost your conkers?

Queen
So you won?

Richard, Duke of York
Yes, of course! We won! We won! *Victory!*

All
Hurrah!

Queen
(*With a sigh*) So, I suppose now you want
to ravish me?

Richard, Duke of York
Yes, yes. In a moment. The woman's insa-
tiable! Three cheers for Good King
Richard! Hap hap!

All
Huzzah!

Richard, Duke of York
Hap hap!

All
Huzzah!

Richard, Duke of York
Hap hap!

*Edmund has now crept back and joined
them having realized his mistake.*

Edmund
Huzzah!

Richard, Duke of York
All we need now is King Richard with us
here, and the day shall be complete.

Queen
Yes, what a pity he's dead.

Richard, Duke of York
What?!

All are horrified.

Who told you that?

Queen
Edmund.

Richard, Duke of York
Is this true?

*All turn on Edmund, who two seconds ago
thought he was so safe. He backs himself
along the wall.*

Edmund
Yes, well I wouldn't know really. I mean I
was nowhere near him at the time. I just
heard from someone that he'd, er . . . I
mean I don't know where he was killed. I
was completely on the opposite side of the
field. I was nowhere near the cottage. Not
that it was a cottage. It was a river. But
then I wouldn't know, because I wasn't
there. But apparently some fool cut his
head off. Or at least killed him in some
way: perhaps took an ear off. In fact I
think he was only wounded. Or was that
somebody else? Yes, it was: he wasn't even
wounded, in fact. Why, did someone say
he was dead?

*Everyone is still facing him intently, when
from behind them comes Prince Harry,
carrying Richard III's body in his weary
arms.*

Prince Harry
Yes.

Richard, Duke of York
What?

Prince Harry
It is true, my lord. I stumbled upon his
body myself.

*He lays the body on the ground and kneels
beside it.*

Oh, pardon me, thou bleeding piece of
earth. Goodnight, sweet king. And flights
of angels sing thee to thy rest.

This isn't at all to his father's taste.

Richard, Duke of York
Yes, yes, yes. Very good, Harry. That's
enough of that. We all know who did this
dreadful deed, don't we?

*He turns to Edmund. Edmund nods slowly.
He thinks death must be seconds away.*

Henry Tudor!

Edmund nods vigorously.

Yes, and he still roams free. Harry, call
for silence.

*Prince Harry gets up, carrying Richard
III's crown.*

Prince Harry
Silence!

He places the crown on the head of the new king.

Long live the king.

All
(*Kneeling*) Long live King Richard IV!

The new king responds in a manner most sombre and Shakespearian.

King
This day has been as 'twere a mighty stew,
In which the beef of victory was mixed
With the vile turnip of sweet Richard slain
And the gristly dumpling of his killer fled.
But we must eat the yellow wobbly parts
the Good Lord serves
In life, each man gets what he deserves.

There is a moment of philosophical consideration by all.

Come on, let's go and kill some more prisoners.

SCENE NINE: EDMUND'S TOWER ROOM

The door opens and Edmund, Percy and Baldrick enter gravely. But then they explode with pandemonic joy.

Edmund
We're safe! And I'm a Prince of the Realm! Hap hap.

Baldrick
Huzzah!

Percy
Huzzah!

Edmund
Can you imagine the power?

Percy
Ours, all ours.

Edmund
What?

Baldrick
Yours, all yours . . .

There is a knock. They dramatically settle into gravity, and Prince Harry enters with a ledger under his arm.

Prince Harry
Ah, Edmund. I know it's a little early, but I would just like to get these battle averages sorted out. Who did you kill today?

Edmund
Ahmmm: no one.

Prince Harry
No one. Oh, dear. Right, I'll put you down for a duck, which I'm afraid takes you out of the running for the Legion of Honour.

Edmund
Oh, I see. Sorry: I thought you meant had I killed King Richard?

Prince Harry
What?

Edmund
What . . . what was the question?

Prince Harry
Who did you kill today?

He is very formal and organized.

Edmund
Oh, I see, right. Oh, well, let's think: ahm . . . well . . .

Baldrick tries to help.

Baldrick
(*Whispers*) Peasants.

Edmund
Pedants . . . pleasant pedant . . . peasants! Peasants! But they don't really count, do they?

Prince Harry
Only in the event of a tie. Nevertheless how many did you kill?

Baldrick sticks up four fingers, Percy five fingers to prompt him. Edmund is slightly puzzled.

Edmund
Ahm . . . four . . . four hand . . . hand . . . handred . . . hand . . . hand . . . hand . . . fifty. Four hundred and fifty.

Prince Harry
Four hundred and fifty! Good Lord! That's three times as many as myself.

Edmund
Yes, well, I had a couple of lucky breaks.

Prince Harry
And nobles?

Edmund looks at Percy and Baldrick but they are stumped.

Edmund
Ahm, well, there was, let's see. I think, Lord Coverdale . . .

Prince Harry
Who fought on our side, I believe.

Edmund
Yes, I think Lord Coverdale saw me slaying . . .

Baldrick impersonates someone – he tilts his hat and purses his lips.

. . . ahm, Warwick.

Prince Harry
Warwick the Wild of Leicester?

Edmund
Yes, that's him. I must say, he was pretty wild too: took some finishing off.

Prince Harry
Yes, indeed. I killed him myself at one point. Anyone else?

Edmund
Ahm. Oh, it's trying to put names to faces, isn't it?

Prince Harry
Here is a list. These lords, I think, are the ones as yet unaccounted for.

Edmund strains forward interestedly.

Roger de Runcie.

Edmund
Oh, yes, right: Roger de Runcie. He was one of mine.

Prince Harry
Lord Thomas of Devon.

Edmund
Yes, him too: backslash. (*Re-enacting it*) Right.

Prince Harry
Lord Yeovil.

Edmund
(*Getting into his stride*) Oh, yes: right. Groin job: yes.

Prince Harry
Well, that's remarkable, Edmund. Oh, and the Bishop of Bath and Wells.

Edmund
Will never walk again!

Prince Harry
. . . will conduct the thanksgiving service.

Edmund
Oh, Bath and Wells!

Prince Harry
Ah, Percy! Edmund tells me you managed to turn up to the battle late, so there's no point in asking you your score, is there?

And Prince Harry leaves. Percy is left behind, looking disappointed.

Edmund
Ha ha!

Baldrick and Percy
Huzzah!

Edmund crosses to the bed.

Edmund
At last I can relax!

He tears open the curtains around his bed: there lies Henry VII, dying.

Who the hell is this?

Percy
Ahm . . . you remember that dying man we saw in the cottage . . .

Edmund
The one I specifically told you not to bring back to the castle under any circumstances?

Percy
Mmmmmm? Yes, that's the one, yes!

Edmund
So what is he doing in my bed?

Percy
He claims he is a wealthy man. I thought if we nursed him back to health, he might reward us.

Edmund
Be quiet, Percy. I think I've got an idea. If he is a wealthy man, and we nurse him back to health, he may reward us.

Baldrick
Brilliant. That was quick thinking, my lord.

Edmund and Percy
Thank you, Baldrick.

Edmund glares at Percy.

Edmund
Yes, well, what would you expect? Who has the fastest brain in the land?

Baldrick
Prince Edmund, Duke of Edinburgh!

Edmund
Who is the boldest horseman in the land?

Baldrick
(*With Percy joining in*) Prince Edmund, Duke of Edinburgh!

Edmund
Who is the bravest swordsman in the land?

Percy
Oh yes, don't tell me! That's that earl from Norfolk . . .

Edmund turns round threateningly.

Edmund
Prince . . .

Baldrick and Percy
. . . Edmund, Duke of Edinburgh!

Edmund
Precisely. Or, as I shall be known from now on . . .

It is a great heroic moment, the birth of a legend . . .

The Black Vegetable!

He turns for applause.

Baldrick
Erm. My lord, wouldn't something like the Black Adder sound better?

Edmund
No, wait . . . (*he steps back*) I think I have a better idea. What about (*he steps forward*) the Black Adder?

They all cheer. A hero is born.

SCENE TEN: EDMUND'S TOWER ROOM

Three doublets are being held in front of Edmund: one orange, one gaudy green, one black. Edmund points at the black one.

Edmund
That one!

SCENE ELEVEN: EDMUND'S TOWER ROOM

Edmund, now with the black doublet on, is faced by three pairs of shoes – two different shades of brown, one pair black and with very pointed toes. Edmund points at the black pair.

Edmund
That one!

SCENE TWELVE: EDMUND'S TOWER ROOM

Edmund, now in a black cloak and doublet, is faced by three metal pots: one copper, one silver, one black iron. Edmund points at the roundish one, the smallest, black one.

Edmund
That one!

A few minutes later. The pot is just about to be lifted off Edmund's head, as the final cut is made to the hair. The pot is lifted off. Edmund stands up. Everything is just right: the hair, the black clothes, all the way down to the pointy-toed shoes. He smiles. He is perfection. With a now spectacularly daft hairstyle.

SCENE THIRTEEN: A CORRIDOR IN THE CASTLE

Edmund, Percy and Baldrick are walking along.

Baldrick
Very witty, my lord.

Edmund
Thank you, Baldrick.

Percy
Oh, yes, very, very, very witty, my lord.

Edmund
Thank you, Percy.

Baldrick
You're certainly wittier than your father, my lord.

Percy will not be outdone.

Percy
And head and shoulders over Richard III.

Edmund turns in fury.

Edmund
Is that supposed to be witty?

Percy
(*Scared*) No, my lord: just an example of the sort of thing you wouldn't stoop to.

Edmund
Go away!

Percy
Yes, my lord.

They leave and Edmund ducks up to his room.

SCENE FOURTEEN: EDMUND'S TOWER ROOM

Edmund enters and looks around to check no one is there. He goes to his bed and draws back its black curtain. The man who was dressed in armour is sitting there in bed. It is Henry VII.

Edmund
Oh, you're still here are you?

Henry VII
Ah, yes.

Henry is eating soup. Edmund has a vague flash of inspiration. He leans over the bed.

Edmund
Wait a moment, haven't I seen you somewhere before?

Henry VII
I don't know. I feel I have seen you before
also.

Edmund
Well, yes: I'm Prince Edmund, son of
Richard IV, in fact. Who are you?

*Henry is terrified, as he realizes the dead-
ly danger he's in.*

Henry VII
I'm . . . not important.

Edmund
Not important? So, you're not rich?

Henry VII
Oh, yes! I'm extremely rich, an incredibly
rich, modest person, who wishes to remain
nameless.

Edmund
Well, you'd better be rich: get better, get
your money and get out of my bed! Is that
clear?

*He reaches for a black parcel on a small
table, closing the bed curtains again. He
unwraps it, to reveal a small princely
crown. Edmund is aware of the presump-
tion, so he looks around his room again
before trying it on in front of the mirror.
He is very proud. And very alone. Then
suddenly he hears a voice.*

Richard III
Oh, yes, very fetching.

*Edmund turns and sees Richard III sitting
calm and relaxed in the chair behind him.
He screams, covers his mouth and continues to scream. Suddenly he stops and
looks at Richard in wide-eyed terror.*

And hello to you.

Edmund
Hello! Hello, sorry: it's a . . . I didn't
expect to see you like this.

Richard III
What, sitting down you mean?

Edmund
Yes. Yes. Sitting down. Good Lord, there
you are, sitting down. Why, I haven't seen
you sitting down since . . .

Richard III
Yesterday.

Edmund
Was it only yesterday? Yes it was. Good
Lord. How was your battle?

Richard III
Oh, fine, somebody cut my head off at one
point, but apart from that it went swim-
mingly. And how are you, Edna?

Edmund
Edmund.

Richard III
Oh, your father told me Edna.

Edmund
No.

Richard III
So, Edna, you loathsome little fairy mag-
got, how are you?

Edmund
How kind of you to ask, your Majesty. I'm
very well. It's very good to see you,
because frankly . . .

*He moves over to Richard III, who is still
seated.*

Richard III
Yes.

Edmund
Well, well, frankly . . . gosh, you look
well . . .

Richard III
Frankly what? Spit it out, you horrid little
scabby reptile.

Edmund
Well, frankly, everyone thought you were
dead.

Richard III
Well, frankly . . .

*His head lifts off his shoulders and flies
up to Edmund's face.*

I am!

Edmund screams, at which moment there is a knock on the door. Richard III replies politely . . .

Do come in!

Edmund
No, don't come in.

Queen
(*From behind the door*) Why not? Have you got someone in there with you?

Edmund
Ahm, not as such.

Queen
Is it a woman?

Edmund
No.

Queen
Is it a man?

Richard III's head flies playfully around the room.

Edmund
Ahm: well . . . yes, yes, it is.

Queen
You hesitated, Edmund. It's not a sheep, is it?

Edmund
No, it certainly isn't a sheep.

Queen
Well then, let me in.

Richard III's body and head are now together again.

Richard III
So, farewell, Edna: you'll be seeing me later.

His body and head separate once more and the body walks backwards. Edmund addresses the head.

Edmund
Have you got transport? If you want to borrow my horse again, or at all . . . not that you borrowed it before . . .

Richard III's body summons his head.

Richard III
Coming.

He disappears into the cupboard as the queen enters.

Queen
Edmund, are you all right? You look as though you've just seen a ghost.

Edmund
Yes.

Queen
Well, hurry up anyway. You're expected at the banquet.

She looks in the cupboard trying to find out what was going on earlier.

Edmund
Oh, yes, all right. Mother, you won't tell anyone about my oversleeping this morning and what have you, will you?

The queen closes the cupboard.

Queen
Would I? Do I tell people that your brother Harry is scared of spoons, or that your father has very small private parts?

Edmund
Ahm, no.

The queen moves towards the bed. Edmund panics.

Mother!

The queen turns to him.

Henry VII
(*Hidden behind curtain of bed*) Baa! Baa!

Queen
Oh, Edmund. It's the *lying* I find so hurtful . . .

Edmund
(*Looking sheepish*) Baa!

~

SCENE FIFTEEN: THE GREAT HALL

A lordly banquet is in progress again. Edmund enters; he is late.

Edmund
(*Greasily*) So sorry I'm late . . .

He tries to take the chair next to the king.

King
Hold! You dare sit there, boy? That was King Richard's seat – would you insult his ghost?

Edmund
Er. No. No. Sorry.

And suddenly Richard III materializes in the chair. Only Edmund can see him.

Richard III
Yes, find your own chair, you smelly little dog's pizzle.

Edmund
Wha . . .!!

He backs off hurriedly.

King
How many prisoners have we got left, Harry?

Richard III starts talking across them, but obviously he can't be heard.

Richard III
Well I'm not Harry, he's Harry.

Prince Harry
About a couple of dozen, my liege.

King
Well, send a brace up to my room, will you?

Prince Harry
Do you want them hung?

King
No, no, fresh ones. I must put in some work on my backhand.

Richard III
Hello, hello. Anybody there?

King
I wish Uncle Dicky were here.

Richard III
Don't Dicky me, ducky.

The king bangs the table for silence. Richard III reacts with irritation to the noise.

King
Tonight, honoured friends, we are gathered to celebrate a great victory and to mourn a great loss. A toast to our triumph.

All
Our triumph.

King
And I raise our royal curse upon the man who slew Richard, our noble king.

Richard III stands and points to Edmund.

Richard III
It was him!

Edmund
Oh, my God!

King
(*Annoyed*) Silence at the end there.

He continues with his speech.

Whoever it was . . .

Richard III
It was him . . . Edna.

Unfortunately no one except Edmund can hear him.

King
Wherever he be . . .

Richard III
He's down there at the end.

King
He shall be struck down.

Richard III
Then get on with it, you stupid oaf: there he is!

The 'Black Vegetable' reconsiders his chosen sobriquet

Edmund
It wasn't me.

King
Who said that?

Richard III
The idiot who killed me this afternoon.

Edmund
I didn't.

King
Well then, who did?

Prince Harry
It *was* actually Edmund who interrupted, sire.

Richard III
Hang the little slug.

Edmund
No! No! No!

He climbs under the table.

King
I will have silence! Come, dear friends, another toast to dead King Richard!

Richard III
(*Bored*) Oh, my God!

They all rise.

King
Gentlemen!

King and Lords
Richard!

Richard III
So, thanks for nothing. Thanks a lot. Thank you very much indeed. That's the last you'll be seeing of me, not that you've seen anything anyway.

Richard disappears and Edmund peeks out from under the table. He is soaked in sweat and very relieved.

King
Now we have silence, we shall continue with the ceremony of desecration. Produce the portrait of the Pretender, Henry Tudor.

The portrait is brought in at floor level and is just about to be held up. Edmund,

who is still under the table, sees it. He has an immediate flashback of Henry Tudor in his bed, eating soup.

Edmund
Oh, my God!

He crawls out from under the table and across the floor to the door. Percy and Baldrick look bemused at his behaviour.

~

SCENE SIXTEEN: EDMUND'S TOWER ROOM

Dead, ghostly Richard opens the door, and Edmund bursts in.

Richard III
Good evening.

Edmund
Where's Henry Tudor?

He crosses to the bed and throws open the curtains. Richard III is lying in the bed making baaing noises.

Oh, no!

Edmund crosses to the cupboard and opens it. Richard III is inside making ghostly noises.

Where is he? Where is he?

Edmund dashes to the window in a panic . . . in time to see Henry VII riding off outside. He runs to the door. Richard III opens it for him.

Er, thank you so much.

He runs out.

~

SCENE SEVENTEEN: THE WOODS

Edmund rides off in hot pursuit of Henry. He reaches some woods and comes across three witches, Cordelia, Goneril and Regan, wailing over a fire. He coughs self-consciously and they all jump.

Cordelia
Hail!

Goneril
Hail!

Regan
Hail!

Cordelia
Ruler of Men!

Goneril
Ravisher of Women!

Regan
Slayer of Kings!

This particularly worries Edmund.

Edmund
Begone, hideous crones!

Cordelia
Be not amazed!

Goneril
Be not overcome with fear!

Regan
Be not paralysed with terror!

This is a little strange, since they are a foot shorter than him. And he's not even slightly nervous.

Edmund
Why have you lured me here, loathsome drabs?

Regan
We bear good news!

Edmund
What news could such repulsive harbingers convey?

Goneril
Today has brought misfortune . . .

Cordelia
But one day . . .

All
Oh, glorious day!

Goneril
One day . . .

All
Oh, happy day!

Edmund
Yes?

All
You shall be king!

Edmund
Really?

All
Yes, your Majesty . . .

They bow low.

Edmund
Well, that *is* good news! God be with you, you snaggle-toothed vultures! History, here I come!

And he mounts his horse and rides off to glory.

~

SCENE EIGHTEEN: THE WOODS AGAIN

A few hours later. The three old crones are sitting round discussing Edmund.

Cordelia
He wasn't as I expected.

Regan
I thought he was *very rude.*

Cordelia
I thought Henry Tudor would be better looking.

Goneril
Yes, and not so Jewish.

Regan
More like that man who rode by just before.

All three of them realize their mistake simultaneously and hit their foreheads in one motion.

All
Oh, no!

Born to be King

SCENE ONE: THE COURTYARD
OUTSIDE A MIGHTY CASTLE

*In 1486, the second year of Richard IV's
historic reign and also the year in which
the egg replaced the worm as the lowest
form of currency, King Richard departed
England on a Crusade against the Turks.*

*People are milling around, waiting for the
king to appear. He rides out of the castle
into the courtyard.*

King
As the Good Lord said: 'Love thy neigh-
bour as thyself unless he's Turkish: in
which case, kill the bastard!'

*He left behind him his beloved son
Prince Harry to rule as regent in his
stead.*

*Prince Harry isn't quite sure of his father's
biblical accuracy.*

Farewell, dear Harry.

Prince Harry
Farewell, father.

*And his slimy son Edmund to do the tasks
most befitting him.*

*Edmund is smiling. The king looks briefly
at him.*

King
Edward.

*The King rides off, accompanied by a
splendidly dressed entourage. Harry
waves, anxiously; Edmund tries to look
concerned. Baldrick sidles up to him and
whispers.*

Baldrick
My lord, with the king gone …

Edmund
Of course! At last, a chance for some real
power!

SCENE TWO: OUTSIDE THE CASTLE WALLS

It is twelve months later. Snow is thick on the ground. Edmund is on horseback, imperiously shouting instructions, and waving his sword.

Edmund
Come on, you scum! Move it: I want you back to the castle by sundown, or you'll all be slaughtered. Onward!

However, all is not as grand as it seems. Edmund is actually herding a small flock of sheep.

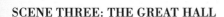

SCENE THREE: THE GREAT HALL

Prince Harry is reading a letter by the fire and beaming.

Prince Harry
Splendid. Splendid!

He looks up at the sound of a door opening. Edmund is trying to close the door on the sheep, who have evidently followed him home. Loud baaing noises from outside.

Edmund
Now look! You're not supposed to be here! That's far enough. Now get out!

He finally slams the door on the determined sheep.

My God, just wait till I get my hands on that bastard brother Harry.

He turns and sees Prince Harry, and tries to hide behind the wall.

Prince Harry
Ah, Edmund. There you are. Splendid news. (*He blocks the fire*) Father's coming home. He'll be here by St Leonard's Day. So we can celebrate both events together. I'll handle the visiting royalty, the guards of honour, and the papal legate. And you can sort out the frolics.

Edmund
The frolics?

Prince Harry
Yes, the Morris dancers, the eunuchs, and the bearded women. You know, the traditional St Leonard's Day entertainment. Damnation, I won't have enough time to attend to the drains. Edmund, you'll have to look into those as well.

Edmund
Um. Yes. Fine, fine. Ahm, I'd be honoured.

Prince Harry
Good. You won't let me down, will you?

Edmund
No, no. I won't. I'm really looking forward to it already. Thank you so very much.

Prince Harry
Splendid.

Edmund
Oh, no! Twelve months of chasing sheep and straightening the royal portraits, and now this. The bastard! The bastard!

Baldrick suddenly appears. A strange, insinuating figure.

Baldrick
If only he *were*, my lord.

Edmund
What?

Baldrick
If only he were a bastard, my lord: then you would be regent now!

Edmund
Ah, yes! And then one day …

Percy also appears as if from nowhere.

Percy
You would be king, my lord.

Edmund
Ah, yes, I would be king. And then what?

Baldrick and Percy
You'd rule the world, my lord.

Edmund
Precisely! It's just not fair, you know:

every other woman in the Court has bastard sons, but not my mother. Oh, no! She's so damn pure she doesn't dare look down in case she notices her own breasts.

SCENE FOUR: THE GREAT HALL

The queen is by a fire with a rather fulsome lady-in-waiting, yarning wool.

Lady-in-waiting
You must be *so* looking forward to the king's return, your Majesty.

Queen
No.

Lady-in-waiting
No, my lady? But think, he will come to your chamber and make mad, passionate love to you!

Queen
Yes, and I wish he wouldn't do that. It's very difficult to sleep with that sort of thing going on, you know. Being used all night long. Like the outside of a sausage roll.

Lady-in-waiting
Still, my lady: we've got the St Leonard's Day celebrations to look forward to. The jesters, the jugglers . . .

Queen
The great brown ox, steaming and smouldering all night long.

Lady-in-waiting
Oh yes: the feast!

Queen
Sorry. No, I was thinking of something else.

Lady-in-waiting
I particularly hope they've got the Morris dancers: I *love* them.

Queen
Yes: I like the eunuchs.

Lady-in-waiting
Oh, yes! The *eunuchs*! I wish I owned one.

Queen
I wish I'd married one.

SCENE FIVE: EDMUND'S TOWER ROOM

Baldrick is on the bed. Percy is sitting at the table reading a scroll. A well-built woman is just leaving Edmund's room.

Edmund
No, that's all right! Fine, fine. Could have happened to anyone.

He shuts the door. Percy and Baldrick are looking wary.

Oh, my God. We've only got one act, and she's shaved her beard off.

Percy inspects the scroll closely.

Percy
There are the eunuchs, my lord.

Edmund
Oh, yes. So? The eunuchs and the

Amazing Beardless Woman. There must be someone else, there must be!

Percy
Well, there's the Jumping Jews of Jerusalem.

Edmund
What do they do?

Percy
They jump, my lord.

Edmund
What?

Percy
They come in and they . . . they jump a lot, my lord. It's a humorous act.

Edmund
Argh! There must be something else, surely? The Death of the Pharaoh! (*He grabs the scroll and reads from it*) Sir Dominic Prick and his Magnificent Strolling Wooferoonies perform the tragic ancient Egyptian masterpiece, the Death of the Pharaoh. Well, that sounds funny.

Percy
Oh, no, no, no, I found it very moving, my lord.

Edmund
Well, it'd better be funny or Prick'll get his come-uppance, I can tell you. Book him.

Baldrick is also reading a scroll. He gets off the bed.

Baldrick
What about Jerry Merryweather and his Four Chickens, my lord?

Edmund
What do they do? Lay eggs?

Baldrick
Yes, my lord.

Edmund
All right, book them.

There is a knock on the door. Percy opens it, takes a message and slams the door in the messenger's face. He hands the message to Edmund, who reads it and looks furious.

Percy
What is it, my lord?

Edmund
The eunuchs have cancelled.

Baldrick
Oh, dear.

Edmund
Ha! I should have known: never trust a eunuch.

Percy
What are we going to do?

Edmund
Well, I know what I'm going to do. Baldrick, give me an execution order.

Baldrick takes an order from his belt and hands it to Edmund.

I'm going to teach them a lesson they'll never forget. I'm going to remove whatever extraneous parts of their bodies still remain.

Edmund opens the door, where the messenger is still standing, and hands the order to him.

Take that to the Lord Chancellor.

He turns back to Baldrick and Percy. This is desperate.

Percy
We could have the Morris dancers, my lord.

Edmund
Not that desperate. Morris dancing is the most fatuous tenth-rate entertainment ever devised by man: forty effeminate blacksmiths waving bits of cloth they've just wiped their noses on. How it's still going on in this day and age, I'll never know.

Percy
Sorry, so do you want them or not?

Edmund hits Percy with the scroll. Prince Harry enters without knocking.

Prince Harry
Ah, Edmund.

They do not want Harry to know that

they're panicking, so . . . they all start bouncing and waving scrolls like the best Morris dancers. Edmund hits Baldrick. Percy hits Edmund. And Edmund brings it gently to a close.

Edmund
And rest.

Prince Harry
Oh! splendid. (*He claps*) And how are the entertainments coming along?

Edmund
Erm . . . well, very, very well indeed. I think it's going to have a slightly *spartan* look.

Prince Harry
What, Greek?

Edmund
Yes, that's right. Yes, a Greek look.

Prince Harry
So everyone's turning up?

Edmund
Absolutely everyone . . . So many people, in fact, that I've had to let the eunuchs go.

Prince Harry
Oh, no, no, no, no!

Edmund
No?

Prince Harry
No, that won't do at all! Not on St Leonard's Day: because, correct me if I'm wrong, Lord Percy, St Leonard himself was a eunuch.

Percy
Yes, that's right.

Edmund
Yes: that's why I thought it might be more tactful ... if ...

He looks up to heaven respectfully.

Prince Harry
No, no, no. To leave out the eunuchs on St Leonard's Day would be like, well, leaving out the Morris dancers, or the bearded woman.

Edmund
Ah, yes.

Prince Harry
And besides, as you know, we are expecting Father's Supreme Commander, Lord Dougal McAngus, at the feast and, as you know, eunuchs are his particular favourite. He's Scottish, you see.

Edmund
Oh, I see.

Prince Harry
Well, I'm relying on you, Edmund. Carry on.

Prince Harry leaves. Edmund is very angry.

Edmund
Oh, I see, so some carrot-faced, thistle-arsed Scottish orang-utan would like some eunuchs, would he?

Percy
Apparently he's a great warrior, my lord.

Edmund
Oh, that's what they all say. These Scots are all the same. Barbarians: half of them can't even speak English.

Baldrick
What do they speak?

Edmund
I don't know: it's all Greek to me.

Percy
They speak Greek?

Edmund
No – I mean it sounds like Greek.

Percy
Well, if it sounds like Greek, it probably is Greek.

Edmund
It's not Greek!

Percy
But it sounds *like* Greek. What's not Greek, but sounds *like* Greek? That's a good one, my lord!

Edmund
Look, it's not meant to be a brain teaser, Percy. (*Shouting*) I'm simply telling you that I cannot understand a blind word they're saying.

Percy
Well, no wonder, my lord! You've never learned Greek, of course.

Edmund
Percy, have you ever wondered what your insides look like?

Percy
Sometimes, my lord, yes.

Edmund draws his dagger.

Edmund
Well, then, I'd be perfectly willing to satisfy your curiosity. Oh, God, this Scotsman's annoying me already. I am the Duke of Edinburgh, you know! And Laird of Roxburgh, Selkirk and Peebles. I could make things difficult for him. As for the entertainments, oh, I don't know. Baldrick, you've got a beard: go and get yourself a nice dress.

Baldrick
Oh, great, my lord.

He is delighted at this splendid opportunity.

~

SCENE SIX: THE GREAT HALL

A small banquet is laid out.

Prince Harry
(*Standing up*) A toast, Mother, to Father's return!

There are hoofbeats outside, followed by the mighty entrance of McAngus actually on a horse. He dismounts.

McAngus
Noble Harry, Prince of Wales, Dougal McAngus places at your feet the spoils of an enemy at war.

He shakes his bag and a head falls out.

Oh, no, sorry: that's my overnight bag … here, behold treasures torn from the tor-

sos of the Turks.

He shakes another bag and various treasures fall out.

Prince Harry
Oh, McAngus, it fills me with joy and hope to see you. What news of the king?

McAngus
When we parted, he said he would return by St Leonard's Day or die in the attempt.

Prince Harry
Then we pray for his return: join us, join us, you must be starving.

McAngus
What about young Lochnivar?

Prince Harry
Ah, yes, him too.

McAngus
Come on, boy.

He brings the horse to the table, leaps over to Edmund's seat and they both start to feed.

And you must be the king's bit of rumpy-pumpy.

Queen
I am the queen.

McAngus
Aye, aye. I've got a message for you. My father sends you his regards.

Queen
Oh, do I know him?

McAngus
(*Insinuating*) Well, you might say that. He's the third Duke of Argyll.

The queen jumps at the sound of his name.

Queen
Oh!

Her embarrassment is covered by a little tweak on the trumpets. Edmund enters.

Prince Harry
Ah, and here's Edmund. This, McAngus, is the man who is providing the entertainments for us tomorrow.

McAngus
Ah, the eunuch! Pleased to meet you.
There's a groat for your trouble.

Edmund
I'm not a eunuch.

McAngus
You sound like one to me.

Edmund
I am not a eunuch. I am the Duke of
Edinburgh.

McAngus
Oh, you are, are you?

Edmund
Yes.

McAngus
(*To the queen*) Same old story, eh? Duke of
Edinburgh and about as Scottish as the
Queen of England's tits.

Edmund squeals a bit.

Oh, no offence. Sorry, your Majesty.

Edmund
I'm sorry: you're in my chair.

McAngus
Don't apologize.

*Edmund kneels at the other side of the
table.*

Prince Harry
Well, now we've all got to know each other,
I've got rather a special announcement to
make.

McAngus
Don't tell me. You are a eunuch as well?

Prince Harry
McAngus, as reward for your heroic deeds
in battle, my father here empowers me to
grant you anything you may desire of me.

Edmund
(*To the horse*) If he's got any sense, he'll
ask for a haircut.

McAngus
My lord, I am honoured: all I ask you for
is a scrap of land: grant me fair Selkirk
and the noble shire of Roxburgh.

Edmund
(*Stands*) What?

Prince Harry
Very well. By the power vested in me . . .

Edmund
Ah, excuse me . . . I'm sorry to dip my little fly in your ointment, but those lands do
in fact belong to me.

Prince Harry
Yes?

He doesn't see the problem.

Edmund
Well, so perhaps he'd like to choose somewhere else.

Prince Harry
McAngus?

McAngus
No, no, I'll have Roxburgh and Selkirk.

Edmund
But that leaves me with Peebles!

McAngus
Oh, and Peebles!

Edmund
Urgh!

Prince Harry
Splendid. Are you trying to say something,
Edmund?

Edmund
Well, I don't know. (*Utter frustration*) I
mean, some people might say, 'Well what
an absurd idea, giving half of Scotland to a
kilted maniac for slaughtering a couple of
syphilitic Turks' . . .

McAngus grabs Edmund by the neck.

. . . but no, *au contraire*, I say, let's
reward him.

Prince Harry
Good, good. So be it. Granted.

*McAngus shakes Prince Harry's hand and
twists Edmund's collar. Edmund squeaks
out his response.*

Edmund
Hurray!

SCENE SEVEN: EDMUND'S TOWER ROOM

Edmund enters in a rage. Percy and Baldrick are in his room. Baldrick is in drag doing a turn.

Edmund
I'm going to kill him. And I'm going to kill him now.

Percy
Who, my lord?

Edmund
That stinking Scottish weasel.

Baldrick
Why, my lord?

Edmund
Because he's a thieving, stinking Scottish weasel.

Percy
How?

Edmund
I'm going to stab him.

Baldrick
Where?

Edmund
In the Great Hall and in the bladder.

He sharpens his knife.

Percy
But if you stab him in front of everybody, won't they suspect?

Edmund
Yes, a drawback. Perhaps we need some-thing . . . a little more cunning.

Baldrick
I have a cunning plan.

Edmund
Yes, perhaps, but I think I have a more cunning one.

He looks through the scrolls, which are still on the table.

Baldrick
Mine's pretty cunning, my lord.

Edmund
Yes, but not cunning enough, I imagine.

Baldrick
Well, it depends how cunning you mean, my lord.

Edmund
Well, I mean pretty damn cunning. How cunning do you think I mean?

Baldrick
Mine's *quite* cunning, my lord.

Edmund
All right then, let's hear it, let's hear what's so damn cunning.

Baldrick
Well, first of all you get him to come with you.

Edmund
Oh, yes, very cunning, brilliantly cunning, I ask him to come with me and then stab him perhaps. How cunning can you get?

Baldrick
No, my lord, you get this enormous great cannon . . .

Edmund
Oh, I see, take him outside, get him to stick his head down a cannon, then blow it off. Oh yes, Baldrick, that's a wonderful idea. No . . . I think I have a plan that will give us a little more . . . entertainment . . . heh-heh-heh.

He goes to the window and looks out.

SCENE EIGHT: THE COURTYARD OUTSIDE THE CASTLE

McAngus is in the courtyard of the palace. Edmund sees him out of the window. McAngus rides off, out into the snowy woods.

Edmund appears in the courtyard as the queen rides up. He pushes her off her horse, and climbs on.

SCENE NINE : A GLADE IN THE
WOODS NEARBY

*McAngus arrives at the wood, and dis-
mounts. Edmund is following him.*

SCENE TEN: A WOOD NEAR THE
CASTLE

*McAngus is hunting in the wood. Edmund
arrives nearby, sees his horse, dismounts
and creeps up behind him. As he gets
closer, he steps into a noose round his
ankle, which swiftly leaves him dangling
upside down from a tree. McAngus does
not even turn round, but carries on
skinning the animal he's just caught.*

McAngus
Can I help you?

Edmund
Ehm, no, no, I'm fine, thank you.

McAngus
Good.

Edmund
I'm not in your way over here, am I?

McAngus
No.

Edmund
There is one thing, I was wondering if you
could do me a favour?

*McAngus stands up, and goes over to
Edmund, who is still hanging upside
down.*

McAngus
Uh . . . huh?

Edmund
I was wondering if you could help us with
the celebrations tonight?

McAngus
What, by staying away, do you mean?

He takes an axe and suddenly cuts the

rope. Edmund falls to the ground.

Edmund
The thing is, we are presenting a mystery
play by one of our leading thespianic
troupes, but unfortunately one of their
number is ill and I thought you'd be the
perfect person to take his place.

McAngus
Hah. Well, I warn you, I'm no actor.

*He plunges a knife casually into a passing
badger.*

Edmund
Yes, there won't actually be much acting
required. It's an ancient Egyptian piece
called the Death of the Scotsman.

McAngus
All right then, I'll have a crack at it.

*He throws his knife again and there is a
squawk.*

Edmund
And you can play the Scotsman, if you
like, who dies at the end of the play.

McAngus
Acting dead. Now that I *can* do.

He walks off to see what he has killed.

Edmund
(*More to himself than to McAngus*) Yes,
well, as I say, there may not be much acting required . . .

He turns and walks away.

McAngus
Oh, and mind the weasel pit.

*Too late. Edmund disappears into a hole
in the ground.*

SCENE ELEVEN: THE GREAT HALL

*The Jumping Jews are on stage, perform-
ing a routine of great pointlessness and
aimlessness: mainly hopping. In fact,
that's it. They hop a bit.*

*The audience has just finished a large
feast: there is food and drink everywhere.*

The queen and Prince Harry are looking pained, but trying to enjoy themselves.

SCENE TWELVE: BACKSTAGE

The Jumping Jews can still be heard onstage. Edmund appears, looking furtive, and carrying a bundle which he puts down on the table. There are three knives already lying there; he picks up one and tests it: it is retractable. He grimaces evilly and opens his bundle, which contains three apparently similar knives. Percy appears and takes the old knives away, then Edmund picks up one of the new knives and stabs it into the table. It does not retract.

He hears voices and is struggling to remove the knife when three men, dressed as Egyptians, enter.

It is Sir Dominic and two of his troupe of articulating actors, warming up by pretending to be trees, crouching on the ground and springing up as they walk in a line.

Sir Dominic
Tall as a tree! Let's see those branches waving and swaying in the breeze! Tall, taller! Now small, smaller.

Edmund
Sir Dominic! Have you made the necessary changes?

Sir Dominic
Yes, my lord.

McAngus enters, wearing an Egyptian headdress too.

Edmund
McAngus: meet your murderers!

The actors are pretending to be trees growing tall. McAngus looks unimpressed.

SCENE THIRTEEN: THE GREAT HALL

Back to the Jews again: it is the climax of their routine. They perform the first irregular movement, turn a bit on one of their hops, and then stop and bow.

The audience claps half-heartedly.

SCENE FOURTEEN: BACKSTAGE

The Jews are coming offstage.

Second Egyptian
How did it go?

One of the Jews takes off his big beard to reveal his own smaller beard.

Jew
Not *bad*: I don't think they really understood it, though.

SCENE FIFTEEN: THE GREAT HALL

The audience is clapping, politely.

The three Egyptians take to the stage with classical panache: they are very noble and conspiratorial.

Backstage McAngus swigs some wine.

Sir Dominic
We three are gathered with most bold intent.

Second Egyptian
Here by the banks of the graceful Nile.

Sir Dominic
Where camels ride and deserts blow.

Third Egyptian
To spill the blood of this Scotsman vile.

The queen and Prince Harry are puzzled.

Queen
What's a Scotsman doing in Egypt?

Prince Harry
I'm not sure: but apparently they've had very good reviews.

SCENE SIXTEEN: BACKSTAGE

McAngus and Edmund are watching the audience.

McAngus
Heh, heh. See your mother there. I met my father on my way back through France: apparently he and her used to whey-hey-hey . . .

That's a delicate sexual euphemism.

Edmund
Oh, don't be absurd. Such activities are totally beyond my mother. My father only got anywhere with her because he told her it was a cure for diarrhoea.

McAngus
Don't you believe it. There are some letters I found in my father's tent – and, by God, they're hot stuff. I tell you they certainly cast a wee shadow of doubt over the parenthood of young Harry for a start!

Edmund
Look, don't be absur . . . what?

His life may be on the point of changing for ever.

SCENE SEVENTEEN: THE GREAT HALL

Second Egyptian
A bagpipe strums,
Behold this way our victim comes,
For never was there tyrant,
This dusty desert here amid

As him born beneath the shadow of yonder mighty . . . Ben Nevis.

SCENE EIGHTEEN: BACKSTAGE

McAngus
Oh, that's my cue: I'm on.

He starts towards the stage.

Edmund
(*Frantic*) Letters? Letters? Where are these letters?

McAngus
Och, they're hidden away. I'll show you them later.

Edmund
All right.

McAngus exits on to the stage. Edmund realizes his mistake. If his plan works, McAngus will be dead in about two minutes.

SCENE NINETEEN: THE GREAT HALL

McAngus enters, and is greeted by the Egyptians.

Third Egyptian
Tutankhamun Macpherson, you come not a whit too soon. Say: is not the weather fair for this, the Ides of June?

He nudges McAngus.

McAngus
Aye, it is. What business do you mean? Delay me not, for I am bound for Aberdeen.

SCENE TWENTY: BACKSTAGE

Edmund rushes up to Percy and Baldrick, who are watching the action onstage.

Edmund
Quick! Help! Oh, my God! McAngus is going to die.

Percy
And not a moment too soon, my lord.

Baldrick
Carrot-faced orang-utan!

Percy
Thieving Scots weasel!

Baldrick and Percy
Death to the Scot!

Edmund
No, look, he knows too much.

Percy
That is why he must die!

Edmund
No! He mustn't! He mustn't – he has vital information . . . I've changed my mind . . . Oh, my God, what are we going to do?

Baldrick
Stop the show, my lord.

Edmund
How? How?

Percy
Well just say 'Stop!'

Edmund is getting extremely flustered now.

Edmund
What's our reason? What's our reason for stopping the show?

Percy
Because the knives are real and McAngus is just about to get killed.

No – he can't take the stupidity any more.

Edmund
Oh, you bastard.

Edmund leaps at Percy and stabs him with the retractable knife. At which point the penny drops . . . Edmund knows what he must do. The play is reaching the climax. There is not a second to lose.

Baldrick
My lord: quick!

Edmund suddenly galvanizes himself, grabs a makeshift headdress and leaps on to the stage with a false knife.

SCENE TWENTY-ONE: THE GREAT HALL

The actors have their knives poised, ready to stab McAngus. Edmund leaps in front of them.

Edmund
Stop! Sorry I'm late.

He stabs McAngus with the retractable knife. McAngus doesn't act dead, so he stabs him again. He is unmoved, so Edmund, exasperated, pushes him over.

It's not good drama, but at least McAngus is still alive.

There is half-hearted, polite clapping; Prince Harry looks relieved that it's over.

SCENE TWENTY-TWO: EDMUND'S TOWER ROOM

A bit later that plotty night Edmund is sitting at the table with McAngus. He is reading the promised, saucy letters.

Edmund
Good, good. Excellent. It's certainly my mother's writing. When did you say these were written?

McAngus
1460.

Edmund
The year my brother was born. Heh, heh! Baldrick, get in here.

Baldrick enters, still in drag.

Get out there and tell everyone the rest of the entertainments have been cancelled.

Baldrick
Why?

Edmund
Why? Because I've told you to, you snivel-

ling little rat.

Baldrick
No, why have they been cancelled, my lord?

Edmund
Oh, I see. Because I have a very important announcement to make.

Baldrick
Does that mean I have to take the dress off?

Edmund
Oh, get out! Get out!

Baldrick leaves. Blackadder laughs manically.

McAngus
You know, if you played your cards right, you could be king.

Edmund
Yes, one day.

McAngus
It might be sooner than you think: last time I saw your father, he'd just charged into Constantinople when they shut the gates on him.

Edmund
No!

McAngus
Yes: there were ten thousand of the Turks in there, armed with scimitars. And your

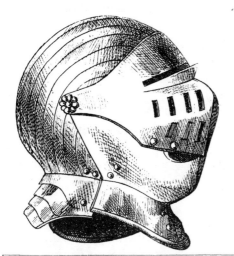

father with a small knife for peeling fruit.

Edmund
Oh, God!

But he smiles.

~

SCENE TWENTY-THREE: THE GREAT HALL

Onstage a man is shooing chickens.

Prince Harry
Jerry Merryweather – another nail in the coffin of variety.

Queen
I liked Bernard the Rabbit Baiter.

Edmund appears on stage.

Edmund
Thank you, thank you.

Prince Harry
Is this announcement going to take long, Edmund? I haven't seen hide nor hair of a eunuch yet.

Edmund steps up onto the table, followed by Percy, who is carrying the letters.

Edmund
No, don't worry, Harry: it will soon all be over. My dear mother, my dear brother; Lords and Ladies of the Court. Today there came into my possession from the hands, my lord, of your faithful servant Dougal McAngus, certain letters – rather *extraordinary* letters – concerning the lineage of Prince Harry.

The queen begins to turn a pleasant shade of scarlet.

Queen
Letters? What's so extraordinary about them?

Prince Harry
Letters?

Edmund
Well. They were written, Harry, by your mother. To . . . your father!

An immediate relaxation in the atmosphere, some laughter, some chatter.

Your father, Harry, being of course Donald, Third Duke of Argyll.

Prince Harry is totally outraged.

Prince Harry
I beg your pardon?

Edmund
These letters are of quite an intimate nature.

Percy is handing him samples of the letters.

Let me give you an example . . . Arundel, Thursday. 'My dear hairy-wairy. Often as you sit at the table with my husband probing deeply into the affairs of state, I long for the day when you will probe . . .'

The queen faints. Prince Harry leaps up.

Prince Harry
Edmund, are you sure you know what you're saying?

Percy hands Edmund another letter.

Edmund
As sure as our mother was, Harry, when she wrote these words: 'Dear Bigboy, sail south. As you know, your galleon is always assured a warm welcome in *my* harbour.'

Percy is mouthing the words of the letter along with Edmund. He loves this stuff.

There is a moan from the queen.

Prince Harry
Bigboy! Mother, do you know anything about this?

Queen
What chance did I have? I was just a little foreign girl.

Prince Harry
Then I must renounce the Regency: and hie me to a monastery. Edmund, you shall be regent until your father returns.

Edmund
The king will not be returning.

Prince Harry
What?

Queen
(*Not upset at all*) Oh, dear!

Edmund
No, the last time McAngus saw him he was facing half the Turkish army armed only with a small piece of cutlery . . . Percy, if you'd like to start things off.

Edmund walks down the table and off and up to the throne.

Percy starts chanting and everyone gradually joins in.

Percy and others
The king is dead! Long live the king.

Prince Harry is leaving, but he turns around and observes sternly . . .

Prince Harry
Probably dead.

Percy
The king is probably dead . . .

All
The king is probably dead, long live the king. The king is probably dead, long live the king.

At which moment, trumpets sound and the king bursts through the doors, a battered, bloody, but vibrant man.

Percy creeps up to join Edmund by the throne.

The king is . . . not dead. Long live the king. Hurray!

The king stands, arms and legs akimbo, waving a spear.

King
Blood! Death! War! Rumpy-pumpy! Triumph! McAngus! (*McAngus leaps up to the king*) My companion in blood and most trusted friend.

McAngus
You made it!

King
Yes! I made it. Thanks to my trusty fruit knife.

As he says this he looks around and notices for the first time that things are looking unsettled and Edmund is sitting on the throne.

Wait a minute: what's going on here? Who are you?

He climbs on to the table.

Queen
It's our son.

King
What? Oh, yes, of course . . . Enid.

Edmund
My beloved father, certain letters have just come to light which I think might . . . change things a bit.

King
Letters, what letters?

Edmund
Well, they speak of acts of love between your wife and Donald, the Gay Dog of the Glens: 'How I long to be in that kingdom between the saffron sheets where you and your ruler are the only ruler.'

The queen faints again.

. . . and then acts of love consummated: 'Oh, you enormous Scotsman' etc., and these letters are dated November and December 1460, which, Harry, in relation to your date of birth is precisely nine months . . .

He is staring at Prince Harry with a look that seems to suddenly contain a hint of panic. There is a pause.

Prince Harry
. . . after I was born.

Utter shock registers on Edmund's face. He cannot believe it.

McAngus
But about nine months before your birth, Edmund.

There is a pause as Edmund slowly turns to McAngus with a look of complete fury and inward despair. He says rather quietly and calmly . . .

Edmund
You bastard!

Prince Harry
No, I think you're the bastard, Edmund.

King
Silence! I will have an explanation.

Edmund
(*Improvising*) My liege, the reason I have gathered you all here today is to try to get some proper justice meted out (*rising to a crescendo*) against this Scottish turd who has clearly forged these obviously fake letters.

King
Let me see them . . .

Edmund
I rip them up in his face so no hint of their filthy slander can remain.

He tears up the letters and throws them into the fire.

You come in here, fresh from slaughtering a couple of chocos when their backs were turned, and you think you can upset the harmony of a whole kingdom? I challenge you (*throwing down his gauntlet*) . . . to a duel!

McAngus
To the death!

Edmund
Ermmmmmm . . . yes, all right.

King
Excellent idea: after all it is St Leonard's Day: there's meant to be some entertainment.

The king leaps off the table. This is his kind of fun.

Take your places!

Edmund produces his fine épée. Two seconds later, McAngus produces his enormous broadsword. There is despair in Edmund's face. McAngus and the king are joshing like old friends, the king comparing his fruit knife with McAngus's sword.

Good to see old Glenshee again, McAngus.

McAngus
Yes, my lord: remember the night with

Glenshee and the Turk and the human kebab!

King
Yes, how could I forget it.

Edmund looks on in panic.

Very well: let the killing begin!

Silence falls. Edmund waves his elegant épée around with purpose, trying to look threatening. McAngus tolerates this for a minute, then brings his heavy sword down, breaking Edmund's feeble instrument in two.

McAngus
Right now, let's see the Black Adder wriggle out of this one.

He draws his sword back against Edmund's neck for the kill.

Edmund
No, wait!

King
Come on, what's the hold-up?

Edmund
I'll give you everything I own. Everything.

McAngus
Uh-huh?

Edmund
Yes. I'm hardly a rich man.

King
You're hardly a man at all!

Edmund
But my horse must be worth a thousand ducats. I can sell my wardrobe, the pride of my life, my swords, my curtains, my socks, and my fighting cocks, my servants I can live without, except perhaps he who oils my rack. And then, my most intimate treasures. My collection of antique codpieces. My wigs for state occasions, my wigs for private occasions, and my wigs for humorous occasions. My collection of pokers, my grendle stretchers – my ornamental pomfries. And, of course, my autographed miniature of Judas Iscariot.

McAngus
Ha ha ha ha ha ha ha. (*He laughs loud and long*) No: that's nowhere near enough.

He rises to strike and then stops.

I'm only kidding: (*Quietly*) I'm quite interested in the wigs.

The fight is over. McAngus is satisfied with the deal. Percy and Baldrick scramble to Edmund's aid.

I hope life doesn't get too dull for you, not being able to pass laws over Scotland any more. Ha-ha!

Edmund
(*To himself*) Yes. Ha ha ha ha. I wouldn't pass water over Scotland.

~

SCENE TWENTY-FOUR: THE BAY WINDOW

The king is sitting in the bay window looking out and muttering. Prince Harry stands by him.

Prince Harry
We're so pleased you're back, Father.

King
I'm not. I miss the smell of blood in my nostrils, and the queen's got a headache.

Prince Harry
But we do have a fascinating week ahead. The Archbishop of York has asked me if you'd care to join his Italian formation dancing class, and I really ought to give him an answer.

King
Do you want me to be honest or tactful?

Prince Harry
Oh, tactful, I think.

King
Tell him to get stuffed! Has that little hooligan McAngus left?

Prince Harry
No, Edmund's just giving him a last look around the castle.

SCENE TWENTY-FIVE: THE RAMPARTS

Edmund and McAngus are now the very best of mates. Edmund is giving him a tour of the castle. They inspect the view, then move on.

Edmund
While this . . .

Edmund points to a large cannon.

McAngus
Yes, very interesting.

He bends over and puts his head into the cannon.

SCENE TWENTY-SIX: THE BAY WINDOW OF THE GREAT HALL

King
Well I'll be sorry to see him go.

Prince Harry
Yes, so will Edmund. He and McAngus have become quite firm friends.

There is the sound of a huge explosion.

What the devil . . . ?

King
The Turks!

Prince Harry
The drains!

Edmund rushes in.

Edmund
Father, Harry, you must come quickly! There's been a rather messy accident!

Prince Harry
Oh, my God! I shall need my plunger!

He and the king exit hurriedly, leaving Edmund. He leans against the wall, then leaps ecstatically into the air . . . It is doubtful that McAngus will cause trouble again.

the Archbishop

SCENE ONE: THE DUKE OF WINCHESTER'S BEDCHAMBER

England, November, 1487. The battle between the Church and the Crown continues to rage and the Duke of Winchester, the greatest landowner in England, is dying.

The duke lies in bed. The Archbishop of Canterbury is on one side of the bed, the king on the other, both holding his hands. Behind the king stands Lord Tavis, in a spiked helmet. Other lords and doctors look on.

Duke
Dying, my lords, am I dying?

Archbishop
Never!

King
Never!

Archbishop
And yet, my son, to pass away the idle hours until your recovery . . .

The duke has an almost terminal spasm, which speeds the archbishop up a bit.

. . . let us imagine you yourself were to pass away: to whom would you leave your lands?

They both produce pre-written wills they are keen the duke should sign.

King
Why, to me! Of course.

He holds his will under the duke's nose.

Duke
Yes: to my beloved king.

The duke prepares to sign the will. The king guides his hand.

Archbishop
I hope then your filthy soul is prepared for hell, my son.

Duke
Hell?!

The king glares at the archbishop.

Archbishop
Yes, hell, where Satan belches fire and enormous devils break wind both night and day.

Duke
Alas!

Archbishop
Hell, where your mind is never free from the torments of remorse and your bottom never free from the pricking of little forks.

Duke
No, spare me the little forks!

He reaches for the archbishop's will.

King
What is this nonsense?

Archbishop
Hell, where the softest bits from your nether regions are everyone else's favourite lunch.

Duke
(*Stabbing pain in his chest*) Alas! Argh! Forgive me, noble sire: I will change my will and leave my lands to the Church!

The will comes out from the archbishop. The duke signs it.

King
What?!

Archbishop
Blessed be thy stainless soul.

King
You will change your mind later, I know it.

And the duke dies.

Archbishop
I think not.

The king is very cross about this indeed.

~

SCENE TWO: THE BAY WINDOW OF THE GREAT HALL

Edmund and Percy are, as usual, doing very little.

Edmund
Ah, Baldrick, what news?

Baldrick
Well, my lord, an informed source tells me that the Duchess of Gloucester has given birth to twin goblins.

Edmund
No, no, no. About the Duke of Winchester.

Baldrick
Oh, he's still hanging on.

Percy
He must be on his last legs by now, my lord.

Edmund
Tssk: how many sets of legs has the man

got? Really, I wish he'd make up his mind: either he dies, or he lives for ever. It's this shilly-shallying that's so undignified.

A messenger enters.

Messenger
My lord, I come with tragic news.

Edmund
What, died at last, has he?

Messenger
Who, my lord?

Edmund
Oh, I see. Now the idea is that you ask me what the message is before you tell it to me. Quite brilliant, I must say. I was referring to the Duke of Winchester.

Messenger
Who, my lord?

Edmund
Right, now let's try and sort this out in words of one syllable, shall we? Someone has died, yes?

Messenger
Yes, my lord.

Edmund
Who is it that has died?

Messenger
The Archbishop of Canterbury, my lord.

Edmund
Are you a cretin?

Messenger
Yes, my lord.

Edmund
Oh, dear. The Archbishop of Canterbury, eh? The king has done it again. That's the third this year. How did this one die?

Messenger
Horribly, my lord.

Edmund
Any details?

Messenger
Ah, no: 'horribly' was all I was given.

Edmund
Ah!

Prince Harry enters.

Messenger
My lord, I come with tragic news . . .

Prince Harry
I've heard it – will you go away. Edmund, the Archbishop of Canterbury has met with a most tragic accident and there seems to be some confusion but I think I've fathomed out how it came about.

Edmund
Yes, I think I've got a pretty shrewd idea myself.

Prince Harry
Apparently, Archbishop Godfrey had just come out of the Duke of Winchester's room . . .

Edmund
Who had just died leaving all his lands to the Church?

Prince Harry
Well, as a matter of fact, yes.

Edmund
And so the king was really out for his blood presumably.

Prince Harry
I dare say. Anyway the point is at that moment Sir Tavis Mortimer . . .

Edmund
The king's hired killer?

Prince Harry
No, no. Mortimer, that tall, rather striking fellow with no ears.

Edmund
Yes, that's him.

Prince Harry
Well, he came round the corner, saw the archbishop, rushed towards him with his head bowed in order to receive his blessing – and unfortunately killed him stone dead.

Edmund
How?

Prince Harry
Mortimer was wearing a Turkish helmet.

Edmund
One of those things with a two-foot spike coming out of the top?

Prince Harry
Yes, the ones they normally use for butting their enemies in the stomach and killing them stone dead.

Edmund
Presumably he had forgotten he was wearing it?

Prince Harry
Yes, that's right. A tragic accident.

Edmund
Almost as tragic as Archbishop Bertram being struck by a falling gargoyle whilst swimming off Beachy Head.

Prince Harry
Yes, or Archbishop Wilfred slipping and falling backwards on to the spire of Norwich Cathedral. The Lord works in mysterious ways – I just don't know how I'm going to break it to his catamite.

Prince Harry moves away. Percy is mortified by all this bitter news.

Percy
What a tragic accident, my lord.

Edmund
Accident, my codlings.

~

SCENE THREE: THE GREAT HALL

Edmund, Percy and Baldrick are sitting in front of the fire warming their hands.

Percy
Who do you think will take over?

Edmund
Oh, it'll be one of those bishop fellows, I should imagine. They tend to go for religious types.

Baldrick
Yes: rumour has it, my lord, that the king wants to choose Prince Harry.

Edmund
Oh, really.

Baldrick
(*With deep meaning*) Prince Harry, archbishop, my lord.

Edmund
Good lord! Prince Harry, archbishop – and we all know what happens to archbishops, don't we?

Percy
Yes, they go to Canterbury.

Edmund
No, you fool, I mean . . .

He does a slitting throat action.

Percy
Oh, yes!

So does he. All three laugh gleefully.

Edmund
Are you sure about your source, Baldrick?

Baldrick
Yes, it was Jane Smart: she was the one who told me about the Duke and Duchess of Kent and the chocolate chastity belt.

Edmund
Well, with Harry gone – the Black Adder will be king next.

Another gleeful laugh. All three pretend to slit their throats.

Today could be one of the most important days of my life. I want my most splendid garments for the ceremony.

Percy
Certainly, my lord. Hat, my lord?

Edmund
The Trojan, I think.

Percy
Boots, my lord?

Edmund
The Italian.

Percy
And codpiece, my lord?

Edmund
Let's go for the Black Russian, shall we?

It always terrifies the clergy.

They laugh. It is a great day.

~

SCENE FOUR: THE GREAT HALL

People are gathered for the announcement of the new archbishop. Edmund is wearing a black helmet with a plume, boots with toes so long they attach to the knee with a golden chain, and a very large black codpiece.

Edmund
Any further rumours, Baldrick?

Baldrick
Not really, my lord. Apparently Lord Wilders is keeping a sheep in his bedroom, but nothing on the appointment, no.

Edmund
Fair enough.

The queen comes across to talk to her son, as a bishop faints at the sight of his codpiece.

Queen
Why are you dressed like this, Edmund?

Edmund
Like what?

Queen
Well, this enormous nonsense here.

She pats the codpiece and walks on to the throne as trumpets blow and the king enters.

Edmund
Ah, fingers crossed.

King
Members of the court and clergy, I have, at last, after careful consultation with the Lord God, his son Jesus Christ and his insubstantial friend, the Holy Ghost, decided upon the next archbishop. May he last longer in his post than his predecessors.

Edmund
Fat chance.

King
I appoint to the Holy Seal of Canterbury my own son . . .

A trumpet blows.

Edwin, Duke of Edinburgh.

Edmund
(*In total panic*) Eurgh!

King
Archbishop, we salute thee.

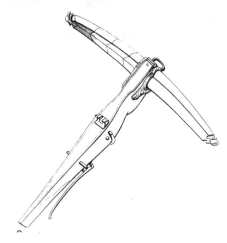

Everyone kneels except Percy, who goes to shake Edmund's hand.

Percy
Congratulations, my lord.

Edmund angrily gestures Percy to kneel. Then he takes a hat from a kneeling bishop and covers his now slightly unsuitable enormous codpiece with it.

SCENE FIVE: SECTION OF THE GREAT HALL

The king and Prince Harry are kneeling and arm wrestling over a stool.

King
Keep going! Keep going! Use both hands if you want to. Very good. Well done, Harry.

There is a polite knock at the door.

Prince Harry
Excuse me.

King
Enter.

Edmund
Your Majesty.

Edmund enters politely: he has changed into modest attire with a tiny codpiece.

King
Ah, my Lord Archbishop.

Edmund
Yes. There were just a couple of points about my appointment before things are really firmed up.

King
Yes?

Edmund
Well, firstly, could I . . . ?

King
No, you couldn't.

Edmund
Secondly, I was wondering . . .

King
Don't misunderstand this appointment, Egbert. I have always despised you.

Edmund
Well, you are my father, of course. I mean you're biased.

King
You, compared to your beloved brother Harry, are as excrement is compared to cream.

Prince Harry
My lord, you flatter me.

Edmund
And me also, my lord.

King
So now, my boy, when I have at last found a use for you, don't try to get out of it.

Edmund
Oh, no, my lord. Certainly not, no. I just wondered whether perhaps another man, equally weak-willed and feeble, might do just as well.

King
Ha! There is no such man.

Edmund
No, of course not, silly me. I thought per-haps someone (*casually*) who believed in God . . .

King
No, no, no. If I needed someone who believed in God, I'd have chosen Harry . . . not an embarrassing little weed like you.

Edmund
Oh, well, I think that's everything cleared up then. Goodness, almost time for even-song: must be going.

King
Egbert, come here.

He beckons Edmund towards him and gets hold of him by the throat.

King
Archbishop. A word of advice. If you cross me, now or ever, I shall do unto you what God did unto the Sodomites, under-stand?

He lets Edmund go.

Edmund
Good, good. I shall make myself available for all eventualities. Thank you so much.

Edmund goes out into corridor. He is crazed with panic, pressed to the wall.

Flee!

~

SCENE SIX: THE CASTLE COURTYARD

Early morning. It is very cold. Edmund stands in front of a loaded cart with Baldrick and Percy. They are fully pre-pared to steal quietly away . . . for ever.

Edmund
We've got the thumb screws, the foot crusher, the nose hooks, those long rods . . . Where's the dwarf?

Dwarf
(*From under a sheet*) Here, my lord.

Edmund
Right, let's go.

He goes round the corner and comes slap bang upon the king, Lord Chiswick and Prince Harry.

King
Archbishop!

Edmund
Ah! Hail!

King
Going somewhere?

Edmund
Ahm . . . yyyyes.

King
Where?

Edmund
Canterbury.

King
Good. Prince Harry here will accompany you. I would hate to see you murdered before your investiture.

Edmund
Well, yes.

King
Chiswick, fresh horses!

Percy has not been paying attention, unfortunately.

Percy
My lord, if we are going to catch the boat to France, we'll have to hurry.

Prince Harry
The boat to France?

Edmund
Ahm . . . You off to France, Percy?

Percy
I thought we all were.

Edmund
No, Harry and I are off to Canterbury, aren't we, Harry?

Percy
Oh, I see. You've changed your plan.

Edmund
No, no, not really. The only change is, per-haps, Percy, if you could go and put your face in some manure and then follow along at a reasonable distance. That will be fine.

~

SCENE SEVEN: ON THE WAY TO CANTERBURY

Edmund and Prince Harry are riding

along, with Percy, Baldrick and the luggage following behind.

Prince Harry
And another thing. What bothers me, your Grace, is suppose my right hand offends me and I cut it off – what happens if my left hand offends me as well, I mean what do I cut it off with?

Edmund
Yes. That is a knotty one.

They pass two workmen, called Cain and Abel.

Cain
Who was that?

Abel
I don't know, but that tall fellow had a face full of manure.

Cain
That's what I call style.

~

SCENE EIGHT: THE ALTAR OF A GREAT CATHEDRAL

Edmund is kneeling in full regalia before a large bishop. The king sits on a throne nearby.

Bishop
Do you, Edmund, Duke of Edinburgh, believe in God the Father . . .

Edmund makes to answer, but suddenly realizes there is more to come.

God the Son, and God the Holy Ghost?

Edmund checks his answer with the king, who nods vigorously.

Edmund
Ahm, yes.

Bishop
I then name thee Archbishop of Canterbury and Primate of all England.

The music swells and the nearby incense burner swings more enthusiastically: its smoke gets to Edmund who sneezes, with extraordinary violence, then wipes his

nose on the vestments of a bishop. A good start to his Primacy.

As the ceremony draws to a close, Edmund, Percy and Baldrick set off down the aisle. Edmund is swinging the incense, but rather too enthusiastically. Two people fall over, and he lets go of it, and it flies out of his hand. He looks anxious. It is not an auspicious beginning.

~

SCENE NINE: THE CLOISTERS OF THE CATHEDRAL

His Investiture over, Archbishop Edmund the Unwilling swiftly adopted the ways of the cloth. But ever the shadow of his father's threat hung over him, until at last one day . . .

Edmund and Baldrick are walking through cloisters. Edmund is in his purple robes. Baldrick is in a simple monk's sackcloth.

Edmund
Tell me, Brother Baldrick: exactly what *did* God do to the Sodomites?

Baldrick
I'm not sure, my lord. Though it is hard to imagine it was anything worse than what they did to each other.

Edmund
Mmmmmmm.

He walks round the corner and straight into a knight who is wearing a pointy hat.

Oh, my God.

Edmund is sure he is facing certain death. The messenger pulls out what he thinks will be a sword, but is in fact a scroll with a message. Edmund reads it.

This is it. Baldrick, get the Bishop of Ramsgate.

Baldrick
Who?

Edmund
Percy, get Percy. My life is hanging by a thread.

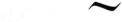

SCENE TEN: LORD GRAVENEY'S BEDROOM

Lord Graveney is dying. A bishop leans over him, holding a will.

Graveney
And if I don't leave my lands to the Church, then what?

Bishop
Then, Lord Graveney, you will surely go to hell!

Graveney
Alas!

Bishop
Hell, where the air is pungent with the aroma of roasted behinds!

Graveney
(*Signs bishop's will*) No! No! *Argh!* I place my lands in the hands of the Church, and so bid the world farewell.

He dies: at that instant, the king crashes through the door and rushes to the bed.

King
What! The archbishop not yet arrived?

Bishop
No, my lord, and even if he does arrive . . .

Edmund bursts in, in a serious panic.

Edmund
Wait!

Bishop
Too late!

Edmund
Get out of my way.

King
I'll kill the pair of you. (*To the bishop*) I'll abolish the Church!

Edmund
My lord, my lord.

He shakes Graveney's corpse, causing his head to flop sideways. Edmund snaps at the bishop.

I said . . . *out!*

Baldrick opens the door and shoves the bishop through. Now Edmund takes violent action with Graveney, sitting and hitting him.

Edmund
My lord, my lord. Wake up! Wake up!

Graveney's eyes open.

Graveney
Am I in paradise?

Edmund
Phew! No, not yet.

Graveney
Then this must be hell! Alas, spare my posterior!

Edmund
No, no, you're all right. It's England.

Graveney
And you are not Satan!

Edmund
No, I'm the Archbishop of Canterbury.

Graveney
Oh, your Grace! I have left all my lands to the Church. Am I to be saved?

King
No, you treacherous swine! I'll kill you.

Edmund gestures for the king to stop and the turns back to Graveney.

Edmund
No, wait! Let's just deal with this in stages, shall we? You see . . . the Church you know, it doesn't really *need* your land.

King
No! What it needs is a damn good thrashing.

Graveney
But if I do not gain its blessing, I will surely go to hell!

The bishop, who has been listening, bursts in.

Bishop
Yes, hell, where tiny tweezers . . .

King
Get out!

Baldrick hustles him out again.

Edmund
Someone like you go to hell? Never. Never!

Graveney
But I have committed many sins!

Edmund
Haven't we all, haven't we all!

Graveney
I murdered my father.

Bishop
(*Opens door*) Alas!

Percy and Baldrick slam door shut. Edmund moves even closer to Lord Graveney, puts his head nearly on the pillow and whispers to him . . .

Edmund
I know how you feel.

King
Hurry up, Edgar!

Graveney
And I have committed adultery . . .

Edmund
Ha! Who hasn't?

Graveney
More than a thousand times?

Edmund
Well, it's 1487 after all!

Graveney
. . . with my mother!

Edmund
Ah.

Everyone is shocked. There is a moment's silence.

Graveney
You see. I will go to hell!

Bishop
(*Opens door again*) Hell, where growths like turnips sprout from your nose and ears.

King
Kill that bishop!

Percy and Baldrick leap on him, pushing him to the floor. Baldrick knocks the bishop unconscious with cross.

Edmund
Uhm, well, let's take hell. You know, it isn't as bad as it's cracked up to be.

Graveney
(*Incredulous*) What?

Edmund
You see, the thing is, heaven is for people who like the sort of things that go on in heaven. Like, well, singing, talking to God, and watering potplants. While hell, on the other hand, is for people who prefer, well, you know the other sort of things: adultery, pillage, torture, those . . . areas.

Graveney
Really?

Edmund
Yes, leave your lands to the Crown, and once you're dead you'll have the time of your life.

Graveney
(*In wonder*) Adultery, pillage . . . for all
eternity?

Edmund
Yup.

Bishop
(*Coming round*) And the smacking of large
sticks against your tender portions.

*Baldrick hits him in the stomach. Percy
hits him on the shoulder. He collapses and
they kick him.*

Graveney
Very well . . . I leave my lands to the
Crown.

He signs the king's will.

And my soul in the hands of the Lord:
may he treat me like the piece of refuse
that I am and send me to hell where I
belong.

King
Amen.

Edmund
Amen: you're a very lucky man. I wish I
could be coming with you, but, being archbishop . . .

Graveney
I'm sorry.

Edmund
No, no, that's all right.

Graveney
Ah!

*He dies and the king waves the will tri-
umphantly.*

King
My son!

Edmund
Father!

*The king kneels, Edmund pats him on the
head.*

King
Father!

Edmund
My son!

It's going very well again.

~

SCENE ELEVEN: COUNTRYSIDE

*The two same peasants are still walking:
two knights splash past them.*

Cain
Who's that?

Abel
Looks like the sort of pair who'd kill the
Archbishop of Canterbury to me.

Cain
Tssk. Typical.

~

SCENE TWELVE: THE GREAT HALL

*The queen is eating alone in the Great Hall.
The loud clashing of swords and shouting
is heard. The king and Prince Harry
enter fighting. Prince Harry is thrown
backwards on to the table.*

King
You Turkish pig! You Turkish dog!

Prince Harry
Father! Father! It's me!

The king lets Prince Harry go. He stands up.

King
It's all right, my boy, you're improving.

Prince Harry
Thank you, Father, goodnight, Mother.

King
He's gaining on me! He's gaining on me!

Queen
How was Edmund?

King
Oh, well, well, well. Chiswick, fresh horse!

Queen
And how are his dear little sheep?

King
Whose sheep?

Queen
Edmund's sheep.

A haunch of horse arrives and the king tucks in.

King
What sheep?

Queen
Well, the ones in Canterbury. His flock that he was talking about.

King
(*Utterly exasperated*) Oh, my God.

~

SCENE THIRTEEN: COUNTRYSIDE

As they feast, the two knights ride even faster towards the castle.

~

SCENE FOURTEEN: THE GREAT HALL

Queen
I can't understand it. Edmund doesn't even like religion.

King
But that's impossible. He's the Archbishop of Canterbury!

Queen
Yes, and the Archbishop of Canterbury is also a naughty little boy whose bottom I had to smack for relieving himself in the font.

King
Well, that was a long time ago.

Queen
It was last Thursday.

King
Ha ha ha!

He roars with laughter.

~

SCENE FIFTEEN: CASTLE ENTRANCE

The knights crash through the main door, cloaks off, and drinking.

~

SCENE SIXTEEN: THE GREAT HALL

King
Well, the boy's turned out well! (*Clinks glasses and breaks the queen's*) A long and healthy life to him! Ah! I thank God that in my lifetime never again shall I have to say, 'Who will rid me of this turbulent priest?'

~

SCENE SEVENTEEN: CASTLE CORRIDOR

The knights career along a corridor.

~

SCENE EIGHTEEN: THE GREAT HALL

Queen
What is that?

King
Something my ancestor, Henry II, once said, when he was having trouble with Thomas à Becket: he was sitting at a table . . . like this with these two drunken

knights, and yelled out . . . 'Who will rid me of this turbulent priest?'

Queen
What?

King
God save us. I said:

The knights burst in through the door into the Great Hall, unnoticed.

(*Yells*) 'Who will rid me of this turbulent priest?'

The knights exchange an excited look with each other.

Queen
Meaning who?

King
The Archbishop of Canterbury, of course.

That's that for the knights. They leave the room determinedly.

Queen
And then what happened?

King
Well, they went straight off and killed him, of course.

SCENE NINETEEN: CASTLE GATES

The two knights crash back out of the main gates of the castle.

SCENE TWENTY: EDMUND'S CATHEDRAL ROOM

Edmund, Percy and Baldrick bound into the room at the abbey.

Edmund
Right, now, let's get down to business, shall we?

Percy
Business, my lord?

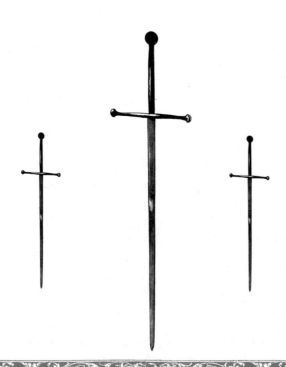

Edmund
Yes, Baldrick has been looking at some of
the ways we can actually make a bit of
money in this job.

Baldrick
Well, my lord . . . there seems to be four
major profit areas. Curses, pardons, relics
and selling the sexual favours of nuns.

Edmund
Selling the sexual favours of nuns . . . do
some people actually pay?

Baldrick
Well, foreign businessmen, other nuns, you
know.

Edmund
Let's start with pardons, shall we?

Baldrick
Well, here's a fair selection. (*Lifts papers
from floor*) Basically you get what you pay
for. It runs from this one which is a pardon
for talking with your mouth full, signed by
an apprentice curate in Tewkesbury.

Edmund
How much is that?

Baldrick
Two pebbles. All the way up to this one,
which is a pardon for anything whatsoever,
including 'murder, adultery or dismember-
ment of a close friend or relative'.

Edmund
And who's that signed by?

Baldrick
Both popes. Curses are pretty much the
same really. I bought this one for half an
egg.

He hands it to Edmund.

Edmund
Aha. 'Dear Enemy, I curse you and hope
that something quite unpleasant happens to
you, like an onion falling on your head.'

Baldrick
That's the lower end of the market, you
can get a real belter for four ducats.

He hands another to Edmund.

Edmund
'Dear Enemy, may the Lord hate you and
all your kind: may you be turned orange
in hue. May your head fall off at an awkward moment.'

Percy
Does this work?

Baldrick
Yes.

Percy
Really?

Edmund
Really?

Baldrick
No.

~

SCENE TWENTY-ONE: COUNTRYSIDE

*Hugely exciting flash of the knights riding,
thrilled by the thought of blood.*

~

SCENE TWENTY-TWO: EDMUND'S CATHEDRAL ROOM

Baldrick
Moving on to relics, we've got shrouds
from Turin, wine from the wedding at
Cana, splinters from the true Cross . . .
then of course there's all the stuff made by
Jesus in his days in the carpentry shop.
Pipe racks, coffee tables, cake stands,
book ends, crucifixes, nice cheeseboard,
waterproof sandals, fruit bowls; oh I
haven't finished this one yet.

It is a brand new, uncompleted thing.

Percy
But this is disgraceful, my lord – all of
these are obviously fake!

Edmund
Yes.

Percy
How will people be able to distinguish
between these and real relics?

Edmund
They won't: that's the point.

Percy
Yes, well, you won't be able to fool everyone. Look: I have here a true relic.

He very dramatically reveals a wooden box.

Edmund
What is it?

Percy
A bone from the finger of our Lord. It cost me thirty-one pieces of silver.

Edmund
Good Lord: is it real?

Percy
It is, my lord. You stand amazed, Baldrick.

Baldrick
I am. I thought they only came in boxes of ten. I could have let you have one for a couple of groats. Fingers are very big at the moment.

Percy
What?

Baldrick
Mind you, for a quick sale you can't beat a good nose. Here's the sacred appendage compendium party pack.

He opens up a couple of boxes. Percy is flabbergasted as he inspects and sees they are the same as his.

Baldrick
Here's Jesus's nose, St Peter's nose, a couple of St Francis's and a box of . . . (*He opens a box which turns out to have a pair of breasts in it*) Oh, no, those are Joan of Arc's.

Percy
That bastard verger! I'll show him! I'll show him!

SCENE TWENTY-THREE: THE CORRIDOR OUTSIDE EDMUND'S CATHEDRAL ROOM

Percy
I'll show him!

He moves fast to the door, opens it and is greeted by the sight of the two utterly martial knights, their swords drawn. They are very suave, very calm.

Good evening.

De Boeuf and De Boinod
Hail!

For De Boeuf and De Boinod are their names.

Percy
And what can I do for you?

De Boinod
We are here to murder the Archbishop of Canterbury.

De Boeuf
We're his enemies. We fear he may be in danger.

Percy
Really? How?

De Boeuf
Well, I mean . . . let's see (*improvises calmly; they are both very smooth and polite*), perhaps good King Richard, angry with the archbishop for some reason, might well send two drunken knights, freshly returned from the Crusades on a mission to wreak vengeance on him.

Percy
Good point: it's happened before. By the way, I didn't quite catch your names?

De Boinod
We are George de Boeuf and Justin de Boinod, two drunken knights freshly returned from the Crusades and here on a mission for good King Richard. God bless us.

It's all very affable.

Percy
Your mission?

De Boinod
Well, as I said, we're here to kill . . .

De Boeuf
A bit of time until the next Crusade.

De Boinod
Yes.

Percy
Oh, fine, well, I'll go and get him.

The knights raise their swords. At that point, Baldrick pops his head round the door. The knights quickly drop their swords.

Percy
Ah, Baldrick.

Baldrick
(*Inspecting the knights, terrified*) Yes?

Percy
Two knights here, to see the archbishop.

Baldrick
Oh, my God!

SCENE TWENTY-FOUR: EDMUND'S CATHEDRAL ROOM

Baldrick
My lord, I've got something to say that's going to shock you.

Edmund
If it's about the nuns of Uppingham and the candelabra, don't bother, I've already heard.

Baldrick
No, my lord. The fact is, there are two men outside who've come to kill you.

Edmund
What?

SCENE TWENTY-FIVE: CATHEDRAL CORRIDOR

Percy
I'm terribly sorry about this. I'll just see what the delay is.

He turns away and enters Edmund's room.

SCENE TWENTY-SIX: EDMUND'S CATHEDRAL ROOM

Edmund and Baldrick are frantically looking for places to hide: under shrouds, in trunks, fireplaces, on top of beds.

Percy
What's going on?

Baldrick
Those men outside: they're here to kill us.

Percy
Oh, come on! Honestly, Baldrick! Just because a couple of people obviously have a bit of breeding, you assume they're bound to be mindless killers.

Two swords smash through the door.

De Boeuf and De Boinod
Prepare for death, heretics!

Edmund turns in panic to a cross on a little altar.

Edmund
Oh, my God! There's no way out! Oh, God! Help me!

He grabs the cross and it miraculously pulls forward like a lever. A door opens in the wall.

Good Lord!

Baldrick
Quick!

They rush through the door and it closes behind them. The knights finally smash through the door.

De Boeuf
Ssssh! They've dozed off.

They creep to the bed and hit it violently, then realize it is a bundle of bedding.

De Boinod
They've gone down the secret passage to the nunnery!

The knights operate the secret door and charge down the corridor, swords uplifted.

~

SCENE TWENTY-SEVEN: NUNS' DORMITORY

The knights burst in, and register with shock that they are in what is obviously a nuns' dormitory. There are three nuns praying.

De Boinod
Sisters! Three men came in: which way did they go?

Edmund
(*A nun*) They went that way . . .

The knights set off towards the door. Then suddenly they stop.

De Boeuf
Wait a second! They'll be watching out for us dressed like this. Quick, in here.

They go into a cubicle.
Percy, Edmund and Baldrick, all nuns, meet the knights coming out of the cubicle, also nuns.

Baldrick
Have you sisters pray seen two burly knights pass this way?

De Boinod
No sister, more's the pity.

De Boeuf
Why don't you try that way?

Percy
(*Speaking normally*) Thank you.

De Boinod
(*Speaking normally*) You're welcome.

They all turn away. Then realization dawns. The fight begins. It is an epic encounter: lives hang by a thread, always on the point of being severed by a swishing sword.

SCENE TWENTY-EIGHT: A CORRIDOR IN THE NUNNERY

The Mother Superior and Sister Sara are strolling towards the dormitory.

Sara
And yet, Mother Superior, does not St Paul say in the Ephesians, 'a woman is like a bat: often heard, but never seen'.

Mother Superior
No, I don't think so, Sara. Shall we check the dormitory?

Sara
Oh, yes, Mother Superior: what a good idea.

SCENE TWENTY-NINE: NUNS' DORMITORY

A strange sight greets the Mother Superior as she enters the dormitory. Five nuns locked in mortal combat.

Mother Superior
Girls, girls! If I've told you once, I've told you a thousand times. Fighting in the dormitory is completely forbidden. Who's the ringleader here? Yes, yes, you, the plain girl.

She tears the headdress off the nearest nun. It is Edmund.

Oh, my God. It's . . . the Archbishop of Canterbury.

Sister Sara removes another headdress.

Sara
And a man . . . aaaaah!

Edmund
Ah, yes. Look, I think I can explain.

SCENE THIRTY: NUNS' DORMITORY

Edmund is standing before the Mother Superior's desk. Sister Sara stands behind Edmund, whipping him gently.

Edmund
And that, sweet lady, is the whole story.

Mother Superior
Let us just go over the facts again. Having been appointed archbishop, you found that all your interest lay in the beauty of your vestments.

Edmund
Alas, the fine embroidery.

Mother Superior
And unable to resist the slide into depravity, you began to dress up in the habit of a nun.

Edmund
I couldn't resist the texture of the hessian underthings.

Mother Superior
Oh, I can understand that, but then you forced the Bishop of Ramsgate and one Brother Baldrick to do so also.

Edmund
May I be cursed for it!

Mother Superior
And finally you got two knights drunk and invited them to come and wrestle with you inside the nunnery in an orgy of heathen perversity.

Edmund
That's right, yes.

Mother Superior
This shameful tale bears the unmistakable ring of truth. And I must therefore tell you that this morning I have written urgently to all three popes recommending your immediate excommunication. Never more may you be Archbishop of Canterbury.

Edmund
Oh, dear.

Mother Superior
That's enough, Sister Sara. I think he's learnt his lesson.

Sister Sara stops beating him.
Go, sinner, and meet thy doom.

The doors of the room mysteriously open. There is a long stretch of darkness outside, into which Edmund walks, head held high, archbishop no more, thank God.

SCENE THIRTY-ONE: NUNS' DORMITORY

Later that night, a final glimpse of religious life.

Mother Superior
Alas, the corruption of the world.

Sara
Yes, alas, Mother Superior.

Mother Superior
I am tired and weary. You may leave me now.

Sara
Very well.

Mother Superior
Alas.

Sara
So presumably you won't be needing the unicorn tonight?

Mother Superior
No, Sara. No. Not tonight.

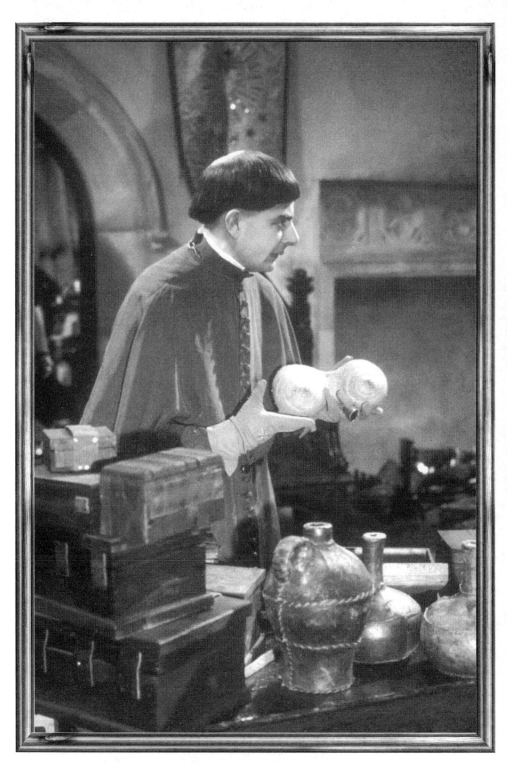

Archbishop Blackadder contemplates the sacred chest of St Matilda

the Queen of Spain's Beard

SCENE ONE: FALCONBREAST CASTLE

It is midnight and the moon is high. Two mysterious shrouded figures are up on the highest battlements.
A dog barks far below them.

And now the two figures have reached opposite ends of the same battlement: they sweep together and meet. The lady is passionate in her speech. The man is very passionate in his breathing.

Lady
Oh, noble prince, your secret note of love has won my heart. (*Deep excited breathing from the man.*) The castle of my body is yours by right of conquest. Come, let your tongue dive into the moat of my mouth, and your hands take possession of the ramparts of my plumpies. For I am yours, and yours alone.

She throws off her cowl, and is a beautiful brunette.

Edmund
(*For it is he*) And I yours!

He throws off his.

Lady
Urgh: Prince Edmund. I thought you were your brother.

She pushes him away in disgust. He topples over the battlement and is savaged by the savage dog below.

~

SCENE TWO: THE KING'S WAR ROOM

In 1492, after the death of Randolph XII of Saxony and the collapse of the Treaty of Insects, Europe was in disarray. Kingdoms rose and fell; borders, even languages, changed; men were killed by their own side and women raped by soldiers of up to seven different nations every week. The Courts of Europe throbbed with activity, and none more so than England . . .

The room is packed with globes, maps and military plans. On the floor is a map of Europe peopled with knee-high soldiers: the king and his lords are very busy. A messenger bursts in.

Messenger
My lord: news! The Swiss have invaded France!

King
Excellent! Wessex: take 10,000 men and pillage Geneva.

Lord Chiswick
But the Swiss are our allies, my lord.

King
Oh, yes. Well, get them to dress up as Germans. Chiswick, remind me to send flowers to the King of France in sympathy for the death of his son.

Lord Chiswick
The one you had murdered?

King
Yes, that's the fellow.

Prince Harry enters.

Messenger
My lord . . .

Prince Harry
Will you get away from me!

Messenger rushes out.

King
Ah, Harry, the gentle art of diplomacy! But you know, Harry, where real diplomacy starts, don't you, my boy?

Prince Harry
Actually I don't, my lord: but I'd like to know.

The king lifts up Prince Harry's skirt.

King
Here . . .

Prince Harry
Are you sure, my lord? I can't imagine anything of real interest down there.

King
Very well: let me explain. What's this for, Harry?

Now he really is getting intimate.

Prince Harry
Well, a couple of things.

King
Correct! And one of those things is . . .

Prince Harry
Best not mentioned really.

King
Right! And the other is fornication, and without fornication there is no marriage, and without marriage there is no diplomacy.

Prince Harry
Oh, I see!

The king then kneels and points to the map.

King
I have decided to ally to a nation most threatening to France. The answer of course is Spain . . . the best way to cement

an alliance of course is by marriage, that is why I have decided that you are to marry the Spanish Infanta.

The lords clap enthusiastically.

Prince Harry
Actually, I don't think I can.

King
What? Why not?

Prince Harry
I am already engaged.

King
What! Who to, boy?

Prince Harry pulls out a list.

Prince Harry
Princess Leia of Hungary, Grand Duchess Ursula of Brandenburg, Queen Beowulfa of Iceland, Countess Caroline of Luxembourg, Bertha of Flanders, Bertha of Brussels and Eunice of Estonia, Bernard of Saxe-Coburg . . . (*Some mistake, surely*) Sorry, that should have been Bertha of Saxe Coburg . . . And Jeremy of Estonia.

King
Damn! If I haven't got a son to marry her then the whole plan falls apart.

The lords look nervously at one another while the king studies the map, not to be disturbed. Chiswick finally takes courage.

Chiswick
Your Majesty.

King
(*Snapping violently*) Yes!

Chiswick
You do have . . . another son, my lord.

King
What . . . Oh, my God, you're right. Of course, the slimy one. What's his name?

Chiswick
Edmund, my lord.

King
Ah, yes, Osmond. Osmond can marry the Infanta. Then, with the Spanish alliance, we can massacre both the Swiss and the French!

Applause and cheers.

Lords
Huzzah!

King
By dividing them for us in two!

Lords
Hurray!

King
Preferably their top halves from their bottom halves!

Lords
Hurray!

~

SCENE THREE: EDMUND'S TOWER ROOM

Edmund tends to the wounds from his earlier fall from the battlements. He has vicious dog bites along his neck. Percy and Baldrick enter.

Percy
Good morning, my lord.

Baldrick
Morning, my lord.

Edmund
Good morning.

Baldrick
My God. What happened to your neck?

Edmund
Ah, yes. They are love bites actually.

Baldrick
Look more like dog bites to me.

Edmund
Well, yes. She was a bit of an animal.

Percy
Really, my lord. A fight to the death, eh? Ha ha!

Edmund
Yes. Well, as my tutor, old Bubbleface, used to say: make love and be merry, for tomorrow you may catch some disgusting skin disease.

He and Percy laugh heartily.

Baldrick
Actually, I'd be prepared to swear those were dog bites.

Edmund
They are not dog bites; she was very attractive.

Baldrick
What, shiny coat, wet nose, clear eyes . . .

Edmund
No, Baldrick, it was a woman.

Baldrick
Fair enough, my lord.

Edmund
Right, now that's sorted out. Percy, what are we up to today?

Percy
Well, my lord. First I thought that you and I might get out a couple of prisoners and . . . actually I think Baldrick may have a point there, they do look rather like dog bites.

Edmund
All right, all right, they're dog bites, they're dog bites. I got bitten by a dog. Some woman pushed me off the top of a rampart because I am so hideously ugly and I got savaged by a rabid dog. Does that satisfy you?

Baldrick
Yes, my lord.

Edmund
Right. Excellent. Good. Yes, Percy?

Percy
Right, my lord. I thought we might . . . so it wasn't a woman?

Edmund
No, it wasn't. It was a dog, it was a dog, it was a bloody great dog!

Percy
Oh, right. Harry, of course, gets all the women.

Edmund
Shut up. I never want women mentioned in my company again.

Baldrick
What about dogs?

Edmund
Or dogs. Shut up you. I never want to see a woman again. If any woman tries to talk to me, warn her: the Black Adder is a venomous reptile and women are his prey.

Knock on the door.

Enter; unless you're a woman, in which case, prepare to be thrown out of the window with your dog!

Messenger
My lord, I bring a message.

Edmund
Yes, obviously. You're a messenger.

Messenger
You are engaged to be married to the Infanta Maria of Spain.

Edmund
What?!

Messenger
My lord, I bring a message. You are . . .

Edmund
Yes, yes, yes, yes. Well, boys, did you hear that? I am to marry the Infanta of Spain!

Percy
Yes! Shall I go and tell her, my lord!

Edmund
What?

Percy
The Black Adder is a venomous reptile and women and dogs . . .

Edmund
No, no, no! This is no ordinary woman. We're talking about a beautiful royal princess, Percy! Imagine what the Spanish Infanta must be like.

Baldrick and Percy
Howwwl!

Edmund has rarely been more excited.

SCENE FOUR: THE GREAT HALL

A crowd of people are gathered round to receive the Infanta. They are looking admiringly at Edmund, who is with Baldrick and Percy. Prince Harry approaches with a beauty on his arm.

Prince Harry
Bienvenido a nuestro castillo–Espero que encuentras los desagües a su satisfacción.

Edmund
Ha ha ha ha. Mmm?

Prince Harry
It's Spanish. It means, 'Welcome to our castle, and I hope you find the drains to your satisfaction.' Here you are. I've jotted it down for you. It should help you break the ice with the Infanta. I don't think you've met Countess Caroline of Luxembourg.

Edmund
Hello, Caroline.

Prince Harry
Actually, I've only just met her myself. Excuse me. *Bienvenue à notre château, Caroline. J'espère que vous trouvez satisfaisant le robinet de purge.*

Prince Harry moves away.

Edmund
Ha ha: Luxembourg.

Baldrick
Have you ever seen a man so obviously seething with jealousy?

Edmund
No, I haven't.

Baldrick
Seethe, seethe, seethe, my lord. If he goes on seething like that much longer, he'll turn into a seethe.

Edmund
Baldrick, what are you talking about?

Percy
My lord.

Edmund
Yes, what is it?

Percy
They say the Infanta's eyes are more beautiful than the famous stone of Galveston.

Edmund
The what?

Percy
The famous blue stone of Galveston, my lord.

Edmund
What's that exactly?

Percy
Ah, well, my lord. It's a famous blue stone, and it comes from Galveston.

Edmund
I see. And what about it?

Percy
Well, the Infanta's eyes are bluer than it, my lord, for a start.

Edmund
I see. Have you ever seen this stone?

Percy
Ahm, not as such, my lord, no. But I know a couple of people who have and they say it is very blue indeed.

Edmund
I see. And have these people seen the Infanta's eyes?

Percy
I shouldn't think so, my lord.

Edmund
And neither have you?

Percy
No, my lord.

Edmund
So, what you're telling me is that something that you have never seen is slightly less blue than something else you have never seen?

Percy
Yes, my lord.

There is a polite fanfare and the Infanta enters. She is an extraordinarily capacious woman. A dragon. But a dragon who is sure she is the most attractive woman in Europe, and the most sensual in the world. She is instantly, passionately, in love with Edmund.

Accompanying her is her interpreter, a thin weaselly cove with a beard, called Don Speekingleesh.

Edmund carries on regardless of her presence.

Edmund
Percy, in the end, you are about as much use to me as a hole in the head, an affliction with which you must be familiar, never having had a brain.

Interpreter
Hello.

Edmund
Hello. (*And he turns back to Percy*) Here I am awaiting the arrival of the most ravishing . . .

The interpreter and the Infanta have approached Edmund, the interpreter closest to him, the Infanta behind him, so the latter is largely blocked from Edmund's view.

Interpreter
Hello.

Edmund
Look, leave me alone, will you. I'm trying to talk to someone.

Edmund continues talking to Percy.

. . . While you're wittering away like a pox-ridden parakeet . . .

Infanta
Eres el verdadero amor de mi vida. Amor mío, amor mío . . .

The interpreter translates the Infanta's whispers.

Interpreter
You are the true love of my life: my love, my love . . .

Edmund
What?

Infanta
Tú eres mi único amor. Quiero besarte y abrazarte . . .

Interpreter
You are the only one for me. I want to hug and kiss you . . .

Edmund bops him on the nose.

Infanta
Soy la Infanta . . .

Interpreter
No, I am the Infanta!

Edmund
What! No one told me you had a beard.

Percy
It must be Jeremy of Estonia!

Infanta
(*Grabbing him*) *Non! Soy la Infanta!*

The horror of realization hits Edmund.

Edmund
Well, absolutely. Waah!

Infanta
He esperado este momento toda mi vida.

Interpreter
I have waited for this moment all my life.

Infanta
Tú nariz es más pequeña de lo que espera-ba.

Interpreter
Your nose is smaller than I expected.

Edmund
I have suffered no similar disappointment.

Interpreter
(*To Infanta*) *No he sufrido igual desengaño.*

Infanta
Amor mío . . .

Interpreter
My love, my love.

The Infanta makes a grab for Edmund and launches into the most passionate kiss in the history of European love. Edmund tugs and pulls and finally breaks free: a broken man.

Infanta
Me gustan tus labios.

Interpreter
Your lips I like.

Infanta
Es el resto de tu cuerpo lo que me interesa.

Interpreter
It is the rest of your body I wish to find out more about.

The Infanta gives Edmund her killer look of lust and desire: he is frozen with horror.

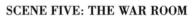

SCENE FIVE: THE WAR ROOM

Messenger One
My lord, news.

King
What?

Messenger One
Your Highness! The Spanish Infanta has arrived!

King
Ah! Good news! Soon we will have Spain in our grip!

A second messenger rushes in.

Messenger Two
My lord, news!

King
What?

Messenger Two
The King of France sends his greetings.

King
Ah! Good news! My diplomacy triumphs!

A third messenger rushes in.

Messenger Three
My lord, news!

King
What?

Messenger Three
Lord Wessex is dead!

King
Ah! This news is not so good.

Messenger Three
Pardon, my lord.

King
I like it not: bring me some other news.

Messenger Three
Pardon, my lord?

King
I like not this news! Bring me some other news!

Messenger Three
Yes, my lord.

He exits and the king returns to the map. Messenger Three re-enters immediately.

My lord, news!

King
Yes?

Messenger Three
Lord Wessex is not dead.

King
Ah, good news. Let there be joy and celebration: let jubilation reign!

Messenger Three
Yes, my lord.

King
Oh, yes, and tell Osmond that to further strengthen ties with Spain, he marries tomorrow!

SCENE SIX: EDMUND'S TOWER ROOM

Edmund sprints into his room and locks the door. Baldrick and Percy are with him.

Edmund
Oh, my God. In twenty-four hours I'll be married to a walrus.

Baldrick
My lord: you can't just lock her out, you know.

Edmund
No, you're right. But it should hold her for at least a minute.

He leaps on to his bed and tugs a small rope. A little portcullis crashes down in front of the door. Baldrick produces an axe from under the bed.

Percy
Wait a moment, my lord! I think I may have a plan to get you out of this marriage.

Edmund
Yeees: but it's going to be a stupid one, Percy, let's face it.

Percy thinks for a while.

Percy
Yes, you're right.

Edmund
Still . . . tell me what it is anyway.

Percy
Actually, no, my lord. I don't think I'll bother.

Edmund
No, go on. Please tell me.

Percy
All right. I go to the Infanta's room and tell her that you've gone mad. She comes to the door, and you meet her, disguised as a little pig. But then, and this is the cunning bit, instead of saying 'oink, oink', you say 'moo'!

Edmund
Then?

Percy
Well, then she'll know you're mad, and leave.

Edmund
You were right. You shouldn't have bothered.

Baldrick
I also have a plan, my lord.

Edmund
Yes?

Baldrick
Why not . . . make her think you prefer the company of men?

Edmund
Well, I do Baldrick, I do.

Baldrick
No, my lord, I mean, the . . . intimate company . . . of men.

It dawns on Edmund.

Edmund
You don't mean . . . like the Earl of Doncaster!

Baldrick
I mean just like the Earl of Doncaster!

Edmund
That great radish, that steaming great left-footer. The Earl of Doncaster, Baldrick, has been riding side-saddle since he was seventeen.

Baldrick
But who would marry the Earl of Doncaster?

Edmund
Well, no one . . . Brilliant! Of course! No one would marry the Earl of Doncaster. Except perhaps the Duke of Beaufort. Quick – what are we going to do?

Baldrick
First I'll get you looking right. We just need something effeminate draped round your shoulders.

Edmund
Either of the Beaufort twins would do.

SCENE SEVEN: EDMUND'S TOWER ROOM

Edmund is now dressed absurdly in extravagant, colourful clothing.

Baldrick
Right, perfect. Now, all we need to do is practise with Percy.

Edmund
(*Very suspicious*) Practise what?

Baldrick
Presentation, my lord. Percy, you stand over here and my lord, just there. Now, Percy, Lord Edmund is going to try and make himself attractive to you.

Percy
Attractive?

Edmund
You know. Like the Earl of Doncaster.

Percy
Good Lord. Oh, well, fair enough.

Percy immediately clicks into his perfect imitation of the famous earl.

Edmund
No, Percy, you act normally. I'm the Earl of Doncaster. Right.

Baldrick
Right. Go.

Edmund tries imitating, but in vain.

Edmund
Oh, I can't do this. It's impossible.

Baldrick
Never mind. I've got a couple more things
might help.

Edmund
Percy, what am I going to do?

*Baldrick leaves in search of more props.
Percy and Edmund stand awkwardly,
Edmund still half trying to get into char-
acter.*

Percy
Perhaps we should try to strike up a conversation . . . Hello there.

Edmund
Hello . . . Er . . . how are you?

Percy
(*Very camp*) I'm fine. Have you heard?
Prince Edmund's going to marry the
Spanish Infanta.

*Edmund physically attacks Percy for this
obviously provocative comment.*

Edmund
No, he damn well isn't, and anyone who
suggests otherwise is going to have his head
torn off.

*He gets Percy flat on his face in a compro-
mising position. Baldrick re-enters.*

Baldrick
Yes, that's the kind of thing.

~

SCENE EIGHT: THE GREAT HALL

*Standing like a man posing for a painting in
the middle of the hall, Edmund is fully
dressed in his campest regalia: Percy is acting it too, and Baldrick is fussing round,
just fixing those crucial little details.
Trumpets blow.*

Edmund
Here she comes.

*They stand to further attention. The king
enters. He is en route to the war room and
isn't at all shocked by this sight.*

King
Morning, Doncaster. Chiswick, take this to
the Queen of Naples.

The king hands Chiswick a vase.

Chiswick
What is it, my lord?

King
The King of Naples.

They exit.

Edmund
Quick . . .

*The doors open and Prince Harry enters
with another beautiful princess on his arm.
He looks at Edmund vaguely askance.*

Oh, my God.

Prince Harry
Some lark for the stag party, eh?

Edmund
Yes, that's right.

Prince Harry
I don't think you have met the Grand
Duchess Ursula of Brandenburg?

Edmund
No, hello. How do you do, Ursula.

Prince Harry
Look, I did just want to have a word about
my speech at the wedding. I thought perhaps I'd go for a fruit motif.

Edmund
Yes?

Prince Harry
Something like this: 'It is with exstrawber-
ry pleasure that we welcome you. May you
be the apple of your husband's eye, and
may he in turn cherries you' – cherish,
you see – 'even though it is an orange'd
marriage.' What do you think?

Edmund
Brilliant, brilliant, quite brilliant.

Prince Harry
Yes, I think it is rather good. I'm actually

hoping to squeeze in a banana by the end of the day. *Willkommen nach unser Schloss, Ursula.*

Prince Harry and Ursula exit. Trumpets blow.

Baldrick
OK, my lord. This is it.

The queen pops her head round the corner.

Edmund
For Christ's sake, mother: what do you want?

Queen
Nothing, nothing.

The queen halts as the doors fling open and the Infanta enters with the interpreter. She sees Edmund; in a second she is sobbing.

Edmund
It's working, it's working!

Infanta
Te abrazo y te amo totalmente.

Interpreter
Oh, I embrace you and love you totally.

Edmund
What?

Infanta
Qué amor es éste que te dizfrazas como un español para complacerme.

Interpreter
Oh, what a love this must be, that you dress like a Spanish man to delight me.

Edmund
Baldrick.

Infanta
O, qué amor, o, qué amor.

Interpreter
Oh, what a love, oh, what a love.

Edmund
Baldrick, you fool.

The Infanta embraces Edmund.

Queen
Oh, look at the two lovebirds . . .

Edmund
(*Over the Infanta's shoulder*) One love-bird, and one love elephant.

Queen
It's almost as if they were married already.

Edmund
(*Suddenly alert*) What?

Queen
It's almost as if you were married already.

Edmund
That's what I thought you said.

He wrestles round to a different angle so he can speak to Baldrick and Percy.

Boys.

Percy and Baldrick
Yes, my lord.

Edmund
I think I have another plan.

SCENE NINE: A CORRIDOR

The Reverend Lloyd is walking along innocently when he is knocked unconscious by a stick wielded by Baldrick.

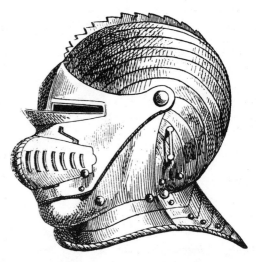

SCENE TEN: A PEASANT'S COTTAGE

*A quintessential wishy-washy clergyman,
the Reverend Lloyd, has made a
makeshift altar out of a table in this peasant's cottage: he is assembling his arte-
facts for a wedding service, and rubbing
his head where he was hit: he looks a little
insecure. As he potters, we hear voices
and a woman, Mrs Applebottom, giggling.*

Edmund
Percy, is she the best you could do? I
mean, I am marrying the woman.

Percy
Yes, but it is only for a couple of days, isn't
it?

Edmund
Oh, yes, I suppose so. Come on, hurry up,
Father.

Reverend
Very well. We are gathered here, O gra-
cious Lord, to bear witness, at very short
notice . . .

*Edmund is standing next to Tully
Applebottom, a solid peasant woman.
Percy and Baldrick flank the odd couple.*

. . . to the marriage of these two God-fearing Christians, Edmund, Duke of
Edinburgh, and . . . (*consulting a piece of
paper*) Tully Applebottom. Is that right?

Tully Applebottom
(*Giggling*) Yes, that's right. Who ever
would have thought it? The Duke of
Edinburgh, consumed with passion,
whisks away little Tully . . .

Edmund
Shut up. (*She giggles: Edmund turns to
the reverend*) Come on, get on with it,
Father.

Reverend
Very well. Are you Prince Edmund, Duke
of Edinburgh?

Edmund
No, I'm a bowl of soup. For goodness'
sake, hurry up!

Loud giggles from Tully.

Reverend
And are you Miss Tully Applebottom?

Tully Applebottom
Mrs.

Reverend
Mrs. Ah!

Edmund
Ah!

Percy
Ah!

A moment's silence.

Edmund
Yes. Well? Get on with it, Father.

Reverend
But surely if she's . . .

Edmund
Oh, for heaven's sake, the Church is never
going to progress if it isn't a bit adaptable.

Reverend
Yes, but this is very unusual . . .

Baldrick places a knife at his throat.

Although hasn't the Church always dealt
with the unusual? The miracle with the
fishes, for example. We continue . . .
Does . . . anyone here . . . know any just
cause or impediment why these two
should not be joined together in holy mat-
rimony?

Edmund
No!

Baldrick
No!

Percy
No!

*At which moment a door swings open and
a large peasant with a scythe enters.*

Mr Applebottom
Yes!

Reverend
Ah, and you are . . .

Mr Applebottom
Mr Applebottom.

Reverend
Are you the father of the bride?

Mr Applebottom
No, I'm the husband of the bride.

Mrs Applebottom
This is my husband Thomas. Thomas, this is my fiancé, the Duke of Edinburgh. Prince Edmund, this is Thomas; Thomas, this is Father . . .

Reverend
Smith, I called about the ducking stool fund.

Mr Applebottom moves threateningly towards Edmund.

Edmund
The thing is, I was just wondering . . .

Mr Applebottom
Yes?

Mr Applebottom has them all cornered by the altar.

Edmund
Whether I could have a temporary arrangement with your good lady.
I only need her for a very short stint.

Mr Applebottom
Get out of here.

Edmund
Look, you stupid peasant. All I want to do is marry your wife.

Mr Applebottom
Get out.

Edmund leaves, without ceremony or dignity or wife.

Mrs Applebottom
That was the Duke of Edinburgh, you know.

Mr Applebottom
Ah, no. That would be the Earl of Doncaster.

SCENE ELEVEN: BAY WINDOW OF THE GREAT HALL

The Infanta, interpreter and queen are having a 'get-to-know-you' session.

Infanta
Ah, esto está bien.

Interpreter
Well, this is nice.

Queen
Yes.

Infanta
Hablemos un poco de cosas de mujeres.

Interpreter
To have a little talk about ladies' things.

Infanta
Las dos solas.

Interpreter
Just the two of us.

Infanta
Bueno. Hábleme de los hombres ingleses, señora.

Interpreter
So tell me, Mrs Queen, about Englishmen.

Queen
Well, they spend most of their time with animals, you know, and other men: and when they do come to the women, they only want one thing.

Infanta
¿Qué?

Interpreter
And what is that?

Queen
Well, it's a kind of pudding made with bread and butter and raisins. That and . . . the other thing, of course.

Infanta
¿Y qué es so?

Interpreter
What is the other thing?

Queen
Well, custard.

Interpreter
Crème.

Infanta
¿Y Edmundo, qué tal es?

Interpreter
And Edmund, now what's he like?

Queen
Well, I told you, this pudding . . .

Infanta
No, no, en la cama.

Interpreter
No, what's he like . . . in bed?

Queen
Oh, I see. Well, in bed he likes hot milk, with just a little cinnamon.

Interpreter
No. What. Is. He. Like?

Queen
Well, he's like a little rabbit really, isn't he?

Infanta
¡Mamá, mamá cuánto le quiero!

Interpreter
Oh, mummy, mummy: how much I love him!

Nothing can put this woman off.

~

SCENE TWELVE: EDMUND'S TOWER ROOM

Edmund is wearing a large set of stag horns on his head. Percy and Baldrick are wearing them as well. There is a roasting stag in front of the fire.

Edmund
I would never have believed that my stag party would be like this . . . the most depressing night of my life.

Baldrick
Well, at least you can take solace in one thing, my lord.

Edmund
What's that?

Baldrick
You can be pretty sure your wife's a virgin.

Edmund
At least, there are no living witnesses to the contrary. If she wasn't we might still stand a chance. Officially you've still got to be a virgin.

An idea hits Edmund. He looks at Percy.

Percy
What, my lord? (*He suddenly realizes*) Oh!

They both look across at Baldrick.

Baldrick
Oh, no, my lord. No.

Edmund
Yes, yes, *yeees!*

This is the definitive plan.

~

SCENE THIRTEEN: A CORRIDOR

Edmund, Percy and Baldrick stand in a dark corridor outside the Infanta's room. Baldrick's coat is removed, as before execution.

Baldrick
My lord, please, I beg you to reconsider.

Edmund
If there were any other way, Baldrick, you know I'd take it.

Baldrick
But I'll die in there.

Edmund
Yes, and we'll give you a hero's funeral: bury you at sea; say you died in combat with an enemy vessel. Right, in you go. Little boy with big job to do. Percy, let's get the king.

Percy turns to follow Edmund, but stops, turns again and goes slowly to Baldrick.

They hug ceremonially, like men before a battle. Tears shed, Percy leaves.

SCENE FOURTEEN: THE INFANTA'S ROOM

Baldrick enters the pitch darkness of the Infanta's room.

Baldrick
Infanta . . . Infanta.

Infanta
¡Ooooooo! Edmundo, amor mío.

Interpreter
Oh, Edmund, my love.

Yes, he's there too.

SCENE FIFTEEN: THE WAR ROOM

The king is still hard at work, waging war, when Edmund bursts in with Percy.

Edmund
My lord, your Majesty!

King
What?

Edmund
I bring the gravest of news!

King
What? Our armies on the Rhine slaughtered, their heads cut off and melted cheese poured down their nostrils in the traditional Swiss manner?

Edmund
No, my lord.

SCENE SIXTEEN: THE INFANTA'S ROOM

Back in the dangerous darkness.

Infanta
Amor mío, amor mío. No te detengas, mi serpiente . . .

Interpreter
Oh, my love, oh, my love. Don't hold back, please my little worm.

SCENE SEVENTEEN: THE INFANTA'S ROOM

Baldrick
Help!

Interpreter
Socorro!

SCENE EIGHTEEN: THE WAR ROOM

King
Then do you bring news of the Russian royal family, mistaken for bison due to their excessive winter clothing and hunted down, chopped to pieces and eaten as sweets by Mongolian bandits?

Edmund
No, my lord.

King
Well, what then?

Edmund
(*His most grand manner*) My lord: the Spanish Infanta is not a virgin.

SCENE NINETEEN: THE INFANTA'S ROOM

There is some panting.

Infanta
¡Más! ¡Más!

Interpreter
Again, please.

SCENE TWENTY: THE WAR ROOM

King
What?!

Edmund
The Infanta I am to marry tomorrow is
not a virgin.

King
Oh, yes. I know, her uncle told me . . . We
took five hundred off the dowry because
of it.

Edmund
But I thought . . .

King
Only one of you has to be a virgin.
Anything else?

Edmund is aghast and leaves with Percy.

SCENE TWENTY-ONE: THE GREAT
HALL

*All Edmund's plans have failed.
The Great Hall is decked for a wedding. A
grand archbishop is ready to go.*

*Edmund and the Infanta stand surround-
ed by lords and ladies. Baldrick is present. He is half the man he was the day
before: battered, hair straight up in the
air, two black eyes, and a stoop.*

*The interpreter is still interpreting every-
thing loudly in the Infanta's ear.*

Archbishop
Dearly beloved, we are gathered together
here in the sight of our Lord to witness the
marriage of two God-fearing Christians ...
Are you Edmund, Duke of Edinburgh?

Edmund
Yes, I am.

Archbishop
And are you María Escalosa Fienna
Infanta?

The interpreter whispers it in her ear.

Infanta
*Si, stupido, date prisa: deja que mis volu-
minosos muslos te abracen.*

Interpreter
(*To archbishop*) Yes, you stupid person:

hurry up. I wish to entwine him again in
my broad thighs.

*The king is standing near the back sur-
rounded by lords with maps and globes
and soldiers: he clearly has not really had
the time to take time off, so he has
brought his war room with him.*

Archbishop
Marriage is an holy state, conceived by
God . . .

Edmund
Dear Lord, please help me now.

Archbishop
. . . so if any man here knows just cause
why they should not be married, let him
speak now, or for ever hold his peace.

Edmund
Now is your chance.

Archbishop
So be it.

Edmund
Thanks. Thanks a lot.

The king is impatient to get back to work.

King
Come on. Hurry up.

Archbishop
Do you, Edmund Plantagenet, take
María Escalosa to be your lawful
wedded wife . . . to have and to hold, to
cherish and to delight, to chastise and
to beat until death, until death do you
part?

Edmund nods weakly.

King
Speak up. Can't hear a thing back here!

Edmund
I do.

King
Still can't hear!

Edmund
I do! I do! I do!

The Infanta, overcome by Edmund's obvi-

ous burst of passion, embraces him.

Archbishop
And do you, María Escalosa Infanta take Edmund Plantagenet to be your lawful wedded husband . . .

Infanta
¡Si, si, si!

Interpreter
Yes, yes, yes.

Edmund
Oh, no!

Archbishop
I then declare you . . .

But suddenly there is a smashing of doors and the entrance of a messenger. He waves a scroll in his hand.

Messenger
Stop!

They all turn to face him to the exasperation of the archbishop.

Archbishop
Christ!

Messenger
I bring absolutely incredible news which must halt the wedding.

King
What – have the Swiss and the French made sudden peace with each other at a mountain pass rendezvous, then forged a clandestine alliance with Spain, thus leaving us without friends in Europe unless by chance we make an immediate pact with Hungary?

Messenger unrolls and consults the scroll and looks up a little puzzled.

Messenger
Yes.

King
As I thought. Are there any Hungarian Princesses in the castle?

Suddenly a ray of hope for Edmund.

Prince Harry
I've got one I think, my lord. Princess Leia of Hungary.

Edmund
What's she like?

Prince Harry
Princess Leia is young and beautiful. Her eyes are like opals and her hair a cascade of perfect chestnut.

Edmund
Oh, well, that sounds all right.

The Infanta is in a state of utter confusion, as the interpreter whispers frantically into her ear.

Infanta
¿Qué pasa aquí?

Interpreter
Excuse me. What is happening, please?

King
Call Leia into Court. And as for that great Spanish dumpling there . . .

The interpreter relays this to the Infanta. She hits him, and hits him hard.

. . . get her out of my sight at once before I eat her.

Infanta
O, amor mío, sálvame.

Interpreter
Oh, my love, save me.

Edmund
Sorry, what can I do? Politics.

He shrugs his happy shoulders.

King
Come on, come on. Where is she?

Edmund smooths his hair and strikes an attractive pose.

Through the crowd walks the very young and beautiful Princess Leia. She is very young indeed. Maybe just ten.

Edmund's face registers surprise. The trumpets accompany the little girl's walk to where Edmund is. They stand facing each other, all others having moved away to give space for this romantic meeting.

Ah, good. Osmund, meet your new wife.

Leia
Hello, Edmund.

Edmund
Hello, Leia.

Leia
Are we getting married now?

Edmund
Er, yes I believe we are.

Leia
Come on then!

Archbishop
Dearly beloved, we are gathered here today . . .

SCENE TWENTY-TWO: EDMUND'S TOWER ROOM

There are now two single beds in Edmund's room. Princess Leia is in one, Edmund is in the other, reading a book. Princess Leia is listening intently.

Edmund
And so it came to pass that the Big Bear had to leave all his friends in the wood, and go to live in a land far away, where the fairies and the elves would look after him until the day he died.

Edmund closes the book. The princess yawns.

Leia
Oh, that was lovely, Edmund. What a happy story. Isn't it time to put the light out?

Edmund
Yes, my dear, I think it is. It must be at least six o'clock.

Edmund blows the candle out between the beds.

Leia
Goodnight, Edmund.

Edmund
(*Wearily*) Goodnight, my dear.

Edmund emits a deep sigh.

Leia
Can I have a drink of water please?

Edmund
Yes, yes, all right.

Witchsmeller Pursuivant

SCENE ONE: THE TYLER'S HOUSE

Four peasants are eating a hearty meal and conversation is flowing with the mead.

Mrs Tyler
What about the plague? Rumours from the north say it's worse there than ever.

Piers
No, no. Now that we've found out about the rats, we'll never have plague again.

Mrs Field
You know what they say – a rat a day keeps the plague away.

Piers
Believe me, madam, there'll be no more plague in our lifetime.

Mrs Tyler rises to get the pie from the side table.

Mrs Tyler
Well, I hope you're right.

She picks up the pie, and when she turns back, all her guests have died from the plague. She screams and drops the pie.

~

SCENE TWO: COUNTRYSIDE NEAR THE CASTLE

By the autumn of the Year of Our Lord 1495, the Black Plague once again howled westwards across Europe from the Indies, carried by seamen and entering England by the South-west Passage.

Each day, thousands died.

Village after village disappeared in its

evil wake, and not even the best and noblest escaped its horror.

~

SCENE THREE: CASTLE CORRIDOR

Edmund is just unhooking a picture of a naked female saint from the wall. Prince Harry comes round the corner.

Prince Harry
Ah, Edmund, I'm glad I've caught you.

Edmund
(*Very guilty*) Er . . . Doing what?

Prince Harry
I'm afraid Father's feeling a bit under the weather.

Edmund
Oh dear, any idea what?

Prince Harry
Not sure. I think it's probably Black Death. Nevertheless, I am sure he would appreciate a little visit from you.

Edmund
Ah! Well, I could probably pop my head around the door.

Prince Harry
Sort of now-ish.

~

SCENE FOUR: THE CORRIDOR OUTSIDE THE KING'S BEDROOM

The queen is knitting, guarding the door. Edmund enters the corridor.

Edmund
(*By door*) Mother, would you like to . . .

Queen
No, dear, he won't let me near him.

Edmund goes in – and is greeted by the king, screaming madly and swinging his sword about.

King
HHHHHaaaaaahhhhhh!

Edmund shoots out and closes the door

behind him. A sword smashes through it.

Queen
How is he?

Edmund
Well, he's up.

~

SCENE FIVE: A MEETING ROOM IN THE CASTLE

Lords are gathered round the table. Edmund is also there looking a little ill at ease. Percy and Baldrick are at his shoulder.

Prince Harry sits at the end of the table, firmly in control of the meeting.

Prince Harry
My lords of the council, we face today the gravest crisis this country has known since the Roman Invasion.

Lords
Here, here.

Prince Harry
Therefore I propose . . .

A messenger bursts in.

Messenger
Your Highness, the king has stirred and calls for you.

Prince Harry gulps and rises.

Prince Harry
Very well. Gentlemen, I must leave.

All rise with Prince Harry. It's pretty definite he's facing certain death.

Prince Edmund is in charge.

Lords
Shame!

Prince Harry exits with the messenger. The lords look to Edmund with expectation; he beckons Baldrick to pick up Prince Harry's papers.

Edmund
Ahm, right, gentlemen. As you know, we face today the gravest crisis this country has known since the Roman Invasion.

Lords
Rubbish! Nonsense!

Lord Lindsey
What about the Viking Invasion?

Lord Broxtable
And the Norman Invasion?

Lord Tablett
And the Swiss Invasion?

Edmund
Well, the greatest crisis for some time.

Lord Broxtable
And we all know why!

Edmund
Why?

Lord Tablett
Because . . . the king is possessed.

Edmund was totally not expecting this.

Edmund
What?

Lord Broxtable
True, true, the land is full of omens, of bewitchment. Only last week in Cornwall a man with four heads was seen taking tea on the beach, and two women in Windsor claim to have been raped by a fish.

Lord Lindsey
I, too, have heard such tales. In Harrogate it rained phlegm, and in Edinburgh it is said the graves did open, and the ghosts of our ancestors rose up and competed in athletic sports.

Other Lords
Horror! Horror! . . .

Percy
Yes, and a friend of mine had this awful pimple inside his nose.

Lord Tablett
A farmer in Rye swears he heard a cow reciting Geoffrey Chaucer, and a girl in Shropshire saw Geoffrey Chaucer in a field, mooing and suckling a young heifer.

Edmund
Yes, gentlemen – surely we aren't the kind of people who believe this sort of thing. I mean, start believing this and next you'll be telling me that washing your hair in bat's droppings stops you going bald.

Lord Broxtable
It is true. I couldn't find enough bats and look what happened.

He reveals he is bald. Shock from all.

Lord Tablett
I move we do the only thing that we can do to remove this curse from the kingdom.

Edmund
Ah yes, well, that sounds like the answer, doesn't it!

Lord Lindsey
Call for . . . the Witchsmeller Pursuivant!

Edmund
Who?

Lord Broxtable
Root out the witches, call for the Smeller!

By now, they are all on their feet, spitting.

Lord Lindsey
The Witchsmeller! Burn, burn, burn!

Lord Tablett
We must inform the Prince of Wales.

They leave, riding a wave of hysteria.

Lords
The Witchsmeller! The Witchsmeller! Burn the witches! Send for the Smeller! Burn, burn, burn!

Edmund sees he's lost control. Percy also follows the lords, equally overcome with passion. Edmund stops him.

Edmund
Percy. What the devil do you think you're doing?

Percy
Look, I just can't take the pressure of all these omens any more.

Edmund
Percy . . .

Percy is almost in tears.

Percy
No, no really, I'm serious. Only this morning in the courtyard I saw a horse with two heads and two bodies.

Edmund
Two horses standing next to each other?

Percy
Oh yes, I suppose it could have been.

Edmund
Honestly, I suppose you're one of those people who think sticking your finger up a sheep's bottom on Good Friday makes you fertile.

Baldrick
That's rubbish.

Edmund
Precisely.

Baldrick
It's Easter Monday.

Edmund
Yes. Remind me not to shake your hand during a religious festival. I don't believe it. I mean, who is this Witchsmeller Pursuivant anyway?

Baldrick
I don't know, my lord, but Mistress Scott would.

Edmund
Of course, the old crone with the cat.

Percy
Oh, the cat, lovely. But she lives in the village.

Edmund
So?

Percy
But everyone's dying of plague.

Edmund
Yes, that's what they claim. Any excuse for getting out of a decent day's work.

Edmund exits, followed by Percy and Baldrick.

SCENE SIX: THE GATES OF THE TOWN

Edmund, Percy and Baldrick make their way into town stepping over bodies as they go.

Edmund
Well, obviously there are some genuine cases.

They pass a pilgrimage of the dead, dying or fleeing. Those who greet Edmund are depressed and downtrodden.

A Peasant
Morning, Prince Edmund.

Edmund
Morning, peasant.

Another Peasant
Morning, Prince Edmund.

Edmund
Morning, peasant.

Yet Another Peasant
Morning, Prince Edmund.

Baldrick
My lord, shouldn't we disguise? We don't want anyone with a grudge coming up and infecting us on purpose, do we?

Edmund
Yes, you're right.

They dive through a market stall selling clothes. Edmund emerges in his 'disguise': a small piece of cloth tied loosely across his face.

Peasant
Morning, stranger.

Edmund
Morning, friend.

One More Peasant
Morning, stranger.

Edmund
Morning, friend.

Peasant Number Six
Morning, stranger.

He turns to the seventh peasant beside him.

Who is that dark stranger?

Peasant Number Seven
Oh, that'll be Prince Edmund.

Peasant Number Six
Oh yes, course it is.

Percy
This way, my lord.

Percy efficiently lays down his cloak for

Edmund on a particularly mucky part of the road. Edmund looks at it and steps round it, walking on. Percy picks up his cloak and runs after him. They walk through the terrible village and arrive at Mistress Scott's house. There is no sign of life coming from the house. The town-crier passes by.

Town-crier
Bring out your de . . .

He drops dead.

Edmund
Where's Mistress Scott?

Yet Another Peasant
You've just passed her.

Edmund
What?

Edmund looks back to see two stakes in the ground. There is a pile of ash at the bottom of each stake – one is five foot high, the other one foot high.

My God. And this?

Percy
The cat, my lord.

Edmund
(*To everyone*) Does anyone know what happened?

A peasant raises his hand and looks

rather suspicious.

Suspicious Peasant
No, I don't.

Thick Peasant
Me neither. I was right on the other side
of town when we burned her.

His friend whacks him.

Suspicious Peasant
Sssssssssssssh!

They are a suspicious pair.

Edmund
You burned her! What for?

Suspicious Peasant
I don't know.

Thick Peasant
Well, it was because she was a witch,
wasn't it?

Suspicious Peasant
Sssssh!

Edmund
You burned Mistress Scott for being a
witch? Why?

Thick Peasant
Can't say. It's a secret.

Edmund
A secret! Do you know who I am?

Suspicious Peasant
A stranger.

Edmund
Oh yes, that's right. Well, tell me anyway.

Suspicious Peasant
No, we can't. And I'll tell you why,
because if you'd been part of a secret
committee to invite the Witchsmeller
Pursuivant into town and he'd already
burned four of your best friends, would
you go telling everyone?

Edmund
No, no, I suppose I wouldn't . . . so is it
the Witchsmeller Pursuivant who's
burned her?

First Peasant
He's guessed!

Another Peasant
He's clever.

Baldrick
They don't call him Clever Jake for nothing, you know.

Edmund
Well, they don't call me Clever Jake. Oh,
I see . . . (*He realizes he's
meant to be in disguise*)
And what does this
Witchsmeller man look
like?

Yet Another Peasant
No one knows, my lord.
No one. He is a master of
disguise, and mostly
appears only at night.
That's right, isn't it?

*It suddenly gets darker. At
which moment, the
Witchsmeller appears, in
all his holy terror, coal-
red eyes glowing beneath
his deathly dark cloak.*

Witchsmeller
I believe so.

Edmund
All right, so he won't be around now, but still, let me tell you something: if the so-called Witchsmeller burned Mistress Scott . . .

Percy
(*Deeply moved*) And her cat.

The Witchsmeller goes and stands next to Edmund, who is oblivious to him.

Edmund
And her cat, then there's something wrong with his nose and I should know – they don't call me Clever Pete for nothing.

Baldrick
Jake, my lord.

Edmund
What about him?

Baldrick
Clever Jake, my lord.

Edmund
Where?

Baldrick
You're Clever Jake, my lord.

Edmund
Oh yes, they don't call me Clever Pete at all, they call me Clever Jake. If I were you and I'd asked the Witchsmeller into town . . . I'd throw the big-nosed bully straight out again. What do you think?

He turns, still totally oblivious to the terrifying figure beside him.

Witchsmeller
I think it's worth serious consideration.

Edmund
There we go. Take Clever Tom's advice and send him back to the madhouse he came from. Come on, boys, Mistress Scott is obviously in no state to help us today.

He strides off.

SCENE SEVEN: CASTLE MEETING ROOM

Two hands are visible, one says 'GOOD' on the fingers, the other says 'EVIL'. The Witchsmeller is in residence.

Witchsmeller
I have two functions: to protect the good . . .

He turns over the GOOD hand, to reveal an egg in it.

And to crush the evil.

Likewise the EVIL hand, with its own egg.

Watch!

He squeezes his hands and both eggs smash.

Prince Harry
Fascinating, absolutely fascinating. Um . . . actually, you have crushed both eggs, you know.

Witchsmeller
Some that seem good sometimes proveth to be evil.

A man with a bowl appears behind the Witchsmeller. He turns to wash his hands in it. At that moment the door behind him opens and Baldrick enters.

Baldrick
My lords, the Duke of Edinburgh!

And Edmund enters.

Prince Harry
Ah, Edmund. Come in. The Witchsmeller's arrived.

Edmund
Oh yes. Old Big-Nose is back, is he?

The Witchsmeller turns, a truly nasty piece of work. Edmund hopes he won't be recognized from the village episode. Vain, vain hope.

Oh, hello. I'm delighted to meet you. I'm one of your greatest admirers.

Witchsmeller
'Old Big-Nose is back'?

Edmund
Yes. Old Big-Nose's . . . back . . . is in a terrible state. I was talking to him just now. He's a great admirer of yours as well.

Percy
Who's this?

Edmund
(*Pointing behind him vaguely*) Oh, Old Big-Nose. In fact, I've just been hearing about your work in Taunton. Imagine that – every single person in the village having an affair with the same duck.

Witchsmeller
The Duck of Taunton was a tragic circumstance.

Edmund
And I hear you very kindly burned our Mistress Scott for us.

Witchsmeller
Oh, yes. And her pussy cat.

Percy looks upset.

Edmund
And have you found our chief witch yet?

Witchsmeller
I feel I may be very close.

Edmund
Wooohh. Get the kindling ready! Make sure that stake is well done! Ha ha ha.

Prince Harry
Do tell me. If you do happen to come across someone who's a bit . . . witchy, you know, how do you find him guilty?

Witchsmeller
By trial, or by ordeal.

Edmund
Ah – the ordeal by water?

Witchsmeller
No, by axe.

Edmund
Ooh.

Witchsmeller
The suspected witch has his head placed upon a block, and an axe aimed at his neck. If the man is guilty, the axe will bounce off his neck. So we burn him. If the man is not guilty, the axe will simply slice his head off.

Edmund
What a very fair test that is!

Witchsmeller
Would you like to attempt a less violent test yourself, your Highness, by way of demonstration?

Edmund
How much less violent?

Witchsmeller
I place before the suspect a dagger and a crucifix.

Prince Harry
How interesting!

Witchsmeller
The suspect is blindfolded. If he picks up the dagger from the table, he is Satan's bedfellow.

Prince Harry
Oh yes, Edmund, I think you should do it! At least take yourself out of the running! Eh?

Prince Harry is in very high spirits, the occasion is going well, there is no sense of fear and the other lords join in the jollity.

Lord Broxtable
I haven't seen your broomstick recently, your Highness!

They all laugh.

Edmund
Ha, ha, I'm not sure, you know.

He is frantically checking where the crucifix and dagger are on the table. But now the Witchsmeller is behind him and has applied the blindfold.

Witchsmeller
You will all notice it has become much darker suddenly.

Everyone turns to the window.

Edmund
Yes, so it has.

It is indeed darker, but while everyone is turned away, the Witchsmeller swaps the crucifix and dagger round.

Witchsmeller
Choose!

All turn round to watch Edmund lift the dagger confidently from the table.

Edmund
There we are!

There is absolute horror in the room.

All
Prince Edmund! The witch! Sorcery!

Prince Harry
How the devil did that happen?

The Witchsmeller is in a new state of excitement, leaping and prancing in the most horrific fashion.

Witchsmeller
As I thought, my lord, this man is the source of evil in your kingdom, this is your witch! Behold Lucifer's brother! Humble bubbbbbilass jjjjjjjjjjkklu-

peeeeeeeaaaaaaakkkkkk seeee! Burn the witch! Burn! Burn!

Edmund
Sorry, I don't think I quite caught the first part of that?

Witchsmeller
Try him tomorrow and you will know the truth.

Prince Harry
Well, if that's what you recommend.

Edmund
Harry, you can't let him do this!

Prince Harry
He is very highly thought of, you know.

Edmund
But he's a quack!

Shocked silence falls.

Witchsmeller
What did you say?

Edmund
I said, 'quack, quack, quack'!

Witchsmeller
See how the Duck of Taunton lives within him.

Prince Harry
Yes, I'm afraid so. Let him be tried tomorrow.

Edmund's face registers the fact he is in very serious trouble.

SCENE EIGHT: THE MEETING ROOM

The meeting room has been transformed into a courtroom. The lords and ladies are in one area, the peasants in another. Prince Harry is on a podium.

Officer
Lords and ladies of England, this court is summoned to adjudge the most heinous of all crimes, that of witchcraft.

A lady screams and faints.

All the more heinous this day as the accused is a Prince of the Realm. Step forward Edmund, Duke of Edinburgh.

Edmund gets up.

Peasant
Look at his hair!

Peasant's Wife
Yes, the hair proves it.

Rather unfair, that – it's just Edmund's usual styling.

Officer
Who will defend the accused . . . ?

Percy stands up and smiles graciously.

And thus condemn himself to certain burning at the stake as a partner in Satan if the accused is found guilty?

Percy sits down.

Baldrick
Lord Percy will defend his Royal Highness.

Percy
Oh yes, me, sorry, yes, hello.

The Witchsmeller suddenly enters, his hatred now turned on to Percy.

Witchsmeller
Witch! Witch! Witch!

Percy
What?

Peasant
Yes, look at his hair.

Peasant's Wife
The hair proves it.

Witchsmeller
Will you force us to listen to the pleadings of a man who may be a witch himself?

Prince Harry
No, you're absolutely right. Well, that concludes the case for the defence. Thank you, Lord Percy. Let the Prosecutor begin.

Witchsmeller
Prince Edmund, are you a Christian?

Edmund
Yes, of course I am.

Witchsmeller
Can you say the Lord's Prayer?

Edmund
I can say it backwards, if you like.

Witchsmeller
Confession!

Everyone claps.

Edmund, you have, I believe, a cat?

Edmund
Yes.

Witchsmeller and Crowd
Ah . . .

Witchsmeller
Its name is Bubbles?

Witchsmeller and Crowd
Ah . . .

Edmund
Right.

Witchsmeller
Or, to give it its full name, BEEZLEBUBBLES!

Huge screams.

Edmund
Eh?

Witchsmeller
Do you deny that you were seen on the feast of St Jacob the Turgid speaking to this same cat, Bubbles?

Edmund
Of course I deny it.

Witchsmeller
But the chambermaid, Mary, heard you saying, and I quote: 'Hello, little Bubbles, would you like some milk?'

Edmund
I might have said that.

Witchsmeller
Aha ha ha! What did you mean by that?

Edmund
I meant, would the cat like some milk?

Witchsmeller
Milk, what did you mean by 'milk'?

Edmund
I meant milk, bloody milk.

Witchsmeller
Bloody milk! A mixture of milk and blood.

Crowd
Ahhhh . . .

The hysteria is building. This man is guilty.

Edmund
No, just milk.

Witchsmeller
The blood was to come later.

Edmund
There wasn't any blood.

Witchsmeller
(*Shouting*) So you had to make do with milk! (*General gasps from the crowd*) Let us move on, my lord. You have a horse called Black Satin?

Edmund
Yes.

Witchsmeller
And do you confess that on the thirteenth day of Jerebothstide you did say unto this horse Black Satin, and I quote: 'Satin, would you like some carrots?'

Edmund
Well, I might have done. He likes carrots.

Witchsmeller
Carrots!

Edmund
Yes, carrots.

Witchsmeller
But, ladies and gentlemen, we all know that carrots are the devil's favourite food.

All agree.

Percy
(*Leaping to his feet*) Er, no, we don't! If the devil likes carrots, why isn't it mentioned in the Bible, then? Why doesn't it say: 'And he took the Lord up to the top of an high mountain and offered him a carrot'?

Edmund
Or why isn't 'Thou shalt not eat carrots' in the Ten Commandments?

Witchsmeller
It is!

Cheers from the crowd.

Edmund
What?

The Witchsmeller takes out a holy book.

Witchsmeller
The Ten Commandments of Jereboth in the Appendix to the Apocrypha: 'And the Lord said unto the children of Bednebott, "Neither shalt thou eat the fruit of the tree that is known as the carrot tree" .'

He closes the book and slams it down on the podium.

Baldrick
But carrots don't grow on trees.

Witchsmeller
Really! And how did you get to know so much about carrots? Ha! Ha! Witch!

Baldrick's in it now too.

My lord, I call my first witness.

He turns to reveal that Black Satin is in the witness box.

Satin. Just relax. You are amongst friends. Good. Now, tell me, in your own words, did you, Satin, on a certain night last Jerebothstide indulge, albeit I accept quite innocently, in frenzied, naked and obscene Satanic orgies with your master, known to you as the Great Grumbledook?

Edmund
What?

Witchsmeller
Silence, Grumbledook! You are not replying, Satin. My lord, are we to assume this horse has something to hide?

Edmund
Either that or he can't talk.

Witchsmeller
A likely story. Black Satin, known in the hierarchy of evil as Black Satin the Loquacious. Are you, or are you not, a servant of Satan?

A man screams and faints. The horse neighs, many scream.

Prince Harry
Sorry, was that a yea or a neigh?

Witchsmeller
A neigh, my lord, but I don't believe a word of it. I call for a recess. (*He turns on the horse*) He may think he can fool us, but we have ways of making him talk!

Many screams.

~

SCENE NINE: THE PRISON

Edmund is in prison. His mother is talking through the bars of his cell.

Queen
Well, I suppose this is what comes of being a witch.

Edmund
Mother, I'm not a witch.

Queen
Oh, Edmund, you always were a bit of a fibber.

Edmund
Mother, I beg of you, use whatever power you have to help me.

Queen
Mmmmm. I haven't had any power for years, you know.

Edmund
Yes, but father's sick. You must do something, otherwise . . .

Queen
Otherwise what?

Edmund
Otherwise I'll be burned.

Queen
Oh yes. Oh yes, this would be a pity.

Edmund
Thanks.

Queen
Well, I'll see if I can sort out something.

The queen leaves, Percy and Baldrick emerge from the shadows.

Percy
My lord, I had an idea how to get out of this.

Edmund
Yes?

Percy
Send for all the greatest lawyers in the land, and they could save you.

Edmund
Brilliant, contact them at once.

Percy
I've already done it, my lord!

Edmund
Are those the replies?

Percy
Ah, yes, my lord.

Edmund
Read them.

Percy
Ahm . . . very well. Robert Wyatt writes from Somerset: 'What you ask is against reason and God. I spit on you and your master, and look forward to passing water over both your graves at a later date.'

Edmund
What does that one say?

Baldrick
It's from John Watts.

Edmund
(*Relieved*) Oh, Stinker Watts!

Baldrick
'Dear Percy, of course I remember being at school with Prince Edmund and your-self, and so was very interested by your letter . . .'

Edmund
Yes?

Baldrick
'May you both die horribly. Yours, John Watts.'

Edmund
Oh no, I'm doomed.

Baldrick
Maybe not, my lord. I have a cunning plan that cannot fail.

Edmund
What is it?

They huddle. Two guards appear and obscure our heroes as they hatch their plan.

Guard One
My wife wondered if you'd like to come to dinner tonight?

Guard Two
No, thanks.

Guard One
Why not?

Guard Two
The food always tastes like manure, and frankly I find you both very boring.

Guard One
Oh, fair enough, then. How about next Thursday?

Guard Two
That's fine by me.

They walk away to reveal Edmund, Baldrick and Percy.

Edmund
Brilliant, brilliant. Ha ha. Well done, Baldrick, very cunning.

Baldrick
Thank you, my lord.

Edmund
You may capture the eagle, but you cannot clip its wings.

The guards enter once more and stand in front of Edmund, Percy and Baldrick.

Guard One
By the way, how's that eagle of yours?

Guard Two
Fine. Had a bit of trouble at first, but now I've clipped its wings, no problem.

Guard One
Glad to hear it.

They walk off again.

Edmund
Tomorrow I shall not be so meek. Heh, heh!

SCENE TEN: THE COURT

The trial has recommenced. Edmund is looking very self-assured now. He is hissed at by the crowd, but he, Baldrick and Percy hiss back.

Witchsmeller
My lord, unhappily, the horse, blessed Satin the Confessor, who was to have been our first witness today . . .

Prince Harry
Yes?

Witchsmeller
Cannot be with us.

Prince Harry
Oh.

Witchsmeller
However, before he died . . .

Edmund
You bastard!

Witchsmeller
He made this signed confession. I will read it to you: 'I, Black Satin, confess that my former master Edmund is the servant of Satan, and I spoke to him on the matter frequently over a gallon' – a gallon! – 'a gallon of stableboy's blood.'

The Witchsmeller turns around full circle showing the confession to the horrified crowd. He reveals a hoofmark signature. Lots of screams and fainting.

My lord, this tragic, horrid, nasty and most evil case draws to an end. In pursuing this end I call my last witness.

Loud cheers.

Edmund
What is it? A cow? A talkative badger? An easily bribed ant?

Witchsmeller
Call Jane Firkettle.

Jane Firkettle enters. She is an amiable old lady.

Witchsmeller
Jane Firkettle, do you know the man standing before you?

Jane
Which?

Witchsmeller
That's him.

Jane
Of course I recognize him.

She waves and blows big kisses.

Edmund
She's seen me on a coin.

Witchsmeller
And have you or have you not committed sins of the flesh with him?

Jane
I have.

Edmund
You must be joking.

Jane
To my deep shame.

Edmund
And mine. I mean, look at her.

Witchsmeller
Can you describe these foul deeds?

Jane
Yes. After we had just kissed once, he transformed into a wild animal.

Edmund
Or perhaps I do remember her.

Witchsmeller
Anything else?

Jane
Yes, my lord. Three months later, I was great with child.

Edmund
Oh, for God's sake!

Witchsmeller
And did you give birth to a son?

Jane
I did. My little Johnny.

Witchsmeller
And do you see this son of Satan anywhere in court?

One by one, the spectators shake their heads – including a friendly-looking red man dressed in black with horns on his head, sitting among them. But where is the son? Finally, the Witchsmeller produces a small white poodle.

Jane
Yes, that's him.

Huge screams from the crowd.

Witchsmeller
I give you John Grumbledook!

Lord Tablett
Yes, look at his hair.

Lord Broxtable
His hair gives him away.

Edmund
Oh, come on – he doesn't look a bit like me!

Witchsmeller
Of course he does, my lord. I give you three proofs of witchcraft. A cat that drinks blood, a horse that talks, and a man who propagates poodles. These men must burn.

Crowd
Burn! Burn. Burn! Let the witches fry!

Officer
Silence. Silence for the Prince of Wales!

Prince Harry stands.

Prince Harry
The verdict of this court is that the accused are guilty of witchcraft. The maximum penalty the law allows is to be burned to death. However, in view of your previous good background I am disposed to be lenient. I therefore sentence you to be burned alive. (*Cheers*) Do you have anything to say?

Edmund is smiling, resigned to all this madness. Percy decides to fight back.

Percy
Well, yes I'd certainly like to say something!

Edmund
Shut up, Percy.

Percy changes his mind.

Percy
No, thank you.

Prince Harry
And you, Grumbledook?

Edmund
Yes. *Now!*

As one, Percy, Baldrick and Edmund raise their arms and jump in the air.

~

SCENE ELEVEN: THE CORRIDOR OUTSIDE THE KING'S BEDROOM

Edmund, Percy and Baldrick land in the corridor.

Edmund
Oh, brilliant, Baldrick. How you did that I will never know.

They run to the king's bedroom.

Percy
Quick, in here.

All three enter the king's bedroom. The door shuts.

King
Aaaaaahhh!

There is much confusion and noise. They all run out and the king appears, still mad.

You Turkish pigs!

Percy
Oh, sorry – it was that door.

He points to another.

Edmund
Oh, Percy.

It is too late. They are by now surrounded by soldiers.

~

SCENE TWELVE: THE TOWN SQUARE

A notice is being pounded on to a stake. Peasants watch. It reads:

Public execution by burning.
Friday.
Indoors if wet.

~

SCENE THIRTEEN: A BARRACKS ROOM/DUNGEON

Edmund, Percy and Baldrick are all bald, shaved for frying. Two guards are waiting near the door. Edmund calls out to them.

Edmund
Uhm, look, you two. For a pretty hefty reward, you wouldn't consider helping us to . . .

The guards get the plan instantly.

Guards and Edmund
Escape?

Edmund
. . . then dressing up as . . .

Guards and Edmund
. . . washerwomen . . .

Edmund
. . . and carrying us out to safety in . . .

Guards and Edmund
. . . three large wicker laundry baskets . . .

Edmund
Would you? No, obviously not.

The guards exchange a look of mutual cynical amusement – prisoners always try that one.

Guard One
Oh-oh. Here comes the wife.

They straighten up as the queen and little Princess Leia enter.

Leia
Hello, Edmund.

Edmund
Hello, dear.

Leia
(*Giggling*) You look funny.

Edmund
Yes, I've had all my hair cut off.

Leia
Oh yes, that's it.

Edmund
Look, there's no word of a reprieve is there?

He looks to the queen, who shakes her head unhappily.

Leia
Oh no, everyone's really looking forward to it. Hello, boys.

Baldrick and Percy
Morning.

Leia
I have to go to my room, which isn't fair, but . . . (*going near to Edmund confidentially*) in fact, I think I might even get a better view from the window.

Edmund
Oh, great.

Leia
Well, I'd better be going.

She turns, but returns as the queen motions to her, reminding her of something.

Oh yes, and your mummy asked me to give you this.

She hands a bag to Edmund.

Edmund
(*Very excited*) What is it? A knife? A file? A bucket of water?

Leia
(*Loud, so the guards can hear*) No, silly, it's a dolly.

Edmund opens the bag frantically, only to find the truth.

Edmund
Oh yes. So it is. Well, great, great. Thanks. Just what I needed.

Leia
Goodbye, Edmund.

She starts to leave.

Edmund
Goodbye, dear.

Leia and the queen start to leave.

Uh, Mother . . .

Queen
Yes? Oh, bye bye, dear.

They exit and the guard locks the door.
All hope is gone.

~

SCENE FOURTEEN: TOWN SQUARE

Percy, Baldrick and Edmund are tied to
ladders on a huge pyre. A crowd bays
and yells, led by the Witchsmeller.

Witchsmeller
Burn the witches!

Crowd
Burn them! Burn them! Let's give Satan a
sizzling supper!

The Witchsmeller reaches Prince Harry.

Prince Harry
(*Trying to make conversation*) This really
must be one of the most difficult parts of
the job for you.

Witchsmeller
Yes.

He grabs a lighted torch with glee.

Prince Harry
And for the witch as well, of course.

Edmund, Percy and Baldrick, strapped
to the pyre, exchange their final words.

Baldrick
My lord, I have a cunning plan.

Edmund
Oh fuck off, Baldrick. I'm going to try to
stall him.

The Witchsmeller addresses Edmund.

Witchsmeller
Well, Grumbledook, your time has come.
Do you wish at last to confess?

Edmund
No. Oh sorry, yes, yes. I do, in fact.

Witchsmeller
Confession!

The crowd cheer.

Edmund
Ahm, yes, I would like to confess before
God and this rather small crowd . . .
that I have occasionally done things
wrong.

Witchsmeller
Be more specific.

Edmund
Ahm, yes, I have erred and strayed like a
lost ox.

Witchsmeller
Sheep!

Edmund
Ah yes, sheep, sheep. I have coveted my
father's adultery.

Witchsmeller
Get on with it!

Edmund
I have not always honoured my neigh-
bour's ass.

Witchsmeller
(*Annoyed*) Oh, light the fires!

They do.

Edmund
I'm a witch, I'm a witch.

Baldrick
And so am I!

Percy
Me, too!

Witchsmeller
Too late.

The crowd cheer as they go up in flames.

Edmund
Oh damn! I'm not even comfortable.

He wriggles a little and drops the doll his
mum gave him, which has been pressing
into his back. The doll hits the fire. And
suddenly, spookily, the Witchsmeller
starts to look unhappy.

Witchsmeller
How fast the heat travels!

Prince Harry
Yes, it is rather warm, isn't it.

Witchsmeller
I feel as if I am on fire!

He's right. His body has actually started smoking.

Prince Harry
Yes, I'm rather regretting my own choice of undergarments, too.

And the Witchsmeller explodes into flames.

Witchsmeller
I am burning, burning!

Prince Harry
Yes, but I bet you're jolly glad of that cloak in winter.

The Witchsmeller staggers away, in flames. He collapses. He dies. The earth is free of its vilest scourge.

Prince Harry
Good Lord!

Suddenly, the fire on the pyre dies down and Edmund, Baldrick and Percy's ropes fall off them.

Edmund
Ahm . . . well done, Baldrick.

Percy
Yes, that was a close shave. Well done, Baldrick.

Baldrick is not quite so sure how he is responsible for this miracle.

~

SCENE FIFTEEN: OUTSIDE THE KING'S CHAMBER

The doors of the king's room are thrown open. The king appears, clearly perfectly well, doing a healthy stretch to greet the bright new dawn.

The queen is sitting with her tapestry in the window, and Leia is standing on the seat, looking out of the window keenly.

King
Morning, my love!

Queen
Ah! Good morning, dear.

King
Morning, Princess!

Leia
Good morning!

King
What's going on out there?

Leia
Well, Uncle Harry was going to burn Edmund alive, when . . .

Queen
Darling, sssh! (*To the king*) Nothing, my dear: it's all sorted out now.

King
Oh, good.

The queen winks and wrinkles her nose. Stars fly out of it. Leia turns and sees this – she looks amazed. There's something bewitching going on here.

~

SCENE SIXTEEN: OUTSIDE THE CASTLE

Percy, Baldrick and Edmund arrive back in the castle. Two guards lift their pikes.

Percy
I said he shouldn't have burnt that cat.

And the Blackadder Three walk on to freedom.

Edmund, Duke of Edinburgh and Lord Warden of the Royal Privies, proudly shows visitors his extensive chin collection

the Black Seal

Many are the tales told of the Black Adder, and of his faithful henchmen, Lord Percy Percy and Baldrick, son of Robin the Dung Gatherer. But none is told so oft, with so much hitting of heads in wonder and repeating of exciting parts as this, the final chapter in the Book of . . . the Black Adder.

SCENE ONE: THE GREAT HALL

England 1498. St Juniper's Day, the day on which the king would lavish new honours upon his kinfolk.

It is an important state occasion. The king is flanked by the queen and his guards. Edmund stands, handsome and proud.

King
St Juniper once said: 'By his loins shall ye know him, and by the length of his rod shall he be measured.' The length of my rod is a mystery to all but the queen and a thousand Turkish whores; but the fruits of my loins are here for all to see. I have two sons: Harry and . . . another one. Step forward Harry, Prince of Wales.

Prince Harry steps forward, arms folded. He bows low, and then spreads his arms out and lies completely prostrate on the floor in front of the king.

I hereby name thee Captain of the Guard; Grand Warden of the Northern and Eastern Marches; Chief Lunatic of the Duchy of Gloucester; Viceroy of Wales; Sheriff of Nottingham . . .

While the list is being read, Edmund is tapping his feet, looking at the sky, inspecting his fingernails. He is bored.

. . . Marquess of the Midlands; Lord Polemaker in Ordinary; and Harbinger of the Doomed Rat.

He hands Prince Harry the scroll. Prince Harry bows and walks back.

Step forward, the other one.

Edmund folds his arms and goes forward to the king, bowing extravagantly, lying prostrate on the floor as Prince Harry did.

Until now, thy titles have been but few: Duke of Edinburgh and Warden of the Royal Privies.

Edmund
Even so, my lord.

King
We thank thee, Egbert, for your work in Edinburgh. Know now we do relieve thee of thy heavy task, and give the dukedom to our loyal cousin, Hastings.

The king folds the scroll and passes it to Hastings – it seems it is a birthday present.

Many happy returns, Tom.

Edmund
What?

King
Thus have I discharged the duties of Juniper.

He steps forward, placing his feet on either side of Edmund's head.

Chiswick: fresh horses! We ride at once for Stoke, where it is my sworn intent to approach the city walls, bare my broad buttocks and cry, 'Behold, I honour thee most highly!' Come, all who are brave!

The king walks over Edmund and the room swiftly empties. Percy and Baldrick run to Edmund and crouch by his head.

Percy
Well, it could have been worse, my lord.

Baldrick
There was a moment there I thought you were going to lose the Privies.

Edmund leaps to his feet.

Edmund
No!

Baldrick and Percy recede, frightened. It is a hugely dramatic and scary and defining moment.

It will *not* do.

Percy
No, my lord, you're right. It won't.

Edmund
I must clear away the chaff from my life and let shine forth the true wheat of greatness.

Percy
Do it at once, my lord.

He thinks Baldrick is in for the sack.

Edmund
Very well: Percy. You are dismissed from my service.

Percy
Me? Why, my lord?

Edmund
Why? Because, Percy, far from being a fit
consort for a Prince of the Realm, you
would bore the leggings off a village idiot.
You ride a horse rather less well than
another horse would. Your brain would
make a grain of sand look large and
ungainly and the part of you that can't be
mentioned, I am reliably informed by
women around the Court, wouldn't be
worth mentioning even if it could be. If
you put on a floppy hat and a funny codpiece, you might just get by as a fool, but
since you wouldn't know a joke if it got up
and gave you a haircut, I doubt it. That's
why you're dismissed.

*Edmund heads out, followed by Baldrick.
Percy stands stock still, shocked to his
very soul.*

Percy
Oh, I see.

Edmund
And as for you, Baldrick.

Baldrick
Yes.

Edmund
You're out, too.

And he walks out.

Baldrick
Fair enough.

~

SCENE TWO: THE CASTLE COURT-
YARD

*So Edmund spurned his friends and
began his quest for glory.*

*Edmund and Baldrick walk out into the
courtyard.*

Edmund
I suppose you'll go back to shovelling dung
in the gutter where I found you?

Baldrick
I shouldn't think so.

Edmund
No?

Baldrick
No such luck. I had to wait years for that
job: that's quite a good position. I'll probably be milking pigs or mucking out the lepers or something.

Edmund
Really?

Baldrick
Yes. It'll be years before I get back to shovelling dung again.

*Edmund walks away and Baldrick wipes
away a tear.*

~

SCENE THREE: THE CASTLE GATES

A hundred yards later.

*Edmund rides his horse out of the gates
and almost knocks over an old man. The
horse rears.*

Edmund
Get out of my way!

Old Man
Going on a journey, my lord?

Edmund
No, I thought I'd stand here all day and
talk to you.

Old Man
You'll be needing someone to tend to your
horse, then.

Edmund
No, and if I did, I wouldn't take you. I
mean, look at you. What is your profession?

*Old man takes out a rag and begins a
foolish dance.*

Oh, God. A retired Morris dancer. That's
all I need. Oh well, never mind. If you can
keep up, you can come.

*Edmund rides off as fast as he can. Then,
perhaps rather unexpectedly, the old man
on his donkey rides up easily and passes
Edmund.*

Thus did Edmund set forth into England with his rather irritating new old servant. His purpose to scour the land and search out the six other Most Evil Men in the kingdom. Only then would the time have come for . . . the Black Adder.

SCENE FOUR: A WOOD

Sir Wilfred Death

Edmund and the old man are behind a tree.

Edmund
Here he comes now.

Edmund steps out as Sir Wilfred Death rides proudly towards them. Suddenly a horse rears out in front of him, and two other men, on horseback, appear on either side.

Oh, my God.

Robber
So, Sir Wilfred Death. Your tyranny is at an end! Prepare to be strung by your codlings from the boughs of that tree.

Wilfred
Never!

Loud screams and scuffling ensue. Within seconds the two robbers are swinging by their testicles from a tree. Sir Wilfred strides away and Edmund steps out in front of him.

Edmund
Sir Wilfred Death!

Wilfred
Edmund!

There is a butch double-handed hand-shake between them.

Edmund
I'm looking for some men – to take over the kingdom.

Wilfred
How many have you got so far?

Edmund raises one finger. Wilfred mean-

ingfully gives him a two-fingered salute. He's in.

SCENE FIVE: A FIELD

Three-Fingered Pete

A very villainous man indeed is standing in the field. It is Three-Fingered Pete. Beside him stands a sturdy peasant. Near them is a horse.

Pete
So we are agreed: he who wins takes the horse?

The peasant nods wisely and confidently. He's sure he's a crack shot and this is an archery contest! Pete points at the target across the common.

There is our mark: you shoot first.

The peasant raises his bow deliberately and shoots. It hits the bull's eye.

Yes. Good. Very good. So good in fact . . . (*He takes out his arrow and lines it up*) I'm going to have to . . . (*He aims at the target and then at the last moment turns and shoots the peasant*) . . . cheat.

Sir Wilfred is on the horizon.

Wilfred
Three-Fingered Pete!!

Pete looks up and then at his hand. Edmund raises three fingers. It's going well.

SCENE SIX: A COPSE

Guy de Glastonbury

A coach is approaching. A bandit appears on horseback. It is Guy. The coach slows down. The lord inside looks out.

Guy
Good evening, and surrender: your money or your life.

Lord
Here, take it! It is all the money I have.

He tosses him a bag of gold.

Guy
Thank you.

Lord
Now, let me pass.

Guy
Oh, damn: I'm always doing this. Did I say, your money or your life?

Lord
You did.

Guy
Sorry, slip of the tongue. Your money *and* your life.

He shoots a cross bow and politely kills the poor fellow.

Sorry.

He rides on and turns to the driver of the coach.

Thanks, Ned. See you Thursday?

There is a smatter of applause and Wilfred, Edmund and Pete step out.

Wilfred
Guy!

Guy
Wilfred!

Wilfred
Now what we need is a real bastard.

Pete
Sean the Irish Bastard?

Wilfred nods and smiles.

SCENE SEVEN: A VILLAGE SQUARE

Sean the Irish Bastard

It is night. A man armed to the teeth, knives everywhere, is slinking along a wall. Another man, the over-fat figure of the local squire, is walking along the pavement, his feet clacking. He passes two beggars.

First Beggar
Money for the blind!

The squire raises his nose in the air and walks on. Sean is waiting behind a corner. The squire's footsteps pass. Sean leaps out and quickly darts left to steal the money from the beggars, letting the squire pass on. The First Beggar feels in his hat. Nothing there.

Here, business is very quiet this morning.

Second Beggar
Aye, everyone's gone to lunch, I think.

Sean moves off and runs into Wilfred.

Wilfred
Sean!

SCENE EIGHT: A HILLSIDE

Next morning. All are riding along. Edmund gives the sign: five fingers. They all do five, including the confident Pete, who does three.

SCENE TEN: THE EDGE OF THE WOOD

Friar Bellows

Edmund and the others peer through a bush, to reveal a clearing within which is the friar himself. He is heartily rogering the daughter, a contented smile on his features as he whistles and takes in the flora and fauna.

Wilfred
Friar Bellows . . . doing the Lord's work?

Friar
Er . . . just administering extreme unction.

The others smile at each other. The task is almost done.

SCENE ELEVEN: OPEN COUNTRY

Jack Large

The Black Seal, for so must they now be known, are riding along.

Edmund
And who shall be the seventh, Wilfred?

Wilfred
Why, need I say? . . . Jack.

The horsemen all stop in horror simultaneously.

Guy
What, Mad Bully Boy Jack, the Grave-Robbing Assassin of Aldwych?

Wilfred
No.

Pete
Then Crazed Animal Jack, the Cattle-Rustling Cannibal from Sutton Coldfield?

Wilfred
No.

Sean
Then your man is Sane Jack O'Hooligan,

SCENE NINE: THE EDGE OF A WOOD

A friar, a father and his virginal daughter are present. It is an obvious parting place, and the father and girl have just hugged goodbye. The father is very concerned.

Father
Friar, I fear greatly for her chastity.

Friar
Alas, such is the way of the world. The sweetest rose too often is . . . plucked too soon . . .

Father
I wonder whether you might take her while I am gone.

The holy friar registers a tiny surprise. Then inspects her.

Friar
Yes. The answer is yes, I shall.

the Man-Hating Goat-Murderer of Dingle Bay?

Wilfred
No.

Friar
Surely not Canon Jack Smollett, Senior Archdeacon of the Diocese of St Wotan, the Entrail-Eating Heretic of Bath and Wells?

Wilfred
No. I'm talking about Unspeakably Violent Jack, the Bull-Buggering Priest-Killer of no fixed abode.

They are all profoundly shocked.

Edmund
Are you sure he's the kind of chap we're looking for?

Wilfred
Yes. And here he comes.

They are on the brow of a hill. Wilfred points at a giant of a man in the distance.

This huge man is walking boldly through the countryside. But suddenly a tiny man appears and keeps getting under his feet. The giant turns and with huge strength grips the little man, first the left hand on his shoulder, then the right, and lifts him up to his own face level.

Giant
What do you think you're doing?

The small man viciously butts the giant, who falls unconscious, and heads on. For he is Jack Large. And suddenly, there are the Black Seal.

Jack
Boys!

Wilfred
Are you with us?

Jack
Aye!

Edmund lifts both hands and makes a mighty seven. These deeply bad men will change the world.

~

SCENE TWELVE: A FILTHY TAVERN

Edmund's old servant sits outside with his donkey and the horses. The others are still laughing as they enter the tavern.

They sit around a table. Edmund is trying to be as at ease with these people as he can be: he is endlessly aspiring to their level of evil and camaraderie. The Seal are all laughing and toasting each other.

Edmund
And, Jack, tell me, what is your second name?

Jack
Large, Jack Large.

Edmund
Ha, then in our band, you shall be known as Large Jack.

He laughs. There is silence from the others, who seem less amused, particularly Jack.

Jack
Why?

Edmund
Because you are so little.

Jack
I see. Why not Little Jack, then?

Edmund
Ahm, because Large Jack is more amusing.

Jack
Is it?

Edmund
Very well, then, Little Jack.

Jack points his sword at him.

Jack
You wish to mock my size?

Edmund
No, no, no, of course not. Ahm, innkeeper, more beer.

All
Hurray!

Edmund
Six large beers . . . and another large beer. Let us then go on to the plan!

All
Yes, the plan, the plan!

Friar
But first – a motto for our enterprise. 'Blessed are the meek . . .'

There is general consternation.

. . . 'for they shall be slaughtered!'

All
(*Raising weapons*) Hurray!

They all stand and rush to the door.

Edmund
But wait. The plan, the plan; you have forgot the plan!

Pete
I thought that was the plan.

Sean
Let's get those meek bastards now!

All
Hurray!

Edmund
No, quiet! Quiet!

They fall quiet. There is a pause.

Wilfred
Yes, who wants quiet? I want chaos!

His sword swipes at the table and knocks everything off it.

Jack
And slaughter!

Pete
And flowers!

All
What?

Pete
Mercilessly crushed under foot.

All
Hurray!

Friar
Silence!

All
Silence!

Guy
Peace, for the word of the Lord.

They all sit.

Friar
For Christ's sake, let's hear the plan.

Edmund gathers himself.

Edmund
Very well. The plan is simple.

General annoyance from the Seal.

Wilfred
I thought it was cunning!

All
Down with the plan!

Edmund
It's cunning in its simplicity. Tonight, I ride for home . . .

The Seal turn on Edmund. Wilfred grabs him.

Wilfred
I say strike now while the iron is hot!

Edmund
But the iron isn't hot!

Wilfred
Isn't it?

Edmund
No, it's just warming up. When it is hot, then we will strike.

Sean
What, are we going to have to wait till summer?

Edmund
No: when the iron is hot.

Pete
What iron?

Edmund quivers with frustration, but finally gathers himself and continues.

Edmund
When my brother returns, I shall send for you all.

Friar
How?

Edmund
By a message, a sign.

Guy
What sort of sign?

Edmund
Well, something black probably.

Jack
Black pudding?

Edmund
No.

Pete
A messenger with Black Plague, perhaps?

Edmund
Yes, that's better.

Friar
He means to kill us!

Edmund
A messenger with black hair.

Wilfred
A black-headed messenger.

Edmund
Yes, and when he comes to you, drop what you are doing and speed with all haste to Jaspar's tavern.

All
Hurray!

Sean
Ah, I know it well. How is Jolly Jaspar these days?

Pete
Dead.

Jack
How?

Friar
I killed him.

Wilfred pats him on the back.

Guy
Oh, well done.

Edmund
From there, I shall take you to the castle, where we shall capture the king and the queen and the prince.

All
Hurray!

Edmund
(*Stands*) And say: 'The Kingdom of Albion is ours!'

All
Hurray!

Edmund
'You are doomed to lives of exile! Get out!'

Pause. There is dead silence where there should have been applause.

Pete
Exile?

Edmund
Yes, exile! For life!

Guy
But why don't we just kill them?

Edmund
Well, yes, I suppose we could kill them.

All
Yes, *kill, kill, kill!*

They charge for the door again.

Edmund
No! Wait! Remember! Wait until I send the sign.

Sean
If I get a messenger with blackheads all over his face, I'll kill the ugly bastard.

Wilfred
How do we know it's not a trap?

*Utter suspicion is suddenly directed
against Edmund.*

Edmund
Because, look. The Black Adder gives you
his word.

Wilfred
But we want your word, not this Black
Adder fellow's.

Edmund
I am the Black Adder.

Pete
Oh, I see.

Edmund
And when all is done, the Black Seal shall
rule England. We few, we happy few, we
band of ruthless bastards!

He stands triumphantly on the table.

All
Hurray!

Edmund
All for one!

All
And each man for himself!

*There is a final dramatic show of
weapons and then they all leave.*

SCENE THIRTEEN: A FOREST GLADE

*Night time. The old man and Edmund are
throwing sticks into the fire they have lit.
It is a rare moment of confident peace
and beauty.*

Old Man
You're in a merry mood, my lord.

Edmund
Oh yes. No one can stop me now!

Old Man
No one?

Edmund
No, no one. Except perhaps . . . no, not
even him.

Old Man
And whom might that be, my lord?

Edmund
Well, there was a man, Philip of
Burgundy, known to his enemies as the
Hawk. We were deadly childhood rivals.
Of course, in those days he was known as
the Thrush. But no one's heard of him for
years. Come on, let's go. We've got work
to do.

Old Man
Not so fast, Edinburgh.

*Suddenly the old man's voice changes into
a deep and noble bass.*

Edmund
(*Whipping round*) What?

Old Man
This Hawk, did he look something like . . .
this?

*There is a blinding white light and sudden-
ly the old man is transformed from someone rather scruffy into a grand gentleman,
with elegant clothes and a noble bearing.*

Edmund
Erm . . . Not really, no.

*The old man tears off his bushy eyebrows,
revealing almost identical ones underneath. Edmund jumps.*

Oh, my God, Philip of Burgundy!

Hawk
Known to my enemies as . . . (*with
panache he puts on a Robin Hood-style
cap*) the Hawk!

Edmund
But your horse . . . it was a huge
brown . . .

A huge brown horse appears at his side.

Yes, that's the one. Well . . . (*Smiles*) It's
very good to see you, er, Phil.

*He turns round to go, but the Hawk steps
on the end of his pointy shoes, trapping
him.*

Hawk
This time, not fast enough!

Edmund
Oh, God. What do you want with me?

Hawk
I'll tell you later.

He knocks Edmund unconscious, and laughs like evil villains should.

SCENE FOURTEEN: A DARK AND DISMAL DUNGEON

The Hawk pushes Edmund downstairs into the dungeon and follows him in. He holds a sword to Edmund's back.

Hawk
Ha, ha, ha! I return at last, after fifteen years.

Edmund
(*On the floor*) And what have you been up to?

Hawk
Waiting, plotting, nurturing my hatred and planning my revenge.

Edmund
So, you've kept yourself busy?

Hawk
Yes. Fifteen years in France teaches a man to hate. Fifteen years of wearing perfume, fifteen years of eating frogs, fifteen years of saying '*Pardon?*' . . . All because of *you*.

Edmund
But surely the scenery . . . ?

Hawk
I never went outside: I couldn't stand the smell.

Edmund
(*Whimpering*) But what has all this got to do with me?

Hawk
Because, Edmund, it's going to take you fifteen years to die.

Edmund
Fifteen years?

Hawk
Yes.

Edmund
How?

Hawk
I think it would be more amusing if you found out for yourself. Let me just say it has something to do with snails.

He opens a trapdoor in a rock with his sword. The rock swings down to reveal several small snails clinging to it. The Hawk makes to leave.

Edmund
Oh, my God. Where are you going?

Hawk
Why, to the castle, to kill the royal family and claim the throne that isn't mine by right.

He exits. Edmund stares at the snails in terror. Outside, the Hawk, astride his horse in matching colour, rides off to the castle.

SCENE FIFTEEN: THE DUNGEON

Back inside, Edmund is kneeling and praying to the god who has featured very little in his life so far.

Edmund
Dear Lord, who made the birds and the bees . . . and the snails, presumably, ahm, please help me, a little animal too, in my despair. I have been a sinner, but now I intend to follow the path of the saints: particularly the very religious ones. In the name of the Father, Son and the Holy Ghost. Amen.

Mad Gerald
Amen.

His voice comes out of the darkness. Edmund had no idea anyone else was there. He leaps in terror.

Edmund
What?

Mad Gerald leaps out.

Mad Gerald
Amen, I said. Did I get it wrong? Ha, ha. Haven't heard that word for twenty years, you see.

Edmund
Who are you? I . . . didn't realize I had company.

Mad Gerald
(*With relish*) Ha, ha, ha. 'Company' – haven't heard that word for twenty years either. Or 'realize' – I'd completely forgotten! 'Realize'!

Edmund
Oh no, you're not mad, are you?

Mad Gerald
Arr, yes, I'm very mad, thank you. 'Mad'! That's a word I know – I say it to myself every morning: 'Morning, Mad Gerald, how are you?' I say, 'I'm completely mad, today thank you.' 'So, no change there,' I reply. 'No, you'd be mad to expect any.' 'I am mad, aren't I?' 'Yes, you are, you're mad, Gerald.'

Edmund
Quiet! Shhh!

Mad Gerald
Shhh!

Edmund
Look, I know this may seem a stupid question . . .

Mad Gerald
Question.

Edmund
. . . but you don't know if there's a way out of here, do you?

Mad Gerald
A way out?

He laughs manically, for a long time.

SCENE SIXTEEN: THE DUNGEON

Twelve months later. Edmund is sitting in the cell looking desolate. Mad Gerald is still laughing manically and dancing around.

Mad Gerald
Ha, ha, ha. A way out, you say?

Edmund
Yes.

Mad Gerald
I haven't heard those words 'a way out' for o . . .

Edmund
Twenty years?

Mad Gerald
Yes, twenty years! Not like Mr Rat. I'm always saying Mr Rat.

Edmund
What?

Mad Gerald
Well, I tend to say, 'Good morning, Mr Rat. How are you today?' And then Mr Rat says (*rubbing his nose*), 'Myim, myim.' Ha, ha, ha!

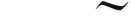

SCENE SEVENTEEN: THE DUNGEON

Still more months have passed. Edmund is sitting with Mad Gerald on the straw.

Mad Gerald
No, no, you mustn't be rude about Mr Rat, you know. He's my best friend.

Edmund
Really?

Mad Gerald
Well, there's him and Mr Key.

Edmund
What?

Mad Gerald
Mr Key. I made him out of my own teeth.

He takes out a pretty white key and holds it in front of his mouth. Edmund isn't very interested.

Good morning, Mr Key.

Edmund suddenly looks at the key again. It looks strangely convincing. He grabs it, unlocks the door and sprints up the stairs outside the dungeon. From inside Mad Gerald shouts to him.

Mad Gerald
Hey! Close the bloody door!

SCENE EIGHTEEN: A ROAD

Edmund reaches a road and meets a man on a cart.

Edmund
Stop! Where are you going?

Man on cart
I'll tell you where – wherever I can sell these six black homing pigeons I've got in the back, that's where.

Edmund
Black homing pigeons?

This is too good to be true. Black pigeons . . . the Black Seal . . . the summoning . . .

Man on cart
Well, mostly.

Edmund
How much are they?

Man on cart
Six shillings.

Edmund feels desperately in his pockets.

Edmund
Damn.

Man on cart
(*Merrily*) Although I suppose if you beat me and gagged me and tied me to that tree over there, you could have them for less.

Edmund
Oh, right.

Two minutes later, the man on the cart is tied to a tree, gagged, and Edmund is riding away. He arrives back at the castle. From the battlements he releases the pigeons, and in the courtyard releases a small black chicken.

Across England the five pigeons make very fast landings on five members of the Black Seal. The sixth bird is seen in the sky, and then it is shot.

A few minutes later, Jack Large roasts the chicken on a spit. Suddenly he spits out a black ring and the relevance of it hits him.

~

SCENE NINETEEN: A STOCKROOM IN THE CASTLE

The room is empty. The Hawk enters in his messenger disguise. He rips it off and is revealed in his full glory. He takes out his sword and holds it high above his head.

Hawk
Ha! At the striking of ten bells, I shall claim the throne.

The bell strikes three times. But then, at the next six strikes, each of the Black Seal bursts out of suitable hiding places in the room. On the tenth strike, the Hawk addresses them.

Gentlemen, to what do I owe this pleasure?

There is an irritated banging on the inside of the largest wardrobe. Edmund can't get out. Guy slashes off the lock and Edmund emerges heroically.

Edmund
To me, Burgundy!

The Hawk is genuinely shocked.

Hawk
Edmund! I had not expected to see you again.

Edmund
No, dead men don't tend to make social calls, do they?

The Seal all laugh.

Prepare to die!

Five weapons arrive at the Hawk's throat. Jack Large's knife is at his testicles.

Hawk
No, wait. Let me just say one last thing . . . if these men are indeed, as they seem to be, the six most evil men in the land . . .

Edmund
Yes, they are! Your last sentence please.

Hawk
Then they've made a pretty damn peculiar choice for their leader, haven't they? My Lord Warden of the Privies.

Edmund
What? Do you think they should have chosen you, Thrush?

The Seal laugh.

A man twisted by unbridled ambition!

Rebellious murmuring is heard from the Seal.

A man tortured by insatiable greed!

The Seal become louder.

The evillest man in the world! Do you think they should have chosen you?

Black Seal
Yes!

And with a swooshing sound the six weapons are suddenly at Edmund's throat and codlings.

Edmund
But he's a mindless killer!

Black Seal
Hurray!

Edmund
He'll destroy the kingdom!

Black Seal
Hurray!

Edmund
He murdered his whole family!

Pete
Who didn't? I certainly killed mine.

Wilfred
And I killed mine.

Friar
And I killed yours.

Sean
Did you?

Friar
Yes.

Sean
Good on you, Father.

Hawk
Are you with me, then?

Black Seal
Yes!

Hawk
(*To Edmund*) Prepare to die.

It is about to happen, when . . .

Wait! I have a more amusing method.

Edmund
Amusing for whom, I wonder?

The Hawk pulls back a curtain to reveal the most terrible and complex instrument of terror. The Seal take a step backwards in shock and admiration. They cheer and clap. Minutes later Edmund is imprisoned in the device.

Hawk
In precisely one minute . . .

He turns a one-minute hourglass.

. . . the spike will go up your nethers, the shears will cut off your ears.

Edmund
Both of them?

Hawk
Yes. The axes will chop off your hands. I don't think we need to go into the attributes of the coddling grinder. And these two little feathers here will tickle you under what's left of your arms, which is the amusing part. Gentlemen, let us go and slaughter everyone else in the royal family.

Black Seal
Hurray!

Hawk
God Save the King.

Black Seal
Because nobody else will!

They leap from the room. Edmund gives a

terrified look at the hourglass: the sand is slipping by.

SCENE TWENTY: A CORRIDOR OUTSIDE THE STOCKROOM

The Black Seal emerge dramatically into the corridor.

Hawk
On!

He heads round a corner, then stops them.

Stop!

Two maidservants emerge from around the corner, each carrying a tray of drinks. The Hawk, with his sword drawn, laughs.

Let us first relieve these two old warhorses of their delightful burden, and drink a toast to our enterprise.

They all grab a drink.

May God thrive!

Black Seal
Over our dead bodies.

They gulp down the wine and charge down the corridor. Suddenly, they die by vicious poisoning. Only Sean survives, who gets up calmly and totters over towards the women.

Sean
Mmm, it's got a bit of a sting in its tail.

He takes another goblet, drinks it, and dies as well. The women tear off their headdresses: they are Percy and Baldrick. They hug and shake hands enthusiastic-ally, but are frozen by Edmund's dreadful cries as each part of the torture mechanism takes its effect. A little giggle caused by the feathers is finally heard.

Baldrick and Percy look uncomfortable. Maybe they left it a teensy bit late.

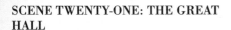

SCENE TWENTY-ONE: THE GREAT HALL

A psalm is playing on a full organ. Edmund is in bed looking in a very rough state: bloody, bandaged ears and hands, and deathly pale.

Queen
Oh, Edmund, Edmund!

Prince Harry
Edmund.

King
Edmund!

Edmund's eyes jerk open.

He lives!

All around stand the lords of the court. A huge cheer goes up. Edmund whispers.

Edmund
Father, you called me Edmund!

King
Sorry, Edgar. How are you?

Edmund
Not so well. Harry, what do you think my chances are?

Prince Harry
Oh good, good.

Queen
He will live?

Prince Harry
Oh no, sorry, I thought you meant chances of going to heaven.

Edmund
Oh damn.

King
But have no fear. My son, your body may have been mutilated beyond recognition, but your spirit will live for ever. My lords!

He raises his glass.

SCENE TWENTY-TWO: A CORRIDOR IN THE CASTLE

Percy and Baldrick have been sitting quite happily in the castle, waiting for news of Edmund, but Percy has just shattered the calm. Baldrick looks aghast.

Baldrick
What did you say?

SCENE TWENTY-THREE: THE GREAT HALL

The king is in mid-toast.

King
. . . I give you – Edgar!

Everyone takes their glasses and raises them to Edmund.

SCENE TWENTY-FOUR: A CORRIDOR IN THE CASTLE

Percy and Baldrick are sprinting down the corridor.

Baldrick
I told you to poison the Black Seal's goblets, not to poison the whole vat!

SCENE TWENTY-FIVE: BACK IN THE GREAT HALL

All
Edgar!

Edmund pulls the king down to whisper in his ear the name by which he would wish always to be remembered.

King
The Black Dagger!

All
The Black Dagger!

They all drink.

King
May his name last as long as our dynasty.

Prince Harry, the queen and then the king

and court all drop down dead.

Edmund
Good Lord! I wonder if it was the wine?

He takes a polite sip.

No, seems perfectly all right to me. Now I shall be King of E . . .

And he dies. For ever.

Instruments of Torture
in the late Middle Ages

The interminable wars, rebellions and religious schisms of the Middle Ages necessitated the growth of an extremely sophisticated torture industry. Combining both physical and mental cruelty, this inventively devilish trade provided employment for literally tens of thousands of blacksmiths, ropewefters, chainforgers, holemakers and bollock-pummellers. In 1376 there were almost as many professional torture workers as there are celebrity diarists today.

M'Baron's Fancy
Instrument for scraping the victim's amputated nails across a blackboard made of his own charred and pressed relatives.

Pruty's Lathe
Machine for carving the buttocks into wafer-thin slices and then using them to wallpaper the victim's cell.

La Brilliantine
Device for ruining the victim's hairdo or cutting it off entirely.

Scavenger's Ladyhole
Makes infuriating ticking noise when you are trying to sleep.

Spaniard's Rack
A simple peasant torture from the Valladolid region. The victim is tied to an iron restaurant and their mouth stuffed with a large, blanched onion. Ideally, this should be a Spanish onion – when in season – but, if not, a whole swede or a cannonball may be substituted. The victim is then presented with a rack of lamb, unacceptably overdone, but, because of the onion, he finds himself unable to complain to the maître d'. Exquisite agonies of embarrassment result, particularly if someone whom the victim is particularly keen to impress is tied to the same establishment.

The Dog

A big dog is introduced into the victim's front garden and encouraged to go to the lavatory. The prisoner is blindfolded after having his contact lenses removed with a red-hot pepper and strewn on his lawn.

Sir Beastly

One of these is attached to a tender part of the victim's anatomy and then flicked with a ruler.

Boiled Arse

Victim is made to sit in a bath of red-hot lead and then teased mercilessly about the colour of his behind (see below).

Hengist and Horsa

Two identical Danish pastries are put before the prisoner. He is commanded to confess which of the two apricots he has flattened. Whichever one he chooses, he is told he is a liar, that only God can squash an apricot. After which he is beaten about the thighs and neck with a red-hot iron bar and his remains thrown in the moat.

Medieval Medicine

By 1380, medicine had advanced to the point where, though doctors* were able to diagnose and give Latin names to over 3000 diseases and conditions, only three known cures had been discovered. These were:

1. Herbs   2. Leeches   3. Saw it off.

Purveyors of medical supplies did a roaring trade, and no medieval town was complete without its sawyers, lechers and herberts (as they were known). Leech ranching was a respectable and lucrative profession, akin to management consultancy or merchant banking today. Once a year, the Leech Fair was held at Spitalfields when leech-herds drove vast clusters of leeches from all over the country for the leech auctions, with their 'merrie cries of "Leech-ho!" and "Giddy-yap, l'il leechies!" ' (Chaucer). Below follows a list of popular remedies.

Appendicitis
Leeches applied to flesh over the affected part and allowed to gorge themselves until the appendix itself is exposed. This is then sawn off.

Arthritis
Bunches of dried thyme inserted into patient's gloves and socks.

Asthma
Cough mixture made of crushed leeches and garlic.

Blood-poisoning
Examine any attached leeches for symptoms of illness (boils, lesions, etc.). Remove any unwell leeches and apply fit ones to poisoned areas.

Broken limbs
Chives strapped to limb.

Bubonic Plague
Fennel bulbs, leeches and hacksaw posted to patient.

Burns
Buttered leeches applied to affected skin.

Cataract
Leech inserted under each eyelid.

Diarrhoea
Aniseed or attar of roses inserted into patient's bucket to reduce smell.

* Or 'murderers' as they were known.

Earache
Two or more leeches worn as earrings while symptoms persist.

Flat feet
Insert coriander leaves between toes. If ineffective, saw off feet.

Foot and Mouth Disease
Saw off all affected areas.

Hiccoughs
Balance leech on key and drop it down patient's back.

Impetigo
Leeches.

Indigestion
Leeches.

Leechbite
If leech no longer present, apply sage as poultice to wound. If leech still attached, saw it off.

Measles
Young leech applied to each measle individually.

Nosebleed
Fat leech crammed up each nostril to staunch the flow.

Palsy
Allspice.

Pleurisy
Cumin seed.

Pneumonia
Flat-leaved parsley.

Root-canal work
Leeches.

Surfeit of Lampreys
Live leeches, three times a day during meals, to be taken internally.

Syphilis
Apply leeches indiscriminately.

Toothache
Leech applied to scrotum to take patient's mind off pain in jaw.

Verruccas
Poke repeatedly with cinnamon stick.

Warts
Charm wart by engaging it in flattering conversation.
When you have got it alone, saw it off.

The Blackadder Chronicles
PART TWO:
THE EARLY TUDORS

After the death of Prince (and, briefly, King) Edmund at the hands of his sinister adversary 'The Thrush', a huge queue of impostors seized the English throne one after another – including Edward IV,* Henry IV, Henry VI, Edward V, William IV, some bloke called Derek and Lady Jane Wellesley. However, none of them showed any staying power, and the crown was finally seized by Henry Tudor, a tall, dark, blue-eyed, man with a face like a stoat, whom the Black Adder himself had saved from certain death at the Battle of Bosworth.

Henry, donning a 'VII' borrowed from an aunt, was immediately attacked from all sides by hundreds of pretenders – amongst them Lambkin Warmneck, Scrumnel Basset, Timpson Pertscrew, Singelton Crampon, Crimplene Gusset,** Gareth Gwenlan and Grimly Feendish. Only one of these – a certain Bernard Baldrick – need detain us here.

Baldrick, an unemployed dung-taster from Stoke, had sought to better himself by taking the Deputy Village Idiot Test at Hoathly Posset in Staffordshire. In the course of the practical, however, he accidentally burnt the examiner at the stake, and thus caught the eye of the evil Earl of Lincoln, who was looking for a cloth-eared, frog-faced, total moron to place on the throne as his puppet.

In 1486, the earl ordered Baldrick to raise an army and march on London. Baldrick unfortunately misheard and, two days later, armed a raisin, marched on Londonderry and was never seen again. The Earl of Lincoln, humiliated, retired to his estates and devoted the rest of his life to perfecting the art of eating biscuits without getting any crumbs on his napkin.

Meanwhile, Henry VII cunningly married Elizabeth of York, daughter of Edward IV and Henry VI, thus confusing any remaining pretenders, enabling him to keep a firm grip on her baronies, and uniting the Houses of York and Lancaster into the House of Tudor and the House of Pancakes. Too late Henry realized this left his children with far too many surnames to fit on their school nametapes, and he died an angry and embittered man.

On the accession of his son Henry VIII in 1509, the whole country heaved a sigh of relief. Here, at last, was a king they had heard of! Henry initially took little interest in affairs of state. He appointed Cardinal Wolsey as Lord Chancellor, Cardinal Sprunt as Lord Scrivener and Cardinal Blackadder as Keeper of the Privy Rolls, leaving the king himself free to write 'Greensleeves' and tuck into a large bowl of syphilis. He immediately became deranged, fat and covered in pustules, and insisted on being known as either Keith or Michelle.

* William VI of Scotland
** Malcolm XII of Scotland

Henry VIII executed at least 50,000 people during his reign, especially singling out for punishment anyone suspected of laughing at people who were slightly chubby. Unsurprisingly, this plump nutcase and Cardinal Blackadder got on like a house on fire, spending long evenings at Hampton Court wassailing, simonizing, dissolving monasteries, tinkling with virginals and stuffing each other's orifices with lightly-oiled lampreys. Such was the rich inner life of the new Supreme Head of the Church of England.

Henry, as is well known, had seven wives: Katherine of Aragon, Anne Boleyn, Anne of Cleese, Moll of Flanders, Catherine Howard, Catherine Seymour and Catherine the Other One. This last was in fact Baldrick – dressed up in an old brocade curtain and with a dab of anchovy paste behind each ear. The king, insane, half-blind, halt, lame and stone-deaf was grateful for anything he could get, and Baldrick, of course, felt very much the same way.

It is sometimes said, quite inaccurately, that Henry VIII died of a surplus of Lamborghinis. In fact, he was almost certainly murdered by Cardinal Blackadder, who strangled him with an eel after being caught in the act of helping himself to a couple of peerages from the king's bureau.

Henry was succeeded by his only son, Edward VI. As he was just nine years old, England was ruled on his behalf by two 'Protectors', enabling the young king to enjoy his childhood to the full, playing with his friends and executing anyone who beat him at rounders. The exiled Cardinal Blackadder's attempts to get in on the act from his French hideaway, tempting the Boy King with gifts of marmite-flavoured sceptres, jellied conkers and bags of emerald-centred toffees were contemptuously ignored.

Edward died young and was succeeded by his sister, Bloody Mary Queen of Scots, a sour, narrow-minded, obstinate woman with a mouth like a bottom, whose idea of a nice mixed grill was twenty Protestants and a tomato. As can be imagined, Cardinal Blackadder and his son, Lord Edmund, kept a low profile while this frightful hag was around. In due time, Mary died – embittered, childless and with nasty singes along the hems of all her dresses – leaving the way clear for her sister Elizabeth, the Virgin Train.

She had been waiting for ages and ages on the sidelines, but when she did arrive she was a bit of a disappointment – being painted a strange colour, not very clean inside or out, and with no buffet car. However, she did have a very jolly, podgy nurse, imaginatively called Nursie, a silly laugh and a bloke called Melchy to help her rule.

Our story continues in dramatized form . . .

Black Adder II

Being a true and japesome historie of
Elizabethan Englande
by Richard Curtis and Ben Elton

Bells
Served by a dungball in a dress and accompanied by a bird-brained
dimwit he can't shake off, Edmund, the bastard great-great-grandson
of the repulsive original, is reasonably normal – until he meets Bob …

Head
Edmund, newly appointed minister in charge of religious genocide and
Lord High Executioner, finds himself in a spot of bother when he com
pletely ruins Lord Farrow's weekend by cutting off his head.

Potato
Blackadder sets off unwillingly to seek out new potatoes and to boldly
go where Sir Rather-a-Wally Raleigh has already gone before …

Money
Trouble is in store for Edmund when the baby-eating Bishop of Bath
and Wells drops by unexpectedly and tries to shove a red-hot poker up
places where a cotton bud would be kinder.

Beer
An embarrassing incident with a turnip, an ostrich feather and a fanat-
ically Puritan aunt leads to a right royal to-do in the Blackadder household.

Chains
Edmund is slightly inconvenienced when a fat-headed German chamber-pot boxes him up in a chestful of iron spikes and leaves him to play
charades with a crazed Spanish interrogator …

The Cast

Lord Edmund Blackadder	Rowan Atkinson
Lord Percy	Tim McInnerny
Baldrick	Tony Robinson
Queen Elizabeth I	Miranda Richardson
Lord Melchett	Stephen Fry
Nursie	Patsy Byrne
Kate/Bob	Gabrielle Glaister
Flashheart	Rik Mayall
Dr Leech	John Grillo
Kate's Father	Edward Jewesbury
Wisewoman	Barbara Miller
Young Crone	Sadie Shimmin
Lady Farrow	Holly de Jong
Gaoler Ploppy	Bill Wallis
Mrs Ploppy	Linda Polan
Earl Farrow	Patrick Duncan
Captain Redbeard Rum	Tom Baker
Sir Walter Raleigh	Simon Jones
Bishop of Bath and Wells	Ronald Lacey
Mollie	Cassie Stuart
Mad Beggar	Tony Aitken
Arthur the Sailor	John Pierce Jones
Mrs Pants	Lesley Nicol
Mr Pants	Barry Craine
Messenger	Piers Ibbotson
Leonardo Acropolis	Philip Pope
Lady Whiteadder	Miriam Margolyes
Lord Whiteadder	Daniel Thorndike
Simon Partridge	Hugh Laurie
Geoffrey Piddle	Roger Blake
Monk	William Hootkins
Prince Ludwig	Hugh Laurie
Torturer	Max Harvey
Guard 1	Mark Arden
Guard 2	Lee Cornes

Bells

SCENE ONE: A ROOM IN A ONE-ROOM COUNTRY COTTAGE

Kate is sitting with her father. She is young and pretty, and he is old and gibbering.

Kate
Father, I must speak. I can be silent no longer. All day long you mutter to yourself, gibber, dribble, moan and bash your head against the wall yelling, 'I want to die'. Now, you may say I'm leaping to conclusions, but you're not completely happy, are you? It's mother, isn't it?

Father
No, it's not.

Kate
You're brooding over her death, aren't you?

Father
Kate, for the final time, your mother is not dead. She's run off with your Uncle Henry.

Kate
Dear Father, I know you only say such things to comfort me.

Father
Your mother is alive and well and living in Droitwich. It's not her I brood over. I'm sad because, my darling, our poverty has now reached such extremes that I can no longer afford to keep us and must look to my own dear tiny darling to sustain me in my frail dotage.

Kate
But Father, surely . . .

Father
Yes, Kate . . . I want you to become a prostitute.

Kate
Never, Father.

Father
Do you defy me?!

Kate
Indeed I do, for 'tis better to die poor

than to live in shame and ignominy.

Father
No, it isn't.

Kate
I'm young and strong, clever, my nose is pretty. I shall find another way to earn us a living.

Father
Oh, please go on the game. It's a steady job and you'd be working from home.

Kate
Goodbye, Father. I shall go to London, disguise myself as a boy, and seek my fortune.

Father
Why walk all the way to London when you can make a fortune lying on your back?

But Kate has gone for ever.

～

SCENE TWO: BLACKADDER'S LODGINGS

Lord Edmund Blackadder is a noble of modest means. When not attending to the needs of his queen, he inhabits lodgings in Drury Lane, not very spacious, not very light, but with lots of nice exposed beams.

Blackadder is taking aim with a bow and arrow. Baldrick is at the door, holding a target above his head. Blackadder shoots a bullseye.

Baldrick
Very good shot, my lord.

Blackadder
Thank you, Baldrick.

The door against which Baldrick is standing suddenly swings open. It is Percy. He carries a bow, and wears a distinctly Robin Hoody hat. Baldrick, still holding the target, is, in fact, pinned to the door. He moves with it as it opens.

Percy
Sorry I'm late.

Blackadder
Don't bother apologizing. I'm sorry you're alive.

Percy
Ah, good, I see the target's ready.

He lines up his bow professionally for a shot.

I'd like to see the Spaniard who could make his way past me.

Blackadder
Then go to Spain, there are millions of them.

Percy lines up, and then turns again.

Percy
I advise them to stay there then – keep their hands off our women.

Blackadder
Oh, God, who is she this time?

Percy
I don't know what you mean.

Percy turns to take his shot again and Blackadder removes a pink envelope from his pocket. Percy lunges to grab it, but Blackadder, without looking up from the letter, stops him clean with a kick in the nether regions.

Blackadder
And who is Jane?

Percy
I am sworn to secrecy. Torture me, kill me, you shall never know!

Another casual but deadly blow from Blackadder to Percy's soft bits.

(*In great pain*) Jane Harrington!

Blackadder
Ah.

Percy
We are very much in love, my lord.

Blackadder
This is *the* Jane Harrington?

Percy
(*Proud*) Yes.

Blackadder
Jane 'bury me in a Y-shaped coffin' Harrington?

Percy
I think maybe there are two Jane Harringtons.

Blackadder
No. Tall, blonde, elegant?

Percy
Yes, that's right.

Blackadder
Goes like a privy door when the plague's in town?

Percy
My lord!

Blackadder
Come on, get on with your shot, you'll get over her . . .

Percy tries to forget it and concentrate on a shot.

I did. (*Percy struggles to control himself*) So did Baldrick actually.

Baldrick smiles in happy memory. Percy is for a moment incensed. He drops his aim and shoots Baldrick in the codpiece. Baldrick looks down at the arrow sticking in his codpiece.

Baldrick
Ow!

Percy
Damn!

Blackadder
You see, she's got a thing about beards, apparently.

Percy
Well, in that case, I'm going to shave.

Percy leaves, opening the door by using the arrow in Baldrick's codpiece. The door swings shut with Baldrick still on it.

Blackadder
Bad luck, Balders.

Baldrick
Not to worry, my lord. The arrow didn't, in fact, enter my body.

Blackadder
Oh, good.

Baldrick
No. By a thousand to one chance, my willy got in the way.

Blackadder
Extraordinary.

Baldrick
Yes, sir. I'd only just put it there, but now I will leave it there for ever.

Blackadder
Quite so, Baldrick. It can be your lucky willy.

Baldrick
Yes, my lord. Years from now, I shall show it to my grandchildren.

Blackadder
Yes, Baldrick, I think that grandchildren may now be out of the question.

Blackadder pulls the arrow out of the codpiece, thereby releasing Baldrick from the door.

Poor old peabrain Percy. Never catch me falling in love, that's for damn sure as mustard.

There is a knock at the door.

Come in.

Baldrick opens the door and Kate enters, now dressed, in classic Shakespearian style, as a girl pretending to be a boy.

Kate
Good day to you, Lord Blackadder.

Blackadder chokes up for a moment: a flash of romantic music; it's jolly nearly love at first sight. But he recovers; after all, this is a boy.

Blackadder
Good day to you, boy. What is it brings you here?

Kate
I'm an honest, hard-working lad, but poor, and I must support my father, who is stark-raving mad. Therefore I have come to London to seek a servant's wage.

Blackadder
Well, yes, indeed. Unfortunately, I already have a servant.

Kate
The word is that your servant is the worst servant in London.

Blackadder
Mmmmm. That's true. Baldrick, you're fired. Be out of the house in ten minutes. Well, young man . . . you've got yourself a job. What do they call you?

Kate
Kate.

Not thinking, she is as much taken with Blackadder as he is with her.

Blackadder
Isn't that a bit of a . . . girl's name?

Kate
It's uhm, short for, uhm, Bob.

Blackadder
Bob?

Kate
Yes.

Blackadder
Well, Bob, welcome on board.

They shake hands in a magical moment. Blackadder notices that Baldrick hasn't moved.

Sorry, Baldrick. Any reason you're still here?

Baldrick
I've got nowhere to go, my lord.

Blackadder and Kate release hands. Blackadder puts his arm around Baldrick.

Blackadder
Oh, surely you'll be allowed to starve to death in one of the royal parks?

Baldrick
I've been in your service since I was two and a half, my lord.

Blackadder
Well, that must be why I'm so utterly sick of the sight of you.

Baldrick
Couldn't I just stay here and do the same jobs but for no wages?

Blackadder removes his arm.

Blackadder
Well, you know where you'd have to live . . .

Baldrick
In the gutter?

Blackadder
Yes, and you'd have to work a bit harder too.

Baldrick
Of course, my lord.

Blackadder
All right. Go and get Bob's stuff in then

and chuck your filthy muck out into the street.

Baldrick smiles.

Baldrick
God bless you, sweet master.

As Baldrick opens the door to leave, Percy enters.

Blackadder
Now, Bob, this is Percy: a smooth-shaving dimwit I don't seem to be able to shake off.

Percy strides forward in a hearty manner which he imagines makes young lads admire and look up to him.

Percy
Hullo there, young Bob, you young roister-doister you.

He tousles her hair, to Kate's alarm.

You look a likely sort of lad, for tricks and sports and all sorts of jolly, rosy-cheeked caperings, eh? Course you do, and more besides, I'll warrant, you young scamp! Ha ha ha.

But Kate has eyes only for Blackadder.

Kate
Thank you so much for letting me stay, Lord Blackadder.

Blackadder
No, not at all, Bob. I'm looking forward to having you . . . (*he panics at the double entendre*) having . . . another man about the house, instead of that animal Baldrick. Excuse me. I'm just going to the lavatory.

Blackadder exits, worried.

Kate
How little he knows! And how much I would have him know.

Percy
I say, Bob, I think this calls for a celebration. How about a game of cup and ball

and a slap-up tea at Mrs Miggins's Pie Shop?

Kate
Get lost, creep.

Percy
I like you, young Bob. You've got balls!

SCENE THREE: QUEENIE'S CHAMBER

Queenie, her advisor, Melchett, and her nurse, Nursie, are in her private chamber. It is not a huge room, but it is highly ornate, with enough gilt to gild a huge field of very large lilies.

Queenie is utterly bored, her arms slung back over her throne. Before her, Melchett is doing some kind of hornpipe dance, like a sailor out at sea.

Queen
Nice try, Melchy, but it's no use. I'm still bored.

Melchett stops.
Melchett
I'm very sorry, madam. Your royal father used to be very amused by my impersonation of Columbus.

Queen
Doesn't surprise me. He used to laugh at those people with the funny faces, and the bells.

Melchett
Ah – jesters, ma'am.

Queen
No. (*Tiny pause to remember*) Lepers. Where's Edmund these days?

Melchett
Well, the whisper on the underground grapevine, ma'am, is that Lord Blackadder is spending all his time with a young boy in his service.

Queen
Oh. Do you think he'd spend more time with me if I was a boy?

Melchett
Surely not, ma'am.

Nursie
You almost were a boy, my little cherry pip.

Queen
What?

Nursie
Yeah. Out you popped from your mummy's tumkin and everyone shouted, 'It's a boy! It's a boy!' And then someone said, 'But it hasn't got a winkle!' And then I said, 'A boy without a winkle! God be praised – it's a miracle! A boy without a winkle!' And then Sir Thomas More pointed out that a boy without a winkle is a girl, and everyone was really disappointed.

Melchett
Yes, well, you see he was a very perceptive man, Sir Thomas More.

Queen
Oh, what has happened to Edmund? There's something very odd about someone who spends all their time with a servant.

~

SCENE FOUR: THE COUNTRYSIDE

These are indeed happy times for Blackadder and 'Bob'. They walk along a beach together laughing. They are in a wood, it begins to rain and, laughing, they run for shelter. They laze in the sun on a grassy knoll. It is sunset; they stroll together.

In the background, music plays, reminiscent of some great Elizabethan love songs:

Greensleeves; The Rain It Raineth Every Day; Hey, Nonny I Love You; My Love is a Prick (on a Tudor Rose);

Hot Sex Madrigal in the Middle of My Tights

~

SCENE FIVE: BLACKADDER'S LODGINGS

It is late at night. Blackadder is seated on a chair and Kate is pouring him a drink.

Blackadder
Well, Bob, we're a couple of fine lads together, aren't we? Let's get ratted and talk about girls. (*He slaps his thigh with false bravado*) Yes, we could sing some really dirty songs and . . . (*He can't help but look at her, but he tries to carry on being masculine*) Oh, God . . . I find you curiously pleasant company, young Bob.

Kate
I am honoured, and for my part want nothing more than to be with you . . . old man.

Blackadder
Well, yes, of course, there's nothing more healthy and . . . normal . . . than having a good . . . chum.

Kate
What think you, my lord, of . . . love?

Blackadder
You mean rumpy-pumpy?

Kate
What would you say, my lord, if I were to say I love you?

Blackadder
Well, of course, it would depend entirely on who you said it to. If you said it to a horse, I'd presume you were sick, if you said it to Baldrick, I'd presume you were blind, and if you said it to me . . .

Kate
Yes, my lord?

Blackadder
Well, I'd naturally assume we were having

a big lads' joke about backticklers, the
way we healthy fellows often do, and so
I'd probably grab you for a friendly wrestle and we'd probably slap each other's
thighs like jolly good chums, and laugh at
what it would be like . . . if we really did
. . . fancy each other.

Kate
In that case, my lord, I love you.

*Blackadder laughs unconvincingly. He
jumps up and they grab each other. There
is a half-hearted effort at wrestling,
which ends with Blackadder sitting on
Kate's stomach. Then a pause, and they
move together as if about to kiss when
Baldrick enters.*

Baldrick
(*Misunderstanding*) Don't worry, Bob. He
used to try and kill me, too.

Blackadder jumps up.

Blackadder
Ah, Baldrick. God, am I glad to see you.
What do you want?

Baldrick
I was just wondering if I could sleep on the
roof. The Town Bailiff says if I lie in the
gutter, I'll be flushed into the Thames with
all the other turds.

Blackadder
By all means, Baldrick, help yourself . . .
I was just off to bed anyway . . . erm,
goodnight, Baldrick, goodnight . . . Bob.

Kate
Goodnight, my lord.

Blackadder
Yes. Oh, God!

Edmund exits, in despair.

~

SCENE SIX: DOCTOR LEECH'S
SURGERY

Dr Leech is keen on leeches. There are
*large pictures of leeches on the wall and
jars of leeches everywhere, and a blackboard with a leech drawn on it, with a little
leech on its back. Dr Leech sits behind the
desk, with Blackadder on the other side.*

Dr Leech
Now then, what seems to be the trouble?

Blackadder
Well, it's my manservant.

Dr Leech
I see. Well, don't be embarrassed. If
you've got the pox, just pop your manservant on the table and we'll take a look at
it, shall we?

Blackadder
No, it's my real manservant.

Dr Leech
And what's wrong with him?

Blackadder
Nothing is wrong with him. That's the
problem. He's perfect. And last night I
almost kissed him.

Dr Leech
I see. So, you've started fancying boys
then, have you?

Blackadder
Not 'boys'. A boy.

Dr Leech
Yes, well, let's not split hairs, it's all
rather disgusting, and naturally you're
worried.

Blackadder
Of course I'm worried.

Dr Leech
Well, of course you are. It's not every day
a man wakes up to discover he's a screaming bender with no more right to live on
God's clean earth than a weasel. Ashamed
of yourself?

Blackadder
Not really, no.

Dr Leech goes to wash his hands.

Dr Leech
Bloody hell, I would be, still why should I complain, just leaves more rampant totty for us real men, eh?

Blackadder
Am I actually paying for this personal abuse, or is it extra?

Dr Leech
No, all part of the service. Mmmm, I think you're in luck, though. An extraordinary new cure has just been developed for exactly this kind of sordid problem.

Blackadder
It wouldn't have anything to do with leeches, would it?

Dr Leech double-takes.

Dr Leech
I had no idea you were a medical man.

Blackadder
No, no. Just I've never had anything you doctors didn't try to cure with leeches. Leech on my ear for earache. Leech up my bottom for constipation.

Dr Leech
They're marvellous, aren't they?

Blackadder
Well, the bottom one wasn't. I sat down and squashed it.

Dr Leech
You know, the leech comes to us on the highest authority.

Blackadder
Yes. I'd heard that. Dr Hoffman of Stuttgart, wasn't it?

Dr Leech
That's right. The great Hoffman.

Blackadder
Owner of the largest leech farm in Europe.

Dr Leech
Yes. I can't spend all day gossiping. I'm a busy man.

Dr Leech goes to the desk, followed by Blackadder. They both sit.

As far as this case is concerned, I've had time to think it through and I can strongly recommend a course of . . .

Dr Leech and Blackadder
. . . leeches.

Blackadder
Oh, just pop a couple down my codpiece before I go to bed.

Dr Leech
Oh, no, no, no, no. Don't be ridiculous. This isn't the Dark Ages. No – just pop four in your mouth in the morning, and let them dissolve slowly.

Dr Leech hands Blackadder a prescription.

Within a couple of weeks, you'll be beating your servant with a stick just like the rest of us.

Blackadder
You're really just an old quack, aren't you?

Dr Leech
I'd rather be a quack than a ducky. Good day.

SCENE SEVEN: BLACKADDER'S LODGINGS

Breakfast. Blackadder is sitting at the table. Baldrick enters, with a plate and a spider.

Baldrick
Anything to follow, my lord? There's this lovely fat spider I found in the bath. I was saving it for myself, but . . . if you fancy it . . .

Blackadder
Shut up, Baldrick. I don't eat invertebrates for fun, you know. This is doctor's orders.

Baldrick eats the spider.

Baldrick
I don't hold with all this newfangled doctoring. Any problems, I go to the wisewoman.

Blackadder
Yes, Baldrick, I'm long past entrusting myself to some deranged Druid who gives her professional address as 1 Dunghill Mansions, Putney.

So he thinks.

SCENE EIGHT: OUTSIDE THE HOVEL

The sign reads '1 Dunghill Mansions'. It is very dark and gungy. Blackadder walks up the path to the young crone.

Blackadder
Tell me, young crone, is this Putney?

Young Crone
That it be, that it be!

Blackadder
'Yes, it is', not 'That it be'. You don't have to talk in that stupid voice to me. I'm not a tourist.

Young Crone
(*Slightly deflated*) Oh.

Blackadder
I seek information about a wisewoman.

Young Crone
Ah! The wisewoman! The wisewoman!

Blackadder
Yes, the wisewoman.

Young Crone
Two things, my lord, must ye know of the wisewoman.

Blackadder
Yes?

Young Crone
First! She is a woman. And second, she is . . .

Blackadder
Wise?

Young Crone
You do know her then?

Blackadder
Oh, no, just a wild stab in the dark, which is incidentally what you'll be getting if you don't start being a bit more helpful. Do you know where she lives?

Young Crone
'Course.

Blackadder
Where?

Young Crone
Here. Do you have an appointment?

Blackadder
No.

Young Crone
Well, you can go in anyway.

Blackadder
Thank you, young crone. Here is a purse of moneys . . . which I'm not going to give to you.

Blackadder enters the hovel.

SCENE NINE: THE HOVEL

There stands the Wisewoman, in full wisewoman regalia.

Wisewoman
Hail, Edmund, Lord of Adders Black.

Blackadder
Hullo.

Wisewoman
Step no nearer. For already I see thy bloody purpose. Thou plottest,

Blackadder! Thou would'st be king and drown Middlesex in a butt of wine.

She cackles.

Blackadder
No, no, no, no. It's far worse than that. I'm in love with my manservant.

Wisewoman gets on to the bed.

Wisewoman
Oh, well, I'd sleep with him, if I were you.

Blackadder
What?

Wisewoman
When I fancy people, I sleep with them. I have to drug them first, of course, being so old and warty.

Blackadder
But what about my position, my social life?

Wisewoman
Very well then. Three other paths are open to you, three cunning plans to cure thy ailment.

Blackadder
Ah, good.

Wisewoman
The first is simple. Kill Bob.

Blackadder
Never.

Wisewoman
Then try the second. Kill yourself.

Blackadder
And the third?

Wisewoman
The third is to ensure that no one else ever knows.

Blackadder
That sounds more like it. How?

Wisewoman
Kill everybody in the whole world.

She cackles.

Blackadder
Ah ha.

It's clear now. She's quite mad. He gets up and leaves.

~

SCENE TEN: BLACKADDER'S LODGINGS

Blackadder is at the door. He steels himself, enters and finds himself absolutely face to face with a bottom. Kate is cleaning some shelves just above the door.

Blackadder
Now . . . look here, Bob. I have something to say to you. And I want you to listen very carefully.

Kate
Yes.

Blackadder
Look, Bob. I have decided . . . that you are to leave my service.

Kate
Oh, no, my lord. My father will starve and I'll have to become a . . . male prostitute and besides . . . I thought we were . . . friends.

Blackadder
We are friends, Bob. Of course, of course, of course, of course, of course, of course, of course, of course, of course. In fact, that's the reason I want you to leave my service and become my, live in . . . chum.

Kate
Oh, my lord.

Blackadder
Now, I want to make it quite clear that I am in no way interested in the contents of your tights.

Kate
You might be, my lord, if you knew what I kept in them.

Blackadder
I flatter myself, Bob, that I know what a gentleman keeps in his tights, thank you very much.

Kate
But, my lord, I have a great secret.

Blackadder
What?

Kate
Prepare to be amazed.

She starts to take her top off.

Blackadder
Oh, no. You haven't got one of those awful birthmarks shaped like a banana, have you?

Kate
No!

Blackadder
Or a tattoo saying, 'Get it Here'?

Kate
No!

Blackadder
Oh, God, you've got one of those belly buttons that sticks outwards, haven't you?

Kate
No, my lord.

Blackadder
Well, what can it possibly be?

She rips open her bodice.

Good Lord!

SCENE ELEVEN: BLACKADDER'S LODGINGS

Two minutes later, after Blackadder has got his breath back.

Blackadder
Well, what was all that Bob stuff about then?

Kate
Because you would have just used me and cast me aside like you have so many women before.

Blackadder
Would I?

Kate
Yes, but now you have had a chance to grow to love me for what I really am.

Blackadder
Yes, that's true. And now . . . I want to marry you . . . Bob.

Kate
Kate!

Blackadder
Then come, kiss me, Kate!

SCENE TWELVE: QUEENIE'S CHAMBER

Melchett enters to a very bored Queenie sitting with Nursie.

Melchett
Madam, I bring grave intelligence of your former favourite, Lord Blackadder.

Queen
Oh, good.

Melchett
It appears he wishes to marry a girl called Bob.

Queen
That's a very odd name for a girl, isn't it? Girls are normally called Elizabeth, or Mary.

Nursie
And Donald.

Queen
Mouth is open, Nursie: should be shut.

Nursie
But it's true, sweet one. I had three sisters, and they were called Donald, Eric and Basil.

Queen
Then why's your name Nursie?

Nursie
That isn't my real name!

Queen
Isn't it?

Nursie
No.

Queen
What is your real name then?

Nursie
Bernard.

Queen
Mmmm. It suits you, actually.

Blackadder sweeps in.

Blackadder
Majesty.

Queen
Oh, hullo, stranger.

Blackadder kneels.

Blackadder
I seek your permission to wed.

Queen
So I hear – Melchy, what do you think of all this?

Melchett
I must profess, madam, I am astonished that Blackadder could possibly have eyes for any other woman than yourself.

Queen
Good point, though slightly grovelly.

Blackadder
But when I fell in love, ma'am, I didn't know she was a woman. I thought she was a boy.

Melchett
Of course, that makes it perfectly acceptable.

Queen
Oh, all right, go on and marry her.

Blackadder
Thank you, ma'am.

Queen
Just tell me one thing. Is her nose as pretty as mine?

Blackadder
Oh, no, no, no, no, no, ma'am.

Queen
Oh, good. Because otherwise I would have cut it off and then you'd have had to marry someone without a nose, and that wouldn't be very nice, would it?

Blackadder
No, ma'am.

Queen
I mean, imagine the mess when she got a cold. Yuk.

Blackadder
Well, quite, ma'am.

Queen
All right – off you go then.

She slaps his bottom as he heads away. But her high humour fades as she closes the door.

Everyone seems to get married, except me.

Nursie
And me, ma'am.

Queen
Oh, shut up, Bernard.

SCENE THIRTEEN: BLACKADDER'S LODGINGS

Very weddingly, Baldrick is fitted into a lovely dress. Kate is fluffing round with the final details.

Kate
You'll make a lovely bridesmaid, Baldrick, and pity me that I have no actual girl chums because we were so poor in our house, we couldn't afford friends.

Blackadder
It is strangely in keeping with the manner of our courtship that your maid of honour should be a man.

Baldrick
Thank you very much, my lord.

Blackadder
I use the word 'man' in its broadest possible sense. For as we all know, God made man in his own image, and it would be a sad look out for Christians throughout the globe if God looked anything like you, Baldrick.

Kate
Ignore Mr Grumpy. There we go, Balders. (*Standing back and admiring*) You look sweet as a little pie.

Blackadder
Kate, he looks like what he is, a dungball in a dress.

Enter Percy.

Percy
Edmund, I . . .

He stops and spies Baldrick, but does not recognize him and, believing himself to be in the presence of a rather petite girl, begins to flirt.

Oh, hullo there. Edmund you didn't tell me we were expecting guests. And such a pretty one, too.

Blackadder
Oh, God.

Percy
Well, you're a little cutie to be hiding yourself away all these years. Tell me, gorgeous, what's your name?

Blackadder
He's called Baldrick.

Percy
Baldrick, that's a pretty name. Edmund used to have a servant called Baldrick, but anyway, away with such small talk, lady, a kiss!

Baldrick
What?

Percy
And so modest too, come on, you little tease, you know you want to. Give us a kiss.

Baldrick
All right, if you say so.

Baldrick kisses Percy passionately. Percy claps a hanky to his nose in disgust.

Percy
Oooo dear, what an original perfume.

Blackadder
Percy, that *is* our Baldrick, he's wearing a dress.

Percy now fears he may die of infection.

Percy
Bleuch!

Blackadder
Anyway, what do you want?

Percy having finally cleaned his lips with a rabbit's-foot-on-a-stick, preens himself for this dialogue.

Percy
Well, erm, Edmund, there has been some discussion around the Court on the subject of who's going to be your best man, and I thought it might be the moment to bring it to a conclusion.

Blackadder
Oh, yes, Percy, I would like you . . .

Percy
(*Overcome*) Oh, Edmund, I'm so proud . . .

Blackadder
Please let me finish. I would like you . . . to take this letter to Dover, where is lately docked the galleon of my old school friend and adventurer, Lord Flashheart! He shall be my best man.

Percy knows that he is outclassed.

Percy
(*Depressed*) Lord Flashheart, the best sword, the best shot, the best sailor, and the best kisser in the kingdom?

Blackadder
Even he. To Dover at once!

Percy
Yes. Actually, I was going to suggest Lord Flashheart for best man myself.

Percy exits and bursts into tears in the corridor.

~

SCENE FOURTEEN: CORRIDOR OUTSIDE QUEENIE'S CHAMBER

It is the wedding day. Kate is waiting with her father, who looks distinctly unkempt. Blackadder enters.

Kate
Oh, Edmund. I can't believe it's really happening.

Blackadder
It is, my sweet.

Kate
Before we go in, I want you to meet my father.

Blackadder
Oh, fine.

He pauses and waits expectantly for his father-in-law. Then he spies the loitering man.

Excuse me, could you move along, please. Look, I'm waiting for my father-in-law. The last thing I want is some scruffy old beggar blocking up the corridor smelling of cabbages.

Father
I am your father-in-law.

Blackadder looks with an utterly depressed squint at Kate, who nods.

Blackadder
Oh, no . . . all right, how much do you want to clear off?

Kate
Edmund, how could you? He is my father, my only living relative.

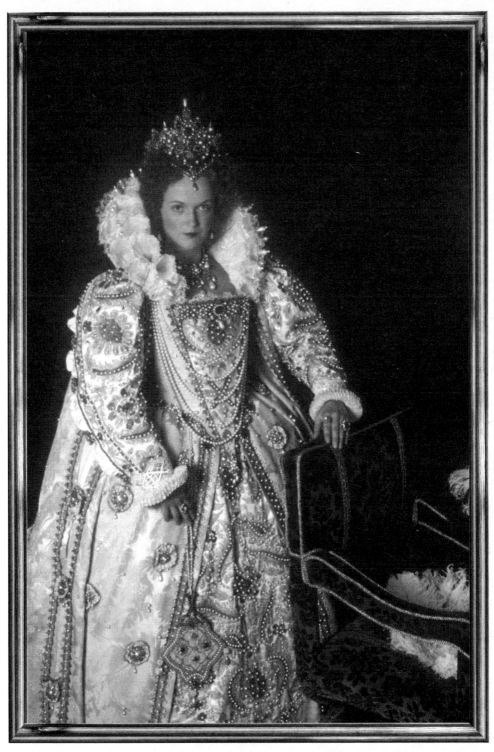

Good Queen Bess in one of her favourite gowns, decorated with the milk teeth of over 50,000 Catholics

Father
Ten pounds should do the trick.

Kate
Father!

Blackadder
All right. There you go.

Blackadder gives him the money. Father leaves.

Kate
Edmund, you mustn't.

Blackadder
Don't worry. I'll get Baldrick to beat him up after the service. We'll get the money back. Come on, we're late.

SCENE FIFTEEN: QUEENIE'S CHAMBER

They are all in attendance for the wedding. Queenie is feeling impatient.

Queen
Edmund, could we get on, do you think? I want to get to the reception so I can get squiffy and seduce someone.

Blackadder
Unfortunately, ma'am, the best man still has not arrived.

Queen
Well, get another one.

Blackadder
There's no one else I can really think of.

Percy coughs.

Sorry, Percy?

Percy
Nothing, my lord. Just clearing my throat.

Blackadder
Good. We don't want you coughing all the way through the ceremony.

Queen
Oh, come on, Edmund, you must be able to think of another best man.

Blackadder
Well, I suppose I could ask Percy. (*He turns to Percy*) Percy . . .

Percy
(*Thrilled*) My lord!

Blackadder
Can you think of another best man?

Percy
(*Hurt, but recovering fast*) Well, one name does spring to mind.

Blackadder
Yes, but I can't ask Baldrick. He's a bridesmaid and, besides, I need a friend, an equal, an old and trusty companion.

Percy
I think there is one person in the room who fits the description.

Blackadder
Of course. Nursie, how do you fancy putting on a pair of hose and being my best man?

Queen
Edmund! Don't be so naughty. You know perfectly well who Percy's referring to.

Blackadder
Of course. I'm sorry. Melchett . . .

Queenie squeaks.

Blackadder
All right, all right! Shamed as I am, and contradiction in terms though it is, Percy, you can be the best man.

Percy
Oh, my lord: noble coz! What an honour. I brought along a ring . . .

Percy produces the ring.

Blackadder
I really did think old Flash would have turned up!

There is a sudden explosion and flash, the doors fly open, masonry falls from the ceiling, as does a rope, and Flashheart appears in the corridor. He is the most glamorous man in the world.

Flashheart
It's me!

Blackadder
Flash!

Flashheart comes down the corridor, knocking over two suits of armour. He enters the chamber.

Flashheart
Flash by name. Flash by nature!

The doors close.

Hurray!

All
Hurray!

Blackadder
Where have you been?

Flashheart
Where haven't I been? (*He is referring to every girl in the world*) But I'm here now, and . . . who is that?

He looks at Percy in total horror.

Blackadder
No idea, but he's in your place.

Flashheart
Not for long.

He draws his sword and hands it to Baldrick. He then pushes Percy through the doors and takes his sword back.

Flashheart
Thanks, bridesmaid. Like the beard, gives me something to hang on to. So, my old mate Eddie's getting hitched, eh? What's the matter? Can't stand the pace of the In-Crowd! (*He turns to Queenie*) Hi, Queenie,
you look sexy. Woof! But listen, wear your hair long, I prefer it that way.

He pulls a pin out of Queenie's hair, some falls down attractively.

Queen
I've got *such* a crush on him!

Flashheart
Hey, Melchy! Still worshipping God?

Melchett
My lord!

Flashheart
Last thing I heard, he'd started worshipping me. Ha ha ha ha ha ha!

All
Ha ha ha ha ha ha!

Flashheart
Nursie – I like it, firm and fruity. Am I pleased to see you, or did I put a canoe in my pocket. Down, boy, down!

Nursie laughs. Percy's head appears through the smashed door and Flashheart bops him again.

And now, where's this amazing bird, the one who's stopped my old pal Eddie doing exactly what he wants ten times a night.

Blackadder
Flash, let me introduce my fiancée, Kate.

Flashheart sees Kate and they twirl to a kissing position.

Flashheart
Hi, baby.

They kiss passionately.

She's got a tongue like an electric eel and she likes the taste of a man's tonsils. You don't want to marry this jerk, baby. Meet me on my horse in eight seconds.

They release each other.

Kate
But I can't run in this frock. You see, I've found I actually prefer wearing boys' clothes.

Flashheart
Weird. I always feel more comfy in a dress!
I've got a plan, and it's as hot as my pants!

*Blackadder is meanwhile talking to
Percy.*

Blackadder
What a man Flash is. Things will certainly
liven up round here now he's back, won't
they, Flash?

*He turns to Flashheart, but he and Kate
seem to have disappeared. But in an
instant they are back. Flashheart in a
dress and Kate in tunic and trousers.*

Flashheart
So long, suckers! Next time you're bored
with your lives, give me a call and I'll
come round and kill you.

Kate
Bye, Edmund, and thanks for everything.

Flashheart
Hurray!

*And in a flash they are gloriously gone.
Smoke settles on the amazed assembly,
then Melchett has an idea with which he is
very pleased.*

Melchett
It is customary on these occasions for the
groom to marry the bridesmaid. I presume
you will honour this.

Baldrick
I do.

Blackadder
Ah-ha.

*He glances at Baldrick, who is looking
seductively his way. The end of the world
is nigh.*

THE BALLAD OF BLACKADDER THE BOYFRIEND

So Flashheart tweaked the Adder's beard,
From now he always shall be single.
To fall in love with boys is weird,
Especially boys without a dingle.

Blackadder, Blackadder,
His taste is rather odd.
Blackadder, Blackadder,
The randy little sod.

Lord Flashheart, Lord Flashheart,
I wish you were the star.
Lord Flashheart, Lord Flashheart,
You're sexier by far.

Head

SCENE ONE: BLACKADDER'S LODGINGS

Blackadder is sitting at the table with Baldrick, who is looking perplexed.

Blackadder
Right, Baldrick, let us try again, shall we? This is called adding. If I have two beans and then I add two more beans, what do I have?

Deep thought, then . . .

Baldrick
Some beans.

Blackadder
Yes and no. Let's try again. If I have two beans and then I add two more beans, what does that make?

Baldrick
(*More thought*) Umm . . . a very small casserole?

Blackadder
Baldrick, the ape creatures of the Indus have mastered this. Now try again. One, two, three, four, so how many are there?

Baldrick
Three.

Blackadder
What?

Baldrick
And that one.

Blackadder
Three, and that one, so, if I add that one to the three, what will I have?

Baldrick
Some beans.

Blackadder
Yes. To you, Baldrick, the Renaissance was just something that happened to other people, wasn't it?

Percy rushes in, wearing an enormous ruff.

Percy
Edmund, Edmund, come quickly, the queen wants to see you.

Blackadder
What?

Percy
I said, Edmund, Edmund, come quickly, the queen wants to see you.

Blackadder
Please, let me finish. What . . . are you wearing round your neck?

Percy
It's my new ruff.

Blackadder
You look like a bird who's swallowed a plate.

Percy
It's the latest fashion actually and as a matter of fact it makes me look rather sexy.

Blackadder
To another plate-swallowing bird perhaps, if it was blind and hadn't had it in months.

Percy
I *think* you may be wrong.

Blackadder
You're a sad laughable figure, aren't you, Percy? What do you think of Percy's ruff, Baldrick?

Baldrick
Four!

Blackadder
What?

Baldrick
Some beans and some beans is four beans.

Blackadder
No, we've moved on from advanced mathematics. We're on to elementary dressmaking. What do you think of Percy's ruff?

Baldrick
I think he looks like a bird who's swallowed a plate, my lord.

Blackadder
No, that's what *I* think, that's what *I*

think, what do *you* think? Try to have a thought of your own, Baldrick. Thinking is *so* important. What do *you* think?

Baldrick
I think thinking is *so* important, my lord.

Blackadder
I give up. I'm off to see the queen.

Percy
Shall I come too, my lord?

Blackadder
No, best not, people might think we're friends. You stay here with Baldrick. Bird neck and bird brain, you should get on like a nest on fire.

~

SCENE TWO: QUEENIE'S CHAMBER

Queenie, Nursie and Melchett are sitting together.

Melchett
Grey, I *suspect*, Majesty.

Queen
I think you'll find it was orange, Lord Melchett . . .

Melchett
Grey is more *usual*, ma'am.

Queen
Who's queen?

Melchett
As you say, Majesty, there were these magnificent *orange* elephants, and . . .

Blackadder enters and drops on to one knee.

Blackadder
Milady. You wished to see me?

Queen
Yes, Edmund, Lord Melchett has bad news.

Blackadder
Lord Melchett *is* bad news, ma'am.

Queen
No. Be serious. Melchett.

Melchett
Unhappily, Blackadder, the Lord High Executioner is dead.

Blackadder
Oh, woe. Murdered of course?

Melchett
Oddly enough, no. They usually are, but this one just got careless one night and signed his name on the wrong dotted line. They came for him while he slept.

Blackadder
He should have told them they had the wrong man.

Melchett
He did. But, you see, they didn't. They had the right man, and they had the form to prove it.

Blackadder
Tsk. Bloody red tape, eh? And the bad news?

Queen
The bad news is that, actually, there are simply hundreds of Catholics who desperately want their heads snicked off, and there's no one to organize it.

Blackadder
I pity the poor sod who gets the job; no one ever survives it more than a week.

Melchett
I have taken the liberty, ma'am, of drawing up a list of suitable candidates.

Queen
Oh, good-o! Let's hear it.

Melchett unrolls a scroll.

Melchett
List for the post of Lord High Executioner. Lord Blackadder . . .

Pause. He rolls the scroll back up again and smiles at Blackadder.

Blackadder
Ah.

~

SCENE THREE: BLACKADDER'S LODGINGS

A large black book with golden lettering is being read by Blackadder and Percy. It is called the Book of Death. Percy is now wearing the tiniest ruff ever seen. Like a high wing collar with a tiny frill.

Blackadder
Right then. Let's take a look, shall we? Who's first into the head-basket then? Admiral Lord Effingham and Sir Francis Drake on Monday . . .

Percy
That should draw a crowd.

Blackadder looks at him questioningly.

Well, sailing enthusiasts.

Blackadder
Yes. Better make sure there's a few anchors and things on the souvenir stall.

Percy
'Aye, aye, sir.'

Blackadder
Never, ever, try to be funny in my presence again, Percy. Right, Buckingham and Ponsonby on Friday, oh, wait a minute, Farrow on Wednesday. Hmm. Who's Farrow when he's not having his head cut off?

Percy
James Farrow, pleasant bloke from Dorchester.

Blackadder
Don't know him.

Percy hands him the official execution scroll, which Blackadder signs.

Never will, either. And he goes on Wednesday?

Percy

Mmm.

Blackadder

It's not right, though, is it?

Percy

(*Suddenly very passionate*) Well, no. Now you come to mention it, my lord, there was absolutely no evidence against young Farrow at all. It was an outrageous travesty of justice!

Blackadder

No, I mean it's not right that he should be stuck on Wednesday, when we could do him on Monday and have half the week off.

Percy

Oh, I see. Yes, that's right.

Blackadder

Pop him in on Monday. Right. Good. Five dead in two days, not a bad start. Oh, yes, Percy, and the new ruff . . .

Percy

Better?

Blackadder

Worse.

Percy

But the fashion of today is towards the tiny.

Blackadder

In that case, Percy, you have the most fashionable brain in London.

~

SCENE FOUR: GUARD ROOM IN THE PRISON

Blackadder and Percy are addressing the staff in this stony and dirty room. There is a horrible-looking man, a rotund woman and an executioner in his mask.

Blackadder

Right, good morning, team. My name is Edmund Blackadder, and I am the new

minister in charge of religious genocide. Now, if you play straight with me, you'll find me a considerate employer . . . But cross me, and you'll soon discover that under this boyish, playful exterior beats the heart of a ruthless, sadistic maniac. Now, my man, you are?

Gaoler

(*Shuffling to attention*) Gaoler, sir, my lord.

Blackadder

Good, well done. And your name is?

Gaoler

Ploppy, sir.

Blackadder

Ploppy?

Gaoler

Yes, sir.

Blackadder

Ploppy the gaoler.

Gaoler

That's right, sir. Ploppy, son of Ploppy.

Blackadder

Ploppy, son of Ploppy the gaoler.

Gaoler

Oh, no, sir. I'm the first Ploppy to rise to be gaoler. My father, Daddy Ploppy, was known as Ploppy the Slopper. It was from him that I inherited my fascinating skin diseases.

Blackadder

You are to be congratulated, my friend. We live in an age where illness and deformity are commonplace, and yet, Ploppy, you are, without a doubt, the most repulsive individual I have ever met. I would shake your hand, but I fear it would come off.

Gaoler

There's no' many bosses would be that considerate, sir.

Blackadder

Thank you, Ploppy. I do my best.

He moves on to the rotund and dirty woman.

Now then, woman, if indeed you *are* a woman, what is your function on Death Row?

Cook
I'm the last-meal cook, sir. The prisoners may ask me for what they fancy for their last meal.

Blackadder
And you cook for them what they desire?

Cook
Oh, yes, sir! Provided they ask for sausages. Otherwise they tend to get a tiny bit disappointed. Saussies is all I got.

Blackadder
You are clearly a woman of principle and compassion, Mistress . . .

Cook
Ploppy, sir.

Blackadder
Ah, so you are married to . . .

Cook
No. Many people think that, but it's pure coincidence. We did laugh when first we found out. 'Good morning, Mistress Ploppy,' he'd say, and I'd say 'Good morning, Mister Ploppy.'

She and the gaoler laugh.

Blackadder
The long winter evenings must just fly by.

He moves on to the third figure, who is wearing an executioner's mask and carrying an axe.

Ah. And you must be the boy who makes the tea.

He laughs at his joke.

Gaoler
Oh, no, sir, he's the executioner. But he does sometimes make the tea.

Blackadder
And your name is?

Baldrick
Baldrick, my lord.

Blackadder whips off the hood.

But I'll change it to Ploppy if it will make things easier for you.

Blackadder
No, thank you. I can cope with more than one name. What are you doing here?

Baldrick
Well, it's a hobby.

Cook
It would be more fun, sir, if he were to change his name – give the place a more family atmosphere.

Blackadder
A family atmosphere! This is meant to be a place of pain and misery and sorrow.

Cook
That's what I mean, sir.

Gaoler
Mistress Ploppy's a bit of a social realist, sir.

Blackadder
Now then, we're going to run a fast, efficient operation and I intend to do as little work as possible. My deputy Percy here will explain.

Percy takes his new job very seriously and stands on a box to deliver his important oration.

Percy
Ahem. Good afternoon, staff. My name is
Lord Percy and if you play fair by me,
you'll find me a considerate employer, but
if you cross me, by Jove . . .

Blackadder
Just tell them the plan, duckface.

Percy
My lord, not in front of the staff.

Blackadder
Get on with it.

Percy
Right, staff, as you know, we are sched-
uled to execute Drake and Effingham on
Monday, Lord Farrow on Wednesday and
Buckingham and Ponsonby on Friday. But
in order to give us the middle of the week
off, Lord Blackadder has decided to move
Farrow to Monday.

A little cheer.

Blackadder
Let's just say he's got time off for good
behaviour.

Another cheer.

SCENE FIVE: QUEENIE'S CHAMBER

*It is Tuesday of the next week. The very
beautiful Lady Farrow kneels before
Queenie and Melchett.*

Lady Farrow
Your Majesty.

Queen
Yes, Lady Farrow.

Lady Farrow
My husband dies tomorrow. I beseech you,
even if you cannot save his life . . .

Queen
Which I don't think either of us would
want, seeing as how he's a horrible
traitor . . .

Lady Farrow
Of course not, your Majesty, but if he
must die, may I see him?

Queen
But of course. (*To Melchett*) What's she
asking me for? Why doesn't she just go
along to the execution with everyone else?

Melchett
Uhm, no, Majesty, I don't believe she
wants to *see* him die, I believe she wants to
see him *before* he dies.

Queen
How odd!

Melchett
Majesty?

Queen
That she hasn't seen him. Well, I wouldn't
marry someone I'd never seen. (*To Lady
Farrow*) You should take marriage a bit
more seriously, next time.

Lady Farrow bursts into tears.

Oh, come now, Lady Farrow, crying isn't
going to help your husband now.

Nursie
No. Ointment. That's what you need when
your head's been cut off. That's what I
gave your sister Mary when they done her.
'There, there,' I said. 'You'll soon grow a
new one.'

Queen
Shut up, Nursie. Of course you may see

your husband, my dear. And if that horrid old Edmund tries to stop you, give him this. It's a warrant for his own execution.

Melchett gives Queenie a scroll which she gives to Lady Farrow.

Lady Farrow
Oh thank you, ma'am. May flights of angels sing you to your rest.

Queen
Yes, I'm sure they will.

SCENE SIX: BLACKADDER'S LODGINGS

Blackadder is at the table. Percy leads Ploppy and Mrs Ploppy in.

Percy
Hup, hup, hup, hup . . .

Blackadder
So, they're all dead, are they?

Percy
Yep. All three. Drake, Effingham, Farrow.

Blackadder
Splendid. Any interesting last words?

Percy
Well, Farrow was rather moving, my lord. A great, strong man, he stood there gaunt and noble in the morning mist and in a loud, clear voice he cried out, 'My wife might have bloody well turned up.'

Blackadder
Ha! She's clearly shacked up with some new pair of tights already. Right. Well, unless Lord Percy has anything to add, you lot can amuse yourselves in whatever foul depraved way you feel fit till Friday.

Percy
Thank you, sir. Well, staff, I've got a few notes on today's show. On the whole, I was impressed . . .

Blackadder
They've gone, Percy.

Indeed they have. Percy follows, annoyed.

Percy
Team . . . Team . . .

There is a knock on the outer door. Baldrick enters.

Baldrick
My lord, there is a lady outside to see you.

Blackadder
Is she pretty?

Baldrick
I don't know, what do you think?

Blackadder
I don't know, do I? I haven't seen her yet, have I?

At which moment, the beautiful Lady Farrow enters.

Make yourself scarce, Baldrick.

Lady Farrow
Good evening, Lord Blackadder.

Blackadder
Well, it certainly is now. Perhaps you'd like to slip into something more comfortable?

Lady Farrow
No, my lord, for there is a great pain in my heart.

Blackadder
(*Seductively*) Probably indigestion. I'll soon take your mind off that . . .

Lady Farrow
It is my husband.

Blackadder
Your husband's got indigestion? Well, he won't be bothering us then . . .

Lady Farrow
No, he dies tomorrow.

Blackadder
Oh, come on, you can't die of indigestion! You're over-dramatizing. Drink?

Lady Farrow
He is to be executed at your order. I am Lady Farrow.

Blackadder
Ah. And what exactly did you want of me?

Lady Farrow
I wish to see my husband tonight.

Blackadder
Not really possible, actually.

She bursts into noisy tears.

Excuse me a second.

He goes across the room, and calls out the door.

Baldrick!

Baldrick
Yes, my lord.

Blackadder
That Farrow bloke you executed today, are you sure he's dead?

Baldrick
Well, I chopped his head off – that usually does the trick.

Blackadder
Yes, don't get clever with me, Baldrick. I

thought you might just have lopped off a leg or something by mistake.

Baldrick
No, the thing I chopped off had a nose.

Blackadder
Fine.

He turns back to Lady Farrow.

So sorry, I've just been consulting my legal people and I'm afraid there really is no chance of a meeting.

Lady Farrow
But the queen told me it would be allowed.

A very big unhappy smile spreads across Blackadder's face.

Blackadder
Really?

Lady Farrow
Yes, and that if you said no, I should give you this.

Blackadder takes the scroll, reads it and does a little jump of shock. Then a huge smile.

Blackadder
Well, yes, fine, fine. Absolutely. Why not?

~

SCENE SEVEN: THE PRISON GUARD ROOM

Baldrick is sitting on a chair, holding a hessian bag, unusually dressed, wearing gentlemen's clothes. Blackadder, Mr Ploppy and Percy are gathered around.

Blackadder
Right, Baldrick, is that all clear?

Baldrick
Yes. I've killed someone I shouldn't have killed, and now you want me to put a lady on my head, and talk to his old bag.

Blackadder
No, I want you to put a bag on your head and talk to his old lady.

Baldrick
Right. Why do I want a bag on my head?

Blackadder
In order, nincompoop, that she should believe that you're her husband.

Baldrick
Did he used to wear a bag on his head then?

Mr Ploppy
Young . . . young Ploppy here has a point, my lord. Lord Farrow never wore a bag. He was an old-fashioned sort of gent.

Percy
Yes, my lord, I hadn't meant to mention it, but I have been wondering all along why you should think that Baldrick with a bag on his head is going to be a dead ringer for Lord Farrow, because he's not.

Blackadder
Look, cretins, the bag is there in order to obscure Baldrick's own features, and many might think, incidentally, that that would be reason enough for him to wear it. Before I bring in Lady Farrow, I shall explain to her, inventing some cunningly plausible excuse, that her husband has taken to wearing a bag. She can then chat to Baldrick, imagining him to be the man she married, and the queen need never know of my little miscalculation.

Mr Ploppy
Why, my lord, that is a brilliant plan.

Percy
Foolproof.

Blackadder
You're very kind.

Mr Ploppy
Although there is something lurking at the back of my head that bothers me.

Blackadder
Probably a flea.

Mrs Ploppy enters.

Mrs Ploppy
Your worship, Lady Farrow awaits your pleasure.

Blackadder
All right, okay. Quick, quick!

He goes to the door and opens it slightly to speak to Lady Farrow. Baldrick is well out of her sight.

Ah, Lady Farrow, what a real pleasure it is to see you again.

Lady Farrow
It is my beloved that *I* shall be pleased to see.

Blackadder
Well, quite, quite. Though I should warn you that . . . he will not be quite as you knew him.

Lady Farrow
You fiend, what have you done to him?!

Blackadder
We have put . . . a bag over his head.

Lady Farrow
Why?

Blackadder
Well . . . the thing *is* . . . you see . . . none of the other prisoners have such shapely widows – wives – as yourself, and therefore in the interests of morale of the condemned community, your husband has nobly agreed to wear a bag, it was either that or have all the other prisoners in there with you.

Lady Farrow
How like him to make such a gesture.

Blackadder
Yes. Yes. Well, I'll just go check he's bagged up.

He closes the door on her and moves back across the room. Baldrick now has the bag over his head, and is feeling about.

Right, Balders, this is it.

Mr Ploppy
My lord.

Blackadder
What is it now, Ploppy?

Mr Ploppy
I have located my nagging doubt, it's a small point, but I do now recall that Lord Farrow was considerably taller, more than a yard taller, than young Ploppy.

Blackadder looks around in angry despair and then grabs the bag off Baldrick's head.

Blackadder
Nhhh! If you want something done properly, you've got to do it yourself. Haven't you anything else I should know?

Mr Ploppy
Yes, he had a very deep voice. Big, deep, booming voice.

Blackadder
Quite like mine then?

Mr Ploppy
No, my lord. A big, deep, booming voice.

Blackadder
Well, mine's quite deep.

Mr Ploppy
Not like his. And in fact, Lord Farrow was taller even than you, my lord. A right giant, Lord Farrow.

Blackadder
Yes, all right, all right. Don't rub it in. Percy, you better go and have another word with her. Go on, go on.

Percy goes to the door and also opens it just a little. He slips outside.

Percy
Sorry about the delay, madam. As you know, you are about to meet your husband, whom you will recognize on account of the fact that he's got a bag over his head.

Lady Farrow
I would know my darling anywhere.

Percy
Well, yes, there are a couple of other things.

Lady Farrow
I am prepared for the fact that he may have lost some weight.

Percy
Yes. And some height. That's the interesting thing. You'll probably hardly recognize him at all, actually.

Lady Farrow
You'll be telling me his arm's grown back next.

Percy is shocked.

Percy
Ah, 'scuse, just for a sec.

He shuts the door quickly and rushes across to the others.

He's only got one arm!

Mr Ploppy
Oh, yes! (*Hits his head in self-dismay*)

Blackadder
Oh, well, I'll just have to stick it inside the shirt. Which one? Which one?

Percy
Hang on.

He goes to the door again.

Erm . . . erm . . . how do we know that you're his wife?

Lady Farrow
What?

Percy
Well, you know, you could be a . . . gloater.

Lady Farrow
I beg your pardon?

Percy
You know, a gloater, come to gloat over a condemned man. I mean, we're up to our ears in gloaters here. 'Can I come in for a gloat,' they shout. And we shout back, 'You heartless gloaters . . .'

Lady Farrow bursts into tears.

All right, tell you what. I'll believe you're not a gloater if you tell me which arm he hasn't got.

Lady Farrow
His left of course. Now let me see my husband!

Percy
Right.

He rushes away in embarrassment and shuts the door on her again.

It's the left, and good luck.

Blackadder pushes his whole left arm inside his jerkin.

Blackadder
(*Shaking his head sadly*) 'Gloaters' . . . you really are a prat, aren't you, Percy? (*Then, to Baldrick*) Right, now don't forget, in two minutes you interrupt me, all right? No more than two minutes, otherwise I'm in real trouble and don't forget because . . .

Baldrick
Because we're not at home to Mr Cock-up.

Blackadder
Correct.

Mr Ploppy
Remember the voice, m'lord.

Percy, Mr Ploppy, Mrs Ploppy and Baldrick exit.

Blackadder
Yes, yes, yes, yes. (*He gathers breath, then calls in a very deep voice*) Enter!

Lady Farrow steps in meekly.

Lady Farrow
James.

Blackadder
My darling.

Lady Farrow
How are you?

Blackadder
Oh, fine, fine. Food's not bad. Apart from the sausages.

Lady Farrow
Your voice is somehow different.

Blackadder
(*Going deeper*) Oh, how?

Lady Farrow
Somehow lighter, not as deep nor booming as once it was.

Blackadder
(*Now absurdly deep*) Is that better?

Lady Farrow
Oh, my darling.

She moves towards him but then stops, a little coyly.

Call me by that name you always called me to show your love is still strong.

Blackadder
Ah yes . . . Aaaahm, look, do you think this is quite the time and the place for that sort of thing?

Lady Farrow
Please.

Blackadder
Ahm, this is the specific, secret little name that I always used to call you. You want to be called it again, is that right?

Lady Farrow
Yes. The one . . . the one like 'your little pumpkin'.

Blackadder
The one like 'your little pumpkin'. But not actually 'your little pumpkin'.

Lady Farrow
No.

Blackadder
Ahm, right then, my little . . . pumpkini-wumpkini.

She rushes at him with great passion: he has got it right.

Lady Farrow
Oh, my darling!

But the moment she gets to hug him, she screams.

Aaaarrrrrgggghhhh! Your arm!

Blackadder
What's wrong with it?

Lady Farrow
What happened to it?

Blackadder
I'm rather hurt you don't remember your-

self, in fact.

Lady Farrow
But it was only cut off at the elbow.

Blackadder
Ah.

Lady Farrow
What happened to the rest?

Blackadder
Ah, well, yes. I got into a little scrap here, with a fellow who called you a nosey little strumpet who's always going blubbing to the queen, and we got into a fight and he cut off the top half.

Lady Farrow
Alas!

Blackadder
Well, quite. Gosh, I think you'd better be going. Lord Blackadder said he was going to be sending in his servant Baldrick to collect me.

Lady Farrow
(*In a new intimate tone*) Perhaps, my lord, he is leaving us for a little longer.

Blackadder
Oh, no, I shouldn't think so. *Baldrick!* is usually very punctual.

Lady Farrow
Perhaps this Baldrick is doing it out of kindness?

Blackadder
Oh, no. I shouldn't think so. *Baldrick!* is a very unkind person.

He couldn't be shouting 'Baldrick' louder – but to no avail.

Lady Farrow
Well, then, let us leap on the moment that we have been given and use it to its full.

Blackadder
What?

Lady Farrow
Let me do this last thing for you. What

wife could do more?

*She kneels in front of Blackadder –
something very intimate is about to occur.*

Blackadder
What? . . . Oh, I see!

At that instant, in pops Baldrick.

Baldrick
Right, that's it. Time's up.

Blackadder
No, it's not!

Baldrick
Oh, yes, it is! Come on, out with you.

Lady Farrow
Oh, my lord, we have had so little time.
May we finish what we began, in paradise.
Farewell.

*Blackadder waves weakly and then turns
to Baldrick.*

Blackadder
Baldrick, you bastard, you utter bastard.
That was the first time ever, in my whole
life. I've been on this paltry boring planet

for thirty years, and that's the first time
anyone has ever . . .

*He is about to strangle him when Lady
Farrow pops her head back round the
door.*

Lady Farrow
But do not despair, my lord. Your brother
petitions the queen tomorrow morning.
There may still be hope!

She leaves.

Blackadder
What?

Baldrick
Shall I prepare the guest room for Mr
Cock-up, my lord?

SCENE EIGHT: QUEENIE'S CHAMBER

*The young, attractive Earl Farrow kneels
before Queenie. Melchett and Nursie are
in attendance.*

Queen
Oh, yes, all right, then. Let him off. He
probably is innocent anyway.

Earl Farrow
My lady, may the heavens rain down radi-
ant jewels and sweetmeats upon you!

Queen
Yes, yes, yes, yes, yes.

Earl Farrow
And may cherubim and seraph . . .

Queen
Out.

*Earl Farrow sweeps out, and Blackadder
bursts in, followed by Percy.*

Blackadder
My lady! About Lord Farrow!

Queen
I've just let him off.

Blackadder
No, no, no. You can't. He's a complete cad of the first water.

Melchett leans down and whispers into Queenie's ear.

Queen
'Can't' is not a word for princes, Lord Blackadder.

Melchett
How very true, Majesty.

Queen
Anyway, I won't be argued with, will I, Nursie?

Nursie
Well, sometimes, my darling, when you want something very naughty . . .

Queenie squeezes Nursie's nose.

No, you won't be argued with! Absolutely not!

Queen
Precisely. So, Lord Blackadder, I want to see Lord Farrow here in one hour. Meanwhile I shall spend the time visiting my old friend Lord Ponsonby, who I believe I'm having killed on Friday. Come along, Nursie. Let's see if there are any good heads in Traitors' Cloister on the way.

Queenie, Melchett and Nursie sweep out. Only Percy and Blackadder remain. Total silence.

Blackadder
Percy, this is a very difficult situation.

Percy
Yes, my lord.

Blackadder
Someone is for the chop. You or me, in fact.

Percy
Uhm, yes.

Blackadder
Let's face facts, Perce, it's you.

Percy
Except, except . . . I may have a plan.

Blackadder
(*Very cynical*) Oh, yes?

Percy
How about if we get Lord Farrow's head and body, and we take it to the queen, except, just before we get in, we start shouting and screaming and then we come in saying we were just on our way when he said something traitorous and so we cut his head off in the corridor to teach him a lesson.

Blackadder
Pathetic. Absolutely pathetic. Contemptible. Worth a try – where did we put the head?

Percy
It's on a spike in Traitors' Cloister.

Blackadder
Oh, God, that's where the queen's gone. Did she know Farrow?

Percy
Oh, yes, they were childhood friends.

Blackadder
Well, if she sees his head on a spike, she'll realize he's dead.

Percy
Yes.

Blackadder sprints out of the room, and returns for a split second.

Blackadder
You fetch the body . . . I'll cover the head.

~

SCENE NINE: TRAITORS' CLOISTER

Blackadder is standing uncomfortably in front of a marble pillar, which has a head impaled on a spike upon it. Queenie approaches with Nursie as Blackadder tries desperately to conceal the head.

Queen
Hullo, Edmund. Look, I'm sorry I snapped at you just now. You know I'm really very keen on you indeed, don't you?

Blackadder
Yes, ma'am. As you were keen on Essex.

Queen
Exactly.

Blackadder
Right up to the point at which you had his head cut off.

Queen
Ha ha, he didn't mind that, he knew it was only little me. And I must say, his head looked super on its spike. Are there no heads on spikes today?

Blackadder
Arrm, no. No.

As Queenie moves round, he moves round too, uneasily twisting the head as he goes.

No, no. We're training up a new executioner, and he's a little immature. Takes him for ever, slash, slash, slash. By the time he's finished, you don't so much need a spike, as a toast rack.

Queen
I love toast. Still, must be off to say bye bye to Ponsonby. Would you care to stroll with me a while, just if you've got time, if you're not too busy . . .?

Blackadder
No, sorry, ma'am. Affairs of office, etc. . . . .

Queen
I *said*, 'Would you like to stroll with me a while, just if you've got time, if you're not too busy . . .'

Blackadder
Ah, yes, of course, it would make the decade worthwhile.

His hands go behind him. There is a tense look on his face, as though he might be

pulling the head off the spike.

A few seconds later . . .

Blackadder and Queenie are talking, ten yards on. Blackadder's hands are behind his back.

. . . and in Genoa 'tis now the fashion to pin a live frog to the shoulder braid, stand on a bucket and go 'bibble' at the passers-by.

Queen
Oh, our Italian cousins!

Blackadder
Well, if you'll excuse me, ma'am, I've got some business to attend to.

Queen
Certainly. But first, Edmund, take my hand, tell me you forgive my former sharpness.

She holds out her arms. There is an awkward pause and then Blackadder does indeed bring his hands forward, smiling.

Blackadder
My lady.

Queen
Sweet Lord Blackadder.

Queenie leaves, waving coyly. Blackadder steps forward to reveal that he has tucked the head into the back of his tights. He backs away as Queenie moves off, dragging Nursie behind her. As she disappears, Percy taps him on the shoulder and scares him.

Blackadder
Ah!

Percy
I've got the body, my lord, and I see you've got the head.

Blackadder
It's no good, Percy. No one'll ever believe we've just cut it off. It's gone green. We're doomed.

Percy
Doomed! But wait a moment. That's not Farrow.

Blackadder
Isn't it?

Percy
No. That's Ponsonby.

Blackadder
Ponsonby? That genius Baldrick has killed the wrong bloke. We're saved!

Percy
Saved!

Blackadder
Farrow is still alive and we're saved!

Percy
Hurray!

Blackadder
Yes, and when the queen gets back from seeing Ponsonby, we'll . . . Oh, God!

Blackadder sprints off, followed by Percy.

Percy
We're doomed, doomed . . .

~

SCENE TEN: PRISON GUARD ROOM

Queenie, Nursie, Mr Ploppy, Mrs Ploppy and Baldrick are present. Baldrick is in his executioner's cowl.

Queen
It's not very nice here, is it?

Nursie
It's not meant to be, my pikelet. This is where all the horrid people who don't like you live.

Queen
I suppose so. It's a bit smelly too, isn't it?

Nursie
Well, course I'm used to that, of course. In the morning, when you were a little baby . . .

Queen
Shut up, Nursie. YOU!

Mr Ploppy comes forward.

No not you, you're too repulsive. You.

Baldrick comes forward.

Baldrick
Yes, your royal majestic Highness.

Queen
Bring in Lord Ponsonby.

Baldrick
Yes, your royal majestic . . . thing.

He slips out.

Queen
So strange Ponsonby turned out to be a traitor. You would have thought that he'd have had problems enough with that hunch and only having one leg.

Nursie
Yes, and that terrible speech problem.

There is a pause, and then the slow opening of the door. Percy and Baldrick enter with a lamp, leading a man with one leg, a hunch and a bag over his head.

Percy
Your Majesty, Lord Ponsonby.

Blackadder
Your royal Majesty. Thowy about ve bag. Didn't have time to thave, tho' I thought . . .

For it is he.

THE BALLAD OF BLACKADDER THE BEHEADER

His great grandfather was a king,
Although for only thirty seconds.
When put in charge of beheading,
He felt that fame and glory beckoned.

Blackadder, Blackadder,
No such blooming luck.
Blackadder, Blackadder,
Elizabethan schmuck.

Blackadder, Blackadder,
Nothing goes as planned.
Blackadder, Blackadder,
Life deals him a bum hand.

Baldrick receives the news that he is to become a rent boy, under the impression that this is a promotion to some form of junior bailiff

Potato

SCENE ONE: BLACKADDER'S LODGINGS

Blackadder is working and fed up. It is a gloriously sunny day outside, and the roar of a crowd, which annoys Blackadder even more, shows there is some kind of public holiday going on.

Percy pops his head round the door. He is dressed in merry gear, with horns on his head and looking suspiciously like a morris dancer. He is very happy and excited.

Percy
Coming?

Blackadder
No.

Percy
It'll be a once-in-a-lifetime experience.

Blackadder
No it won't.

Blackadder slams the door in Percy's face. Another knock.

Percy reappears.

Percy
Everybody's going.

Blackadder
Don't exaggerate, Percy. *I'm* not going. Mrs Miggins from the pie shop isn't going.

Percy
My lord, you are cruel. You know perfectly well that Mrs Miggins is paralysed from the nose down. And besides, she is honouring the occasion in her own special way by baking a great commemorative pie in the shape of an enormous . . . pie.

Blackadder
What an imagination that woman has.

Percy
Oh, come on, Edmund. The greatest explorer of our age is coming home. The streets have never been so gay. Women are laughing, children are singing. Oh, look, look, there's a man being indecently assaulted by nine foreign sailors and he's still got a smile on his face.

Blackadder
Look, Percy, the return of Sir Walter 'Oo what a big ship I've got' Raleigh is a matter of supreme indifference to me.

Now that is too much for Percy.

Percy
If you're not careful, all the children will dance about outside your window singing 'sour puss' and 'grumpy face'. And you wouldn't want that, would you?

Blackadder
I believe I could survive it. Now Percy, get out before I cut your head off, scoop out the insides and give it to your mother as a vase.

He guides Percy out and slams the door on him.

What a clot. The most absurdly dressed creature in Christendom.

Baldrick enters. He has also made an effort to look nautical, with two little oars sticking out of his hat like antlers.

With one exception.

Baldrick
My lord?

Blackadder
Baldrick, you look like a deer.

Baldrick
Thank you, my lord. You look a bit of a duckie yourself.

Blackadder
Oh, God. What do you want?

Baldrick
I was wondering if I might have the afternoon off.

Blackadder
Of course not. Who do you think you are? Wat Tyler? You can have the afternoon off when you die. Not before.

Baldrick
But I want to cheer brave Sir Walter

home. Oh, dear sir, on a day like today, I feel so proud to be a member of the greatest kingdom in the world.

Blackadder
And doubtless many other members of the animal kingdom feel the same way, Baldrick.

There is another roar from the street.

Oh, look, will you shut up. Bloody explorers, ponce off to Mumbo Jumbo land, come home with a tropical disease, a suntan and a bag of brown lumpy things, and Bob's your uncle, everyone's got a picture of them in the lavatory. I mean, what about the people who do all the work?

Baldrick
The servants.

Blackadder
No, me. *I'm* the people who do all the work. I mean, look at this, what is it?

He picks up a potato.

Baldrick
I'm surprised you've forgotten, my lord.

Blackadder
I haven't forgotten. It's a rhetorical question.

Baldrick
No. It's a potato.

Blackadder
Look, to you it's a potato, to me it's a potato, but to Sir Walter bloody Raleigh it's country estates, fine carriages, and as many girls as his tongue can cope with. He's making a fortune out of the things: people are smoking them, building houses out of them. They'll be eating them next.

Baldrick
Stranger things have happened.

Blackadder
Well, exactly.

Baldrick
That horse becoming pope.

Blackadder
For one.

There is a knock on an outer door.

Oh, God.

Baldrick goes to open the door.

Probably some berk with a parrot on his shoulder selling plaster gnomes of Sir Francis Drake and his Golden Behind.

A child is heard from outside.

Child
Sour puss, grumpy face, sour puss, grumpy face, sour puss, grumpy face.

Blackadder
Right. That does it.

Blackadder shoots an arrow out of the window, as Melchett enters. The child screams, seriously wounded.

Child
Mummy!

Blackadder
And another thing. Why aren't you at school?

Melchett
Ah, Blackadder: started talking to yourself, I see?

Blackadder
Yes, it's the only way I can be sure of intelligent conversation. What do you want?

Melchett
Well, I just looked in on my way to the palace to welcome Sir Walter home. I wondered if you'd care to accompany me?

Blackadder
I don't *think* I'll bother, actually. Three hours of bluff seaman's talk about picking the weevils out of biscuits and drinking urine is not my idea of entertainment.

Melchett
As you wish. (*To Baldrick*) Servant, my hat.

Baldrick exits. Melchett opens a little silver box he is carrying and offers its contents to Blackadder.

Potato?

They are raw.

Blackadder
No thanks. I don't.

Melchett has one himself.

I see you haven't succumbed to this fad of dressing up like half an allotment in Nottingham Forest.

Baldrick enters and hands Melchett his hat – the most ridiculous of the garments so far, a huge horned hat.

Baldrick
There you go, my lord.

Melchett
Thank you.

Blackadder
You have.

Melchett
It's probably just as well you're not coming, Blackadder. You're not very popular at Court at the moment and the queen and I have much to talk about.

Melchett exits and Blackadder follows.

Blackadder
Yes, well, I can probably leave all this until tomorrow.

Melchett
No, I shouldn't bother . . .

Blackadder
No, no, no, no problem. I'll be coming with you. Obviously the queen and I are going to be the only ones even vaguely sensibly dressed . . .

~

SCENE TWO: QUEENIE'S CHAMBER

As fate would have it, Queenie is also looking celebratory, in 'explorer' clothing. She has a patch over one eye, an ornate galleon on her hat and gold anchors decorate her hair.

She is by the door with her back to Nursie, who is sitting on a stool. There is a knock on the door.

Queen
Who is it?

Melchett
Melchett, milady.

Queen
(*Crossing to throne*) Stop. Close your eyes. Now enter.

Melchett enters with his eyes closed. Blackadder is with him, and puzzled.

Ahoy there, me shivering matey; heave ho. Right, open your eyes.

Melchett
Thank you, Majesty. And . . .

He opens his eyes, and looks around, apparently perplexed.

Queen
What's the matter, Melchy?

Melchett
I beg your pardon, lady, I was wanting to greet the gallant sailor who hallooed me when I came in.

Queenie squeals with delight.

Perchance he has hauled anchor and sailed away.

Queen
No! It was me!

Melchett
Majesty, surely not!

Blackadder
(*To Melchett through closed teeth*) You utter creep. (*Then to all . . .*) So where's this barnacle-bottomed, haddock-flavoured, bilge rat, Sir 'Rather a Wally' Raleigh? I hear he's about as exciting as one of his potatoes.

Queen
Blackadder's a frightful old lubber, eh, Melchy?

Melchett
Indubitably no sea dog, ma'am, with a yo-ho-ho and, perhaps I might venture, a bottle of rum into the bargain.

A bosun's whistle blows in an outer room.

Queen
It's him! Oh, God! Do I look absolutely divine and regal and yet at the same time very pretty and rather accessible?

Melchett
You are every Jolly Jack Tar's dream, Majesty.

Queen
I thought as much. If he's really gorgeous, I'm thinking of marrying him.

Blackadder
My lady, is that not a little rash?

Queen
I don't think so.

Nursie
It wouldn't be your first little rash if it was.

Another whistle and in walks Walter. He is the picture of arrogant swagger. Queenie screams with joy. Queenie and Nursie rise. Walter bows.

Walter
Majesty!

Queen
Splice my timber, Sir Walter; it's bucko to see you, me old matey.

Walter
I'm sorry?

Blackadder
She says hello.

Walter
And well she might, for I have brought her gifts and dominions beyond her wildest dreams.

Queen
Are you sure? I have some pretty wild dreams, you know. I'm not sure what they mean, but the other day, there was this enormous tree, and I was sitting right on top of it . . .

Melchett
Ma'am . . .

Queen
And then I dreamt once that I was a sausage roll . . .

Melchett
Majesty!

Queen
I'm sorry. I'm so excited I don't know what I'm saying. Come on, Sir Walter, I want to hear about absolutely everything.

Walter
Then prepare to hear tales of terrible hardship, endurance and woe. We set sail from Plymouth in the spring of 1552.

Blackadder yawns a little loudly.

Queen
You remember Lord Blackadder.

Walter turns and inspects him carefully.

Walter
No. But I can see he is the sort of pasty landlubber I have always despised.

They all laugh at Blackadder.

Queen
Well, quite. Don't crowd Sir Walter, Edmund.

Walter
Twice last week, I fought in hand-to-hand combat with a man with two heads and no body hair. I'll warrant the most exciting

thing that has happened to that limpid prawn in a whole year was the day his servant forgot to put sugar in his porridge.

Blackadder tries to laugh this off. Queenie is utterly enthralled.

Queen
Gosh, you've got nice legs.

Walter
While I hold the six seas of the world in my hand, this fellow here couldn't even put six gobstoppers in his mouth.

Queen
Ha ha ha – he's a complete no-hoper, isn't he, Walt!

Walter
He certainly is.

They both laugh.

Queen
My bedroom's just upstairs, you know.

Melchett
I apprehended, Sir Walter, that there were only seven seas.

Walter
Only numerically speaking. We sailors do not count the sea around the Cape of Good Hope. It is called the Sea of Certain Death, and no sailor has crossed it alive.

Blackadder
Well, well, well. What an Extraordinary Coincidence.

Queen
What's an Extraordinary Coincidence?

Blackadder is so, so, so casual.

Blackadder
Yes, it's just that I was planning a jaunt around the Cape of Good Hope myself, leaving a week on Thursday, I think.

Queen
Really?

Blackadder
Yes. And now that – sorry, I've forgotten your name – has returned and the whole Court smells of fish, I've half a mind to set off this afternoon.

Walter
If you attempt that journey, you've no mind at all.

Blackadder
Or perhaps a mind that knows no fear?

Queen
Is that true Edmund? Do you know no fear?

Blackadder
Well, yes, I do rather laugh in the face of fear and tweak the nose of terror.

Queen
Gosh, Edmund, I'd forgotten how dishy you are.

Walter
You'd never dare. Why, round the cape, the rain beats down so hard, it makes your head bleed.

Blackadder
So some sort of hat is probably in order.

Walter
And great dragons leap from the water and swallow ships whole.

Blackadder
I must remember to pack the larger of my two shrimping nets.

Queen
Oh, Edmund, you're completely wonderful. If you do this, I'll probably marry you.

Now things are definitely slipping away from Walter.

Walter
Oh, yes, and who'll be your captain? To my mind, there's only one seafarer with few enough marbles to attempt that journey.

Blackadder
Oh, yes, and who's that?

Walter
Why Rum, of course, Captain Redbeard Rum.

Blackadder
Well done. Just testing. And where would I find him on a Tuesday?

Walter
Well, if I remember his old habits, he's normally up the Old Sea Dog.

Blackadder
Oh, yes. And where is the Old Sea Dog?

Walter
Well, on Tuesdays, he's normally in bed with the captain.

~

SCENE THREE: A TAVERN

A dark and rummy place, where sits Redbeard Rum, a huge red-bearded pirate. Blackadder has tracked him down.

Rum
Aaaaaarrrrrgggggghhhhh, me laddie!

Blackadder
Aaaarrrrgghh, indeed. So Rum, I wish to hire you and your ship, can we shake on it?

They shake hands: Rum inspects Blackadder's hand.

Rum
You have a woman's hand, my lord. I'll wager these dainty pinkies never weighed anchor in a storm.

Blackadder
(*With a hint of sarcasm*) Well, you're right there.

Rum pinches Blackadder's cheeks.

Rum
Ha! You have a woman's skin, my lord. I'll wager it's ne'er felt the lash o' the cat, been rubbed with salt, and then flayed off by a pirate chief to make fine stockings for his best cabin boy.

Blackadder
This is uncanny. I don't know how you do it, but you're right again.

Rum
So, why should I let a stupid cockle like you aboard my boat?

Blackadder
Perhaps for the money in my purse.

Blackadder holds up his purse, which Rum takes.

Rum
You have a woman's purse, my lord . . . I'll wager that purse has never been used as a rowing boat, I'll wager it's never had sixteen shipwrecked mariners tossing in it.

Now he's beginning to test Blackadder's patience.

Blackadder
No, right again, Rum. I must say when it comes to tales of courage, I can see I'm going to have to keep my mouth shut.

Rum
You have a woman's mouth my lord. I'll wager that mouth never had to chew through the side of a ship to escape the dreadful spindly killer fish.

Blackadder
Yes. I must say when I came to see you I had no idea I was going to have to eat your ship as well as hire it, but since you're clearly as mad as a mongoose, I'll bid you farewell.

Rum
You damned courtiers to the queen, you're nothing but lap dogs to a slip of a girl!

Blackadder
Better a *lap-dog* to a *slip of a girl* than a . . . git!

Rum
So you do have some spunk in you! Don't worry, laddie – I'll come. I'll come!

They shake on it.

Blackadder
Well, let us set sail as soon as we can. I will fetch my first mate, and return as fast as my legs will carry me.

Rum
Aye, you have a woman's legs, my lord. I'll wager those are legs that have never been sliced clean off by a falling sail and swept into the sea before your very eyes.

Blackadder
Well, neither have yours.

Rum
That's where you're wrong. (*He knocks over the table vigorously to reveal two wooden stumps*) Ha-ha!

Blackadder
Oh, my God.

Rum
No point in changing your mind now: no one else will come, the whole thing's suicide anyway. What's the first mate's name?

Blackadder
Percy.

Rum
A nautical cove?

Blackadder
Yes, well, he's a sort of wet fish.

~

SCENE FOUR: BLACKADDER'S LODGINGS

Percy looks set for sailing and paces the room nervously. Baldrick also has on a hat, and is very calm: he is packing clothes into the trunk. Suddenly, Percy explodes with emotion.

Percy
I'm not coming. I'm just not coming. I mean, of course I'm very keen to go on the trip. It's just unfortunately I've an appointment to have my nostrils plucked, next year.

Baldrick
Oh, I'm sorry, my lord, I thought it was because you were a complete coward.

Percy
Don't be ridiculous, Baldrick. You know me. I mean, I laugh in the face of fear and tweak the nose of the dreadful spindly killer fish. I'm not one of your milksops who's scared out of his wits by the mere sight of water.

Baldrick hands him a glass of water. Percy screams and runs to the door.

Yes, all right. I admit it. I admit it. I'm terrified. You see, Baldrick, when I was a baby, I was savaged by a turbot. Baldrick, you can't think of a plan to get me out of this, can you?

Baldrick
You could hide, my lord.

Percy
Hide. Brilliant. Where?

They both look round and Baldrick spots a chest.

Baldrick
In the box?

Percy
Which one?

Baldrick
This one.

Percy
Perfect. All right, let's practise. (*He sits inside the chest*) Edmund comes in and says, 'Hullo Baldrick. You haven't seen Percy, have you?' and you say . . .

Baldrick
No, my lord: I haven't seen him all day.

Percy
Brilliant!

There is a noise outside.

Oh, my God! Here he comes.

Percy shuts the lid and hides as Blackadder enters.

Blackadder
Oh, hullo, Balders. Where the hell's that cretin Percy? You haven't seen him, have you?

There is a short pause. Baldrick cannot quite bring himself to lie for Percy.

Baldrick
Yes, my lord, he's hiding in the box.

Baldrick steps away from the chest as Blackadder kicks it and addresses Percy . . .

Blackadder
Come on, jellybrain. Hurry up, otherwise we'll miss the tide.

Blackadder exits.

~

SCENE FIVE: QUEENIE'S CHAMBER

Later that day. Blackadder in sailing gear. Queenie, Nursie, Melchett and Sir Walter are opposite him.

Queen
Oh, Edmund, I'm so proud, you're just my complete hero . . . Oh dear, I'm going all gooey now.

Blackadder
Ma'am, I am moved, and if during my journey, I could believe that occasionally you did spare me a thought and perhaps . . . go gooey again, I would deem my certain death a minor inconvenience.

Queen
Oh, Ned. I've written a poem.

Blackadder
Madam, I am honoured.

Queenie clears her throat: rapt attention.

Queen
When the night is dark,
And the dogs go 'bark',
When the clouds are black,
And the ducks go 'quack'
When the sky is blue,
And the cows go 'moo',
Think of lovely Queenie:
She'll be thinking of you.

Everyone claps.

It's called 'Edmund'. Shakespeare gave me a hand with the title, but the rest is all my own work.

Nursie
Tush and fie, my tiddly: you didn't always make such pretty speeches. 'Tis but the twinkling of a toe since you could say nothing but 'Lizzie Go Plop Plop. Lizzie go . . .'

Queen
Put a bung in it, Nursie. Now. I'm sure that Melchy and Wally want to say something as well.

Walter
Yes, indeed. (*He crosses to Blackadder*) Goodbye, Blackadder: I'd say 'Bon Voyage', but there's no point: you'll be dead in three months.

Blackadder
I love you, Walter: I hope you know that.

Melchett presents Blackadder with a map.

Melchett
Farewell, Blackadder. The foremost cartographers of the land have prepared this for you. It's a map of the area that you will be traversing.

It is blank.

They'd be very grateful if you could just fill it in as you go along. Goodbye.

From outside there is a strange and chilling cry.

Queen
What's that?

Enter Rum, being pushed by Baldrick.

Rum
To Tilbury, me hearties: the wind is in the sails, the oars are in the rollocks, and we must away!

Blackadder
Lady, it is my captain. Long on beard, short on legs.

Queen
Oh, Captain: I wish you luck from the bottom of my heart.

Baldrick pushes the captain to Queenie.

Rum
You have a woman's bottom, my lady. I'll wager that sweet round pair of peaches has never been forced twixt two splintered planks to plug a leak and save a ship.

Queen
It certainly hasn't and I'm quite pleased about it. Anyway, what's wrong with women's bottoms?

Rum
Not big enough, ma'am.

Nursie
Mine might be.

Rum clocks her and crosses to her. It's love at first glimpse.

Rum
In that case, my little pudding of delight, let us beat around the bush no longer. I know I'm only a bluff old cove with no legs and a beard you could lose a badger in, but if you'll take me, I'm willing to be captain of your ship for ever. What do you say?

Nursie
Oh, yes, please.

Rum
I'll be back. We'll all be back.

Baldrick and Percy wheel Rum out.

Queen
Oh, Edmund: then this is it. Have you got clean underwear, and don't eat foreign food and watch out for strange men and discover me a country and bring me back a vegetable and . . . oh, everything.

Blackadder
Madam, I shall do all I can. Farewell . . . And . . . don't wait up.

Blackadder closes the door on Queenie.

She turns to face Melchett, Nursie and Sir Walter.

Queen
Gosh!

Walter
Well, that's the last we'll see of him. In three months' time he'll be dead as a . . . dead dodo.

Queen
(*Sadly*) Oh, Sir Walter, really.

Melchett is very amused by her ditty.

Melchett
Sir Walter Really. Ha!

~

SCENE SIX: RUM'S CABIN

It is a cramped, wooden cabin, home to seafarers for hundreds of years. The table is laden with food. Baldrick is serving Rum, Blackadder and Percy. Rum and Blackadder have large tankards in their hands.

Rum
Aaaarrrrrgggghhhhh!

Blackadder
Aaaarrrrrgggghhhhh!

Baldrick
Aaaarrrrrgggghhhhh!

But Percy does not 'Aaaarrrrrgggghhhhh'.

Blackadder
Not joining us in the 'Aaaarrrrrgggghhhhhs', Percy?

Percy
No. I'm thinking of England and the girl I left behind me.

Blackadder
Oh, God. I didn't know you had a girl.

Percy
Oh, yes. Lady Caroline Fairfax.

Blackadder
Caroline! I didn't know you knew her.

Percy
Oh, yes. I even touched her once.

Blackadder
Touched her what?

Percy
Her, once. In a corridor.

Blackadder
I've never heard it called that before. Still when you get home in six months, you'll be a hero: she might even let you get your hands on her twice.

Percy
I fear not.

Blackadder
Why not?

Percy
(*With massive passion*) Because we'll never get home. We're doomed, doomed! Condemned to a watery grave with a captain who's legless.

Rum
Rubbish. I've hardly touched a drop.

Percy
No, I mean, you haven't got any legs.

Rum
Oh, yes, you're right there. Carry on. Sorry.

Percy
Oh, God! We've got no hope! No hope of ever returning!

Blackadder
On the contrary: we are certain to return.

Percy
What?

Blackadder
Because, me old salts, we are not going to the Cape of Good Hope at all.

All
What?

Blackadder
We are, in fact, going to France.

All
France?

Percy
But Edmund, surely France has already been discovered – by the French for a start?

Blackadder
Precisely. It's a trick – we just camp down in the Dordogne for six months, get a good suntan, come home, pretend we've been round the cape and get all the glory.

Percy
Hurray!

Rum
A masterly plan, me young master, and one that leads me to make an announcement meself.

Blackadder
And what's that, Rum?

Rum
Truth is, I don't know the way to the Cape of Good Hope anyway.

Blackadder
Good Lord. What were you going to do?

Rum
Oh, what I usually do. Sail round and round the Isle of Wight until everyone gets dizzy and head for home.

Blackadder
You old rascal! Still, who cares? By the day after tomorrow, we shall be in Calais! Captain, set sail for France!

Rum
Aye, aye, sir!

The light fades on our intrepid heroes.

~

SCENE SEVEN: RUM'S CABIN

It is the day after the day after tomorrow . . .

Blackadder
So you don't know the way to France, either?

Rum
No, I must confess that too.

Blackadder nods. Takes in this important news.

Blackadder
Bugger.

~

SCENE EIGHT: QUEENIE'S CHAMBER

Time is hanging heavy back home.

Queen
He's only been gone three days and I'm missing him already.

Walter
Well, perhaps, ma'am, I might amuse you still further with tales of my adventures.

Queen
Like what?

Walter
Perhaps you would like to hear the one about the mad pirate king whose crew consisted entirely of men called Roger?

Queen
Heard it.

Walter
Well, maybe I could distract you with the tale of the time I fell into the water and was almost eaten by a hammerhead shark.

Queen
Yes, all right. Try that one.

Walter
Well, ma'am. I fell into the water, and was almost eaten by a shark, and the funny thing is, its head was exactly the same shape as a hammer.

Pause. Total boredom.

Queen
Oh, God. You'd better come up with some

presents, or I'm going to go off explorers completely, you know.

Queenie starts to leave.

Walter
Ma'am.

But just before she does, she turns to face Walter.

Queen
And I'll tell you something else. Edmund was right. You do smell of fish. Pooey!

SCENE NINE: RUM'S CABIN

Blackadder finally lifts his head from his hands.

Blackadder
Look, there's no need to panic. Someone in the crew will know how to steer this thing.

Rum
The crew, milord?

Blackadder
Yes, the crew.

Rum
What crew?

Blackadder
I was under the impression that it's common maritime practice for a ship to have a crew.

Rum
Opinion is divided on the subject.

Blackadder
Really?

Rum
Yes. All the other captains say it is, and I say it isn't.

Blackadder
Oh, God. Mad as a brush.

SCENE TEN: QUEENIE'S CHAMBER

It is six months later. Queenie is swiping the globe in bored impatience. Nursie and Melchett stand by.

Melchett
Sir Walter's death warrant for your signature, ma'am.

Queen
Good. Any news of Edmund?

Melchett
Well, ma'am. If they are on course, they should be nearing the urine-drinking stage by now.

Queen
Oh, don't be horrid, Melchy. Edmund would rather die.

Melchett
I fear that may be wishful thinking, Majesty.

SCENE ELEVEN: RUM'S CABIN

Blackadder, depressed. There is a knock on the door.

Blackadder
Enter.

Percy and Baldrick come in, carrying empty wine bottles.

So soon?

Percy
You said today.

Blackadder
Yes, well, I'm not feeling very thirsty at the moment. I mean, I had an eggcup full of stagnant water three weeks ago.

Pause. He stares at the empty glasses on the table.

Oh, all right. Come on, let's get on with it.

And he takes his bottle.

Baldrick
Shall we drink each other's, or stick to our own?

Blackadder
Baldrick!

Baldrick
Sorry, my lord.

Blackadder
Is Captain Rum joining us for this bring-a-sample party, or is he going to sit this one out?

Percy
Oh, no, he's been swigging his for ages. Says he likes it. Actually, come to think of it, he started before the water ran out.

Blackadder
Oh, God. Well, let's get on with it.

A mysterious darkness falls over the proceedings. Ten minutes later . . .

It's always the same, isn't it? You get all keyed up then you can't go.

Percy
Me too.

Baldrick
I've done two bottles.

Blackadder
All right then, pour it out. That it should come to this. Drinking Baldrick's water.

Baldrick
Say when.

Blackadder
When.

He is handed a bottle. They are about to drink.

Baldrick
Down the hatch!

The terrible moment is upon them – when . . .

Rum
Land ahoy!

They all look up. Blackadder's face beams with instant satisfaction. They hit land with a bump.

Blackadder
Ah – France at last!

Rum
No, me young master, for through fair winds and fine seamanship, our vessel has once more fetched up on the shores of old Blighty.

All
Hurray!

Rum
By a lucky chance, we have landed at Southampton Dock.

All
Hurray!

Rum
Fare thee well. Last one up the Old Sea Dog gets a lick of the cat.

Rum leaves and Baldrick peers out the window.

Baldrick
Doesn't look much like Southampton to me, my lord.

Blackadder
What?

Baldrick
All those streams of molten lava, the steamy mangrove swamp and that crowd of beckoning natives rubbing their tummies and pointing to a large pot.

Blackadder
Oh, God.

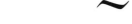

SCENE TWELVE: QUEENIE'S CHAMBER

Two years later. Melchett, Nursie and Queenie are in their traditional positions. Sir Walter Raleigh is standing in the corner.

Queen
And where are they now?

Melchett
If they haven't been eaten by cannibals, ma'am, they should be back any minute now.

Blackadder bursts in with Percy and Baldrick.

Blackadder
Ma'am.

Queen
Edmund, you're alive!

Blackadder
Yes.

Queen
And your silly friend.

Percy
Lord Percy, ma'am.

Queen
And your monkey.

Baldrick
Your Majesty.

Queen
But where is Captain Rum?

Blackadder
Bad news, milady. Rum is dead.

Nursie cries – the sorrow and disbelief of true love lost.

Percy
Do not despair, good woman. He died a hero's death, giving his life that his friends might live.

Blackadder
And that his enemies might have something to go with their potatoes.

Nursie
You mean they put him in the pot . . .?

Blackadder
Yes. Your fiancé was only a third-rate sailor, but a first-rate second course.

Nursie cries again.

However, we did manage to save something of him as a memento.

He produces Rum's beard.

Nursie
Oh, my lucky stars. I shall wear it always to remind me of him.

She puts it on.

Blackadder
However, ma'am, I am now returned, and my mind cannot help remembering talk of wedding bells.

Queen
No. I'm completely bored with explorers and if you haven't brought me any presents, I'm going to have you executed.

Blackadder
Ma'am!

Queen
I only let Raleigh off because he blubbed on his way to the block. Presents please.

Blackadder searches for an idea.

Blackadder
Yes, ma'am, yes. Well, there was *one* thing, ma'am.

Queen
Good.

Blackadder
A most extraordinary gift from the island paradise we visited.

Queen
Hurry up.

He takes out a boomerang, gives it to Queenie.

What is it?

Melchett
A stick.

Queen
Is it a stick, Lord Blackadder?

Blackadder
Yes, ma'am, but 'tis a very special stick, because when you throw it away . . . it comes back.

Queen
Well, that's no good, is it? Because when I throw things away, I don't want them to come back. You! (*To Percy*) Get rid of it!

Percy
Certainly, ma'am.

He throws it out into the corridor.

Queen
What else have you brought?

Blackadder
Yes, well. There was very little time, what with picking the weevils out of biscuits, and . . .

Queen
Melchy, what did I do with that spare death warrant?

Melchett and Sir Walter look smug at Blackadder's downfall. At which moment the boomerang comes back and knocks Percy unconscious. Queenie is highly amused.

Oh, Edmund, it's wonderful.

Blackadder
Ma'am.

Queen
But what about Melchy and Wally? You must have brought something for them as well. Nursie's got her beard, I've got my stick, what about the two boys?

Blackadder
Ah, yes. There was one thing, ma'am.

Queen
Good.

He goes to Baldrick and turns, smiling, with a very familiar bottle, filled with yellowish liquid.

Blackadder
A fine wine from the Far East. A most delicious beverage.

Baldrick produces two tankards from his bag and Blackadder fills them for Melchett and Walter. They are eager to try it.

Queen
Oh, good. Have a taste, boys. Tell us what you think.

Walter
Mmm, it certainly has plenty of nose.

Melchett
Ah, yes, this is very familiar.

Blackadder
I'm sure you'll be glad to hear there is an inexhaustible supply of the stuff.

He turns and hands the bottle back to Baldrick. They smile at each other.

THE BALLAD OF BLACKADDER THE BAD EXPLORER

Sir Francis and Sir Walter had
Discovered New Worlds and new nations,
And though Blackadder thought them mad,
He tried his hand at navigation.

Blackadder, Blackadder,
He saw the oceans foam.
Blackadder, Blackadder,
He should have stayed at home.

Blackadder, Blackadder,
He heard the new world call.
Blackadder, Blackadder,
Discovered bugger all!

Nursie, Queenie and Beardie-Wierdie

The Favourites of
Queen Elizabeth 1

ROBERT DUDLEY,
EARL OF LEICESTER
Tall, bearded man with a 'merrie laugh';
favourite of the queen for nine years until
she discovered she much preferred chewing
gum. Executed for High Treason and 'too
muche laughinge'.

FRANCIS BACON,
EARL OF SANDWICH
Tall, rubicund man with much-admired
'shapely calves'; poet, playwright, philoso-
pher, alchemist and chewing-gum merchant. Favourite of the queen for five
years. Executed for High Treason and
'because I am fedde uppe of sharinge my
bedroome with a loade of calves, whiche,
though shapelie, do also smelle'.

FRANCIS BUDLEIGH,
EARL OF ESSEX
Short, choleric man with fierce hatred of
beards, cattle, chewing-gum and bacon.
Favourite of the queen for twelve minutes.
Executed for High Treason and 'cominge in
the roome and annoyinge me'.

HENRY CUDDLY,
EARL OF DUDLEY
Small, woollen squirrel. Favourite of queen
for twenty-six years. Knighted 1559.
Created Earl of Dudley in 1562. Appointed
to Privy Council 1568. Lord Chancellor of
England 1571. Washed 1580. Executed for
High Treason after one of his eyes fell out
in 1594, and replaced in the queen's affec-
tions by a small piece of eiderdown.

SIR WALTER RALEIGH
Small, bearded pirate. Discoverer of potato
(1554), tomato (1556), tobacco (1559),

avocado (1561) and rumpipumpo (1565).
The latter, a small, foul-smelling Central
American buffalo-tick which Raleigh
claimed was delicious when set on fire and
poked up the nose, led to his downfall. He
was imprisoned in the Tower, where he
ended his days reading, composing poetry,
being executed for High Treason and
'sittinge arounde in the Towere being a
paine in the bottome'.

SIR WALTER POTATO
Large, amusingly shaped potato with a
moustache and big ears. Favourite of the
queen for several weeks in 1555. Tried by
his peers and executed for High Treason
after first having his ears and moustache
pulled off, and being sliced, boiled, fried
and thrown in Traitor's Moat, and then
transported round England on a cart under
a large sign reading 'Warninge to Traitores'.

EDMUND BLACKADDER, ESQ.
Of little academic interest.

ROBERT FRANCIS,
EARL OF BURLEIGH
A brilliant soldier, sailor, scholar, physi-
cian, wit, athlete and master of disguise, he
was favourite of the queen under a variety
of names and beards, including that of
'William Shakespeare' in which identity he
wrote forty-two award-winning plays and
13,500 sonnets. Executed for High Treason
and 'sonnetes'.

WILLIAM VASTCOCK,
EARL OF WOLVERHAMPTON
Little is known of this shadowy figure, or of
the reason the queen was reputedly so
fond of him.

Money

SCENE ONE: BLACKADDER'S BEDROOM

It is half light. A bed is set up in the corner of the room. We see Blackadder asleep, and then notice that there are feet on the pillow next to him. There is a knock on the door.

Blackadder
Go away.

Baldrick opens the door. He is carrying a lamp and wearing a night cap. He pops his head round the door.

Baldrick
My lord, there is someone at the door to see you.

Blackadder
Oh, God. (*Rubs his eyes*) What time is it?

Baldrick
Four o'clock.

Blackadder
Baldrick, I've told you before, you mustn't let me sleep all day. This woman charges by the hour.

Baldrick crosses to the side of the bed.

Baldrick
My lord, it's four o'clock in the morning.

Blackadder
Someone wants to see me at four in the morning? What is he, a giant lark?

Baldrick
No, he's a priest.

Blackadder
Tell him I'm Jewish.

He rolls over to go back to sleep but, by this time, the woman is inclined to chat, having been woken. She is Mollie.

Mollie
Aren't you going to introduce me then?

Blackadder
What?

Mollie
Aren't you going to introduce me to your friend?

Blackadder
Oh, very well, but I think you're making a

mistake. Baldrick, I am delighted to introduce you to . . . I'm sorry, I've forgotten your name.

Mollie
Mollie.

Blackadder
Of course. Mollie. Baldrick, this is Mollie, a dear friend of mine.

Mollie
I'm not dear. I'm very reasonable, actually, Baldrick. Most girls would charge an extra sixpence for all the horrid things he wants a girl to do . . .

Blackadder
(*Interrupting*) Yes, all right then. Baldrick, this is Mollie, an inexpensive prostitute. Mollie, this is Baldrick, a pointless peasant. Now may I go to sleep, please?

Baldrick
What about this priest?

Blackadder
Tell him to take his sacred backside out of here. And what's more, if he comes begging again, tell him I shall report him to the Bishop of Bath and Wells, who drowns babies during christenings and eats them in the vestry afterwards.

Baldrick
Very good, my lord.

Mollie
Goodbye, Baldrick.

Baldrick
Goodbye, Mollie.

There is a little crush developing here . . .

Blackadder
For God's sake, get out!

Baldrick exits.

Well, you're a one, aren't you? When you should be whispering sweet conversational nothings like 'Goodness, something twice the size of the Royal Barge has just hoved into view between the sheets', you don't say a word. But enter the Creature from the Black Latrine and you won't stop jabbering.

Mollie
He treated me like a human being.

Blackadder
Look, if I'd wanted a lecture on the rights of man, I'd have gone to bed with Martin Luther.

Baldrick bursts back through the door, obviously hurled through it, smashing it in the process. He lies on the floor. Mollie moves up so her head is resting on the pillow.

Blackadder
Yes, Baldrick. What is it now?

Baldrick
It's the priest – says he still wants to talk to you.

Blackadder
And did you mention the baby-eating Bishop of Bath and Wells?

Baldrick
I did, my lord.

Blackadder
And what did he say?

In reply, the door swings open. In the shadows, dark and threatening, stands a priest.

Bishop
He said, I *am* the baby-eating Bishop of Bath and Wells.

Blackadder is a touch uneasy, and checks that Mollie is covered which, fortunately, she is.

Blackadder
Good Lord!

Bishop
You haven't any children, have you, Blackadder?

Blackadder
No, I'm not married.

Bishop
In that case I'll skip breakfast and get straight down to business. Do you know what day it is today?

Blackadder
No, I don't.

Bishop
It is exactly one year ago to the day that the Bank of the Black Monks of St Herod – 'Banking with a Smile and a Stab' – of which I am the Assistant Manager, lent you £1000. Our motto is 'Repayment or Revenge'.

Blackadder
Of course. And naturally I would have paid you back, but unfortunately, and this is the real bugger, I've gone and lost my wallet. Disastrous! It had all my addresses in it, all my little notes saying 'forget-ye-not' and, of course, *all my money*.

Bishop
That is no concern of mine. The debt is now due. Not to repay a loan is a sin and we Black Monks – we hate sin.

He whips the sheets off Blackadder's bed, revealing Mollie. Blackadder is disconcerted for a moment.

Blackadder
Ah, yes. Your Grace – may I introduce my mother. Mother . . .

The bishop sits on the bed.

Bishop
Good morning, my dear. I hope you have not forgotten our appointment?

Mollie
Of course not, Pumpie.

Bishop
You know, I have a mind, my pretty, to play 'Nuns and Novices', so don't forget your wimple.

Mollie
(*Giggles*) Saucy.

Bishop
But as for you, *you* come with *me*.

He drags Blackadder out of bed.

Blackadder
Where . . . ?

Bishop
To visit the last poor fool who 'lost his wallet'.

And he pushes Blackadder out of the room with his sword.

~

SCENE TWO: A BLASTED HEATH

A violent sky, a mound of earth, and two or three twisted crosses. A mad beggar cavorts in the background. Blackadder reads a tombstone that the bishop has directed his attention to.

Blackadder
'William Grieves. Born 1513: in Chelmsford, with the love of Christ. Died 1563: in agony, with a spike up his bottom.'

Mad Beggar
Ha ha, 'tis ever and so nuncle, with the Black Monks. Scream did he, scream and gurgle as they skewered his cat flap for want of a farthing.

Bishop
I think you . . . get my message.

The beggar hangs on to Blackadder's leg and is dragged along as they walk.

Blackadder
Yes, yes, indeed. But tell me, Bishop, let me test the water here, so to speak. Supposing I was to say to you something like 'I'm a close friend of the queen's and I think she'd be very interested to hear about you and Mollie and the wimple, so why don't we just call it quits, eh, fatso?'

Bishop
I would say, firstly, the queen would not believe you, and secondly . . . you'll regret calling me fatso, later today.

He reveals a red-hot poker

Blackadder
Ah.

Bishop
I will have my money by Evensong tonight or . . . your bottom will wish it had never been born.

The Bishop leaves, in great sweeping splendour, coughing and hissing.

Mad Beggar
Poor Tom's cold. Pity poor Tom, for his nose is frozen, and he does shiver and is mad.

Blackadder
Oh, shut up.

He casually pushes Poor Tom into a big, wet pond.

~

SCENE THREE: BLACKADDER'S LODGINGS

Blackadder is pacing up and down, very worried. Percy and Baldrick stand by.

Blackadder
Well, lads, I'm up a certain creek, without a certain instrument. Either I raise £1000 by this evening, or I get murdered. What should I do?

Baldrick
It's obvious.

Blackadder
What?

Baldrick
You'll have to get murdered. You'll never raise that sort of money.

Percy
Oh come now, Baldrick, a piffling thousand! Pay the fellow, Edmund, and damn his impudence.

Blackadder
I haven't got a thousand, dung-head. I've got eighty-five quid in the whole world.

Percy
But you are always boasting to the queen about how wealthy you are.

Blackadder
A cunning web of deceit subtly spun about the Court to improve my standing, unfortunately.

Percy
(*Shocked*) You mean you've been . . . fibbing?

Blackadder
Yup. My whole life has been a tissue of whoppers. I consider myself one of England's finest fibsters. (*Looks out into the corridor*) Oh, my God! Percy!

Percy
Mmm?

Blackadder
A giant humming-bird is about to eat your hat and cloak.

Percy
Oh, no!

He rushes out.

Blackadder
You see? I'm terrific at it.

Percy returns.

Percy
It seems to have gone now. Couldn't you just dip into the family fortune?

Blackadder
There isn't one. My father blew it all on wine, women and amateur dramatics. At the end he was eking out a living doing humorous impressions of Anne of Cleves.

Percy
Oh, Edmund, I'm sorry. I had no idea. But do not despair, for I have some small savings, carefully harvested from my weekly allowance set aside against my frail old age.

This is a very moving moment. A moment of pure friendship, of pure generosity.

By lucky hap, it's just over a thousand methinks, and has for years been hidden beyond the wit of any thief . . .

Percy and Blackadder
. . . in an old sock under the squeaky floorboard . . .

In fact, even Baldrick is in on it.

All
. . . behind the kitchen dresser.

Percy is very surprised at this.

Percy
You've seen it?

Blackadder
Seen it, pinched it, spent it. And the same goes for the two farthings Baldrick thinks he's got hidden inside that mouldy potato.

Baldrick
Oh, bloody hell!

Percy
Then you are doomed. (*He goes to sit on the floor*) Alas. For God's sake, let us sit upon the carpet and tell sad stories . . .

Blackadder
Certainly not. When Lord Blackadder is

Lord Percy Percy standing on a chair in his tights in order to
show off his long thin thing to best advantage

in trouble, he doesn't sit about.

Baldrick
You won't be able to sit about with a spike up your bottom.

Blackadder
Well exactly. Still, I've got eighty-five quid and that's a start. I'm sure I'll think of something as long as I'm not disturbed.

Enter a messenger.

Messenger
My lord, the queen does demand your urgent presence on pain of death.

Blackadder
Damn! The path of my life is strewn with cowpats from the devil's own satanic herd.

SCENE FOUR: QUEENIE'S CHAMBER

Melchett and Queenie are playing chess. Nursie is watching. Blackadder bursts in.

Blackadder
Madam – you sent for me.

Queen
Did I? I don't remember. What a naughty scatterbrain I am. Snap!

Blackadder
Well, perhaps, ma'am, if I might be allowed to withdraw, I have one or two tiny matters to attend to.

Queen
Certainly.

He opens the door and they all burst into giggles.

That was a terrific joke, wasn't it?

Melchett
Magnificent!

Nursie
Ever so naughty!

Blackadder
What, my lady?

Queen
I *do* know why I wanted to see you, and I just pretended I didn't and I fooled you and it worked *brilliantly*, didn't it?

Blackadder
It was terrific, madam. Thank God I wore my corset, because I think my sides have split.

Queenie bursts into giggles.

So why did you want to see me?

Queen
To crack the lovely joke!

Melchett
Or perhaps, Blackadder, you don't think the queen's jokes are funny enough for you to be troubled with?

Blackadder
Au contraire, I'm ecstatic about the whole incident. I only didn't laugh out loud because I was afraid, if I did, my head would have fallen off.

Queen
If you don't start soon, your head *will* fall off. Now pay Melchy his £85 and run along.

Melchy holds out his hand.

Blackadder
Eighty-five pounds?

Queen
Yes. We had a bet. I said that you wouldn't fall for my trick and Melchett said you would, because I'm so super and you're so stupid. So you owe him £85.

Blackadder
Fine, fine. I mean, it's only money, isn't it?

He puts his hand into his purse.

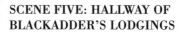

SCENE FIVE: HALLWAY OF BLACKADDER'S LODGINGS

Blackadder charges into the corridor.

Baldrick is there.

Blackadder
I cannot believe it. She drags me all the way from Billingsgate to Richmond to play about the weakest practical joke since Cardinal Wolsey got his nob out at Hampton Court and stood at the end of the passage pretending to be a door. (*Baldrick snorts with merriment*) Oh shut up, Balders. You'd laugh at a Shakespeare comedy.

Percy emerges from Blackadder's room and hugs Blackadder emotionally.

Percy
Edmund, oh Edmund, I have awaited your return.

Blackadder
And thank God you did, for I was just thinking, 'My God, I die in twelve hours. What I really need now is a hug from a complete prat.'

He pushes Percy away, goes into his room and pours himself a stiff drink.

Percy
But fear not, for I have a plan to save the life of my dear, dear friend.

Blackadder
Look, I'm not interested in your bloody friends. What about me?

Percy
(*Thinks he's joking*) Ha ha, not bad, Edmund, that's a good one.

Blackadder
Oh, all right then. What's your big plan, blockhead?

Percy
I intend to discover, this very afternoon, the secret of alchemy, the hidden art of turning base things into . . . gold.

Blackadder
I see. And the fact that this secret has eluded the most intelligent people since the dawn of time doesn't dampen your spirits?

Percy
Oh, no. I like a challenge.

Percy strides out.

Blackadder
Balders, I lost the £85. The grave opens up before me like a . . . big hole in the ground.

Baldrick
I did have one idea, my lord, but . . . no . . . it's stupid . . .

Blackadder
What is it?

Baldrick
Well, I have heard there is good money to be made down the docks, doing favours for sailors.

Blackadder
Favours. What do you mean? Delivering messages, sewing on buttons, that kind of thing?

Baldrick
Not *quite* . . .

Blackadder
(*Light beginning to dawn*) Baldrick?

Baldrick
My lord?

Blackadder
Are you suggesting that I become . . . a rent boy?

Baldrick
Well, a good-looking bloke like you, posh accent, nice legs, could make a bomb. Just stick a pink carnation in your hat and make the old sign.

Blackadder
I'd rather die.

Baldrick
Oh, fair enough, that's all right then. I'll put the kettle on while we wait shall I?

Baldrick is about to go. Blackadder stops him. He's had a thought.

Blackadder
With a *slight* alteration, your sick and sordid plan might . . . just . . . work!

SCENE SIX: DOWN BY THE DOCKS

Baldrick is dressed up tarty. He looks nervous and leans against the wall. He wears a carnation and carries a sign saying 'Get it here'. A large rough-hewn sailor approaches. Blackadder is hidden behind the wall.

Arthur the Sailor
Give me a kiss, I'll give you a penny.

Blackadder pops out as from nowhere, on the bargain.

Blackadder
A penny?!

Arthur
All right. Tuppence.

Blackadder
All right. Go on.

Blackadder nods and pops out of sight again.

Arthur
Nothing fancy, just a peck. I miss my mum, you see. When I was a little kid, my mother always used to . . .

Blackadder pops up again.

Blackadder
Get a move on, he's a prostitute, not an agony aunt.

Arthur
Oh, go on, please. Just a peck on the cheek and say, 'There, there Arthur, Mummy kiss it better and you shall have a story.'

Blackadder
Well, I don't know. Do you do requests, Baldrick?

Baldrick
What . . . kinky stuff? Yeah, I'm game.

Arthur
Please. (*He is crying now*) I miss my mother so much. I mean, she was like a mother to me.

Blackadder
Oh, all right. Go on, Baldrick.

Blackadder disappears.

Baldrick
I've forgotten what I'm supposed to say.

Blackadder reappears, takes Baldrick to one side and grabs the sign from him.

Blackadder
Oh, get out of the way: I'll do it. There, there, Arthur. (*He kisses Arthur – horrible experience*) Mummy kiss it better and you shall have a story.

Arthur
(*So happy*) What kind of story?

Blackadder
I don't know. One about a squirrel, I suppose.

A little later . . . Arthur has his arms around Blackadder and Baldrick.

. . . and then Squirry the Squirrel went . . .

Arthur and Baldrick
. . . *Neep, neep, neep.*

Blackadder
And they all went home for tea.

Arthur
Oh, thanks very much, me old shivering mateys. That was wonderful. (*Takes his arms down*) Now then, what do you charge for a good, hard shag?

Pause.

Blackadder
A thousand pounds.

Arthur
A thousand pounds! You've got to be joking!

Blackadder
Well, I'm sure we could negotiate.

Blackadder hands Baldrick the sign.
Arthur winks at Baldrick.

~

SCENE SEVEN: BLACKADDER'S LODGINGS

Blackadder and Baldrick walk straight in. Baldrick is carrying the 'Get it here' sign.

Blackadder
Right: so we've got sixpence.

Baldrick
Yeah. Now all we need to do, my lord, is to go down to the cock fights and put it on a bird that is a dead cert, but has got odds of 40,000 to 1.

Pause as Blackadder stares at Baldrick.

Blackadder
Know you of such a bird?

Baldrick
No. But we could make one.

Blackadder
No, Baldrick, we couldn't. Oh, God. I suppose you have to be told some time. Sit down. What happens is, a mummy bird and a daddy bird, who love each other very much, get certain urges . . .

Baldrick
No, no, my lord. What I mean is we could get a mad wild killer bull and disguise it as a bird.

Exasperated look from Blackadder.

But it'll be such a strange-looking bird so no one else will back it: but we'll know it's a killer bull, so we'll put money on it.

Blackadder
Only we will know?

Baldrick
Yes. If we stick enough feathers on it and hang an egg between its legs.

Blackadder
Yes, all right, Baldrick. A chat with you

and somehow death loses its sting.

Messenger enters.

Messenger
My lord, the queen does demand your urgent presence on pain of death.

Blackadder rises.

Blackadder
You're not making any friends here, you do know that, don't you, messenger?

~

SCENE EIGHT: QUEENIE'S CHAMBER

Queenie is pacing up and down. Melchett and Nursie nearby. Blackadder comes running down the corridor and enters, breathless and panicky.

Blackadder
Madam, you wished to see me . . . again.

Queen
Yes, Edmund. I wanted to apologize for the silly trick I played on you.

Blackadder
Ah.

Queen
It was naughty and bad of me.

Nursie
It was, my little rosebud, and if you weren't quite so big, it would be time for Mr and Mrs Spank to pay a short sharp trip to Bottieland.

Queen
Thank you, Nursie. And thank you, Edmund.

Blackadder
That's all?

Queen
Yes, thanks for coming.

Blackadder and Queenie shake hands. He turns and opens the door and hears a scream of giggling. He turns around.

Melchett collapses on to throne and puts his arm around Nursie.

That was very funny too, wasn't it?

Blackadder
My lady?

Queen
Dragging you all the way across town again just to say sorry for dragging you all the way across town the first time. It was Melchett's idea. I think it's wonderful, don't you?

Blackadder
It's fantastic. Melchett, I prostrate myself at the feet of the world's greatest living comedian.

Queen
Oh, you are *super*, Edmund. Oh, Edmund, I promised Lord Melchett that I would play shove ha'penny with him, but we have no coin. Do you have a ha'penny?

Blackadder
Unfortunately only a sixpence, madam. What a shame . . .

Queen
Oh no, a sixpence will do just as well.

Blackadder is trapped.

Blackadder
Oh good.

~

SCENE NINE: HALLWAY OF
BLACKADDER'S LODGINGS

Blackadder appears in the corridor outside his room. The place is full of smoke.

Blackadder
Oh, God! This place stinks like a pair of armoured trousers after the Hundred Years War. Baldrick, have you been eating dung again?

Baldrick is just visible with a pair of bellows. Percy emerges blasted and bruised. He is ecstatic.

Percy
My lord! Success!

Blackadder
What?

They go across to the table in Blackadder's room, on which there is an alchemy set.

Percy
After literally an hour's ceaseless searching, I have succeeded in creating gold, pure gold!

Blackadder
Are you sure?

Percy
Yes, my lord . . . behold!

He uncovers a silver platter, which has a lump of something green on it.

Blackadder
Percy . . . it's green.

Percy
That's right, my lord.

Blackadder
Yes, Percy. I don't want to be pedantic or anything, but the colour of gold is gold. That's why it's called gold. What you have discovered, if it has a name, is some 'green'.

Percy's face holds an expression of joyous amazement. He holds the green out in front of him.

Percy
Oh, Edmund, can it be true? That I hold here in my mortal hand, a nugget of purest green?

Blackadder
Indeed you do, Percy, except, of course, it's not really a nugget, is it? It's more of a splat.

Percy
Well, yes, a splat today, but tomorrow . . . who knows or dares to dream?

Blackadder
So we three alone in all the world can cre-

ate the finest green at will.

Percy
Just so.

Suddenly worried and whispering.

Not sure about counting in Baldrick, actually.

Blackadder
Of course you know what your great discovery means, don't you, Percy?

Percy
Perhaps, my lord.

Blackadder
That you, Percy, Lord Percy, are an utter berk. Baldrick.

Baldrick
My lord?

Blackadder
Pack my bags. I'm going to sell the house.

Baldrick and Percy
What?

Blackadder
There's nothing else for it. I shall miss the old place. I know I've had some happy times here, when you and Percy have been out. But, needs must when the devil vomits into your kettle. Baldrick, go forth into the streets, and let it be known that Lord Blackadder wishes to sell his house.

Baldrick exits.

Percy – just go forth into the street.

~

SCENE TEN: BLACKADDER'S LODGINGS

Blackadder is trying to sell his house, and going at the sales pitch with gusto. His victims are a wealthy but rather timid couple called Mr and Mrs Pants. They have just looked round the house and are entering the main room again.

Blackadder
And this is the den.

Mrs Pants
Oh, dear.

Blackadder
But I have to tell you, Mr Pants, that I have had an extremely encouraging nibble in other quarters, and I think you know me well enough to know that I'm not the sort of man to ignore a nibble for long.

Mrs Pants stands by the fireplace.

Mrs Pants
I noticed some dry rot in the bedrooms, Timothy.

Blackadder
Well, Mrs Pants, dry rot is as dry rot does. Stop me if I'm getting too technical.

Mrs Pants
And the floors are perhaps a little uneven.

Blackadder
Indeed yes, madam, and at no extra cost.

Mrs Pants is now by Baldrick's door.

Mrs Pants
Strange smell.

Blackadder
Yes, that's the servant; he'll be gone.

Mr Pants
(*Laughing*) You've really worked out your banter, haven't you?

Blackadder
No, not really. This is a different thing; it's spontaneous and it's called wit.

Mrs Pants
What about the privies?

Blackadder
When the master craftsman who created this home was looking into sewage, he said to himself, 'Romeo', for 'twas his name, 'Romeo, let's make 'em functional and comfortable.'

Mr Pants
Oh, well that seems nice, doesn't it, dear?

Blackadder
I think we understand each other, sir. So, sold then. Drink?

Blackadder pours and picks up two goblets from the small table.

Mrs Pants
But what about the privies?

It is clear she is not going to let this one go.

Blackadder
Uhm, well, what we are talking about in privy terms, is the very latest in front-wall fresh air orifices combined with a wide capacity gutter installation below.

Mrs Pants
You mean you crap out of the window?

Blackadder
Yes.

Mrs Pants
Well, in *that* case, we'll definitely take it. I can't stand those dirty indoor things.

~

SCENE ELEVEN: BLACKADDER'S LODGINGS

It is an hour later. Blackadder is counting his money. Percy sits beside him, wearing a strange green brooch.

Blackadder
There, that's the lot. He only wanted to pay a thousand but I managed to beat him up to eleven hundred.

Percy
Ha ha, Edmund, you wily trickster you.

Blackadder
Credit where credit's due. I just named the price, it was Baldrick who actually beat him up. Percy, what's that on the front of your tunic?

Percy
(*Proudly*) 'Tis a brooch, my lord, a brooch cunningly fashioned from pure green!

Blackadder
It looks like you've sneezed.

Percy
It is with trinkets such as this brooch, and here, a ring, that I intend to revive your fortunes and buy back your house.

Blackadder
You think there's a big market for jewellery that looks like snot, then?

Percy is hurt.

Percy
My lord.

Blackadder
The eyes are open, the mouth moves, but Mr Brain has long since departed, hasn't he, Perce?

The messenger enters once more.

Messenger
My lord . . .

Blackadder
(With heavy sarcasm) Ah, messenger! Thank God you came. Percy and I could not have waited another second without you.

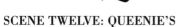

SCENE TWELVE: QUEENIE'S CHAMBER

Blackadder rushes in, panting and dirty. At first he does not see Melchett, Queenie and Nursie, who are playing ships behind the door.

Blackadder
Majesty!

Queen
Thank God you've arrived. Terrible news.

Blackadder
What?

Melchett
The French intend to invade, Blackadder.

Blackadder
My God!

Queen
So I need some money.

Blackadder slumps onto the throne.

Blackadder
Ah.

Melchett
Yes, every nobleman must pay £500 towards the upkeep of the navy.

Queen
But we've decided to make you a special case.

Blackadder
Oh, thank you, ma'am.

Queen
Melchy here hasn't got a bean, so we thought since you're so fabulously wealthy, you could pay for both.

Melchett
It would be awfully sweet of you.

Blackadder
Unfortunately, ma'am, I'm in the middle of a cash-flow crisis, and I just haven't got any money on me.

Queen
But Edmund . . .

Blackadder
Sorry, ma'am.

Blackadder gets off the throne. But he cannot hide from Queenie the huge wodge in his tights.

Queen
But Edmund, what's that in your tights?

Blackadder takes it out, most surprised.

Blackadder
Good Lord!

Queen
It looks like just over a thousand pounds.

Blackadder
So it is!

Queen
I *thought* you said you didn't have any?

Blackadder
Yes, sorry, I meant *real* money: this is just a bit of loose change. I must have left it in the codpiece when I sent these tights to the laundry.

Queen
Gosh! A thousand pounds just loose in your tights! That *is* flash! Anyway, hand it over.

Blackadder
Aahh . . .

knock your block off.

Melchett
But, Majesty, I only acted . . . please.
(*He is weeping*) Oh, please, I so want to
live . . .

*Queenie, who has been looking at him
sternly, can no longer contain herself as
she bursts into a huge guffaw.*

*Melchett sees what has been happening
and wipes away his tears in joyous relief.*

Praise the Lord for the gift of laughter.

~

Queen
Thanks. Bye.

*She takes the cash and turns away
abruptly.*

Blackadder
Fine. Yes, well, goodbye indeed. Goodbye
ma'am, goodbye Melchett. And . . . goodbye Nursie.

*Although this is his final, fatal farewell,
everyone ignores him.*

Byeeeee.

*The second he moves out, Melchett checks
the door, then falls on the floor, followed
by the others.*

Queen
Ha ha ha – silly old Edmund – he was
completely fooled. It was a brilliant trick,
Melchy.

Melchett
Brilliant, ma'am.

Queen
And now I'm going to have you executed.

Melchett
(*Utterly terrified*) Majesty?

Queen
It's for taking the mickey out of my
beloved Edmund so cruelly. I'm going to

**SCENE THIRTEEN: BLACKADDER'S
LODGINGS**

*Blackadder bursts in on Baldrick, who is
packing.*

Blackadder
Right, Balders. I lost the money. I'm going
to have to run away.

Baldrick
Why, my lord?

Blackadder
Well, to avoid these monks, of course.

Baldrick
No point – the Black Bank has branches
everywhere.

Blackadder
Damn!

Suddenly a thought catches him.

If I die, Baldrick, do you think people
would remember me?

Baldrick
Of course they would.

Blackadder
Yes, I suppose so.

Baldrick
People would always be slapping each
other over the shoulder and laughing and

saying, 'Do you remember Old Privy Breath'?

Blackadder
Do people call me 'Privy Breath'?

Baldrick
Oh, yes. The ones who like you.

Blackadder
Am I, then, not popular?

Baldrick
Put it this way, when people slip in what dogs have left in the streets, they do tend to say, 'Oops, I've trod in an Edmund.'

Blackadder
The bloody cheek. I'll show them.

Baldrick
Have you got a plan, my lord?

Blackadder
Yes, I have, and it's so cunning you could brush your teeth with it. All I need is some feathers, a dress, some oil, an easel, some sleeping draught, lots of paper, a prostitute and the best portrait painter in England.

Baldrick
I'll get them right away, my lord.

~

SCENE FOURTEEN: BLACKADDER'S LODGINGS

It is two hours later, at eight o'clock. Blackadder is pacing. Baldrick comes in and announces:

Baldrick
My lord, the finest portrait painter in England. Mr Leonardo Acropolis.

In steps a man who looks exactly the same as Leonardo da Vinci, white beard and all. He crosses in front of Baldrick to Blackadder.

Blackadder
Oh, hello. Are you any good?

Leonardo
No . . . I am a genius.

Blackadder
You'd better be, or you're dead!

There is a violent knocking.

All right – into the bedroom, beard face. Baldrick – get the door.

Baldrick and Leonardo leave. Blackadder takes an absolutely relaxed seated position, reading a book. Two seconds later, Baldrick comes smashing through the door again.

Baldrick
(*Dusting himself off*) My lord, the Bishop of Bath and Wells.

The bishop enters, holding a skull in one hand and his poker at his side.

Bishop
The time has come, Blackadder . . .

Blackadder turns casually.

Blackadder
Oh, hullo, Bish.

Bishop
The Black Monks will have their money . . . or I will have my fun.

Blackadder
You enjoy your work, don't you?

Bishop
Bits of it, yes.

Blackadder
The violent bits?

The bishop puts the skull and poker down and stands behind Blackadder. He starts to massage his shoulders.

Bishop
Yes. You see I am a colossal pervert. No form of sexual depravity is too low for me. Animal, vegetable or mineral, I'll do anything to anything.

Blackadder
Ah – fine words for a bishop. Nice to hear the Church speaking out for a change on

social issues.

Bishop
Have you got the money?

Blackadder
Nope.

Bishop
Good, I hate it when people pay up. Say your prayers, Blackadder. It's poker time!

He brandishes the red-hot poker at Blackadder who stands up and calmly turns to face him.

Blackadder
Fine. Are you ever concerned that people might find you out?

Bishop
No, no, no . . . I kill, I maim, I fornicate, but as far as my flock is concerned my only vice is a little tipple before Evensong.

Baldrick holds out a goblet to the bishop. It is poisoned wine.

Oh, thank you.

The bishop drains the glass.

Bend over, Blackadder – this is where you get yours. Aaaahhhh!

Blackadder bends over. The bishop then grabs his own throat.

Drugged, by God!

Blackadder
No, by Baldrick actually – but the effect is much the same.

~

SCENE FIFTEEN: BLACKADDER'S BEDROOM

It is fourteen hours later. Blackadder enters, and gaily opens the curtains, revealing the bishop in his bed.

Blackadder
Wakey, wakey, Bish! Dear me, you clerics really are slugger-beds.

The bishop's head emerges from the sheets.

Bishop
Where am I? (*He sees Blackadder*) Ah. I remember, drugged!

Blackadder
That's right.

Bishop
Well, you should have killed me while you had the chance. You have looked in wonder at your last dawn, Blackadder.

Blackadder
Well, I'm not so sure about that.

I did wonder, though, what people who saw this might think . . .

He reveals the painting to the bishop.

Bishop
Heavens above! What creatures from hell are these?

Blackadder
Yes, they make an unusual couple, don't they – though, in fact, I think you probably recognize this huge sweating mound of blubber here, eh, fatso?

The bishop cries out and lunges for the painting.

Blackadder
Ah–ah!

He smacks him like a naughty child.

No point. Anyway, we have the preliminary sketches. Now, we can soon bang off a couple of copies. Let's see. One for the queen, one for the Archbishop, a couple kept aside perhaps to form the basis of an exciting exhibition of challenging young artists' work.

The bishop is stunned by the painting and turns sideways to get it in perspective.

Bishop
By the horns of Beelzebub! How did you get me into that position?

Blackadder
And it's so beautifully framed, don't you think? Which is ironic really, because that's exactly what's happened to you!

Bishop
You fiend – never before have I encountered such corrupt and foul-minded perversity. Have you ever considered a career in the Church?

Blackadder
No, I could never get used to the underwear. What I could use, though, is £1100 to buy back my house and £4000 to cover some sundry expenses, 10 shillings for the two doors and, let's say, 3 pence for a celebratory slap-up binge at Mrs Miggins's pie shop.

Bishop
Yes, yes. But first, one question. Who is the second figure? Who could you have got to have performed such deeds, to have gone lower than man has ever gone, to have plunged the depths of degradation in order to save your filthy life?

The bishop pulls back the sheet. It is Percy. He wears a distinctly curious, lurid pink and black girdle arrangement, wrapped up in chains. A black ruff and a pink pointy hat finish off his rather phallic look.

Percy
Oh, hullo.

Blackadder
Percy, may I introduce His Grace, the Bishop of Bath and Wells. Your Grace, Lord Percy Percy, heir to the Duchy of Northumberland.

Percy holds out his hand for a formal handshake.

Percy
Hullo. It was . . . lovely working with you.

THE BALLAD OF BLACKADDER THE BANKRUPT

Take heed the moral of this tale,
Be not a borrower or lender,
And if your finances do fail,
Make sure your banker's not a bender.

Blackadder, Blackadder,
He trusted in the Church.
Blackadder, Blackadder,
It left him in the lurch.

Blackadder, Blackadder,
His life was almost done.
Blackadder, Blackadder,
Who gives a toss? No one!

SCENE ONE: BLACKADDER'S LODGINGS

Breakfast time at Lord Blackadder's place. Percy and Blackadder are eating the Elizabethan equivalent of toast.

Percy
I must say, Edmund, it was jolly nice of you to ask me to share your breakfast before the rigours of the day begin.

Blackadder
It is said, Percy, that civilized man seeks out good and intelligent company so that through learned discourse he may rise above the savage and closer to God.

Percy
(*Delighted*) Yes, I'd heard that.

Blackadder
Personally, however, I like to start the day with a total dickhead to remind me I'm best.

Blackadder rises and goes to sort out the mail.

Percy
(*Laughing*) Beshrew me, Edmund, you're in good fooling this morning!

Blackadder
Don't say 'beshrew me', Percy. Only stupid actors say 'beshrew me'.

Percy
Oh, how I would love to be an actor. I had a great talent for it in my youth – I was the man of a thousand faces.

Blackadder
How did you come to choose the ugly mug you've got now, then?

Percy laughs.

Percy
Oh, tush, my lord.

Blackadder
And don't say 'tush' either. It's only a short step from 'tush' to 'hey nonny nonny' and then I'm afraid I shall have to call the police.

He at last gets round to reading his letter. Immediately, his face lightens.

Well, God pats me on the head and says, 'Good boy, Edmund.'

Percy
My lord?

Blackadder
My aunt and uncle, Lord and Lady Whiteadder, the two most fanatical puritans in England, have invited themselves to dinner here, tonight.

Percy
But aren't they the most frightful bores?

Blackadder
Yes, but they have one great redeeming feature: their wallets. More capacious than an elephant's scrotum and just as difficult to get your hands on. At least until now. For tonight they wish to 'discuss my inheritance'.

Percy
Hey nonny nonny, my lord – good news!

Blackadder
Baldrick!

Baldrick enters with a piece of cheese hanging from his nose on a string.

Why have you got a piece of cheese tied to the end of your nose?

Baldrick
To catch mice, my lord. I lie on the floor with my mouth open and hope they scurry in.

Blackadder
And do they?

Baldrick
Not yet, my lord.

Blackadder
I'm not surprised. Your breath comes straight from Satan's bottom, Baldrick. The only sort of mouse you're going to catch is one without a nose.

Baldrick
That's a pity because the nose is the best bit on a mouse.

Blackadder
Any bit of a mouse will seem like luxury compared to what Percy and I must eat tonight. We are entertaining puritan vegetable folk, Balders, and that means no meat.

Baldrick
In that case, I shall prepare my turnip surprise.

Blackadder
And the surprise is?

Baldrick
There's nothing else in it except the turnip.

Blackadder
So another word for turnip surprise would be a turnip.

Baldrick
Oh, yes.

Blackadder
Good.

A knock on the door.

Get the door, Baldrick.

Baldrick obeys and exits.

Percy
Well, my lord, if things go as planned tonight, it would seem congratulations are in order.

Blackadder
Nice try, Percy, but forget it: you're not getting a penny.

There is a loud crash and Baldrick enters, carrying the door.

Baldrick, I would advise you to make the explanation you are about to give phenomenally good.

Baldrick
You said, 'Get the door.'

Blackadder
Not good enough. You're fired.

Baldrick
But, my lord, I've been in your family since 1532.

Blackadder
So has syphilis. Now get out.

Baldrick
Very well, my lord. Oh, by the way, there was a messenger outside when I got the door. Says the queen wants to see you. Lord Melchett is very sick.

Blackadder
(*Grinning*) Really?

Baldrick
Yes. He's at death's door.

Blackadder
Well, my faithful old reinstated family retainer, let's go and open it for him then!

~

SCENE TWO: MELCHETT'S CHAMBER

Melchett is pale and groaning. Nursie and Queenie are by his bedside when Blackadder enters. Queenie leads him to the bed.

Queen
Oh, Edmund, quick, quick! Melchett's dying. We must *do* something.

Blackadder
Yes, of course: some sort of celebration.

But let's wait till he's actually snuffed it, shall we?

Queen
Nursie's old methods don't seem to be working.

Nursie
(*Rubbing his stomach*) Come on, little tummy.

Melchett groans.

Queen
It all started last night at about two o'clock. I was tucked into bed, having this absolutely scrummy dream about ponies, when I was awakened by a terrific banging from Lord Melchett.

Blackadder
Well, I never knew he had it in him.

Queen
It's true, I promise. He was banging on the castle gates and falling over and singing a strange song about a girl who possessed something called a dickie die doe?

Blackadder
Yes, it's a lovely old hymn, isn't it?

Blackadder crosses to Melchett. Melchett groans again.

Blackadder
Well, ma'am, I think I know what's wrong with Lord Melchett, and unfortunately, it isn't fatal.

Queen
Well, hurry up and cure the horrible man. I'm fed up with him lying there moaning and groaning . . .

Nursie
And letting off such great and fruitsome flappy woof-woofs one can scarcely believe one's tiny noseling.

Blackadder
The truth is, Lord Melchett just can't take his ale.

Melchett rises, rallying under these insults.

Melchett
Madam, I protest! I may be a little delicate this morning but what I drank last night would have floored a rhinoceros!

Blackadder
If it was allergic to lemonade.

Melchett
It's Blackadder here who can't take his ale. He's famous for it.

Blackadder
Yeah?

Melchett
Yeah.

Blackadder
Yeah?

Melchett
Yeah.

Queen
Oh, Nursie, isn't it exciting, the boys are getting tough!

Melchett
I'm sure we all remember the shame and embarrassment of the visit of the King of Austria when Blackadder was found wandering naked among the corridors of Hampton Court singing 'I'm Merlin, the Happy Pig'.

Blackadder
What did you have last night then? A whole half-pint of potato juice?

Melchett
On the contrary, I had two flagons of claret and a double helping of curried turtle. I can assure you it's no holds barred with us at the annual Communion wine-tasting.

Blackadder
Annual – ha! For me and the wild boys, every night is drinky night!

Melchett
Says who?

Blackadder
Says me.

Melchett
Says you?

Blackadder
Yeah.

Melchett
Yeah?

Blackadder
Yeah. You want to come round sometime, have a look at the underside of *my* table.

Queen
(*Loud and firm*) Tonight!

Melchett
(*Still so hung over*) Tonight?

Blackadder
(*Loving it*) Yeah, come on Melchy, what are you scared of?

Queen
Perhaps you're right, perhaps he's a wet and a weed.

Melchett
Oh all right then. Tonight. I'll be there.

Queen
Hurray: and last one under the table gets
10,000 florins from the loser.

*Blackadder is shocked, but gathers him-
self . . .*

Blackadder
Ma'am? Right. Well, I'll get the beer in
then. Right.

*Blackadder sweeps out of the room.
Queenie beckons Nursie to the door.*

Queen
Nursie, do you know what I'm going to
do?

Nursie
What?

Queen
I'm going to go along and find out exactly
what happens at these 'boys' nights'.

Nursie
Good idea, poppet.

Queen
And I'll wear a cloak with a cowl so no one
will recognize me.

Nursie
Another good idea. You're so clever today,
you better be careful your foot doesn't fall
off.

Queen
Does that happen when you have lots of
brilliant ideas – your foot falls off?

Nursie
Certainly does. My brother, he had this
brilliant idea of cutting his toenails with a
scythe and *his* foot fell off.

SCENE THREE: BLACKADDER'S
LODGINGS

*Percy is sitting at the table, thinking hard
with a pen in his hand. Blackadder is
pacing.*

Blackadder
Right. Now, the sort of person we're looking for is an aggressive drunken lout with
the intelligence of a four-year-old and the
sexual sophistication of a donkey.

Percy
Cardinal Wolsey.

*Baldrick enters with a mouse tied to his
nose.*

Blackadder
Baldrick.

Baldrick
My lord.

Blackadder looks hard at him.

Blackadder
Why?

Baldrick
I got fed up with an all-mouse diet, my
lord. I thought I'd try a cat for variety.

Blackadder
Good, well done. And now, returning to
the real world, do you have a knife?

Baldrick
Yeah.

Blackadder
Good, because I wish to quickly send off
some party invitations, and to make them
look particularly tough, I wish to write
them in blood. Your blood, to be precise.

Baldrick produces a knife with some apprehension.

Baldrick
How much blood will you actually be requiring, my lord?

Blackadder
Oh, nothing much, just a small puddle.

Baldrick
Will you be wanting me to cut anything off; an arm, or a leg, for instance?

Blackadder
Oh, good lord, no, a little prick should do.

Baldrick
Very well, my lord. I am your bondsman, and must obey.

He scrunches his eyes, about to do the job. Blackadder turns and sees Baldrick just about to perform the cruellest cut of all.

Blackadder
Oh, for God's sake, Baldrick! I meant a little prick on the finger.

Baldrick
I haven't got one there!

Blackadder
Oh, forget it, forget it.

Baldrick
Thank you, my lord.

Baldrick leaves, relieved and still, technically speaking, a man.

Blackadder
Right. Now, Perce, how's this list going?

Percy
Very well indeed. I thought we could invite my girlfriend Gwendolen.

Blackadder
Sorry, no chicks. Who else?

Percy
That's about as far as I'd got, actually.

Blackadder
Right. I'll dictate. First, Simon Partridge.

Percy
Not Farters Parters, also known as Mr Ostrich?

Blackadder
Even he.

Percy
But he's a fearful oik.

Blackadder
Takes one to know one, Perce. Secondly, Sir Geoffrey Piddle.

Percy
Not 'Here's to the health of Cardinal Chunder' Piddle.

Blackadder
The very same. And thirdly, Freddie Frobisher, the flatulent hermit of Lindisfarne.

Percy
(*Holding his nose*) Oh, pong pong!

Blackadder
Right. That should do the trick.

Percy
Oh, and of course, Lord and Lady Whiteadder, who will be coming anyway.

Blackadder
Oh yes . . .

Suddenly, Blackadder realizes the dreadful contradiction the evening ahead holds.

Oh, no.

~

SCENE FOUR: QUEENIE'S CHAMBER

Queenie and Nursie, are back in their usual positions. Blackadder is kneeling before them.

Queen
I must say, Edmund: it does look a teeny

bit like trying to get out of it.

Blackadder
Quite the wrong impression, ma'am. I just want to make it another night. That's all.

Nursie
Certainly not.

Queenie is surprised at this firm assertion by Nursie.

Queen
I beg your pardon?

Nursie
Well, it's just one excuse after another, isn't it? Next thing he'll be trying to get out of having his bath altogether.

Queen
He isn't talking about baths, Nursie.

Nursie
Well, he should be. How else is he going to keep clean? Soon he'll be saying he doesn't want to have his nappy changed.

Queen
Lord Blackadder doesn't wear a nappy.

Nursie
In that case, it's even more important that he has a bath.

Queen
Shut up, Nursie! I know why you want to get out of it, because I remember the last time you had a party, I found you face down in a puddle wearing a pointy hat and singing a song about goblins.

Blackadder rises, really quite angry now.

Blackadder
Yes, all right, all right. Tonight it is.

Queen
Oh, Edmund, I do love it when you get cross. Sometimes I think about having you executed just to see the expression on your face.

SCENE FIVE: BALDRICK'S ROOM/ THE CORRIDOR/BLACKADDER'S LODGINGS

Blackadder is waiting for the guests to arrive, and giving the boys their final briefing. They enter Baldrick's room to the right of the front door.

Blackadder
Right – now let's make sure you've got this. We are having two parties here tonight.

Percy and Baldrick
Right.

Blackadder
And they must be kept completely separate.

Percy and Baldrick
Right.

Blackadder
Firstly, a total piss-up involving beer-throwing, broken furniture and wall-to-wall vomiting, to be held here in Baldrick's bedroom.

Baldrick
Thank you very much, my lord.

Blackadder then heads out and on into his lodgings at the end of the corridor. Percy and Baldrick follow.

Blackadder
And secondly, Percy will join me in here for the gourmet turnip evening. Is the turnip surprise ready?

Baldrick
Yes, my lord.

Baldrick and Percy start to giggle sheepishly. Percy snorts.

Blackadder
Then what is so funny?

Percy
Well, my lord, when Baldrick and I were preparing the turnip surprise, we had a surprise, for we came across a turnip that was exactly the same shape . . . as . . . a thingy.

He and Baldrick lose the battle against giggle hysteria. They both snort with laughter at the hilarious memory. Blackadder is not convinced.

Blackadder
A thingy.

Baldrick
Yes. A great, big thingy. It was terrific.

Blackadder
Size is no guarantee of quality, Baldrick. Most horses are very well endowed, but that does not necessarily make them sensitive lovers. I trust you have removed this hilarious item?

Baldrick
Oh, yes, my lord.

Blackadder
Good. Because there's nothing more likely to stop an inheritance than a thingy-shaped turnip.

Percy
Oh, absolutely, Edmund. But it was jolly funny.

He and Baldrick start to giggle again.

Baldrick
I found it particularly ironic, my lord, because I've got a thingy that's shaped like a turnip.

Edmund
Yes, all r . . .

Baldrick
I'm a big hit at parties.

Blackadder
Are you?

Baldrick
Yes. I hide in the vegetable rack and frighten the children.

Blackadder
What fun. Perhaps you've forgotten that I'm meant to be having a drinking competition here tonight with Lord Melchett and 10,000 florins are at stake.

Baldrick
Oh dear.

Blackadder
What do you mean?

Baldrick
Well, firstly you haven't got 10,000 florins and thirdly, one drop of the ale and you fall flat on your face and start singing that song about the goblin.

Blackadder
That's nonsense. But just in case it's true . . .

Baldrick
It is true, actually.

Blackadder
Yes, all right, it's true, it's true. So the plan is, when I call for my incredibly strong ale, you must pass me water in an ale bottle. Have you got that?

Baldrick
Yes . . . When you call for ale, I pass water.

Blackadder
Good. And Percy, your job is to stay here and suck up to my aunt.

Percy
I think you can trust me to know how to handle a woman.

Blackadder
Oh, God.

There is a knock on the door.

Right, here goes.

Blackadder rushes into the corridor, followed by Baldrick, who brushes him down with a clothes brush, which he then throws into the cupboard. Percy stands at the entrance to Blackadder's lodgings.

Blackadder opens the front door, and there are the Whiteadders: crosses on hats, shoulders and round necks. Surely the most severe and humourless humans on the planet.

Uncle, Aunt, greetings! How nice it is to see you.

He kisses his aunt on each cheek. She slaps Blackadder firmly on both cheeks.

Lady Whiteadder
Wicked child, don't lie. Everyone hates us and you know it.

Blackadder
May I introduce my friend, Lord Percy.

Percy tries to be roguishly charming.

Percy
Well, well, well, Eddy, you didn't tell me

you had such a good-looking aunt. Good-morrow to thee, gorgeousness. I know what I like and I like what I see.

Lady Whiteadder punches him in the face.

Lady Whiteadder
Be gone, Satan!

Blackadder guides them into his lodgings where a very polite dining table is set up.

Blackadder
Yes, well. Well, I hope you had a pleasant inheritance. Did I say 'inheritance'? I meant journey. If you'd just like to help yourself to a legacy, uhm, a chair . . .

Lady Whiteadder
Chair! You have chairs in your house?

Blackadder
Oh . . . yes.

Lady Whiteadder
Wicked child! (*She hits Blackadder*) Chairs are an invention of Satan. In our house, Nathaniel sits on a spike.

Blackadder
And yourself?

Lady Whiteadder
I sit on Nathaniel. Two spikes would be an extravagance.

Blackadder
Well, quite.

Nevertheless, Lord and Lady Whiteadder sit at the table.

Lady Whiteadder
I will suffer comfort this once. We shall just have to stick forks in our legs between courses. I trust you remember we eat no meat.

Blackadder
Heaven forbid! No, here we feast only on God's lovely turnip, mashed.

Lady Whiteadder stands in horror.

Lady Whiteadder
Mashed?!

Blackadder
Yeees.

Lady Whiteadder hits him.

Lady Whiteadder
Wicked child.

And she whacks him once more.

Mashing is also the work of Beelzebub. For Satan saw God's blessed turnip and he envied it and mashed it to spoil its sacred shape. I shall have my turnip as God intended.

Blackadder
Fine. Baldrick!

Baldrick enters.

Would you fetch my dear aunt a raw turnip, please?

Baldrick
But we've only got the one . . .

Blackadder
Just do it. Thank you.

Baldrick exits.

Uncle, will you have your turnip mashed, or as God intended?

Lady Whiteadder
He will not answer. He has taken a vow of silence. I believe that silence is golden.

Silence falls. After a couple of moments Blackadder coughs. The cough sounds strangely like the word . . .

Blackadder
Inheritance.

There is suddenly a very loud knocking on the door.

Lady Whiteadder
Edmund, I trust you have invited no other guests.

Blackadder
Certainly not.

Lady Whiteadder
Good. For where there are other guests, there are people to fornicate with.

Blackadder
Well, quite.

The knocking again. Blackadder rises.

I'll just tell them to fornicate off. Lord Percy will look after you.

Blackadder exits. Percy is left on the spot.

Percy
Ahm, yes. Well, Lord Whiteadder, a vow of silence. That's quite an interesting thing. Tell me about it . . .

~

SCENE SIX: THE CORRIDOR/ BALDRICK'S ROOM

Blackadder enters the corridor. He goes to a cupboard and takes out a silly hat and a pair of false breasts, which he slips on. He then opens the door.

Sure enough, it is three drunken idiots: Piddle and Partridge, mutated aristocrats, and Frobisher, a gross priest. They all wear silly hats, and grin inanely before bursting into song. Partridge holds a clutch of ostrich feathers. They are all also wearing false breasts.

All three
Happy birthday to you!
Happy birthday to you!
Happy birthday, Eddie Baby!
Happy birthday to you!

Blackadder tries to quieten them down, but fails. He lifts his voice for the benefit of the Whiteadders . . .

Blackadder
But it's not my birthday, *Archdeacon.*

He ushers the lads into Baldrick's room.

Well, get stuck in, boys . . .

Partridge
'Stuck in' – wehey! – geddit?

Piddle
No.

Partridge
Well, it sounds a bit rude, doesn't it?
'Stuck in.'

There is a knock at the door.

Blackadder
Sorry. Back in a tick.

Blackadder goes for the door.

Partridge
Wehey! 'Tick', eh, lads. Now that sounds
a bit rude, doesn't it? That sounds a bit
like 'bum'.

*Blackadder opens the front door. It is
Melchett.*

Blackadder
Ha! Melchers. Late, I see, to avoid the
early drinking. Oh, Melchy, you really are
a beginner – you're not even wearing a
pair of comedy breasts.

Melchett
Au contraire, Blackadder.

*He undoes his coat to reveal a much big-
ger pair, painted gold.*

Blackadder
Yes, well, let's wait till we get down to the
serious drinking, shall we?

*Melchett heads down the corridor towards
the Whiteadders.*

Melchett
In here?

Blackadder
No. It's this way.

*Blackadder opens the door to Baldrick's
bedroom. All three lads are bending over,
their bottoms facing three lit candles on
the table.*

All
Wehey!

Melchett
Good evening.

They all turn round.

Blackadder
Lads, this is Lord Melchett.

All
Hurray!

Blackadder
Give him a large one, will you?

Partridge
'Large one' – wehey! – geddit?

Piddle
No.

Partridge
Yes, you do. Large one, it sounds a bit
rude.

Piddle
Oh yes – large one – get it! Wehey!

Blackadder
You may find the conversation a bit above
your head at first, Melchy, but you'll soon
get used to it.

Blackadder takes a large flagon.

Well, down the hatch!

All
Hurray!

*Blackadder swigs his beer merrily and
exits into the corridor. He opens the door
of the cupboard and throws in the con-*

tents of the flagon, then crosses to his lodgings.

There is an unexpected knock on the front door. He opens it impatiently, and there stands a cowled woman. It is, of course, Queenie. Though Blackadder, strangely, does not recognize her.

Woman
I heard there was a party on.

Edmund
No. Yes. There are two and you're invited to neither.

Blackadder is about to close the door.

Woman
But I'm a friend of Lord Percy's.

Blackadder
Oh, you must be Gwendolen. You were invited anyway. Come in, do.

Woman
Thank you very much.

Blackadder
It's in here.

Woman
Thank you.

He smiles and opens the door of the cupboard. The woman walks in obediently and Blackadder calmly locks her in.

Blackadder
There you go.

He heads for his lodgings, breasts on.

~

SCENE SEVEN: BLACKADDER'S LODGINGS

Blackadder bursts in, breasts and all.

Blackadder
Sorry about that. Carol singers.

Blackadder sits. Everyone freezes, noticing the breasts. Percy coughs, three times, in very unusual ways.

Sorry – he's sick. Leprosy, of the brain.

Lady Whiteadder
What he is trying to tell you is that you appear to be wearing a pair of devil's dumplings.

Blackadder looks down and flinches in shock at the sight of his own breasts. He then covers them with his hands and thinks of a plausible answer.

Blackadder
Oh, my God – my ear muffs have fallen down.

He moves them up, and tries to stretch them round his ears.

Would you like a pair? It's getting rather cold.

Lady Whiteadder
No thank you – cold is God's way of telling us to burn more Catholics.

Blackadder
Well, quite. Which reminds me, Auntie . . .

She hits him.

Lady Whiteadder
Do not call me Auntie. An aunt is a relative and relatives are evidence of sex . . . and sex is hardly a fitting subject for the dinner table.

Blackadder
Or indeed, any table.

Percy
Except, perhaps, a table in a brothel.

Blackadder does not move, but somehow Percy disappears under the table. It is clear that Blackadder has kicked him.

Blackadder
Oh dear, Percy, you seem to have fallen off your chair.

Percy re-emerges just as Baldrick enters with the turnip and crosses to Lady Whiteadder.

Well, now, what was I saying . . . Oh, my God!

Baldrick
Your turnip, my lady.

Percy and Blackadder are horrified. It is the thingy turnip. A chilling moment as Lady Whiteadder inspects it. Then . . .

Lady Whiteadder
Very good. Very good.

She nibbles one end. Baldrick exits.

You know, Nathaniel – this takes me right back to our wedding night.

Blackadder is shocked at this. Lady Whiteadder turns to him to explain.

We had raw turnips that night, too.

Lady Whiteadder takes a huge bite and Blackadder winces. Suddenly, from very near there is a loud, drunken roar. It is part cheer, part crash, and deafening.

What was that?

Blackadder
What was what?

Lady Whiteadder
That noise.

Blackadder
Noise? Did you hear a noise, Percy?

Percy
No.

Blackadder
Good.

Percy
Apart from that colossal drunken roar.

Percy suddenly disappears under the table again.

Blackadder
Oh, *that* noise. It's the Catholics next door, I'm afraid.

Lady Whiteadder
Ah.

Blackadder
I'll just go and burn them. Back in a minute. Percy.

Blackadder rises and exits into the corridor. All eyes turn to Percy . . .

~

SCENE EIGHT: THE
CORRIDOR/BLACKADDER'S
LODGINGS/BALDRICK'S ROOM

There is a violent knocking from the cupboard. Blackadder is about to cross to it, when he notices Baldrick.

Baldrick hands him a red plastic comedy nose. Blackadder puts it on, then crosses to the cupboard and opens it. The woman stumbles out gasping for air.

Blackadder
Yes?

Woman
I'm suffocating!

Blackadder
Well, thank God you knocked. Come on now, take a deep breath. And another. Better?

Woman
Yes.

Blackadder
Good.

And he pushes her back in the cupboard and locks it again. He then heads out towards Baldrick's room; meanwhile, back in his lodgings . . .

Percy
Mind you, I'll say one thing for Catholics: they do have natural rhythm.

Lady Whiteadder lunges to hit Percy.

In Baldrick's room, the lads are all wearing plastic noses. Melchett is seated.

Piddle
Geddit? Yes, wehey!

Melchett
I notice you're not drinking, Blackadder.

Blackadder
Don't you worry about me Melchers, I'm holding my own here.

Partridge
Wehey! Holding my own! Now that sounds *incredibly* rude.

They howl with laughter.

Blackadder
Yes, well, I never went to university, of course.

Melchett
Blackadder, that doesn't explain why you're not drinking with us.

Blackadder
Ah, yes, no, well that's what I actually came to talk to you about. What do you say to the idea of ten minutes' absolute silence to get some really serious drinking in?

Frobisher
Hooray! Sssssh!

Partridge and Piddle
Sssssssssssssh!!

Blackadder
Yes, I said, 'please give me silence', not 'drench me with dribble'.

All
Sorry, Edders.

Melchett
Now. Here's a nice glass of cider.

Melchett hands Blackadder the flagon.

Blackadder
Only cider? I'm going to go and put some brandy in it.

They all cheer, then shush. And Blackadder gets out quick. Once in the corridor, he unlocks the cupboard and throws in the contents of the flagon. A little scream as he throws the flagon in as well, and locks the door again. He takes off his red nose and throws it away.

In Baldrick's room, the lads are sitting on the floor with beer barrels exploding around them.

~

SCENE NINE: BLACKADDER'S
LODGINGS

Blackadder enters once more.

Blackadder
Well, how are we all going then?

Lady Whiteadder
Not well. Let us discuss your inheritance.

Blackadder
Ah, yes. Good. Little drink first?

Lady Whiteadder stands and hits Blackadder.

Lady Whiteadder
Drink! Wicked child! Drink is urine from the last leper in Hell.

Blackadder
Oh, no: this is only water. This is a house of simple purity.

Lady Whiteadder sits. At which moment, Friar Frobisher crashes through the door and vomits into the fireplace.

Frobisher
Great booze-up, Edmund.

And he exits. A pause. A distinctly tricky pause.

Lady Whiteadder
Do you know that man?

Blackadder
No.

Lady Whiteadder
He called you 'Edmund'.

Edmund
'Know' him? Yes, I do.

Lady Whiteadder
Then can you explain what he meant by 'Great booze-up'?

Very long pause. Also tricky.

Blackadder
Yes, I can. My friend is a missionary and on his last visit abroad brought back with him the chief of a famous tribe. His name is Great Boo. He's been suffering from sleeping sickness and he's obviously just woken, because as you heard, Great Boo's up.

Percy
Well done, Edmund.

Blackadder
And I think I'd better just go visit him. Perce, over to you.

Blackadder rises and leaves. Percy claps.

Percy
Yes. How about some sort of game? How about a couple of frames of Shove, Piggy, Shove?

~

SCENE TEN: BALDRICK'S ROOM

The lads are still sitting on the floor. Blackadder enters.

Melchett
Blackadder, you challenged me to a drinking competition earlier today, and I haven't seen you touch a drop.

Blackadder
Nonsense.

Melchett
'Tis true. You twist and turn like a . . . twisty-turny thing. I say you are a weedy pigeon and you can call me Susan if it isn't so.

Blackadder crosses to the door.

Blackadder
All right, all right. Baldrick! Fetch my incredibly strong ale!

Frobisher
My God – not Dr McGlue's Amber Enema?

Blackadder
Pah! A drink for schoolgirls.

Partridge
Surely not Scrollops Lobster Scrumpy?

Baldrick has arrived with a jug of water and a glass.

Blackadder
Ha! No. It is Blackadder's Bowel Basher, a brew guaranteed to knock the backside off a concrete elephant, is it not, Baldrick?

Baldrick
(*Proudly*) No, it's water.

Melchett
What?!

Blackadder
Ha ha ha: but seriously, Baldrick – and presuming you wish to see another dawn . . .

Baldrick
(*A bit doubtful now*) You did call for your incredibly strong ale, my lord?

Blackadder
(*Pleased*) Yes! That's right.

Baldrick
That's a relief. I thought I'd made a mistake.

Baldrick pours water into a glass.

Piddle
My God, he's right! It is water.

Blackadder knees Baldrick.

Frobisher
Come on, lads, let's give him a real drink.

Frobisher hands Blackadder a flagon of ale. All eyes on Blackadder for a second.

Blackadder
Fine.

Frobisher
Hurray! Bums up!

Partridge
Wehey! 'Bums'. Sounds a bit like . . . 'bum', doesn't it?

Melchett
Drink, Blackadder. Drink!

Blackadder drinks.

All
Wehey!

SCENE ELEVEN: BLACKADDER'S LODGINGS

42 seconds later Lady Whiteadder is in the midst of smacking Percy. The door swings open to reveal Blackadder. He is wearing his Cardinal's hat and is looking very merry indeed.

Blackadder
Percy, I lost the bet.

Lady Whiteadder
Edmund, explain yourself.

Blackadder
I can't. Not just like that. I'm a complicated person, you see, Auntie. Sometimes I'm nice, sometimes I'm nasty. And sometimes, I just like to sing little songs like . . . (*singing*) . . . 'See the little goblin . . .'

Lady Whiteadder
I mean, explain why you are wearing a Cardinal's hat, why you are grinning inanely . . .

Blackadder kneels, revealing a large ostrich feather sticking up from his trousers.

. . . And why you have an ostrich feather sticking out of the seat of your breeches.

Blackadder
I'm wearing a Cardinal's hat, because I'm Cardinal Chunder. I have an ostrich feather up my bottom because Mr Ostrich put it there to keep in the little pixies. And I'm grinning inanely because I think I've just about succeeded in conning you and your daft husband out of a whopping great inheritance.

Lady Whiteadder
Is that right? May I remind you cursed creature . . .

She hits Percy as he is within reach.

. . . that your inheritance depends upon your not drinking and not gambling.

Blackadder
Oh, yes, damn. Percy, the devil farts in my face once more.

Lady Whiteadder
'Not mentioning farts' was also a condition.

Blackadder
Shove off, you old trout.

Lady Whiteadder
How dare you speak to my husband like that?! Nathaniel, we're leaving.

She starts to go, then turns to Percy.

And you . . .

Percy
Yes.

Lady Whiteadder
Has anyone ever told you you are a giggling imbecile?

Percy
Oh, yes.

Lady Whiteadder
Good.

She leaves, slamming the door.

Blackadder
Good riddance, you old witch!

There is a knock on the door.

Oops, she's forgotten her broomstick.

But it is Lord Whiteadder who enters.

Lord Whiteadder
Look, just wanted to say, thanks for a splendid evening. Yes, first rate all round. Particularly your jester.

He almost leaves but then has another thought.

And by the way – loved the turnip – very funny – exactly the same shape as a thingy.

~

SCENE TWELVE: BALDRICK'S ROOM

Things are as out of control as ever in Baldrick's room, when Lady Whiteadder
enters, having got the wrong door.

Lady Whiteadder
Good Lord!

Partridge
Well, look who it is!

Piddle
Who is it?

Partridge
Well, it's a boys' party, and she's a girl – so it must be the stripper! Wehey!

~

SCENE THIRTEEN: BACK IN BLACKADDER'S LODGINGS

Percy is trying to comfort Blackadder.

Percy
Oh no, don't get too depressed, Edmund. I mean, money isn't everything. Think of clouds and daisies, and the lovely smiles on little babies' faces.

Blackadder
Be quiet, Percy.

~

SCENE FOURTEEN: THE CORRIDOR

Meanwhile, Lady Whiteadder is trying to keep the door of Baldrick's room closed.

Lord Whiteadder politely opens what he takes to be the front door for her. It is, in fact, the cupboard. As she walks in, Queenie bursts out. At that moment, the boys emerge from the drinking den.

Partridge
Wehey! Another stripper!

Piddle
(*Seeing Lord Whiteadder*) And a . . . a male stripper!

Frobisher
Oh, yes, this is much more like it.

He takes off Queenie's coat and cowl.

There is a moment of shock as she is revealed in full regal costume.

Partridge
And – she's come dressed as the queen!

Piddle
Wehey! Sexy!

Queen
Do you know who I am?

Blackadder bursts out of his room with Percy behind.

Blackadder
Yes, I know who you are.

Piddle
Who?

They all look at him.

Blackadder
You're . . . (*singing*) 'Merlin, the Happy Pig'.

Queen
Wrong, I'm afraid. I am . . . the Queen of England.

She stands to her full height. They all kneel.

I may have the body of a weak and feeble woman, but I have the heart and stomach of a concrete elephant.

Partridge
Prove it!

Queenie grabs a huge flagon for herself and prepares to down it in one.

Queen
Certainly will. First I'm going to have a little drinky . . . and then I'm going to execute the whole bally lot of you.

She takes a huge gulp.

~

SCENE FIFTEEN: BLACKADDER'S LODGINGS

Dawn the next day. Everyone is sitting drunk in a heap around Queenie's feet.

Only Lady Whiteadder is missing.

Blackadder
See the little goblin,
See his little feet.
And his little nosey wose,
Isn't the goblin sweet?

All
Yes.

Blackadder
See the little gob . . .

Queen
Wait a minute! I'm sure there was something very important I had to do to all of you this morning.

All
Wehey!

Melchett
I remember something about 10,000 florins. Was it . . . ?

Lord Whiteadder
No, I think it was something about an inheritance.

Edmund
Look! Do you lot want to hear about this goblin, or not?

All
Yes!

Blackadder
Right, well perhaps this time I might be allowed to continue, and perhaps finish, with any luck.

Lady Whiteadder appears from underneath Queenie's skirt.

Lady Whiteadder
Luck – wehey! – geddit?!

All
Ahmm – no.

Lady Whiteadder
Oh, come on – 'luck' – sounds almost exactly like f . . .

The end of the most immoral episode.

THE BALLAD OF BLACKADDER THE BOOZER

Blackadder couldn't hold his beer,
The art of boozing he's not mastered.
And I, your merry balladeer,
Am also well and truly plastered.

Blackadder, Blackadder,
A bit like Robin Hood.
Blackadder, Blackadder,
But nothing like as good.

Blackadder, Blackadder,
I thought that he had died.
Blackadder, Blackadder,
The writers must have lied.

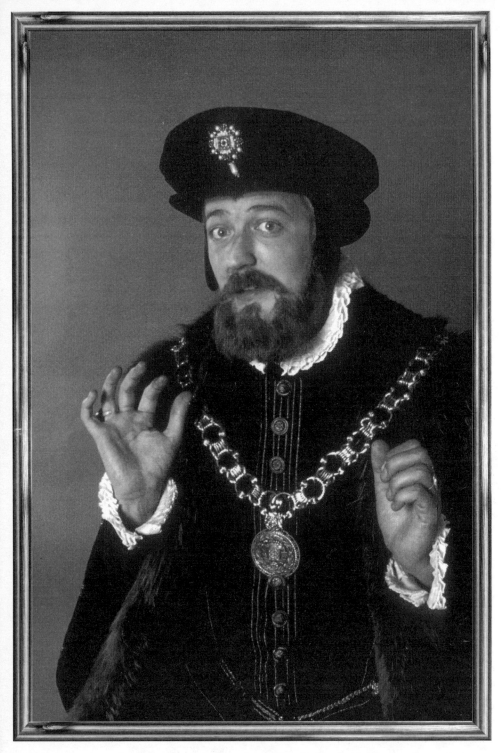

The queen's most trusted advisor and confidant, Lord Melchett, attempts to tiptoe out of the country on a dark and moonless night near Dover

Chains

SCENE ONE: QUEENIE'S CHAMBER

Blackadder is in a towering fury. He shouts at Melchett and Queenie.

Blackadder
Get out, get out, libidinous swine and take that whore slut painted strumpet with you! May you both rot in the filth of your own fornication!

Melchett and Queenie are amazed at his passion. There is a pause.

Queen
Mmmm. And what did you say to him?

Blackadder
(*Massively cool*) Say, madam? I said nothing. I simply pulled up my tights and jumped out of the privy window.

Queen
Oooo, Edmund, you are so naughty!

Blackadder
Well, I try, madam, and then ten minutes later when I've got my breath back, I try again.

Queenie laughs.

Melchett
And perhaps now we can turn to more important matters of state.

Queen
Must we?

Melchett
I fear so, ma'am. It is a very tragic case. My old tutor, Lord Forrest's son, has been kidnapped and he begs you to help him pay the ransom.

Queen
Edmund, what would you say?

Blackadder
(*Suddenly sincere*) Well, as you know, my lady, I have had experience of this dreadful situation. Only last year my aunt came to me to beg for help in the ransom of my Uncle Osric.

Melchett
So you know something of the dreadful pain involved.

Blackadder
Indeed I do, and can suggest no better answer than the one I gave to her.

Queen
Which was?

Blackadder
'Get stuffed.'

Melchett
Blackadder, you would jest over a young man's life?

Blackadder
For 'young man' read 'young idiot'. Look, anyone stupid enough to let some moustachioed dago come up to them in a corridor, say 'Excuse me, Meester' and hit them over the head with a big stick deserves everything they get. Toodle-oo.

Queenie giggles and Blackadder exits with a mighty swagger.

SCENE TWO: THE CORRIDOR OUTSIDE QUEENIE'S CHAMBER

Baldrick meets Blackadder coming out.

Baldrick
My lord.

Blackadder
Yes, Baldrick?

Baldrick
You were in good fooling this morning.

Blackadder
Thank you, Baldrick.

Baldrick
I heard quite an amusing story myself the other day.

Blackadder
Oh, good.

And he walks straight off and shuts the second set of doors between him and Baldrick. A German with a moustache speaks from the shadows. Another German guard is hiding, unseen.

First guard
Excuse me, Meister.

He indicates the other guard to him.

Blackadder
Yes, what is it?

First guard whispers in Blackadder's ear while second guard hits Blackadder on the back of his head.

I said, 'What is it?' not 'Hit me hard on the head with a . . .'

And Blackadder blacks out.

SCENE THREE: QUEENIE'S CHAMBER

Immediately afterwards.

Queen
You know, Melchy, I've completely changed my mind about that Forrest bloke. I mean, he's obviously very stupid, but we can't go round punishing people for that, can we?

Melchett
Certainly not, ma'am.

Queen
If we went around punishing people for being stupid, Nursie would have been in prison all her life.

Melchett
A very piquant observation, Majesty.

Melchett hands her the paper.

Queen
So, I will sign this ransom, but it must be the last, absolutely the last, final, full stop, never again, cross my heart and hope to die.

She scrawls on a piece of paper.

Melchett
Surely not 'hope to die', Majesty.

Queen
Oh, all right. I'll cross that out.

She takes the paper and scrawls on it again.

Here you are. Sorry about the smudge.

Melchett
Thank you, ma'am.

He exits with pomp.

SCENE FOUR: THE CORRIDOR OUTSIDE QUEENIE'S CHAMBER

First guard
Excuse me, Meister.

Melchett
Yes?

First guard indicates to Melchett that second guard wants to speak to him. Second guard whispers into Melchett's ear and first guard knocks Melchett out. Melchett falls to the floor.

SCENE FIVE: A DREADFUL DUNGEON

Blackadder comes round. He is tied to Melchett, back to back.

Blackadder
Oh, God, God, God! What on earth was I drinking last night? My head feels like there's a Frenchman living in it. Where am I?

A groan comes from nearby.

Oh, God. Who's that?

Melchett
'Tis I, Melchett.

Blackadder
Melchett. You ought to get this house of yours cleaned up, you know. It's a real mess.

Melchett
This is no time for jokes, Blackadder. We've been kidnapped.

Blackadder
Oh, God. How *incredibly* embarrassing.

Melchett
As private parts to the gods are we, they play with us for their sport.

The door flies open and an obvious torturer rushes in.

Blackadder
Oh, God. Who's that?

The torturer leans towards Melchett with a torture instrument.

Torturer
Ti prepara para interrogación y suplicio.

Blackadder
Now just wait a minute. If anyone's going to be spoken to round here it's going to be me, all right? Tell him, Melchett.

Melchett and Blackadder swivel round.

Melchett
Certainly. *Parlo con lui; no mi capo.*

Torturer
Bueno.

He turns to Edmund.

Ti prepara para interrogación y suplicio.

Blackadder and Melchett settle in their new position. Blackadder is now facing the torturer.

Blackadder
That's better. Now, what's he saying?

Melchett
He says he'd like a word with you.

Blackadder
Anything else?

Melchett
Yes. He says he would like to torture you as well.

SCENE SIX: THE DREADFUL DUNGEON

Blackadder is in a torturing device and the torturer is tightening the screws.

Blackadder

Right. Now, am I by any chance addressing a senior dignitary of the Spanish
Inquisition?

Torturer

Ti gustava mucho del Inquisición.

Blackadder

Good, because if I am, I wish to make it
quite clear that I am prepared to tell you
absolutely anything.

Torturer

No habla, puerco.

Blackadder

No speako Dago. I demand to see the
British Ambassador, understand?

Torturer

Silencio par comenzar!

Blackadder

Oh, for God's sake. How . . . can . . . you
. . . question . . . me . . . if . . . you . . .
don't . . . speak . . . English?

Torturer

(*Peeved*) No!

He gestures proudly to himself.

Yo pregunto las questiones.

Blackadder

All right, let's start with the basics.
English is a non-inflected Indo-European
language derived from . . .

~

**SCENE SEVEN: CORRIDOR AND
QUEENIE'S CHAMBER**

*Percy and Queenie are passing time play-
ing frisbee in the corridor. Queenie throws
it to Percy, who catches it.*

Percy

How's that?

Queen

(*Warning*) Percy. Who's queen?

Percy drops the frisbee.

Percy

Whoops. Butterfingers!

Queen

So, I win again.

Percy

Yes, well done, your Majesty.

They cross into the chamber.

Queen

And there's definitely been no news of
Edmund?

Percy

I fear not, ma'am.

Queen

Why, then he has vanished. Simply
vanished.

Percy

(*In a reverie of sorrow*) Like an old oak
table.

Queen

Vanished, Lord Percy, not varnished.

Percy

Forgive me, my lady, but my Uncle
Bertram's old oak table completely
vanished. 'Twas on the night of the great
Stepney fire, and on that same terrible
night his house and all his other things

completely vanished too. So did he, in fact. 'Twas a most perplexing mystery.

Queen
Lord Percy.

Percy
Yes?

Queen
It's up to you. Either you can shut up, or you can have your head cut off.

Percy thinks hard.

Percy
I'll shut up.

SCENE EIGHT: THE DREADFUL DUNGEON

They have clearly been having a communication problem for quite some time now. Blackadder is still in his box.

Torturer
Batardo.

Blackadder
Batardo . . . Barrister?

Torturer
Batardo . . .

Blackadder
Embarrassing.

The torturer jumps off the rostrum and mimes walking with a big pregnant belly. He then mimes cradling a baby in his arms before chucking it away . . . Basically it's turned into a game of charades.

You're embarrassing. I'm embarrassing. Erm, rogering! Pregnant? Baby . . . bathwater . . . sounds like . . . bastard! Ah. (*At last he's got it*) I'm a bastard.

Torturer
Si. Esterminado hijo, hijo.

Blackadder
Donkey.

Torturer
Padre y hijo.

Blackadder
Big bastard. Little bastard.

Torturer
Padre . . .

The torturer mimes panting.

Blackadder
Son. I'm a bastard son.

Torturer
Di perra.

Blackadder
I'm a bastard son. I'm a thirsty barking bastard.

Torturer
No, perra.

He barks.

Blackadder
Oh, dog, dog.

Torturer
No . . .

Mimes breasts.

Blackadder
Woman.

The torturer mimes woman and dog simultaneously.

No, woman dog . . . ah, bitch. I'm a bastard son of a bitch.

Torturer
¡Si! ¡Si!

He shakes Blackadder's hand, happy at their mutual success. A triumph for international communication.

Blackadder
In that case, you are a fornicating baboon.

Torturer
¿Que?

Blackadder
Oh, dear. You . . .

Torturer
Tu . . . o . . . you.

Blackadder
Fornicating . . . (*Begins to mime*) Yes, I can't really do it in this box.

Half an hour later. They're actually getting quite chummy now.

Torturer
Tuos testiculos.

Blackadder
Mmm, yes, my . . . yes, those.

Torturer
Sobre un fuego grande.

Blackadder
Over a large . . .

Torturer
Fuego, fuego . . .

He does a delicate little mime of burning his fingers.

Blackadder
Ah, fire, fire. Yes, so, let's recap: if I admit that I am in love with . . .

Torturer
¡No! ¡No!

He does a little somersault mime.

Blackadder
Sorry, head over heels in love with Satan and all his little wizards . . .

Torturer
Si.

Blackadder
Then you will remove my testicles with a blunt instrument . . .

Torturer
Una guadaña. ¡Guadaña!

Blackadder
. . . resembling some kind of gardening tool, but we can't quite get which . . . and roast them over a large fire.

Torturer
(*Exhausted*) *Si.*

Blackadder
Whereas if I don't admit that I'm in love with Satan and all his little wizards, then you will hold me upside-down in a vat of warm marmalade.

Torturer
Y.

Blackadder
And remove my testicles with a blunt instrument resembling some kind of gardening tool and roast them over a large fire. Oh, I see. Oh, in that case . . . I love Satan.

The torturer runs off and returns with a scythe.

Oh, it's a *scythe!*

The torturer raises the scythe and is about to put his testicular promise into action.

SCENE NINE: QUEENIE'S CHAMBER

*Queenie and Percy seem to be in the mid-
dle of a game of hide and seek. Baldrick
is lying on the dais, and Nursie is seated
on the stool. Queenie is just finishing looking behind the tapestry.*

Queen
Well, I don't know. I've looked everywhere.

Percy
(*Thinking hard*) Perhaps . . . they're not
hiding after all . . . Perhaps they've been
kidnapped!
Queenie paces.

Queen
Nonsense. As Edmund said, only real
idiots get kidnapped.

*This makes Percy very nervous: he jumps
and looks behind him.*

Percy
Do they?

~

SCENE TEN: THE DREADFUL
DUNGEON

*The scythe is still poised over the tortur-
er's head. He is about to do his duty, when
an imposing voice cries out:*

Ludwig
Stop!

*A whip curls round the torturer's raised
arm. He is pulled to the floor. He grovels
and cringes. A figure stands silhouetted in
the doorway, in darkness but exuding
power. The torturer is clearly terrified of
him.*

*The man is Prince Ludwig, he is German,
and he has a cool, arrogant manner: the
Blofeld of the sixteenth century.*

Forgive me, Herr Blackadder, I have been
neglecting my duties as a host. Please

accept my apologies.

*He'd like to think his English is perfect. It
isn't, there's something odd about how he
says 'apologies'.*

Blackadder
(*With utter cool, an English gentleman in
adversity*) I accept nothing from a man
who imprisons his guests in a commode.

Ludwig ignores the hint of unfriendliness.

Ludwig
I hope this scum . . .

*He lashes the whip – the torturer screams
and runs off.*

. . . has not . . . inconwenienced you.

*There it goes again. He says 'w' instead of
'v'.*

Blackadder
It takes more than a maniac trying to cut
off my goolies to inconwenience me.

Ludwig
Good. If he had inconwenienced you, I
was going to offer you his tongue.

Blackadder
Believe me, sir, if he had inconwenienced
me, you would not have a tongue with
which to make such an offer.

A tiny smile breaks on Ludwig's face.

Ludwig
Let me assure you, Herr Blackadder, if I
no longer had a tongue with which to make
such an offer, you would no longer have a
tongue with which to tell me that if I had
inconwenienced you, I would no longer
have a tongue with which to offer you his
tongue.

Blackadder
Well, enough of this banter. Who the hell
are you, sausage breath?

*Ludwig steps dramatically into the flick-
ering torchlight to reveal his hard, cruel
face.*

Ludwig
You do not remember me, then, Herr Blackadder?

Blackadder
I don't believe I've had the pleasure.

Ludwig
On the contrary, we have met many times, although you knew me by another name. Do you recall a mysterious black marketeer and smuggler called Otto with whom you used to dine and plot and play the biscuit game at the Old Pizzle in Dover?

Blackadder
My God!

Ludwig
Yes! I was the waitress!

Blackadder
I don't believe it! You! Big Sally!

Ludwig triumphantly puts on a West Country accent.

Ludwig
'Will you 'ave another piece of poi, moi lord?'

Blackadder
But I went to bed with you, didn't I?

Ludwig crosses to Blackadder.

Ludwig
For my country I am willing to make any sacrifice.

Blackadder
Yes, but I'm not. I must have been paralytic.

Ludwig
(*Smiling in triumph*) Indeed you were . . . Mr Floppy!

Blackadder
Yes, all right, very funny, now . . .

Ludwig
(*Back into his Big Sally voice*) 'Such a disappointment fur a girl!'

Blackadder
Yes, all right, you've had your little joke . . .

Ludwig
'It really doesn't matter. We'll try again in a few minutes. Here, have a look through these naughty parchments.'

Blackadder finally snaps.

Blackadder
Oh, well, we are proud of our comic serving-wench voice, aren't we? Just because we can say 'zur' instead of 'sir'. Essential at all social gatherings, the tedious little turd who keeps putting on amusing voices.

Ludwig
Be quiet!

Blackadder
What else have you got in your astoundingly inventive repertoire, I wonder? A brilliant drunk Glaswegian, no doubt! A hilarious black man. 'See you, Jimmy', 'Where am dat warty melon?' Fabulous! I can't wait to see your side-splitting poof and your funny little croaky one who isn't anyone in particular, but is *such* a scream! And most of all, I like the one you do all the time, the

fat-headed German chamber-pot standing in front of me!

Ludwig's pleasant demeanour starts to crack.

Ludwig
You know, you talk too much, Herr Blackadder. I'm thinking it's a case of werbal diarrhoea that you are having. I should perhaps tell you that I have given the qveen only a week to reply to my ransom demand. Unless she pays up, you die – horribly.

Blackadder
She will pay up. And then, in less than a week, *you* die – howwibly, howwibly.

Ludwig
You find yourself amusing, Blackadder.

Blackadder
I try not to fly in the face of public opinion.

Ludwig
You know, I think that in a week from now, you'll be less in the mood for being amusing.

Blackadder ·
At least when I *am* in the mood, I *can* be amusing.

Ludwig
Then choose your next witticism carefully, Herr Blackadder. It may be your last. Guards! Fetch his friend!

The two guards exit and bring in Melchett.

Melchett
Ow, ow, ow!

Ludwig
Ah, Lord Melchett, we meet again.

Melchett
Aaaah, no. I don't think we've had the pleasure.

Ludwig
You do not recognize me then?

Melchett
Nooo.

Ludwig
Let me refresh your memory. You remember when you were in Cornvall, when you were at the monastery, there was an old shepherd with whom you used to talk?

Melchett
Good Lord! Timpkins!

Ludwig faces Melchett.

Ludwig
Yes. I was one of his sheep.

Melchett is suddenly nervous.

Melchett
But . . . uhm . . . one of the sheep, you say? Not . . .

Ludwig
Yes!

Melchett
Flossie!

Ludwig
Yes!

Melchett
But . . . didn't we?

Ludwig
Yes, Lord Melchett! Baaaa!

Melchett
Oh, God.

This is interesting news for Blackadder.

Ludwig
But enough of such pleasant reminiscences. The guard has found an interesting document in your clothing.

He produces the scroll Queenie gave Melchett.

Melchett
(*Nervously*) Oh, I shouldn't pay much attention to that if I were you.

Ludwig opens it and reads it.

Ludwig
The qveen says she will only pay one ransom, and it is, 'the last, absolutely the last, final, full stop, never again, cross my heart and hope to be spanked until my bottom goes purple.' She has a difficult choice in front of her, has she not?

Blackadder
I think not. Bad luck, Melchers. Still – 'life' – overrated, I reckon.

Ludwig
Yes, gentlemen: if you'll excuse me, I have work to do. Evil plots don't just make themselves, you know.

And he exits, laughing.

SCENE ELEVEN: QUEENIE'S CHAMBER

Queenie is facing Nursie, who is seated on the stool. Percy reads to them both from a letter.

Percy
'Dear Qveen, I, evil Prince Ludwig the

Indestructible, have your two friends and you must choose between them. The ransom is one million kroner. Many, many a-poh-loh-ghies for the inconwenience.'

Queen
Golly! What a difficult choice!

Nursie
Not the first difficult choice you've ever had to make, my little tadpole.

Queen
No, that's true.

Nursie
In the old days, it was *all* difficult choices. Should you have Nursie milk, or moo-cow milk? And of course, it was always Nursie milk, but then, left breasty dumpling, or right breasty dumpling? And of course it was always both breasty dumplings; but then, which one first?

Queen
Shut up, Nursie. Oh dear, it's all very confusing. Lord Percy, play a while to calm my spirit.

Percy
Certainly, ma'am.

Percy hands his lute and the letter to Baldrick, and begins to play. That's . . . play . . .

Patacake, patacake, baker's man – ha ha – you're it! (*He tags Nursie*) Ring around a rosie . . . (*Dancing gaily*) All fall down.

Percy falls down.

SCENE TWELVE: THE DREADFUL DUNGEON

A week later. Blackadder and Melchett are manacled to the wall.

Melchett
What say you, Blackadder – I sing a song to keep our spirits up?

Blackadder
That all depends whether you want the slop bucket over your head or not.

Melchett
Well, perhaps some pleasant word game?

Blackadder
Yes, all right. Make a sentence out of the following words: 'Face – sodding – your – shut.'

This is too much for Melchett. He cracks – a hostage who can take no more.

Melchett
Oh for God's sake, man, we must do something to relieve our minds of the terrible fate that awaits us.

Blackadder
Awaits you, Melchy, not me. How's my beard looking?

Melchett
Oh, alas. Shall I never see England more. Her rolling hills. Her swooping swallows . . .

Blackadder
And her playful sheep.

At which moment there is a powerful slamming of doors, heralding an approach.

About time too.

And Ludwig enters, carrying a letter.

Ludwig
Gentlemen, the answer has arrived.

Blackadder
Well, thank God. I'm sick of this place. The conditions are just disgraceful. It's like a prison in here.

Ludwig
I will read it to you.

Blackadder
Typical master criminal. Loves the sound of his own voice.

Ludwig
After long and very careful deliberation,

the qveen has decided to expend the ransom money on . . .

~

SCENE THIRTEEN: QUEENIE'S CHAMBER

Close-up of Queenie thinking and finally putting pen to paper.

Queen
 . . . a big party. Just impossible to decide between my two faves so have decided to keep the cash, have a whizzy jolly and try to forget both of you. Hope you're not too miffed. Byeee.

~

SCENE FOURTEEN: THE DREADFUL DUNGEON

Blackadder
What?!

Ludwig
'Hope you're not too miffed. Byeee.' Well, as you can imagine, my friends, this makes me very unhappy.

Blackadder
(Very sarcastically) Oh, I am sorry.

Ludwig
But . . . if you gentlemen were to tell me a way to . . . let us say, gain access to your qveen, I might be able to . . . commute your deaths to a life sentence.

Blackadder
Are you suggesting we betray her?

Ludwig
Oh, yes.

A moment of great moral choice for Queenie's most faithful servant.

Blackadder
All right.

Melchett
Blackadder, what are you saying? What of

loyalty, honour, self-respect?

Blackadder
What of them?

Melchett
Nothing.

Ludwig crosses to them.

Ludwig
So you will both . . . play ball?

Blackadder and Melchett
Yup.

Ludwig
Ha ha ha – what joy – see how you collapse before me, you great and incorruptible English nobs. So proud of your great big stiff upper lips.

Blackadder
Gloating is a sign of insecurity, Ludwig. Stop it. Now, do you want to get to the queen or not?

Ludwig
Yes. I thought some kind of disguise. You know, I do a very good Mary, Qveen of Scots.

He turns and hunches his head below his shoulders, then speaks in a Scottish accent.

Hoots, mon, where's me heed?

~

SCENE FIFTEEN: QUEENIE'S CHAMBER

Queenie is seated on the throne. Baldrick is lying on the floor. Percy is wearing Melchett's hat.

Queen
What sort of party should it be?

Percy
Oh, fancy dress. I love fancy dress.

Queen
Nursie?

Nursie
I think it should be one of those ones where everybody comes with nothing on at all.

Queen
Shut up, then. I agree with you, Acting Lord Chamberlain. If we're really going to forget our woes, we need to have as much fun as possible, and what could be more fun than a party where people are dressed up as frogs and rabbits and nuns?

Nursie
And bits of wood.

Queen
You're not going to come as a bit of wood.

Nursie
Aren't I?

Queen
No.

Nursie
Oh. How about a pencil then, should I come as a pencil?

Queen
Don't be silly, Nursie, you always talk like this and always end up coming as the same thing.

Nursie
Do I?

Queen
You know you do. Everyone knows it.

She catches sight of Baldrick and addresses him.

Lassie? What does Nursie always come to fancy dress balls as?

Baldrick
I thought everyone knew.

Queen
Yes. Everyone, apparently, except Nursie. Tell her.

Baldrick
She always comes as a cow.

Nursie
(*Utterly thrilled*) Yes, that's right. A lovely,

lovely cow with great big lovely udders, swinging around going 'Mooooo, come to Nursie-cow, you lovely little heifers!' Oh, yes, what fun, I want to be a cow again, please!

Queen
Oh, shut up. Isn't Nursie stupid?

Percy
She certainly is, ma'am.

They both have a laugh at Nursie.

Queen
You see, we're having a good time already. We've completely forgotten about those chaps in prison, haven't we?

Percy chortles for a second and then thinks up a joke.

Percy
What chaps?

And they both chortle.

~

SCENE SIXTEEN: THE DREADFUL DUNGEON

Blackadder and Melchett are sitting in the gloom. The guards are heard outside.

Guards
Eins, zwei! Eins, zwei! Eins, zwei!

The door opens and Ludwig stands there, wearing a splendid travelling cloak.

Ludwig
My friends, I come to bid you farevell. These guards will ewentually die of old age: but their sons will, I'm sure, go on attending to your needs.

Blackadder
Thank you for your concern, but, in fact, we intend to escape.

Ludwig
With your information, gentlemen, I intend to bring down your qveen and country. The Master of Disguise will become the Master of the World.

Blackadder
Tell me, Ludwig, one thing before you go.

Ludwig
What?

Blackadder
Were you ever bullied at school?

Ludwig
(*Suddenly tense*) What do you mean?

Blackadder
Well, all this ranting and raving about power – there must be some reason for it.

Ludwig
Nonsense. No, at my school having dirty hair and spots was a sign of maturity!

Blackadder
I thought so. And I bet your mother made you wear shorts right up to your final year.

Ludwig
Shut up! Shut up! When I am King of England, no one will ever dare call me Shorty Greasy Spot Spot again!

He slams out of the room, with the guards.

Blackadder
Touched a nerve there, I think.

Melchett
But what good is it going to do if we are doomed to rot here until we die?

Blackadder
Nah! Don't worry. I've got a plan.

Melchett
Really?

Blackadder
Yes. Now that Ludwig's gone, we should have no trouble in overcoming the guards. Germans are sticklers for efficiency, and I've been watching their routine and selected the moment when they are at their most vulnerable. That is when we'll attack.

Melchett
Brilliant. How?

Blackadder
That is the most cunning bit.

SCENE SEVENTEEN: THE SAME DUNGEON

Later that same day. The guards are audible outside.

Guards
Eins zwei, eins zwei, eins zwei, eins zwei . . .

Blackadder
Right, this is it. Don't forget, when they're at their most vulnerable.

Guards
(Outside the door) Eins zwei, eins zwei. Halt. Jingle ze keys. (They jingle the keys) Open ze door. (They open the door) Greetings to ze prisoners. (They step forward and wave at Melchett and Blackadder) Guten Abend, Englander scum. March to ze table. (They march to the table) Eins zwei, eins zwei, eins zwei, eins zwei, eins zwei, eins zwei, halt. Food on ze table, eins zwei. (They put food on the table) Spit on ze food, eins zwei. (They spit on the food and Blackadder and Melchett duck) Insulting farewell gesture to ze prisoners, eins zwei, eins zwei! The two guards stand side by side, thrusting their pelvises forward in unison, their insulting gesture.

Blackadder
Now!

Blackadder and Melchett each punch a guard in the groin. The guards collapse, Blackadder shakes his hand and wrist in agony.

Trust me to get the hard one.

Blackadder and Melchett charge towards

the door. Melchett is halfway up the stairs when Blackadder pushes him to one side to get in front of him.

SCENE EIGHTEEN: QUEENIE'S CHAMBER

Percy is gaily clad, Baldrick has a pencil up each nostril, Nursie is in a rather wonderful cow costume, and Queenie is magnificently attired as Henry VIII.

Queen
Yo ho ho. Off with her head.

Percy
Ma'am, it is brilliant. Your father is born again.

Queen
Let's bally well hope not, or else I won't be queen anymore. Yours is pretty good too. What is it?

Percy
Nothing, ma'am. Just a mere trifle I threw together.

Queen
Mmm, doesn't look much like a trifle. Looks more like a fruit salad to me.

Percy
I see Nursie has really excelled herself.

Nursie
Moo.

Queen
Yes she has. I'm not sure about this, though. (*To Baldrick*) What are you meant to be?

Baldrick
A pencil case.

Queen
Oh, yes. It's just like parties I had when I was tiny. We had tea and cakes and venison and then a trip with a couple of little friends to the executions.

Percy
How sweet.

Queen
If I wanted any of my friends executed, that is. Oh, how I do wish Edmund could be here. He always loved parties and always always wore very, very tight tights.

Percy
Edmund who?

Enter Blackadder dramatically . . .

Blackadder
Edmund Blackadder.

He strides in grandly, whacks Percy and kneels before Queenie.

Majesty!

Queen
Edmund! But . . .

Blackadder rises.

Blackadder
Did you ever know me to miss a party!

Queenie is delighted, but then wrinkles her nose.

Queen
Oooh! But what about Lord Melchett?

Blackadder
Yes, unfortunately, he made it too.

And in comes Melchett, prostrating himself before Queenie.

Melchett
Rapture! Joy beyond measure! Bliss which cannot be counted on one's fingers!

Blackadder makes a tiny and subtle interjection.

Blackadder
Baaa.

Queen
Sorry, Edmund?

Blackadder
Nothing.

Queen
Yes. Unfortunately, apart from my nose getting a little prettier, nothing much has changed around here. Your animal still isn't housetrained. Your friend's still unemployed. And Nursie's one stick short of a bundle.

Nursie
Moo!

Blackadder
Ah, yes, thank you for reminding me.

He draws his sword and kills Nursie with a decisive thrust through the heart.

Queen
Nursie! You've killed Nursie!! That's *horrid*! Guards, guards! Take him away and execute him. He's killed Nursie!

At which moment, the real Nursie enters the room, dressed in a very bad and silly cow costume.

Nursie
Can anyone help me with my udders?

Queen
Nursie!

Nursie
Yes.

Blackadder
Yes! And may I introduce our erstwhile captor . . . Prince Ludwig the Indestructible.

He tears off the head of the cow costume to reveal the dying Ludwig.

Ludwig
Ah! Qveen Elizabeth. We meet again!

Queen
Err . . . I don't think so, actually.

Ludwig
Yes! Remember when you were young, and your father used to take you riding on a magnificent grey pony that you used to kiss and fondle in the stable yard?

Queen
(*Embarrassed*) Yes, yes.

Ludwig
I was the tall and attractive German stable lad who held him.

Queen
No!

Ludwig
Yes!

Queen
You?! Shorty Greasy Spot Spot?

Ludwig
No, no, no! You will regret the day you ever mocked my complexion. I will return and wreak my rewenge!

He rushes into the corridor, making a break for freedom.

Blackadder
No, you won't. You will die and be buried.

Blackadder fells him with a well-aimed arrow. All cheer.

Blackadder
Strange man.

Queen
But how did you know it was him?

Blackadder
This was the information with which we bought our lives. We told him that if the queen was having a party, then Nursie always goes as a cow. From that moment, he was doomed. All we had to do was escape, return and kill the cow.

Queen
But how could you be sure it wasn't Nursie?

Blackadder
Because, Lady, Ludwig was a master of disguise, whereas Nursie is a sad, insane old woman with an udder fixation. All I had to do was kill the one that looked like the cow. That was the mistake I knew that Ludwig would make. His disguise was too good.

Queen
Gosh, Edmund, how brilliant – welcome home.

Blackadder
Well, I must say, ma'am, it is good to be back.

Percy crosses to Blackadder.

Percy
Welcome, Edmund. Did you . . . miss me?

Blackadder
I certainly did. Many was the time, Percy, I said to myself, I wish Percy was here . . .

Percy hugs Blackadder.

. . . being tortured instead of me.

Percy
How we have missed your wit!

Baldrick
Did you miss me, my lord?

Blackadder
Ahm . . . Baldrick, isn't it?

Baldrick
That's right.

Blackadder
No, not really.

Queen
And me, did you miss me, Edmund?

Blackadder
Madam, life without you was like . . . a broken pencil.

Queen
Explain.

Blackadder
Pointless.

THE BALLAD OF BLACKADDER THE BOLD

Beware, all ye who lust for fame!
The path of life is most uncertain.
Prince Ludwig thought he'd won the game
But now, the Kraut's gone for a Burton.

Blackadder, Blackadder,
He beat the Hun by luck.
Blackadder, Blackadder,
He's smarter than a duck.

Lord Melchett, Lord Melchett,
Intelligent and deep.
Lord Melchett, Lord Melchett,
A shame about the sheep!

Epilogue

SCENE NINETEEN: QUEENIE'S CHAMBER

Later that day. The dead bodies of Blackadder, Percy, Queenie, Nursie, Baldrick and Melchett are lying on the floor. Yet Queenie also stands proudly on the dais.

Queen
Ha! Ha! Ha! Now this is a disguise I'm *really* going to enjoy. If I can *just* get the voice right.

And that's how the Germans first came to rule the United Kingdom.

Lord Blackadder, Lord Percy and Lord Unows

The Blackadder Chronicles

PART THREE:
FROM GOOD QUEEN BESS TO MAD KING GEORGE

During the next 300 years, the Blackadders continued their ruthless, cruel and uncompromising attempt to become the most hated family in Europe. In this, however, they were no match for the Stuarts, the first of whom arrived to rule England on the death of Queen Elizabeth.

In 1603, James I had been King of Scotland for thirty-six years. He was a fat, misshapen, ugly, knock-kneed, shambling beast of a man who was also extremely vain and conceited.* His arrival was welcomed by the people with open sewers, and almost at once he earned the prized title of 'The Wisest Fool in Christendom' in the All England Open Fools Championship of 1604. Baldrick came 3178th.

Though fireworks had been invented by the Chinese thousands of years before, nobody had been able to think of an excuse to use them in Europe. Now came their big chance. Led by Guy Fawkes, as many people as possible crammed into the cellars under the Houses of Parliament in an attempt to blow up the king. The attempt failed, but the pleasure brought on by countless bonfire nights since, with cocoa and baked potatoes and burnt sausages and 'oohs' and 'aahs' was certainly worth the trouble.

James's heir, Charles I, was a tiny, little, beardy-weirdy, girly-haired squit of a man who made a complete hash of his life. A fanatical believer in the Divine Right of Kings, he insisted that no one sit down in his presence. The whole court had to eat, go to the toilet and play whist whilst standing up. The mess had to be seen to be believed, and finally one of the cleaners, Oliver Cromwell, had had enough.

For seven long years, Civil War raged over England, as the New Model Army, led by Oliver Cromwell and General Thomas Airfix, mercilessly pursued poor Charles I. Father fought against father, brother skirmished with brother, grand-mother hurled small lavender bags at grandmother. Lord Blackadder, a passion-ate Monarchist, got himself in a rather tricky position when the king asked if he could stay in one of his trees for a week or two – and in a rather trickier position when he found himself appointed Chief Executioner with special responsibility for cutting off his king and master's head. However, he made the best of a bad job, sliced it off nice and cleanly and then put on a rather fetching blond wig and started supporting Oliver Cromwell enthusiastically, until he died and Blackadder changed sides once again.

The Restoration of the monarchy in 1660 was greeted with wild enthusiasm. For years everything had been banned as against God's Will. Now, with Charles II, 'Merrie' England returned with a vengeance: morris-dancing, cock-fighting, train-spotting, bear-baiting, coconut-shies, tombola, Bowl-for-a-Pig and rickety

---

* The mirror, a by-product of space technology developed as part of Galileo's telescope programme, did not reach Scotland until 1717.

tables strewn with second-hand books* – all the things that make life worthwhile in the rainiest country on earth. No sooner had this happened than a third of the country died horribly of the plague, and London was burned to the ground. Cromwell was proved right after all: God takes an extremely dim view of village fetes. As a popular Puritan hymn of the time had it:

TUNE: None**

The Lord hateth raffles and cake stalls,

Yea, he approveth not of bric-a-brac,

Lo! All they that throweth wooden hoops over vermouth bottles

Shall die horribly of ye pestilence.

Things then just went from bad to worse, and Charles II's successor, James II, was so useless that the English asked the Dutch to invade them and so William III and Mary showed up, followed by Queen Anne.

Queen Anne was the first and only person in the history of the human race to care in any meaningful way about chair legs. She commissioned hundreds of thousands of chairs and very, very pretty they are too. If anyone tries to tell you that the British monarchy (present company excepted) is one long, sorry parade of psychopaths, perverts, thieves and murderers, this nice-chair thing can be a pretty withering counter-argument.

The Blackadder of this period – the Duke of Blackadder – was perhaps one of the most distinguished of his whole line. He was a great general, and the queen promised him that wherever he won his first battle he would get a palace named after it as a reward. Some historians believe this could be the reason he lost the Battle of Shithole in 1703.

George I, George II and George III all now ascended the throne in turn wearing ever more enormous powdery wigs. At that time, everyone in England was desperate to get rid of the colonies (which by now were crawling with Americans) so the Georges were absolutely the best people to have in charge. Even in those days, the Germans lost virtually everything except football.

We rejoin our dastardly dynasty with the Blackadders having fallen on rather hard times. Where once they had been lords and dukes, the latest of their number was scraping a living as butler to the Prince Regent, the stupidest man in England. Well, stupidest equal. Baldrick's always hard to beat.

---

* The first second-hand book appeared in February 1664 (Barbara Cartland's novelette *Come Soon Strange Horseman*, published November 1663).
** Both music and rhyme were considered papist atrocities.

Blackadder the Third

Mr Curtis and Mr Elton's
much admir'd Comedy

Dish and Dishonesty

The rotten borough of Dunny-on-the-Wold (three cows, a dachshund named Colin and a small hen in its late forties) elects a whelk-brained MP with a distinctly turnippy aroma.

Ink and Incapability

After Baldrick incinerates Dr Johnson's new dictionary, Edmund's plan to rewrite it over the weekend proves to be like fitting wheels to a tomato – time-consuming and completely unnecessary.

Nob and Nobility

At Mrs Miggins's Coffee Shoppe, huge suspicious sausages are all the rage and French aristocrats are all the rouge in this nail-painting tale of revolutionary derring-do and lace hankies.

Sense and Senility

The prince's palace crawls with actors and anarchists and only one man can eliminate them – that renowned vermin-expert Mr Hopelessly-Drivelo-Can't-Write-For-Toffee-Crappy-Butler-Weed.

Amy and Amiability

In a last-ditch attempt to secure a wealthy (if insane) bride for the Prince Regent, Blackadder accidentally plumps for popular highwayman and squirrel-murderer 'The Shadow'.

Duel and Duality

To save his master's life and thus acquire his huge collection of French pornography, Blackadder enlists the prince's jacket, the Duke of Wellington's cigarillo case and a crazed bloater salesman.

The Cast

Performed with appropriate Scenery, Dresses, etc. by

Edmund Blackadder, butler to the Prince...........................Mr Rowan Atkinson

Baldrick, a dogsbody ....Mr Tony Robinson

Prince George, the Prince Regent, their master ....Mr Hugh Laurie

Mrs Miggins, a coffee shoppekeeper ....Mifs Helen Atkinson-Wood

Mr Vincent Hanna, his own great-great-great-grandfather ..Mr Vincent Hanna

Sir Talbot Buxomly, a Member of Parliament ....Mr Denis Lill

Pitt the Younger, the Prime Minister ....Mr Simon Osborne

Pitt the Even Younger, a tiny Whig ....Master Dominic Martelli

Ivor Biggun, a candidate ....Mr Geoff McGivern

Dr Samuel Johnson, noted for his fat dictionary ....Mr Robbie Coltrane

Byron, a romantic junkie poet......................................Mr Steve Steen

Shelley, a romantic junkie poet ....Mr Lee Cornes

Coleridge, a romantic junkie poet ....Mr Jim Sweeney

Lord Topper, a fop...Mr Tim McInnerny

Lord Smedley, a fop ....Mr Nigel Planer

Ambassador, a fearsome revolutionary ....Mr Chris Barrie

Keanrick, a thespian...Mr Hugh Paddick

Mossop, a thespian ....Mr Kenneth Connor

Anarchist...Mr Ben Elton

Amy Hardwood, the elusive Shadow ....Mifs Miranda Richardson

Mr Hardwood, her father...Mr Warren Clarke

Sally Cheapside, a young lady of doubtful virtue ....Mifs Barbara Horne

The Duke of Cheapside ....Mr Roger Avon

The Duke of Wellington, a famous soldier........................Mr Stephen Fry

King George III, a mad Monarch ....Mr Gertan Klauber

Dish and Dishonesty

SCENE ONE: THE KITCHEN

The kitchen in the basement of the home of George, Prince Regent. As the prince's chambers are glorious and drenched in sun, so are these dingy and caked in dirt. A fit home for Baldrick – a squalid necessity for Blackadder, the butler. Baldrick is cleaning Blackadder's shoes. Mrs Miggins has delivered some groceries.

Blackadder
Well, Mrs Miggins, at last we can return to sanity – the hustings are over, the bunting is down, the mad hysteria is at an end. After the chaos of a general election, we can return to normal.

Mrs Miggins
Has there been a general election then, Mr Blackadder?

Blackadder
Indeed there has, Mrs Miggins.

Mrs Miggins
Well, I never heard about it.

Blackadder
Of course you didn't. You're not eligible to vote.

Mrs Miggins
Why not?

Blackadder
Because virtually no one is – women, peasants, chimpanzees, lunatics, lords.

Baldrick
No, that's not true. Lord Nelson's got a vote.

Blackadder
He's got a *boat*, Baldrick. Marvellous thing democracy. Look at Manchester – population 60,000, electoral roll, three.

Mrs Miggins
Well, I may have a brain the size of a sultana . . .

Blackadder
Correct.

Mrs Miggins
But it hardly seems fair to me.

Edmund Blackadder, Esq., Gentleman's Gentleman
and Complete Arse's Butler

Blackadder
Of course it's not fair. And a good thing too. Give the likes of Baldrick the vote and we'll be back to cavorting Druids, death by stoning and dung for dinner.

Baldrick
Oh, I'm having dung for dinner tonight.

Mrs Miggins
So who are they electing when they have these elections?

Blackadder
Oh . . . the same old shower. Fat Tory landowners who get made MPs when they reach a certain weight. Raving revolutionaries who think that just because they do a day's work that somehow gives them the right to get paid. So basically it's a nice old mess. Toffs at the top, plebs at the bottom and me in the middle making a fat pile of cash out of both of them.

Mrs Miggins
You better watch out, Mr Blackadder. Things are bound to change.

Blackadder
Not while Pitt the Elder's Prime Minister. He's about as effective as a cat flap in an elephant house. And as long as his feet are warm and he gets a nice cup of milky tea in the sun before his morning nap, he doesn't bother anyone till his potty needs emptying.

SCENE TWO: THE HOUSE OF COMMONS

Three fat men are sitting against a panelled wall.

Mr Speaker
Honourable Members of the House of Commons. I call upon the new Prime Minister of Great Britain and her empires, Mr William Pitt. The Younger.

A sprightly but very suave fifteen-year-old schoolboy stands up from behind the fat

men. It is Pitt the Younger.

Pitt
Mr Speaker and Members of the House, I shall be brief as I have rather unfortunately become Prime Minister right in the middle of my exams.

Mixture of cheers and boos.

I look forward to fulfilling my duty in a manner of which Nanny would be proud. I shall introduce legislation to utterly destroy three enemies of the state. The first is that evil dictator, Napoleon Bonaparte.

Hum of approval.

The second is my old geography master, Banana-breath Scrigshanks.

Another hum.

But, most of all sirs, I intend to pursue that utter slob, the Prince of Wales.

All
Here, here!

Pitt
Why, this year alone he has spent £15,000 on banqueting.

All
Boo!

Pitt
Twenty thousand pounds on perfume.

All
Poo!

Pitt
And, most astonishingly of all, an astonishing £59,000 on socks.

All
Shame!

Pitt
Therefore my three main policy priorities are: one, war with France. Two, tougher sentences for geography teachers. Three, a right royal kick up the prince's backside.

All
Hurray!

Pitt
I now call upon the Leader of the
Opposition to test me on my Latin vocab.

SCENE THREE: PRINCE GEORGE'S CHAMBERS

Prince George is dressing. Blackadder enters.

Blackadder
Sir, if I may make so bold, a major crisis has arisen in your affairs.

Prince George
Yes, I know Blackadder. I have been pondering it all morning.

Blackadder
You have, sir?

Prince George
Yes, Blackadder. Socks. Run out again. Why is it that no matter how many millions of pairs of socks I buy, I never seem to have any?

Blackadder
Sir, with your forgiveness, there is another, even weightier problem.

Prince George
They just disappear. Honestly, you'd think someone was coming in here stealing the damn things and selling them off.

Blackadder laughs calmly. For the first

time in his life, the prince is actually right about something.

Blackadder
Impossible, sir. Only you and I have access to your socks.

Prince George
Yes, yes, you're right. Still, for me, socks are like sex. Tons of it about but I never seem to get any.

Blackadder
Sir, if I may return to this very urgent matter. I read fearful news in this morning's paper.

Prince George
Oh, no! Not another little cat caught up in a tree?

Blackadder
No sir – there is a vote afoot in the new parliament to strike you from the civil list.

Prince George
Yes, yes, but what are they going to do about my socks?

Blackadder
Sir, if this bill goes through, you won't have any socks.

Prince George
Well, I haven't got any socks at the moment.

Blackadder
Or any trousers, shirts, waistcoats, or pantaloons. They're going to bankrupt you.

Prince George
But they can't do that – the public love me. Why, only the other day I was out in the street, and they sang 'We hail Prince George! We hail Prince George!'

Blackadder
'We hate Prince George', sire. 'We *hate* Prince George'.

Prince George
Was it?

Blackadder
I fear so, sir. However, all is not lost. Fortunately the numbers in the Commons are exactly equal and if we can find one more MP to support us, you're safe.

Prince George
Hurrah! Any ideas?

Blackadder
Yes, sir. There is one man who might just be the ace up our sleeve. A rather crusty loudmouthed ace named Sir Talbot Buxomly.

Prince George
Never heard of him.

Blackadder
That's hardly surprising sir. Sir Talbot has the worst attendance record of any Member of Parliament. On the one occasion he *did* enter the House of Commons, he passed water in the Great Hall and then passed out in the Speaker's Chair. But if we can get him to support us, we're safe.

Prince George
What's he like?

Blackadder
Well, according to *Who's Who*, his interests include flogging servants, shooting poor people and the extension of slavery to anyone who hasn't got a knighthood.

Prince George
Excellent. Sensible policies for a happier Britain.

Blackadder
However, if we are going to get him to support us, he will need some sort of incentive.

Prince George
Hmmm. Anything in mind?

Blackadder
Yes, sir – you could appoint him a High Court Judge.

Prince George
Is he qualified?

Blackadder
He's a violent, bigoted, mindless old fool.

Prince George
Sounds a bit overqualified. Well, get him here at once!

Blackadder
Certainly, sir. I shall return before you can say 'antidisestablishmentarianism'.

Prince George
Well, I wouldn't be too sure. 'Antidisist' . . . 'antidesi' . . . 'antidisestis' . . .

Blackadder leaves.

~

SCENE FOUR: PRINCE GEORGE'S CHAMBERS

Two days later.

Prince George
'Antidistinctly' . . . 'minty' . . . 'monetarism' . . .

Blackadder
Your Highness, Sir Talbot Buxomly, MP.

Sir Talbot Buxomly walks through the door. He is very red-cheeked and very over-fed and he wears red beagling gear.

Prince George
Ah, Buxomly – roaringly splendid to have you here – how are you, sir?

Talbot
Heartily well, your Highness. I dined hugely off a servant before coming to town.

Prince George
(*Nervous*) Uhm . . . you eat your servants?

Talbot
No, sir – I eat off them. Why should I spend good money on tables when I have men standing idle?

Prince George
Why indeed? Now you have probably heard of Mr Pitt's intentions . . .

Talbot
(*Furious*) Young scallywag . . .

Prince George
Ah, so you don't approve of his plans to abolish me then?

Talbot
I do not sir! Damn his eyes! Damn his britches! Damn his duck pond!

Prince George
Hurrah for that!

Blackadder is pleased too.

Talbot
I mind not a jot if you are the son of a certified sauerkraut-sucking loon.

Prince George
Thank you, sir.

Talbot
It minds not me that you dress like a mad parrot and talk like a plate of beans negotiating their way out of a cow's digestive system . . .

Prince George
Good on you, sir.

Talbot
It is no skin off my rosy nose that there are bits of lemon peel floating down the Thames who would make better regents than you . . .

Prince George
Well, bravo. (*Oblivious to all insults*)

Talbot
The fact is, you *are* the Regent. Appointed by God. And I will stick by you for ever,

though infirmity lay me waste and ill-health curse my every waking moment.

He sits down firmly on a chair.

Prince George
Good on you, sir – and don't talk to me about infirmity. Why, sir, you are the hardy stock that is the core of Britain's greatness. You have the physique of a demi-god, purple of cheek and plump of fetlock. The shapely ankle and the well-filled trouser that tells of a human body in perfect working order.

Blackadder
(*Who is feeling Sir Talbot's pulse*) He's dead, sir.

Prince George
Dead?

Blackadder
Yes, your Highness.

Prince George
What bad luck – we were rather getting on.

Blackadder
We must move at once.

Prince George
In which direction?

Blackadder
As you know, your Highness, Sir Talbot represented the constituency of Dunny-on-the-Wold. And by an extraordinary stroke of luck it is a rotten borough.

Prince George
Really! Is it? Well, well. Lucky, lucky us. Yippee. Lucky, lucky, lucky, lucky. Lucky-

lucky. Lucky. Luck-a-doodle-dandy-dingle. Luck lurrck. Lurrrck. Cluck, cluck, cluck. Lurrrrrck-cluck-cluck-cluck.

Blackadder
You don't know what a rotten borough is, do you, sir?

Prince George
No.

Blackadder
So what was the chicken impression in aid of?

Prince George
Well, I didn't want to hurt your feelings. So, what is a robber button?

Blackadder
Rotten borough.

Prince George
Well, quite.

Blackadder
A rotten borough, sir, is a constituency where the owner of the land corruptly controls both the voters and the MP.

Prince George
Good. Yes. And a robber button is . . . ?

Blackadder
Can we leave that for a moment?

Prince George
Right. Yes.

Blackadder
Dunny-on-the-Wold is a tuppenny-ha'penny place. Half an acre of sodden marshland in the Suffolk fens, with an empty town hall in it. Population – three rather mangy cows, a dachshund named Colin, and a small hen in its late forties.

Prince George
No people at all, apart from Colin?

Blackadder
Colin is a dog, sir.

Prince George
Oh, yes.

Blackadder
Only one actual person lives there. He is the voter.

Prince George
Well right, so what's the plan?

Blackadder
We must buy Dunny-on-the-Wold at once, and thus control the voter. I shall need a thousand pounds.

Prince George
A thousand pounds? I thought you said it was a tuppenny-ha'penny place?

Blackadder
Yes, sir. The land will cost tuppence ha'penny. But there are many other factors to be considered. Stamp duty, window tax, swamp insurance. Hen food, dog biscuits, cow ointment. The expenses are endless.

Prince George
Fine, the money's in my desk.

Blackadder
No, sir, it's in my wallet.

Prince George
Splendid, no time to lose, eh?

Blackadder
My own thoughts precisely, sir. The only question is who to choose as MP.

Prince George
Ah – tricky.

Blackadder
What we need is an utter unknown, yet someone over whom we have complete power. A man with no mind, with no ideas of his own. One might almost say, a man with no brain.

He rings the bell.

Prince George
Any thoughts?

Blackadder
Yes, your Highness.

Enter Baldrick.

Baldrick
You rang, sir?

Blackadder
Meet the new Member of Parliament for Dunny-on-the-Wold.

Prince George
But he's an absolute arsehead!

Blackadder
Precisely, sir. Our slogan shall be 'A rotten candidate for a rotten borough'. Baldrick, I want you to go back to your kitchen sink you see and prepare for government.

~

SCENE FIVE: THE KITCHEN
Baldrick and Blackadder at the table.

Blackadder
Right now, all you have to do is fill in this MP application form. Name?

Baldrick
Baldrick.

Blackadder
First name?

Baldrick
Not sure.

Blackadder
You must have some idea.

Baldrick
Well it might be Sod Off.

Blackadder
What?

Baldrick
When I used to play in the gutter I used to say to the other snipes 'Hello, my name's Baldrick' and they used to say 'Yes, we know. Sod off, Baldrick.'

Blackadder
Right. Mr S. Baldrick. Now, distinguishing features? (*He thinks it through*) None.

Baldrick
Well, I've got this big growth in the middle

of my face here . . .

Blackadder
That's your nose, Baldrick. 'Any history of insanity in family?' Hmm . . . tell you what, I'll cross out the 'in' . . . (*Reads*) 'Any history of sanity in the family?' . . . (*Writes*) 'None whatsoever'. Now then, 'Criminal record?'

Baldrick
(*Proudly*) Absolutely not.

Blackadder
Baldrick, you're going to be an MP, for God's sake. I'll put 'fraud, and sexual deviancy' . . . and finally, 'Minimum bribe level' . . .

Baldrick
One turnip. Oh hang on, I don't want to price myself out of the market.

Blackadder
Baldrick, I've always been meaning to ask. Do you have any ambitions in life apart from the acquisition of turnips?

Baldrick
No.

Blackadder
So what would you do if I gave you a thousand pounds?

Baldrick
Oooh. I'd get a little turnip of my own.

Blackadder
And what would you do if I gave you a million pounds?

Baldrick
Oh well, that's different. I'd get a great big turnip in the country.

Violent knocking on the door.

Blackadder
Oh, God. I'll get that. Just sign here.

He holds out the form to Baldrick, who puts a cross on Blackadder's hand.

Blackadder sighs and stamps the paper with his hand.

~

SCENE SIX: PRINCE GEORGE'S CHAMBERS

The Prince is loitering, when Blackadder enters with Pitt.

Blackadder
Your Highness. Pitt the Younger.

Prince George
Why, hullo there, young shaver me lad. I say, here's fun, I've a shiny sixpence here for the clever fellow who can tell me which hand it's in, ha, ha!

He holds out his hands. Pitt the Younger stares impassively at him.

Ah. School, school. Half hols, is it? Bet you can't wait to get your bat in your hand and give those balls a good walloping.

Blackadder
Mr Pitt is the Prime Minister, sir.

Prince George
Go on! Is he? What, young snotty here?

Pitt
I'd rather have a runny nose than a runny brain.

Prince George
Eh?

Blackadder
Uhm, excuse me, Prime Minister, we do have some lovely jelly in the pantry. I don't know if you'd be interested?

Pitt
Don't patronize me, you lower-middle-class yobbo! What flavour is it?

Blackadder
Blackcurrant.

Pitt
Eeeuughhh!

Prince George
I say, Blackadder, are you sure this is the PM? He seems like a bit of an oily tick to me. When I was at school, we used to line up four or five of his sort, tell 'em to bend over and use them as a toast rack.

Pitt
It doesn't surprise me, sir. I know your sort. Once it was I who stood in the big cold school room, a hot crumpet burning my cheeks with shame. Since that day I have been busy every hour God sent working to become Prime Minister and fight sloth and privilege wherever I find it.

Blackadder
I trust you weren't too busy to remove the crumpet.

Pitt
You will regret this, gentlemen. You think you can thwart my plans to bankrupt the prince by fixing the Dunny-on-the-Wold by-election. But you will be thrashed. I intend to put up my own brother as a candidate against you.

Blackadder
And which Pitt would this be? Pitt the Toddler? Pitt the Embryo? Pitt the Glint in the Milkman's Eye?

Pitt
Ha, sirs. As I said to Chancellor Metternich at the Congress of Strasburg, 'Poo to you with nobs on!' We shall meet, sirs, on the hustings.

He exits with bravado.

Prince George
I say, Blackadder, what a ghastly squit! He's not going to win, is he?

Blackadder
No sir, because, firstly, we shall fight this campaign on issues and not personalities. Secondly, we will be the only fresh thing on the menu. And thirdly, of course, we'll cheat.

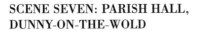

SCENE SEVEN: PARISH HALL, DUNNY-ON-THE-WOLD

It is election night. The small hall has been done up with a few flags and things. A tiny stage is at the end with chairs.

Mr Vincent Hanna, the Town Crier, is reporting on events.

Hanna
Good evening and welcome to the Dunny-on-the-Wold by-election. The first thing I must tell you is that the turnout has been very good. As a matter of fact, the voter turned out before breakfast. And I can now bring you the result of our exclusive exit poll which produced a 100 per cent result for (*rustles papers*) . . . 'Mind your own business, you nosy bastard'.

A journalist outside calls up.

Journalist
Mr Hanna, are you going to talk to any of the candidates?

Hanna
I certainly am. And I can see Prince George now, who is leader of what has come to be known as the Adder Party. Prince George, who has been described in his party news-sheet as a great moral and spiritual leader of the nation, but is described by almost everyone else as a fat, flatulent git. Prince George, hullo.

Prince George appears next to Hanna holding a dachshund.

Prince George
Good evening.

Hanna
And good evening, Colin. Tell me, how do you see your prospects in this election?

Prince George
Well, first – I'd like a word about the disgraceful circumstances in which this election arose. We paid for this seat – I think it's a damn liberty that we have to stand for it as well. And another thing, why is it that no matter how many pairs of socks a man buys, he never seems to have enough?

Hanna
Well, fighting words from the Prince Regent. (*Prince George leaves, satisfied at a job well done*) And now, let's have a word with the Adder Party candidate, Mr S. Baldrick, who so far has not commented on his policies in this campaign. But with him is his election agent, Mr E. Blackadder.

Baldrick appears with a turnip in his mouth. Blackadder is next to him.

Blackadder
We in the Adder Party are determined to fight this election on issues, not personality.

Hanna
Why is that?

Blackadder
Because our candidate doesn't have a personality.

Hanna
Well, he hasn't said much about the issues either.

Blackadder
He's got something wrong with his throat.

Hanna
Well, perhaps he could answer one question at least. What does the 'S' in his name stand for?

Blackadder
Sod off.

Hanna
Fair enough – none of my business really. And now it's time for a result. The tension is very high here. Mr Blackadder assures me that this will be the first honest vote ever in a rotten borough and I think we all hope for a result which reflects the real needs of the constituency. And behind me –

yes – I think I can see the acting returning officer coming to the front of the platform.

Baldrick is on the platform with Prince George, Pitt the Younger, Pitt the Even Younger with his mother Mrs Pitt, an angry-looking boringly dressed man and a fellow in very silly clothes – Ivor Biggun. And Blackadder.

Blackadder
As acting returning officer for Dunny-on-the-Wold . . .

Hanna comments on the proceedings with quiet discretion.

Hanna
The acting returning officer of course, Mr E. Blackadder, and we're all very grateful that he's stepped in at the last minute when the previous returning officer accidentally brutally stabbed himself in the stomach while shaving.

Blackadder
I now announce the number of votes cast as follows. Brigadier General Horace Balsam . . .

Hanna
Keep Royalty White, Rat Catching and Safe Sewage Residents' Party.

Blackadder
No votes.

The angry-looking man stomps off.

Ivor 'Jest ye not madam' Biggun . . .

Hanna
Standing at the Back Dressed Stupidly and Looking Stupid Party . . .

Blackadder
No votes.

Silly-dressed man blows a kazoo and laughs. No one else does.

Sad. Pitt the Even Younger.

Hanna
Whig.

Blackadder
No votes.

Hanna
Oh, there's a shock!!

Blackadder
Mr S. Baldrick.

Hanna
Adder Party.

Blackadder
16,472.

A cheer.

Hanna
And there we have it – victory for the Adder Party, a sensational swing against the Whigs. I'll just try and get a final word with some of the candidates as they come up from the stage. Master William Pitt the Even Younger, are you disappointed?

Pitt the Even Younger is eight years old.

Pitt the Even Younger
Yes, I'm horrified. I smeared my opponent, bribed the press to be on my side, and threatened to torture the electorate if we lost. I fail to see what more a decent politician could have done.

Hanna
Well, quite. And now, Mr Ivor Biggun. No votes at all for the Standing at the Back Dressed Stupidly and Looking Stupid Party. Are you disappointed?

Biggun
No, not really, no. I always say, if you can't laugh, what can you do?

He squirts Hanna with his flower.

Hanna
Take up politics perhaps. Has your party got any policies?

Biggun
Yes, we're for the compulsory serving of asparagus at breakfast, free corsets for the under-fives and the abolition of slavery.

Hanna
Obviously many moderate people would respect your stand on asparagus, but what about this extremist nonsense about abolishing slavery?

Biggun
Oh, we just put that in for a joke – see you next year.

He exits.

Hanna
And now finally, a word with the man who is at the centre of this by-election mystery: the voter himself. (*Consults piece of paper*) And his name is Mr E. Blackadder . . . (*for it is he*) Mr Blackadder, you are the only voter in this rotten borough.

Blackadder
That's right, yes.

Hanna
How long have you lived in this constituency?

Blackadder
Since Wednesday morning. I took over from the original electorate after he very sadly accidentally brutally cut his head off while combing his hair.

Hanna
One voter – 16,472 votes. A slight anomaly?

Blackadder
Not really, Mr Hanna. You see, Mr Baldrick may look like a monkey who's been put in a suit and then strategically shaved, but he's a brilliant politician. The number of votes I cast is simply a reflection of how firmly I believe in his policies.

Hanna
Well, that's excellent. And, that's all from me – another great day for democracy in our country. Vincent Hanna, *Country Gentleman's Pig and Fertilizer Gazette*, Dunny-on-the-Wold.

SCENE EIGHT: THE KITCHEN

Blackadder is in very high spirits.

Blackadder
We are reprieved. It is a triumph for stupidity over common sense.

Baldrick
Thank you very much.

Blackadder
As a special reward, Baldrick, take a short holiday. (*He does not pause at all*) Did you enjoy it? Right.

SCENE NINE: THE HOUSE OF COMMONS

The three fat men again.

Speaker
Will the Honourable Members please cast their votes, Aye or Nay, for the striking of the Prince Regent off the civil lists?

The fat men go off to vote, leaving Baldrick all alone.

Baldrick
Excuse me. Excuse me?

Pitt pops up from behind the bench.

Pitt
Hello, little chappie – are you the new bug?

Baldrick
Yes – I don't know anyone here and I support the prince and I don't know how to vote.

Pitt
Ah! We can soon change all that, can't we? Come along with me.

Baldrick
(*Big smile*) Oh, thanks.

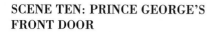

SCENE TEN: PRINCE GEORGE'S FRONT DOOR

Blackadder opens it to Pitt.

Blackadder
Well, well, well, if it isn't the Lord Privy toast rack. Pull up a muffin and sit yourself down.

Pitt
You don't like me, do you, Mr Blackadder?

Blackadder
Well, nobody likes a loser.

Pitt
Oh, then that must be why nobody likes *you*.

Blackadder
What?

Pitt
You lost the vote. Your monkey obligingly voted for us.

Blackadder
Oh, God. If you want something done properly, kill Baldrick before you start.

Pitt
You're beaten, oik, and you and your disgusting master have twenty-four hours to get out.

Blackadder
Twenty-four hours is a long time in politics. Good day.

Pitt
There's just one thing before I go. I've got this sort of downy hair developing on my chest, is that normal? Also, I get so lonely and confused. I've written a poem about it, maybe you'll understand . . . 'Why do nice girls hate me? Why do . . .'

Blackadder
Oh get out, you nauseating adolescent.

He slams the door on the pimply youth.

SCENE ELEVEN: THE KITCHEN

Baldrick is on a spit above the oven. Mrs Miggins has dropped by for the roasting.

Blackadder
How could I have been so stupid? Goodbye Millionaire's Row, hullo Room 12 of the Budleigh Salterton Twilight Rest Home for the Terminally Short of Cash.

Mrs Miggins
Oooh, er! And to think you once dreamed you'd end up in the House of Lords.

Blackadder
What?

Mrs Miggins
The House of Lords.

Blackadder
Of course, the House of Lords! I'd forgotten the House of Lords. They'll never let the bill through. Every man jack of them will be behind the prince.

Mrs Miggins
Hurrah!!

Blackadder
Right! Take Baldrick off the spit.

Baldrick
Hurrah!

Blackadder
I have a plan so cunning you put a tail on it and call it a weasel.

~

SCENE TWELVE: PRINCE GEORGE'S CHAMBERS

Prince George is looking through a telescope. Blackadder enters.

Prince George
Tally-ho, Blackadder! You look happy as a man who thought a cat had done its business on his pie but it turned out to be an extra big blackberry. Did our plan go well?

Blackadder
Excellently, sir. Order a thousand pairs of the finest cotton socks. Take out the drawings for that beach-hut at Brighton.

Prince George
Hurrah!

Blackadder
There, was, however, one slight (*cough*) hiccup.

Prince George
Cough, I think you mean.

Blackadder
No, sir – hiccup. The motion about your impoverishment has now moved on to the House of Lords.

Prince George
Oh, bravo. No worry there then, every man jack of them will be behind me.

Blackadder
(*Very grave*) Ah, would that were so, your Highness. These are treacherous times.

Prince George
Are they?

Blackadder
Yes. It might be wise to appoint a new lord to make sure the old lords vote the right way.

Prince George
Good thinking. A new lord. Any idea who?

Blackadder
Well, sire – one name does leap to mind.

Prince George
Does it?

Blackadder
Yes, sir.

Prince George thinks for a moment. They stare at each other.

Prince George
Ahm . . . you couldn't make it leap any higher, could you?

Blackadder
A young man in your service, sir – who has done sterling work, matching the political machinations of the evil Pitt.

He gently points to his waistcoat.

Prince George
Aha – of course, Blackadder! How can I thank you enough?

Blackadder
And it might be wise to bribe a few lords, just to make sure they vote the way their consciences tell them.

Prince George
Oooh – how many should we bribe?

Blackadder
I think 300 to be sure. At £1,000 each.

Prince George
Three hundred thousand pounds!

Blackadder
Four hundred thousand, I think you'll find, sir.

Prince George thinks hard.

Prince George
Yes, you're right. Thank God I've got you to advise me, Bladder. Just remind me, what do I have to do to appoint this lord chappie?

Blackadder
Very simple, sire. You put on your robes of state, he puts on his, then you sign the document of ennoblement and despatch him at once to the House of Lords.

Prince George
Excellent – I shall change immediately.

Blackadder
And so, sir, shall I.

SCENE THIRTEEN: THE KITCHEN

Blackadder enters in an ermine gown.

Blackadder
Voilà, Mrs Miggins, my robes of state. A thousand pounds well spent, I think.

Mrs Miggins
Oh, very nice! And it's real cat, isn't it?

Blackadder
This is not cat, Mrs Miggins. It is finest leather-trimmed ermine with gold medallion accessories.

Mrs Miggins
Oh, go on, Mr Blackadder, it's cat. Oh, they've left the little collars on!

Blackadder
(*Reads medallion*) 'Mr Friskie. If found please return to Emma Hamilton, Marine Parade, Portsmouth'. Damn! Oh, well. Who cares about a dead cat now that I'm a fat cat?

Mrs Miggins
Oh, you're full of yourself today, Mr B!

Blackadder
Which is more than can be said for Mr Friskie.

SCENE FOURTEEN: PRINCE GEORGE'S CHAMBERS

Blackadder sweeps in, in full lordly regalia.

Blackadder
My lord.

Prince George
My lords.

Blackadder
Pardon, sir?

Prince George
Yes, lords. There is more than one lord in the vicinity. Will you please welcome his Grace, Lord Baldrick.

Baldrick enters in his lordly regalia.

Blackadder
You've made *Baldrick* a lord?

Prince George
Well, yes. One 'who has recently done sterling service, matching the political machinations of the evil Pitt'. Good old Lord Baldrick!

Baldrick
It's all right, Blackadder. You don't have to curtsey or anything.

Blackadder
Sir, might I let loose a short, violent exclamation?

Prince George
Certainly.

Blackadder moves discreetly sideways, then . . .

Blackadder
(*Shouts*) DAMN!

Prince George and Baldrick both jump.

Prince George
I say, that's a bit of a strange get-up, isn't it, Blackadder?

Blackadder
No, sir, I'm just off to a fancy dress party. I'm going as Lady Hamilton's pussy.

He walks towards the door, stops and turns.

There is one little question, sir. About the £400,000 to influence the lords . . .

Prince George
Ah, yes. I gave that to Lord Baldrick.

Blackadder
Ahh! (*Big smile*) Sir, might I be permitted to take *Lord* Baldrick downstairs to give him some instruction in his *lordly* duties?

Prince George
I think that's a splendid idea.

Blackadder
(*To Baldrick*) This way – *my lord.*

~

SCENE FIFTEEN: THE KITCHEN

Blackadder pushes Baldrick in and slams his head on the kitchen table.

Blackadder
Give me the bloody money, Baldrick, or you're dead.

Baldrick
Give me the bloody money, Baldrick, or you're dead, *my lord.*

Blackadder
Just do it, Baldrick, or I shall further ennoble you by knighting you very clumsily with this meat cleaver.

Baldrick
I haven't got it.

Blackadder
What?

Baldrick
I spent it.

Blackadder
You spent it? What could you possibly spend £400,000 on?

Baldrick looks at a massive turnip on the table.

Oh, no . . . oh, God, don't tell me.

Baldrick
My dream turnip.

Blackadder
Baldrick, how did you manage to find a turnip that cost £400,000?

Baldrick
Well, I had to haggle.

Blackadder slams the turnip over Baldrick's head. It stays there.

Blackadder
This is the worst moment of my entire life. I've spent my last penny on a cat-skin windcheater, I've just broken a priceless turnip . . .

There is a knock at the door.

And now I'm about to be viciously slaughtered by a naked Tunisian sock merchant. Well, all I can say, Baldrick, is that's the last time I dabble in politics.

Mrs Miggins's Coffee House
BILL OF FARE

STARTERS

HOG'S BROTH

OR

GLOSSOP SALAD

OR

GREYISH LUMPS WITH TUBES AND VEINS IN (ACCORDING TO SEASON)

ENTREES

STOAT PIE WITH SOFT-BOILED GLOSSOPS

OR

HORSE'S WILLY DU JOUR

OR

ROAST OTTER (CHOICE OF CHEESE, EGG OR GLOSSOP FILLING)

DESSERTS

PUMPKIN CLAMMIES

OR

SCROGGS AND CUSTARD

OR

GLOSSOPS

BEVERAGES

ALE

STOUT

SHERRY

COFFEE

PRICE: 3d (BUCKET NOT INCLUDED)

Ink and Incapability

SCENE ONE: PRINCE GEORGE'S
CHAMBERS

Prince George is in bed asleep.
Blackadder attends. Prince George wakes
violently.

Prince George
Oh! Oh! Blackadder! Blackadder!

Blackadder
Your Highness.

Prince George
What time is it?

Blackadder
Three o'clock in the afternoon, your
Highness.

Prince George
Oh thank God for that. I thought I'd overslept.

Blackadder
I trust you had a pleasant evening, sir.

Prince George
Well, no, actually. The most extraordinary
thing happened. Last night, I was having a
little snack at the Naughty Hell Fire Club
and some fellow said I had the wit and

sophistication of a donkey.

Blackadder
An absurd suggestion, sir.

Prince George
You're right, it is absurd.

Blackadder
Unless of course it was a particularly stupid donkey.

Prince George
You see, if only *I*'d thought of saying that.

Blackadder
It is often the way, sir. Too late one thinks
of what one *should* have said. Sir Thomas
More, for instance, burned alive for refus-
ing to recant his Catholicism, must have
been kicking himself as the flames licked
higher, that it never occurred to him to
say 'I recant my Catholicism'.

Prince George
Well, quite. Why, only the other day
Prime Minister Pitt called me an idle
scrounger. It wasn't until ages later that I
thought how clever it would have been to
have said, 'Oh bugger off, you old fart!' I
need to improve my mind, Blackadder. I

want people to say, 'That George, why he's as clever as a stick in a bucket of pig swill'.

Blackadder
And how do you suggest this miracle is to be achieved, your Highness?

Prince George
Easy. I shall become best friends with the cleverest man in England. That renowned brainbox Dr Samuel Johnson has asked me to be patron of his new book, and I intend to accept.

Blackadder
Would this be the long-awaited dictionary, sir?

Prince George
Who cares about the title, as long as there's plenty of juicy murders in it? I hear it's a masterpiece.

Blackadder
No, sir, it is not. It's the most pointless book since *How to Learn French* was translated into French.

Prince George
You haven't got anything personal against Johnson, have you, Blackadder?

Blackadder
Good lord, sir, not at all. In fact, I'd never heard of him till you mentioned him just now.

Prince George
But you do think he's a genius?

Blackadder
No, sir, I do not. Unless, of course, the definition of genius in his ridiculous dictionary is 'a fat dullard or wobble-bottom; a pompous ass with sweaty dewflaps'.

Prince George
Ha! Close shave there, then! Lucky you warned me. I was about to embrace this unholy arse to the royal bosom.

Blackadder
I am delighted to have been instrumental in keeping your bosom free of arses.

Prince George
Bravo!! I mustn't waste my time with wobble-bottoms. Now fetch some tea, will you, Blackadder?

Blackadder sets off.

Blackadder
Certainly.

Prince George
Oh and make it two cups, will you? That splendid brainbox Dr Johnson's coming round.

Blackadder cannot believe the prince's stupidity.

SCENE TWO: THE KITCHEN

Blackadder enters, slamming the door behind him. He walks down the stairs.

Blackadder
Aagh!

Baldrick
Something wrong, Mr B?

Blackadder reaches the bottom of the stairs and casually throws the prince's tea-tray and its expensive, ceramic contents into an upturned barrel.

Blackadder
Something is always wrong, Balders. The fact that I am not a millionaire aristocrat with the sexual capacity of a rutting rhino is a constant niggle. But today something is even wronger. That globulous fraud Dr Johnson is coming to tea.

Baldrick
I thought he was the cleverest gentleman in England.

Blackadder
Baldrick, I'd bump into cleverer people at a lodge meeting of the Guild of Village Idiots.

Baldrick
That's not what you said when you sent him your navel.

Blackadder
Novel, Baldrick, not navel. I sent him my *novel*.

Baldrick
Novel or navel, it sounds a bit like a bag of grapefruits to me.

Blackadder
(*Bitterly*) The phrase, Baldrick, is a case of sour grapes and yes, it bloody well is. I mean, he might at least have written back, but no, nothing, not even a 'Dear Gertrude Perkins, thank you for your book. Get stuffed, Samuel Johnson.'

Baldrick
Gertrude Perkins?

Blackadder
Yes, I gave myself a female pseudonym. Everybody's doing it these days. Mrs Radcliffe, Jane Austen . . .

Baldrick
Jane Austen is a man?

Blackadder
Of course. A huge Yorkshireman with a beard like a rhododendron bush.

Baldrick
Quite a small one then?

Blackadder
Compared to Dorothy Wordsworth's, certainly. James Boswell is the only real woman writing at the moment and that's just because she wants to get inside Johnson's britches.

Baldrick
Perhaps your book really isn't any good.

Blackadder
Oh, codswallop! It's taken me seven years and it's perfect: *Edmund, a Butler's Tale.* 'A giant roller-coaster of a novel in 400 sizzling chapters. A seering indictment of domestic servitude in the eighteenth centu-

ry with some hot gypsies thrown in.' It's my *magnum opus*, Baldrick. Everybody has one novel in them and this is mine.

Baldrick
Yes, and this is mine.

He produces a single scruffy piece of paper.

My magnificent octopus.

With a flourish he hands it to Blackadder.

Blackadder
This is your novel?

Baldrick
I can't stand long books.

Blackadder
(*Reading it*) 'Once upon a time there was a lovely little sausage called Baldrick, and it lived happily ever after.'

Baldrick
It's semi-autobiographical.

Blackadder
And it's completely utterly awful. Dr Johnson will probably love it.

The bell rings.

Well, speak of the devil. I'd better go and make the great Doctor (*with sarcastic relish*) . . . comfortable. Let's see just how damn smart Dr Fatty Know-It-All really *is*. Oh, and prepare a fire for the prince, will you, Baldrick?

Baldrick
What should I use?

Blackadder
Oh, any old rubbish will do. Paper's quite good. Here. (*He screws up Baldrick's novel and flicks it at him*) Try this for a start.

~

SCENE THREE: PRINCE GEORGE'S CHAMBERS

There is a knock at the door.

Prince George
Enter!

Blackadder opens the door for Dr Johnson. He is sixty, fat and pompous.

Blackadder
Dr Johnson, your Highness.

Prince George
Ah, Dr Johnson. Damn cold day.

Johnson
Indeed it is, sir. But a very fine one for I celebrated last night the encyclopaedic implementation of my premeditated orchestration of demotic Anglo-Saxon.

The prince nods sagely for a good while, then . . .

Prince George
No. Didn't catch any of that.

Johnson
I simply observed, sir, that I am felicitous, since during the course of the penultimate solar sojourn, I terminated my uninterrupted categorization of the vocabulary of our post-Norman tongue.

Prince George
Don't know what you're talking about but it sounds damn saucy, you lucky thing! I know some fairly liberal-minded girls but I've never penultimated them in the solar sojourn or, for that matter, been given any Norman tongue.

Blackadder
I believe, sir, that the Doctor is trying to tell you that he is happy because he has finished his book. It has taken him ten years.

Prince George
(*Sympathetically*) Yes, well, I'm a slow reader myself.

Johnson
Here it is, sire. (*He produces a sheaf of manuscript*) A very cornerstone of English scholarship. This book contains every word in our beloved language.

Blackadder
Every single one, sir?

Johnson
Every single one, sir.

Blackadder
In that case, sir, I hope you will not object if I also offer the Doctor my most enthusiastic contrafibularatories.

Johnson
What, sir?

Blackadder
Contrafibularatories, sir. It is a common word down our way.

Johnson takes a pencil from behind his ear. He is furious.

Johnson
Damn!

He starts writing in the dictionary.

Blackadder
Oh, I'm sorry, sir. I am anaseptic, phrasmotic, even compunctious to have caused you such periconbobulations.

Johnson
What, what, what?

He's now frantic, scribbling down all these new words.

Prince George
Look, what *are* you on about,

A Complete Arse

Blackadder? This is beginning to sound a bit like dago talk to me.

Blackadder
I'm sorry, sir. I merely wished to congratulate Dr Johnson on not having left out a single word. *(He smiles at Johnson, Johnson glares)* Shall I fetch the tea, my lord?

Prince George
Yes, yes – and get that damn fire up here, will you.

Blackadder
(Smoothly) Certainly, sir. I shall return . . . interphrastically.

A smug nod and he leaves.

Prince George
So, Dr Johnson. Sit ye down. Now, this book of yours. Tell me, what's it all about?

Johnson
It is a book about the English language, sir.

Prince George
I see. And the hero's name is what?

Johnson
There is no hero, sir.

Prince George
No hero? Well! Lucky I reminded you! Better put one in pronto. Call him George, that's a good name for a hero. What about heroines?

Johnson
There is no heroine, sir – unless it is our Mother Tongue.

Prince George
Ah – the mother's the heroine. Nice twist. So how far have we got then? Old Mother Tongue is in love with George the hero . . . Now what about murders? Mother Tongue doesn't get murdered, does she?

Johnson
No, she doesn't! No one gets murdered! Or married! Or in a tricky situation over a pound note!

Prince George
Well, now, look Dr Johnson, I may be as thick as a whale omelette, but even I know that a book's got to have a plot.

Johnson
Not this one, sir. It is a book that tells you what English words mean.

Prince George
But I *know* what English words mean. I *speak* English. You must be a bit of a thicko!

That is it. Johnson is seriously angry. He rises to his feet.

Johnson
Perhaps you would rather not be patron of my book, sir, if you can see no value in it whatsoever!

Prince George
Perhaps so, sir, since it sounds to me as though being patron of this complete cowpat of a book will set the seal once and for all on my reputation as an utter turnip head.

Johnson
It is a reputation well deserved, sir! Farewell.

He marches towards the double doors and flings them open. Blackadder is revealed very calmly.

Blackadder
Leaving already, Doctor? Not staying for your pendigestatory interludicule?

Johnson
No, sir, show me out!

Blackadder
Certainly, sir. Anything I can do to facilitate your velocitous extramuralization.

Johnson
(To Prince George) You will regret this doubly, sir. Not only have you impeculiated *(he glares with self-satisfaction at Blackadder, who is not impressed)* my dictionary, you have also lost the chance to

act as patron to the only book in the world that is even better.

Blackadder
And what's that, sir? *Dictionary 2: The Return of the Killer Dictionaries?*

Johnson
No, sir – it is *Edmund: A Butler's Tale* by Gertrude Perkins.

Blackadder nearly drops the teapot he is holding.

A huge roller-coaster of a novel crammed with sizzling gypsies. Had you supported it, sir, it would have made you and me and Gertrude millionaires.

Blackadder
(*With real anguish*) Millionaires!

Johnson
But that, sir, is not to be. I bid you farewell. I shall not return.

He exits in a fury.

Blackadder
Excuse me, sir.

He shoots out.

~

SCENE FOUR: THE VESTIBULE

Outside the door.

Blackadder
Dr Johnson, sir, a word, I beg you . . .

Johnson
A word with you, sir, can mean seven million syllables. You may start it now and not be finished by bedtime. Oh, blast my eyes! In my fury I have left my dictionary with your foolish master. Go and fetch it, will you.

Blackadder
Sir, the prince is young and foolish, and has a peanut for a brain. Give me just a few minutes and I will deliver both the book and his patronage.

Johnson
Oh, will you, sir? I very much doubt it. A servant who is an influence for the good is like a dog who speaks. Very rare.

Blackadder
I think I can change his mind.

Johnson
Well, I doubt it, sir. A man who can change a prince's mind is like a dog who talks Norwegian – even rarer. I shall be at Mrs Miggins's literary salon in twenty minutes. Bring the book there.

He storms out.

~

SCENE FIVE: PRINCE GEORGE'S CHAMBERS

Prince George is standing in front of a raging fire of Baldrick's making.

Blackadder enters.

Blackadder
Your Highness . . . may I offer my congratulations.

Prince George
Thanks Blackadder! That pompous baboon won't be back in a hurry!

He laughs contentedly.

Blackadder
On the contrary, sir. Dr Johnson left in the highest of spirits.

Prince George
What?

Blackadder
He is utterly thrilled at your promise to patronize his dictionary.

Prince George
I told him to sod off, didn't I?

Blackadder
Yes, but that was a joke. Surely.

Prince George
(*Confused*) Was it?

Blackadder
Certainly. And a brilliant one, what's more.

Prince George
Yes, I suppose it was rather, wasn't it?

Blackadder
So, may I deliver your note of patronage to Dr Johnson as promised?

Prince George
Well, of course, if that's what I promised, then that is what I must do. And I remember promising it distinctly.

Blackadder
Excellent. Nice fire, Baldrick.

Baldrick
Thank you, Mr B.

Blackadder
Right, let's get the book. Baldrick, where's the manuscript?

Baldrick
You mean the papery thing tied up with string?

Blackadder
Yes, Baldrick, the manuscript belonging to Dr Johnson.

Baldrick
You mean the batey fellow in the black coat who just left?

Blackadder
Yes, Baldrick, Dr Johnson.

Baldrick
So you're asking where the papery thing tied up with string belonging to the batey fellow in the black coat who just left is?

Blackadder
Yes, Baldrick, I am. And if I do not shortly have an answer, the booted boney thing with five toes on the end of my leg will soon connect sharply with the soft dangly collection of objects in your trousers. For the last time, Baldrick, where is Dr Johnson's manuscript?

Baldrick
On the fire.

Blackadder
On the what?

Baldrick
The hot orangey thing under the stoney mantelpiecey thing.

Blackadder
(*Aghast*) You've burnt the dictionary?

Baldrick
That's right.

Blackadder
You've burnt the life's work of England's foremost man of letters?

Baldrick
Yup. You did say burn any old rubbish.

Blackadder has nearly turned to stone.

Blackadder
Yes, fine.

Prince George
Isn't it going to be rather difficult to patronize this book if we've burnt it?

Blackadder
Yes, it is. If you will excuse me.

Prince George
Of course, now I've got my lovely fire I'm happy as a Frenchman who's invented a pair of self-removing trousers.

Blackadder
Baldrick! Would you join me in the vestibule?

~

SCENE SIX: THE VESTIBULE

Blackadder grabs Baldrick by the collar.

Blackadder
We are going to go to Mrs Miggins's, we are going to find out where Dr Johnson keeps his copy of his dictionary and then you are going to steal it.

Baldrick
Me!

Blackadder
Yes, you.

Baldrick
Why me?

Blackadder
Because you burnt it.

Baldrick
But then I'll go to hell for ever for stealing.

Blackadder
Baldrick, believe me, eternity in the company of Beezlebub and all his hellish instruments of death will be a picnic compared to five minutes with me and this pencil (*He holds it threateningly in his hand*) if we can't replace this dictionary.

~

SCENE SEVEN: MRS MIGGINS'S COFFEE SHOP

Mrs Miggins's Coffee Shop has become fashionable with the literati. Lounging in poses of bored, sensitive, ill health are Byron and Shelley. Coleridge has passed out at the table.

Shelley
Oh love-lorn ecstasy that is Mrs Miggins, wilt thou but bring me one cup of the browned juicings of that naughty bean we call coffee, ere I die?

He coughs pathetically into a handkerchief.

Mrs Miggins
Oh, you do have a way with words, Mr Shelley!

Byron
(*A furious figure*) To hell with his fine talking. Coffee, woman!!
He coughs too.

My consumption grows ever more acute, and Coleridge's drugs are wearing off.

Mrs Miggins
Oh, Mr Byron. Don't be such a big girl's blouse!

She hands Shelley a coffee.

~

SCENE EIGHT: OUTSIDE MRS MIGGINS'S COFFEE SHOP

Blackadder and Baldrick are standing outside.

Blackadder
Don't forget the pencil, Baldrick.

Baldrick
I won't, sir.

SCENE NINE: MRS MIGGINS'S COFFEE SHOP

Blackadder enters. Baldrick sits at a table.

Blackadder
Good day to you, Mrs Miggins. A cup of your best hot water with brown grit in it, unless of course by some miracle your

coffee shop has started selling *coffee* . . .

The three poets sit up.

Byron
Be quiet, sir! Can't you see we're dying?

They slump down again. Blackadder gives them a withering look.

Mrs Miggins
Oh, don't you worry about my poets, Mr Blackadder! They're not dead, they're just being intellectual.

Blackadder
Mrs Miggins, there's nothing intellectual about wandering round Italy in a big shirt trying to get laid. Why are they here, of all places?

Byron
We are here, sir, to pay homage to the great Dr Johnson. As, sir, should you.

Blackadder
Absolutely, I intend to. (*Casually*) You wouldn't have a copy of his dictionary on you, would you, so I can do a bit of revising up before he gets here?

Enter Dr Johnson.

Johnson
Friends, I am returned.

Poets
Hurrah!

Byron
So, sir, how was the prince?

Johnson
The prince was and is, sirs, an utter fool. And his household full of cretinous servants.

The poets laugh.

Blackadder
(*Suavely*) Good afternoon, sir.

Johnson
Ah – and this is the worst of them. Sir, after all your boasting, have you my dictionary and my patronage?

Blackadder
Not quite. The prince begs a few hours more to really get to grips with it.

Johnson
Bah!

Blackadder
However, I was wondering if a lowly servant such as I might be permitted to glance at a copy?

Johnson
Copy? Copy? There is no copy!

Blackadder does turn to stone.

Blackadder
No copy?

Johnson
No. A copy, sir, is like fitting wheels to a tomato – time-consuming and completely unnecessary.

Blackadder
But what if the book got lost?

Johnson
I should not lose the book, sir, and if any other man should, I would tear off his head with my bare hands and feed it to the cat.

Blackadder
Well, that's nice and clear.

The poets draw their swords.

Byron
And I, Lord Byron, would summon up fifty of my men, lay siege to the fellow's house and do bloody murder on him.

He lays his sword threateningly on Baldrick's shoulder.

Coleridge
And I would not rest until the criminal was hanging by his hair with an Oriental disembowelling cutlass thrust up his ignoble behind.

He holds his sword's point at Blackadder's throat.

Blackadder
I hope you're listening to all this, Baldrick.

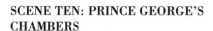

SCENE TEN: PRINCE GEORGE'S CHAMBERS

Blackadder
Sir. I have been unable to replace the dictionary. I am therefore leaving immediately for Nepal, where I intend to live as a goat.

Prince George
Why?

Blackadder
Because if I stay here, Dr Johnson's companions will have me brutally murdered, sir.

Prince George
Good Lord, Blackadder, that's terrible! Do you know any other butlers?

Blackadder
And of course, when people discover that you have burnt Dr Johnson's dictionary, they may go round saying, 'Look, there's thick George, he's got a brain the size of a weasel's wedding tackle.'

Prince George
Well, in that case, something *must* be done!

Baldrick
I have a cunning plan, sir.

Prince George
Hurrah! Well, that's that, then.

Blackadder
Don't get over-excited, sir. I've a horrid suspicion that Baldrick's plan will be the stupidest thing we've heard since Lord Nelson's famous signal at the Battle of the Nile: 'England knows Lady Hamilton's a virgin, poke my eye out and cut off my arm if I'm wrong.'

Prince George
Great, let's hear it.

Blackadder resigns himself to the worst and looks at the ceiling.

Baldrick
It's brilliant. You take the string that's not completely burnt, scrape off the soot, and shove in the pages again.

Blackadder
Which pages?

Baldrick
Well not the same ones, of course.

Blackadder
Yes. I think I'm on the point of spotting the flaw in the plan. But do go on. Which pages are they?

Baldrick
This is the brilliant bit. You write some new ones.

Blackadder
Some new ones? You mean rewrite the dictionary? I sit down tonight, and rewrite the dictionary that took Johnson ten years?

Baldrick
Yes.

Blackadder
Baldrick, that is by far and away without a shadow of a doubt the worst and most contemptible plan in the history of the universe. On the other hand, I hear the sound of disembowelling cutlasses being sharpened, and it's the only plan we've got. So, if you will excuse me, gentlemen . . .

Prince George
Perhaps you'd like me to lend a hand. I'm not as stupid as I look.

Baldrick
I *am* as stupid as I look, sir, but if I can help, I will.

Blackadder
Well, it's very kind of you both, but I fear

your services might be as useful as a barber's shop on the steps of the guillotine.

Prince George
Oh, go on, Blackadder, give us a try!

Blackadder
Very well, sir, as you wish. Let's start at
the beginning, shall we? First 'a'. How
would you define 'a'?

Prince George
Ah – I love this. Quizzes. Ahm . . . 'a' . . .

Baldrick
(*Simultaneously*) Ahm, oh yes. Ahm, let's
see – it's coming – ahm . . .

Prince George
Yes, I've got it!

Blackadder
What?

Prince George
(*Proudly*) Well, it doesn't really mean
anything, does it?

Blackadder
(*With veiled sarcasm*) Good, so we're well
under way then. ' "a" – impersonal pro-
noun. Doesn't really mean anything.' So,
next – 'a' – 'a b'.

Baldrick
A bee. Well, that's a buzzing thing. 'A
buzzing thing'.

Blackadder
Baldrick, I mean something that starts
with 'ab'.

Baldrick
Honey. Honey starts with a bee.

Prince George
He's right, you know, Blackadder. Honey
does start with a bee! And a flower too.

Blackadder
Yes. I'm afraid this really isn't getting
anywhere. And besides, I've left out
'aardvark'.

Prince George
Oh! Well, can't say we didn't try.

Blackadder
No, my lord, it was a brave stab – but I
fear I shall have to proceed on my own.
Baldrick – go to the kitchen and make me
something quick and simple to eat.
Perhaps two slices of bread with something in between.

Baldrick
Like Gerald, Lord Sandwich, had the
other day?

Blackadder
Yes – a few rounds of Geralds.

SCENE ELEVEN: PRINCE GEORGE'S
CHAMBERS

*It is very late at night. Blackadder is sur-
rounded by scrunched paper in Prince
George's study. Prince George wanders
out in his dressing-gown.*

Prince George
How goes it, Blackadder?

Blackadder
Not all that well, sir.

Prince George
Let's have a look.

He takes the piece of paper Blackadder is

working on, as Blackadder leans back in despair.

'Medium sized insectivore with protruding nasal implement.' Doesn't sound like a bee to me.

Blackadder
(*Suddenly cracking with the strain*) It's an 'aardvark'! Can't you see that, your Highness, it's a bloody *aardvark*!

Prince George
Oh, dear – still on 'aardvark' are we?

Blackadder
Yes, we are. If ever I see an aardvark, I'm going to step on its damn protruding nasal implement until it couldn't suck up an insect if its life depended on it.

Prince George
Got a bit stuck, have you?

Blackadder
Yes, I'm sorry, sir. It is five hours later and I've got every word in the English language except 'a' and 'aardvark' still to do. And I'm not very happy with my definition of either of them.

Prince George
Well, don't panic, Blackadder, because I have some rather good news.

Blackadder
What?

Prince George
We didn't take 'no' for an answer, and have, in fact, been working all night. I've done 'b'.

Blackadder
Really? How's it gone?

Prince George
Well, I had a bit of trouble with 'belching' – but I think I've got it sorted out in the end. (*Belches*) Oh, no. There I go again.

He laughs uproariously.

Blackadder
You've been working on that joke for some time, haven't you, my lord?

Prince George
Well, yes, as a matter of fact I have.

Blackadder
Since you started?

Prince George
Basically.

Blackadder
So you haven't done any work at all?

Prince George
Not as such.

Baldrick enters.

Blackadder
Baldrick, what have you done?

Baldrick
I've done 'c' and 'd'.

Blackadder
Let's hear it then.

Baldrick
'Big blue wobbly thing that mermaids live in.'

Blackadder
What's that?

Baldrick
Sea.

Blackadder
Yes, tiny misunderstanding – still, my hopes weren't high. What about 'd'?

Baldrick
I'm quite pleased with 'dog'.

Blackadder
Yes? And the definition of 'dog' is . . .

Baldrick
'Not a cat.'

Blackadder
Excellent, excellent.(*To Prince George*) Your Highness – may I have a word?

Prince George
Certainly.

He takes Prince George aside.

Blackadder
As you know, sir, it has always been my intention to stay with you until you had a strapping son and I one likewise, to take over the burdens of my duties.

Prince George
That's right, Blackadder, and I thank you for it.

Blackadder
But I'm afraid, sir, there has been a change of plan. I'm off to the kitchen to hack my head off with a big knife.

Prince George
Oh, come now, Blackadder, it's only a book! Let's just damn the fellow's eyes, strip the britches from his backside and warm his heels to Putney Bridge! Hurrah!

Blackadder
My lord, these are not the days of Alfred the Great. You can't just lop someone's head off and blame it on the Vikings.

Prince George
Can't I, by God!

Blackadder
No.

Prince George
Oh, well, all right then – let's just get on with it. Boil my brains, it's only a dictionary, no one's asked us to eat ten raw pigs for breakfast. We're British, aren't we?

Blackadder
You're not, you're German. Get me some coffee, Baldrick – if I fall asleep before Monday, we're doomed.

~

SCENE TWELVE: PRINCE GEORGE'S CHAMBERS

Blackadder is asleep and snoring. Baldrick wakes him.

Baldrick
Mr Blackadder, time to wake up!

Blackadder
Ah! What time is it?

Baldrick
Monday morning.

Blackadder
Monday morning! Oh, my God! I've overslept. Where's the quill? Where's the parchment?

Baldrick
I don't know – maybe Dr Johnson's brought some with him.

Blackadder
(*Terrified*) What!

Baldrick
He's outside.

Blackadder screams. Enter Dr Johnson.

Johnson
Are you ill, sir?

Blackadder
(*Wildly*) No – you can't have it. I know I said Monday, but I want Baldrick to read it, which unfortunately will mean teaching him to read, which will take about ten years. But time well spent, I think, because it is such a very good dictionary.

Johnson
I don't think so.

Blackadder
Oh no, we've been burgled! (*Double take*)
What?

Johnson
I think it's an awful dictionary, full of feeble definitions and ridiculous verbiage.
I've come to ask you to chuck the damn
thing on the fire.

Blackadder
Are you sure?

Johnson
I've never been more sure of anything in
my life.

Blackadder
I love you, Dr Johnson, and I want to have
your babies.

They embrace.

(*Looking puzzled*) Excuse me, Dr Johnson,
but my Auntie Margery has just arrived.

*A lady is standing behind him. Blackadder
turns to Baldrick, who has now turned
into a dog.*

Baldrick, who gave you permission to turn
into an Alsatian?

The awful realization dawns.

Oh God, it's a dream, isn't it, it's a bloody
dream . . .

*Auntie Margery, Dr Johnson and Baldrick
the Alsatian dance out of the room.*

Dr Johnson doesn't want us to burn his
dictionary at all.

~

SCENE THIRTEEN: PRINCE
GEORGE'S CHAMBERS

*Baldrick is waking up Blackadder. It is
exactly the same set-up as a few seconds
earlier.*

Baldrick
Mr Blackadder, Mr Blackadder, time to
wake up.

Blackadder
Ah, what time is it?

Baldrick
Monday morning.

Blackadder
Monday morning? Oh my God! I've overslept. Where's the quill? Where's the
parchment?

Baldrick
I don't know. Maybe Dr Johnson's got
some with him.

Blackadder
(*Terrified*) What?

Baldrick
He's outside.

Blackadder
Hang on, hang on. If we go on like this
you're going to turn into an Alsatian again.

Baldrick
Sorry?

There is knocking and roaring from outside.

Blackadder
Oh God, quick – we've got to escape.

~

SCENE FOURTEEN: THE VESTIBULE
OF PRINCE GEORGE'S CHAMBERS

*Dr Johnson and the poets are standing
outside the prince's rooms.*

Shelley
Ho, sir, bring out the dictionary at once!

Byron
Bring it out, sir! Or in my passion I shall
kill everyone by giving them syphilis . . .

Coleridge
Bring it out! And also any opium plants
you might have around!

Johnson
Sir, bring it out or we shall break down
this door!

Blackadder emerges with Baldrick.

Blackadder
Ah. Good morning, Dr Johnson, Lord Byron . . .

Johnson
My dictionary?

Blackadder
And what dictionary would this be?

Dr Johnson starts walking forward, pushing Blackadder back with his cane followed by the poets brandishing their swords. They end up at the doors of the prince's bed-chamber.

Johnson
The one that took me eighteen hours in every day for the last ten years . . . My mother died – I hardly noticed. My father cut off his head and fried it with garlic in the hope of attracting my attention – I scarcely looked up from my work. My wife brought armies of lovers to our house, who worked in droves so that she might bring up a huge family of bastards – I cared not.

Blackadder
Am I to presume, sir, my elaborate bluff has not worked?

Johnson
Dictionary!

Blackadder
Well the truth is, Doctor . . . Now don't get cross. Don't overreact. The truth is . . . we burnt it.

Johnson
Then – you die!

Blackadder is about to die. At which moment, Prince George enters from the bedroom casually carrying a large manuscript.

Prince George
Good morning, everyone. You know, this dictionary is a cracking good read, an absolutely splendid job.

Johnson
My dictionary! But you said it was burnt!

Prince George
I think it's a splendid book and look forward to patronizing it enormously.

Johnson
Well, thank you, sir. Well, I think I'm man enough to sacrifice the pleasure of killing to maintain the general good humour. (*To the poets*) There is to be no murder today, gentlemen.

The poets groan with disappointment.

But retire to Mrs Miggins's – I shall meet you there for a roister you will never forget.

Poets cheer and leave. All is resolved.

Tell me, sir, what words particularly interested you?

Prince George
Ahmm . . . oh, nothing. Just . . . anything.

Johnson
I see you have underlined a few . . . 'bloomers', 'bottom', 'burp' . . .

He turns the pages, worried.

'Fart', 'fiddle', 'fornicate' . . . Sir! I hope that you are not using this first English dictionary to look up rude words.

Blackadder
Well, I wouldn't be too hopeful – that's what all the other ones will be used for.

Baldrick
Can I look up 'turnip'?

Blackadder
'Turnip' isn't a rude word, Baldrick.

Baldrick
It is if you sit on one.

Johnson
Yes, sir. But now we have more important business in hand. I refer of course to the works of the mysterious Gertrude Perkins.

Blackadder
Mysterious no more, sir, it is time for the truth. I can at last reveal the identity of the great Gertrude Perkins.

Johnson
Sir – who is she?

Blackadder
She, sir, is me, sir. *I* am Gertrude Perkins.

Prince George
Good Lord!

Blackadder
And what's more, I can prove it. Bring out the manuscript and I will show you that my signature corresponds exactly with that on the front.

Johnson
Why, I must have left it here when I left the dictionary.

Prince George
This is terribly exciting.

Blackadder
Excellent Baldrick – fetch my novel.

Baldrick
Your novel?

Blackadder
Yes, Baldrick – it's the big papery thing tied up with string.

Baldrick
Like the thing we burnt.

Blackadder
Exactly like the thing we burnt.

Baldrick
So, you want the big papery thing tied up with string exactly like the thing we burnt.

Blackadder
Exactly.

Baldrick
We burnt it.

Suddenly, Blackadder realizes the terrible twist of fate that has occurred and will blight his life for ever.

Blackadder
So we did. Thank you, Baldrick – seven years of my life up in smoke. Your Highness, would you excuse me a moment?

Prince George
By all means.

Blackadder goes out of the room, shutting the doors behind him. Outside, the cry of

a man in total agony is heard.

Blackadder
OH GOD, NO!

He re-enters, calm once more.

Thank you, sir.

Johnson
Burnt you say? That's most inconvenient. A burnt novel, sir, is like a burnt dog . . .

Blackadder
Oh, shut up.

Baldrick
I have a novel, sir . . .

He produces a scrap of paper for Johnson.

Johnson
(*Reading*) 'Once upon a time there was a lovely little sausage called . . .' Sausage! Sausage! Blast your eyes!

Irrationally and unreasonably, Johnson screws up the paper and storms out.

Baldrick
Well I didn't think it was that bad.

Blackadder
(*Leafing despondently through dictionary*) I think you'll find he left 'sausage' out of his dictionary.

He has another thought and looks at the beginning.

Oh, and 'aardvark' . . .

He puts it aside gloomily.

Prince George
Come on, Blackadder, it's not all that bad. Nothing a nice roaring fire can't solve. Baldrick – do the honours, will you?

Baldrick
Certainly, your Majesty.

He looks around, picks up the dictionary, walks behind the other two to the fire, and throws it in.

Freeze. As the greatest work of English lexicography begins to flame.

Duties of the Prince Regent

Attending Privy Council

Acknowledging loyal huzzahs (if any)

Lunch

Duties of a Butler of the Royal Household

Supervising the linen~maids

Announcing

Vintnery

Commissioning moleskins (as and when necessary)

Opening doors

Pinning up duty roster for Windowman
and Underwindowwomen.

Closing doors

Clearing up huge mounds of the
Prince Regent's cock~ups, and his underwear

Duties of an underscrogman

Browting

Lubby~dredging

Frottinage

Emptying the cassops

Cleaning the wulger~hole

Unblocking the mulch~cleats

Removing and making good all squoles,
whiffen~plugs and blunters

Frossocking the hounds

Being log~slammed by the rollickers on Shreeve Monday

Furtling the dove~cot

Quilping

Cliving

Groving

Shaving and pomading the underbutler's jolly~hole

Vunt~duty

Clearing the throssells

Folding the glut~pile

Trimming the scrogs*

Stacking the dried cowpats

Blow~drying the wet cowpats

Arranging the sheep droppings into neat little pyramids

Shit~shovelling

Arse~wiping

Squeezing the horses' pimples

Making sandwiches

* The stout pubic hairs which protrude from a hurriedly-prepared Glossop Pie

Livery of an underscrogman (apprentice dogsbody) circa 1799

Nob and Nobility

SCENE ONE: MRS MIGGINS'S COFFEE SHOP

There is something different about the decoration – it is all tricolour – red, white and blue with strings of garlic hanging everywhere.

Blackadder
Good day, Mrs Miggins.

Mrs Miggins
Bonjewer, monsewer.

Blackadder
What?

Mrs Miggins
Bonjewer, monsewer. It's French.

Blackadder
So is eating frogs, cruelty to geese and urinating in the street. But that's no reason to inflict it on the rest of us.

Mrs Miggins
But French is all the fashion. My coffee shop is full of Frenchies – and all because of that wonderful Scarlet Pimpernel.

Blackadder
The Scarlet Pimpernel is not wonderful, Mrs Miggins. There is no reason whatsoever to admire someone for filling London with a load of garlic-chewing French toffs crying 'ooh-la-la' and looking for sympathy all the time just because their fathers had their heads cut off. I'll have a cup of coffee, and some shepherd's pie, please.

Mrs Miggins
Oh! We don't serve pies any more. My French clientele consider pie uncouth.

Blackadder
I hardly think a nation that eats frogs and would go to bed with the kitchen sink if it put on a tutu is in any position to preach couthness. So, what *is* on the menu?

Mrs Miggins
Today's hot choice is: Chicken Pimpernel in a Scarlet Sauce, Scarlet Chicken in a Pimpernel Sauce or Huge Suspicious-looking Sausages in Scarlet Pimpernel Sauce.

Blackadder
What exactly is Scarlet Pimpernel Sauce?

Mrs Miggins
You take a large ripe frog – squeeze it . . .

Blackadder
Yes. All right. Thank you. I'm off to the pub.

He turns to go. A Frenchman passes him and bows elaborately.

Frenchman
Ah, bonjour, monsieur.

Blackadder
Sod off.

SCENE TWO: THE KITCHEN

Baldrick is in the kitchen. Blackadder storms in, picks up the cat and drop-kicks it.

Baldrick
Sir! Poor little Mildred the cat, what's he ever done to you?

Blackadder
It is the way of the world, Baldrick – the abused always kick downwards. I am annoyed and so I kick the cat, the cat . . . (*There is a squeak*) pounces on the mouse and, finally, (*Baldrick squeals in pain*) the mouse bites you on the behind.

Baldrick
And what do I do?

Blackadder
Nothing, you are last in God's great chain. Unless there's an earwig around here you'd like to victimize. My God, Baldrick – what's happened to your nose?

Baldrick is sporting the most hideous purple blister.

Baldrick
Nice, isn't it?

Blackadder
No, Baldrick. It isn't. It's revolting.

Baldrick
I'll take it off then.

Rather unexpectedly, Baldrick simply peels off the blister.

Blackadder
Baldrick, why are you wearing a false boil? What are we to expect next? A beauty wart? A cosmetic verucca?

Baldrick
It's a Scarlet Pimple, sir.

Blackadder
Really?

Baldrick
They're all the rage down our way. Everyone wants to express their admiration

for the great Pimple and his brilliant disguises.

Blackadder
What has this fellow done apart from pop over to France to grab a few French nobs from the ineffectual clutches of a bunch of malnourished wingeing lefties, taking the opportunity while there – no doubt – to pick up some really good cheap wine and some of their marvellous open fruit flans. Doesn't anyone know? We hate the French! We fight wars against them! Did all those men die in vain on the field of Agincourt? Was the man who burnt Joan of Arc simply wasting good matches?

A bell rings.

Ah! His Royal Highness the Pinhead of Wales summons. And, you know, I feel almost well disposed towards him: utter chump though he may be, at least he's not French.

~

SCENE THREE: PRINCE GEORGE'S CHAMBERS

Prince George is with two pals – Lord Smedley and Lord Topper, utter prats. They are sitting on the bed, very refined in ruffled shirts.

Prince George
Une toast, I say, encore une toast. Le Pimpernel Scarlet!

All
Le Pimpernel Scarlet!

A knock on the door. Blackadder enters and stands in the doorway.

Prince George
Ah, *Le Adder Noir*, come in. (*To pals*) This is the fellow to ask, you chaps, my butler – terribly clever, brighter than a brain pie. Blackadder, we're trying to guess who the Pimpernel is so we can send him an enormous postal order to express

our admiration. Any ideas?

Blackadder
I'm sure if you address the envelope to the Biggest Show-off in London, it would reach him eventually.

Topper
Tish an pish, gadzooks, milarky. How dare you say such a thing! Demme sir, if you're not the worst kind of swine!

Smedley
Dem that swine!

Blackadder
I'm sorry, sir. I was merely pointing out that sneaking aristocrats out from under the noses of French revolutionaries is about as difficult as putting on a hat.

Topper
Sink me, sir, this is treason! The Scarlet Pimpernel is a hero! The Revolution is orchestrated by a ruthless band of highly organized killers, dem them!

Smedley
Dem those organized killers!!

Topper
George, if I remember rightly, we were just discussing the French Embassy Ball in honour of the exiled aristocracy?

Prince George
We certainly were. Where I intend to wear the most magnificent pair of trousers ever to issue forth from the delicate hands of Messrs Snibcock and Turkey, Couturiers to the Very Wealthy and the Extremely Fat. If the Pimpernel does finally reveal himself, I don't want to get caught in boring trousers.

Smedley
Dem those boring trousers.

Topper
Well, what say we all bet your cocksure domestic 1,000 guineas that he can't go to France, rescue an aristocrat and present him at the ball. (*To Blackadder*) Ha!

That's turned you white, hasn't it? That's frightened you, you lily-livered, caramel-kidneyed, custard-coloured cad. Not so buoyant now, are ye? Eh? Eh?

Smedley
Eh?

Little pause. Blackadder is cucumber cool.

Blackadder
On the contrary, sirs. I'll just go pack. Perhaps Lord Smedley and Lord Topper will accompany me? I'm sure it will be a fairly easy trip. The odd death-defying leap, and modest amount of dental torture. Want to come?

Topper
Oh, no.

Smedley
Oh, no.

Topper
Dem.

Smedley
Dem.

They scrabble for excuses.

Topper
Any day now – I've got an appointment with my doctor – I've got a sniffle coming on – I can feel it in my bones.

Smedley
Dem bones. Dem bones.

Prince George
Well, then – how about next week? Come on, chaps – get out your diaries.

Topper
All right. Oh, dem, I've left it behind.

Smedley
Behind.

Topper
And besides, I've just remembered, my father's just died and I've got to be at his funeral in ten minutes. Dem sorry.

Goodbye, your Highness.

Topper exits.

Smedley
Dem. I'm the best man. Dem that dead father! Dem him! Goodbye.

Smedley exits.

Blackadder
See you at the ball.

Prince George
What a shame they were so busy – would have been lovely to have had them with us.

Blackadder
(*Worried*) Us?

Prince George
Yes.

Blackadder
You're coming, sir?

Prince George
Oh, yes, certainly.

Blackadder
Ah. And nothing I can say about the mind-bending horrors of the Revolution will put you off?

Prince George
Oh, no! Absolutely not. Come on, Blackadder, let's get packing – I want to look my best for those fabulous French birds.

Blackadder
Sir, the type of women currently favoured in France are toothless crones who cackle insanely.

Prince George
Oh, ignore that – they're just playing hard to get.

Blackadder
By removing all their teeth, going mad and ageing forty years?

Prince George
That's right, the little teasers! *Well*, come on! I think a blend of silks and satins.

Blackadder

I fear not, sir. (*Rings bell*) If we are to stand any chance of survival, we will have to dress as the smelliest low life imaginable.

Prince George

Oh yes? What sort of thing?

At which moment, Baldrick fortuitously enters. There is a whisper of the catwalk about his gait.

Blackadder

Well, sir – let me show you our Paris collection. Baldrick is wearing a sheep's-bladder jacket with matching dung-ball accessories. Hair by crazy Meg of Bedlam Hair. Notice how the overpowering aroma of rotting pilchards has been woven cunningly into the ensemble. Baldrick, when did you last change your trousers?

Blackadder crosses to Baldrick.

Baldrick

I have never changed my trousers.

Blackadder

Thank you. You see the ancient Greeks, your Highness, wrote in legend of a terrible container in which all the evils of the world were trapped. How prophetic they were. All they got wrong was the name. They called it 'Pandora's Box', when of course they meant 'Baldrick's Trousers'.

Baldrick

They certainly can get a bit whiffy, there's no doubt about that.

Blackadder

We are told that when the box was opened, the world turned to darkness because of Pandora's fatal curiosity. I charge you now, Baldrick, for the good of all mankind, *never* allow curiosity to lead you to open your trousers. Nothing of interest lies therein. However, your Highness, it is trousers exactly like these that you will have to wear, if we are to pass safely into France.

Prince George stares at Baldrick's trousers.

Prince George

Yes. On second thoughts, Blackadder, you know, I think I might give this all a miss. My tummy's playing up a bit. Wish, *wish* I could come, but just not poss with this tum.

Blackadder

I understand perfectly, sir.

Prince George

Also, the chances of me scoring if I look and smell like him are zero.

Blackadder

That's true, sir. We shall return presently to bid you farewell.

Prince George goes into his bedroom. Blackadder and Baldrick walk out together and into the vestibule.

Baldrick

Mr B, I've been having second thoughts about this trip to France.

Blackadder

Oh, why?

Baldrick

Well, as far as I can see, looking and smelling like this, there's not much chance of me scoring either.

And Blackadder hits him.

SCENE FOUR: THE VESTIBULE

Blackadder is in his cloak ready to leave. Baldrick has two huge bags; Blackadder,

a small briefcase.

Prince George
Well, Blackadder, this is it.

Blackadder
Yes, sir. If I don't make it back, please write to my mother and tell her I have been alive all the time, I just couldn't be bothered to get in touch with the old bat.

Prince George
Of course, old man, the very least I can do.

Blackadder
Now, we must be gone. The shadows lengthen and we have a long and arduous journey ahead of us. Farewell, dear master and, dare I say, friend.

They shake hands and briefly hug.

Prince George
Farewell, brave liberator and, dare I say it, butler.

He closes the door, almost in tears.

SCENE FIVE: THE KITCHEN

Blackadder and Baldrick enter with their bags from the back door.

Blackadder
Right, stick the kettle on, Balders.

Baldrick
Aren't we going to France?

Blackadder
Of course we're not going to France. It's incredibly dangerous there.

Baldrick
So, how are you going to win the bet?

Blackadder
As always, Baldrick, by the use of the large thing between my ears.

Baldrick
Your nose?

Blackadder
No, Baldrick, my brain. All we do is lie

low here for a week, then go to Mrs Miggins's, pick up any old French aristocrat, drag him through a puddle, take him to the ball and claim our 1,000 guineas.

Baldrick
But what if the prince finds us here?

Blackadder
He can't find his fly buttons, let alone the kitchen door.

SCENE SIX: PRINCE GEORGE'S CHAMBERS

Prince George is unpacking a stupendous pair of trousers.

Prince George
(*To himself*) What a pair of trousers! I shall be the belle of the embassy ball . . . How do you get them on? (*Shouts*) Blackadder! Oh, no, damn! He's gone to France . . . ah, well, do it myself, shouldn't be too difficult . . .

He puts them on his arms. On second thoughts it is a pretty tricky manoeuvre.

SCENE SEVEN: THE KITCHEN

It is one week later. Blackadder and Baldrick are sitting with their feet up. Blackadder is smoking a pipe and reading a newspaper.

Blackadder
Well, Baldrick, what a very pleasant week. We must do this more often.

Baldrick
Yes, I shall certainly choose revolutionary France for my holiday again next year.

Blackadder
However – time to go to work. Off to Mrs Miggins's to pick up any old French toff.

Loud banging upstairs.

Baldrick
What do you think that could be?

Blackadder
If I were feeling malicious, I would say the prince was still trying to put his trousers on after a week.

~

SCENE EIGHT: PRINCE GEORGE'S CHAMBERS

Prince George re-enters from his bedroom to the drawing room. The trousers are now on his head.

Prince George
Damn!

He bangs his head on the wall.

~

SCENE NINE: MRS MIGGINS'S COFFEE SHOP

Enter Blackadder and Baldrick.

Blackadder
Now, Mrs Miggins, I'd like a massive plate of pig's trotters, frogs' legs and snails' ears, please, all drenched in your delicious Scarlet Pimpernel Sauce.

Mrs Miggins
Not so hostile to the Frenchies now, Mr B?

Blackadder
Certainly not, Mrs M, I'd sooner be hostile to my own servant. (*Slaps Baldrick*) In fact, I came here specifically to meet lovely Frenchies.

Mrs Miggins
Well, *vive* to that, and an éclair for both of us!

Blackadder
Vive indeed. Now, what I'm looking for, Mrs M, is a particular kind of Frenchie. Namely, one who is transparently of noble blood but also short on cash.

Mrs Miggins
Oh, well, I've got just the fellow for you. Over there, by the window, the Comte de Frou Frou. Yes, he's pretty down on his luck. He's made that horse's willy last all morning.

Blackadder and Baldrick move over to him. Blackadder is delighted by his find.

Blackadder
We have struck garlic.

He wipes some crumbs off the table on to a plate and hands them to Baldrick.

Now you can have some lunch, Baldrick.

Baldrick
Thank you.

He exits with the plate.

Blackadder
Le Comte de Frou Frou, I believe.

Frou Frou looks up.

Do you speak English?

Frou Frou
A little.

Blackadder
Yes – when you say a little, what exactly do you mean? Can we talk or are we going to spend the rest of the afternoon asking each

other the way to the beach in very loud voices?

Frou Frou
Oh, no – I can order coffee, deal with waiters, make sexy chit-chat with girls, that type of thing.

Blackadder
Oh, good.

Frou Frou
Just don't ask me to take a physiology class or direct a light opera.

Blackadder
No, I won't. Now, listen, Frou Frou, would you like to earn some money?

Frou Frou
No – I wouldn't. I would like other people to earn it, and then give it to me. Just like in France, in the good old days.

Blackadder
Yes, but this is your chance to return to the good old days.

Frou Frou
Oh, how I'd love that. I hate this life – the food is filthy. This huge sausage is very suspicious. If I didn't know better I'd say it was a horse's . . .

Blackadder
Yes, yes, all right. The plan is this. I have a bet on with someone that I can get a Frenchman out of Paris. I want *you* to be that Frenchman. All you have to do is come to the embassy party with me, say I rescued you and then walk away with 50 guineas and all the vol-au-vents you can stuff in your pockets. What do you say?

Frou Frou
(*Smiling*) It will be a pleasure. If there's one thing we aristocrats enjoy, it's a fabulous party. Oh, the music, the laughter! If only I had brought my mongoose costume.

Blackadder is not enthralled.

SCENE TEN: THE EMBASSY

Blackadder opens the door, Baldrick and Frou Frou follow him. The atmosphere is a bit odd, rather more like a prison cell than an embassy.

Frou Frou
Yes – well, obviously the party hasn't really got going yet.

Blackadder
I think that's a bit of an understatement, Frou Frou. I've been at autopsies with more party atmosphere.

Frou Frou
Don't worry. In a moment we will hear the sound of music and happy laughter.

A dramatic sting of music and then a harsh, cruel laugh. A revolutionary appears from the shadows of the corridor.

Frenchman
Bonsoir, messieurs.

Blackadder
Ah, good evening, my man. Do you speak English?

Frenchman
A little.

Blackadder
Good. Well just take me to the ambassador then, will you.

Frenchman
Pardon?

Blackadder takes stock, then proceeds slowly and clearly with actions to help the stupid foreigner.

Blackadder
I have rescued an aristocrat from the clutches of the evil revolutionaries. Please take me to the ambassador.

The Frenchman replies slowly and clearly with the same actions.

Frenchman
No, I won't. I am an evil revolutionary and have murdered the ambassador and turned him into pâté.

Blackadder
Ah.

Ambassador
(*As he now is*) And you, aristo pig, are trapped.

He and Frou Frou face up like mad things.

Frou Frou
Pig! Ha! You will regret your insolence, revolutionary dog!

Ambassador
Dog! Ha! You will regret your arrogance, royalist snake!

Frou Frou
Snake! Ha! . . .

Blackadder
(*Interrupting*) Sorry to interrupt this very interesting discussion – but this is really none of my business, so I think I'll be on my way. Come on, Baldrick.

He sets off for the door.

Ambassador
Ah-ah-ah-ah-ah-ah, not so fast, English.

He blocks his way.

In rescuing this '*boîte de stinkeeweed*', you have attempted to pervert revolution-ary justice. Do you know what I do to peo-ple who do that?

Blackadder
They're given a little present and allowed to go free?

Ambassador
No . . .

Blackadder
They're smacked and told not to be naughty again but basically let off?

Ambassador
No.

Baldrick
(*Raising his hand*) I think I know.

Blackadder
What?

Baldrick
They're put in prison for the night and brutally guillotined in the morning.

Blackadder
Well done, Baldrick.

Ambassador
Your little gnome is correct, *monsieur*. Gentlemen, welcome, to the last day of your life.

He locks the door. Frou Frou peers through its bars. It's all gone horribly wrong. Far from attending a regal bash, they have ended up in a revolutionary prison in the heart of London.

Frou Frou
How dare you, you filthy weasel.

Ambassador
Weasel! Ha! You're one to talk, aristo warthog.

Frou Frou
Warthog! Ha!

Blackadder
Excuse me, Frou Frou.

He pushes Frou Frou out of the way and confidentially addresses the ambassador.

Look, mate, mate, me old mate. We're both working class, we both hate these rich bastards, come on, me old mucker, just let me go, you've got nothing against me.

Ambassador
On the contrary. I hate you English. With your boring trousers and your shiny toilet paper and your ridiculous preconceptions that Frenchmen are great lovers. I'm French and I'm hung like a baby carrot and a couple of petits pois. Farewell old muckers and death to the aristos!

Baldrick
Death to the aristos!

Blackadder
Shut up, mousebrain.

Baldrick
Oh, yes.

Frou Frou
Monsieur, why waste your words on this scum? Have no fear, the Scarlet Pimpernel will save us.

Blackadder pushes Baldrick casually off the bed and sits on it himself.

Blackadder
Ha! Some hope – he's the most overrated human being since Judas Iscariot won the AD 31 Best Disciple Competition.

Frou Frou
Well, if he should fail us – here, I have these suicide pills. One for me (*plucks it from his ear*), one for you (*from his nose*), and one for the dwarf (*from his bottom*).

Blackadder
Say thank you, Baldrick.

Baldrick
Thank you, Mr Frou Frou.

There is a knock on the door.

Frou Frou
Ah, the Pimpernel.

Baldrick
Hurrah!

But it is the bloody ambassador who walks in.

Ambassador
No – the ambassador, hurrah. I've got nothing to do, so I think I will torture you . . . aristo mongrel!

Frou Frou
Mongrel! Ha! I look forward to it, proletarian skunk!

Ambassador
Skunk! Ha! We'll see about that, aristocratic happypotamus.

Frou Frou
Happypotamus! Ha! We'll see who is the happypotamus, proletarian zebra.

Ambassador
Zebra! Ha! . . .

They exit, shouting.

Baldrick
I'm glad to say, I don't think you'll be needing those pills, Mr B.

He gives a big smile.

Blackadder
Am I jumping the gun, Baldrick, or are the words 'I have a cunning plan' marching with ill-deserved confidence in the direction of this conversation?

Baldrick
They certainly are.

Blackadder
Forgive me if I don't jump up and down with joy – your record in the cunning-plan department is not exactly 100 per cent. So, what's the plan?

Baldrick
We do nothing.

Blackadder
Yep. It's another world-beater.

Baldrick
Wait – I haven't finished. We do nothing *until* our heads have actually been cut off.

Blackadder
And then we spring into action?

Baldrick
Exactly! You know when you cut a chicken's head off, it runs round and round the farmyard.

Blackadder
Yeees.

Baldrick
Well, we wait until our heads have been cut off then we run round and round the farmyard, out the farm gate and escape. What do you think?

Blackadder
My opinion is rather difficult to express in

words, so perhaps I can put it this way.

And he tweaks Baldrick's nose with vigour.

Baldrick
Oh, well – it doesn't really matter because the Scarlet Pimpernel will save us anyway.

Blackadder
No, he *won't*, Baldrick. Either I think of an idea, or tomorrow we die. Which, Baldrick, I have to tell you that I have no intention of doing. I want to be young and wild, and then I want to be middle-aged and rich, and then I want to be old and annoy people by pretending I'm deaf. Just be quiet and let me think.

SCENE ELEVEN: THE CELL

It is night. It is dark. It is quiet. Then . . .

Baldrick
I can't sleep, Mr Blackadder.

Blackadder
I said 'Shut up'.

Baldrick
I'm so excited. To think that the Scarlet Pimpernel will be here at any moment.

Blackadder
I wish you'd forget this ridiculous fantasy. Even if he did come, the guards would be woken by the scraping noise as he squeezes his massive swollen head through the door.

Baldrick
I couldn't sleep when I was little.

Blackadder
You still are little, Baldrick.

Baldrick
Well, when I was even littler, see, we used to live in a haunted hovel. Every night our family was troubled by a visitation from this disgusting ghoul. It was terrible – first

there was this unholy smell, then this tiny, hairy, clammy little creature would materialize in the bed between them. Fortunately I could never see it myself.

Blackadder
Yes. Tell me, Baldrick, when you left home, did this repulsive entity mysteriously disappear?

Baldrick
(*Mysteriously*) That very day.

Blackadder
I think then that the mystery is solved. Now, shut up. Either I think of an idea or tomorrow we meet our maker. In my case, God. In your case, God knows. But I'd be surprised if he's won any design awards.

Pause.

Wait a minute. I've thought of a plan.

Baldrick
Hurray!

Blackadder
Also, I've thought of a way to get you to sleep.

Baldrick
What?

Sound of a sharp hit, followed by a clunk from Baldrick.

SCENE TWELVE: THE CELL

The next morning. The door opens and the ambassador enters.

Ambassador
Good morning, scum. Did you sleep well?

Blackadder
(*Very confident*) Like a top. By jiminee, you must be thirsty after your long night's brutality. A drink?

He cunningly and secretly drops two pills into the offered water.

Ambassador
No, thanks. Not while I'm on duty.

Blackadder
Perhaps later?

Ambassador
For you, *monsieur*, there is no later. Because, gentlemen, I am proud to introduce France's most vicious woman, unexpectedly arrived from Paris this morning. Will you please welcome Madame Guillotine herself.

A horrible hag enters, cackling wildly. Half her face is obscured by a large frilly cap.

Mme Guillotine
Ha ha ha. Are these the English pigs?

Blackadder
Yes, that's us.

Mme Guillotine
Leave me with them, Mr Ambassador – I intend to torture them in a way so unbearably gruesome even you won't be able to stand it.

Ambassador
I don't think I will have a problem, *madame*.

Mme Guillotine
No, you will be sick.

Ambassador
Well, let me stay for the first few minutes and if I feel queasy, I will leave.

Mme Guillotine
You will be sick immediately.

Ambassador
What if I am sick quietly in a bag? I mean, what is it exactly you have in mind?

She whispers. The ambassador backs out, gagging.

Mme Guillotine
So, scum – prepare to be in pain!

Blackadder
Yes, certainly. But first perhaps, a toast to your beauty.

Mme Guillotine
Thank you. OK!

She dances forward, takes the cup and swigs it.

So, I expect you were expecting to be rescued.

Blackadder
Some bloody hope.

The reply comes in a perfect cut-glass English accent.

Mme Guillotine
On the contrary, I'm just sorry I was so late.

Blackadder
What!

Mme Guillotine tears off her frilly cap and wig. She is not Mme Guillotine at all – she is Smedley.

Mme Guillotine
Yes, gentlemen, I have come to take you to freedom.

Baldrick
Hurray!

Blackadder
My God – Smedley! But I thought you were an absolute fathead.

Smedley
Ha ha – no, just a dem fine actor. Thank God I got here before you took any of those awful suicide pills.

Blackadder
I suppose, if the person were to take one and wish he hadn't, he'd be able to do something about it?

Smedley
No, they're very odd things. The symptoms are most peculiar – first of all the victims become depressed. (*Very depressed*) Oh, God, this whole Revolution is so depressing. I mean, sometimes I wonder why I bother. I'm so lonely, and no one loves me.

Blackadder
And after the depression, comes death?

Smedley swaps back with irrational fury.

Smedley
No, after the depression comes the loss of temper, you stuck-up bastard. What are you staring at? (*And thumps Baldrick*)

Blackadder
And after the temper comes death?

Smedley
No. After the temper, comes the . . . er . . . the . . . er . . . ?

Blackadder
Forgetfulness?

Smedley
That's it, the . . . er . . .

Blackadder
Forgetfulness.

Smedley
That's it. Right in the middle of a thingy you forget what it was you . . . ooh, nice pair of shoes.

Blackadder
And after the forgetfulness you die?

Smedley
Oh, no, I forgot one! After the forgetful-

ness comes a moment of exquisite happiness! Jumping up and down and waving your hands and knowing that in a minute we'll be free. Free! Free! *Free!*

Blackadder
And then death?

Smedley
No, you jump into the corner first.

He does and falls down dead in a dark corner.

Baldrick
Hurray, it's the Scarlet Pimpernel!

Blackadder
Yes, Baldrick.

Baldrick
And you killed him.

Blackadder
Yes, all right. I mean what is the bloody point of being the Scarlet Pimpernel if you're going to fall for the old poisoned-cup routine. Scarlet Pimpernel my foot. More like Scarlet Git. But wait – this is our chance to escape – quick!!

Baldrick
But what about Mr Frou Frou?

Blackadder
Forget Frou Frou – I wouldn't pick my nose to save his life. Now come on.

They run into the corridor. And bump straight into Frou Frou.

Frou Frou, my old friend and comrade. What are you doing here?

Frou Frou
I escaped. What happened here?

Blackadder
(*Guiltily*) Oh nothing, nothing.

Frou Frou
I thought perhaps for a moment that the Scarlet Pimpernel had saved you.

Blackadder
Ha! Ha!

Baldrick
Ha! Ha!

~

SCENE THIRTEEN: PRINCE GEORGE'S CHAMBERS

Blackadder, Frou Frou and Baldrick enter. Prince George is doing up his trousers – the same trousers, back to front.

Prince George
Ah, chaps – good to see you. Just trying on my trousers.

Blackadder
Sir, I return as promised, plus one top French aristocrat fresh from the Bastille.

Prince George
(*Bowing*) Ah. Pleased to meet you, *monsieur*, do sit down. Damn sorry about the Revolution and all that caper – most awfully bad luck. So tell me, Blackadder, how the devil did you get him out?

Blackadder
Sir, it is an extraordinary tale of courage and heroism which I blush from telling myself. But since there is no one else . . .

Baldrick
I could try.

Blackadder clips Baldrick.

Blackadder
We left England in good weather – but that was as far as our luck held. In the middle of Dover harbour, we were struck by a tidal wave and I was forced to swim to Boulogne, with the unconscious Baldrick tucked into my trousers. Then we were taken to Paris, where I was summarily tried, condemned to death and then hung by the larger of my testicles from the walls of the Bastille. It was then that I decided I'd had enough.

The prince is completely engrossed.

Prince George
Bravo!

Blackadder
So I rescued the Comte, killed the guards, jumped the moat, ran to Versailles, where I climbed into Mr Robespierre's bedroom, leaving him a small tray of milk chocolates and an insulting note. The rest was easy.

Prince George
That is an incredible story. Worthy of the Scarlet Pimpernel himself.

Blackadder
Well, I wouldn't know.

Frou Frou
I, on the other hand, would. (*He stands up*) Because you see, sir . . .

He takes off his wig and glasses with a flourish. Blackadder closes his eyes in startlement. Frou Frou takes off his nose. Baldrick looks amazed. It is Topper.

I am the Scarlet Pimpernel.

Blackadder
Oh – oh.

Baldrick
Hurray!

Prince George
Good Lord. Topper!

Topper
Yes, your Highness.

Prince George
But egads and by jingo with dumplings, steak and kidneys and a good solid helping of sprouts! I can't believe it! You're the fellow who has singlehandedly saved all those dem Frenchies from the chop!

Topper
Well, not quite singlehandedly, sir. I operate with the help of my friend Smedley – but he seems to have disappeared for the moment, slightly mysteriously.

Baldrick is about to speak.

Blackadder
Shut up, Baldrick.

Baldrick
Yes, Mr Blackadder.

Prince George
So, Blackadder rescued the Scarlet Pimpernel.

Topper
No, sir, he did not.

Prince George
Eh?

Topper
Prepare yourself for a story of dishonour and deceit that will make your stomach turn.

Prince George
(*Fascinated*) I say, this is interesting, isn't it, Blackadder?

Blackadder nods.

Topper
Not only that – but I trust it will lead to the imprisonment of a man who is a liar, a bounder and a cad.

He stares at Blackadder. Blackadder looks behind him, but he's not joking his way out of this one.

Prince George
Well, bravo – because we hate liars, bounders and cads, don't we, Blackadder?

Blackadder
Generally speaking, sir, yes. But perhaps before Lord Topper starts to talk he might like a glass of wine. He looks a bit shaken.

Topper
Shaken but not stirred.

Blackadder goes to the tray. There is the pleasant plop of two suicide pills. Blackadder returns and looks on benignly as Topper quaffs his wine.

It all began sir, last week. I was sitting in Mrs Miggins's coffee shop when . . . (*Suddenly depressed*) Oh, God, all this treachery is so depressing. (*Then angry*) I mean the whole thing makes you so incredibly angry!

He hits Baldrick.

It makes you want to . . .

He grabs Prince George and starts shaking him. But suddenly he becomes forgetful.

Nice waistcoat, your Majesty. Erm, sorry, I've completely forgotten what I was talking about.

Blackadder
A story of dishonour and deceit.

Topper
(*Extremely happy*) Oh yes – that's a great story! Great! Oh, that's a wonderful story! Let me just jump into this corner first.

He does so and dies.

Prince George
Well, roast my raisins, he's popped it. I say, Blackadder, do you think he really was the Scarlet Pimpernel?

Blackadder

Well, judging from the ridiculous ostentatiousness of his death, I would say he was.

Prince George

Well, that's a damn shame, because I wanted to give him this enormous postal order.

Blackadder

Please, sir, if you'd let me finish. I would say he was . . . n't. You see, the Scarlet Pimpernel would never, ever, reveal his identity. That's his great secret. So what you're looking for is someone who has – say – just been to France and rescued an aristocrat, but when asked: 'Are you the Scarlet Pimpernel', he replies, 'Absolutely not.'

Prince George

But wait a minute, Blackadder, you've just been to France and you've rescued a French aristocrat. I say, Blackadder, are you the Scarlet Pimpernel?

Blackadder unleashes a huge smile.

Blackadder

Absolutely *not*, sir.

Prince George gapes with excitement and hands him that postal order.

Baldrick

Hurray!

The Prince Regent relishes the prospect of another evening under the
gaming tables playing 'Hide the Sausage'

Turtle and Son,
Gentlemen's Launderers and Sprucers
3, Bun Lane, Clerkenwell

Name: E. Blackadder (p.p. HRH)   Date: 12-19 June 1815

Hats 14
Cravats 21
Gloves 60
Capes 7
Canes 2
Boots 6
Sporrans 0
Kimonos (Informal) 3
Kimonos (Foulweather) 0
Shoulderettes 8
Scanties 44
Fol–de–Rols 2
Skimpies 9
Underskimpies 9
Overskimpies 4
Arbroath Smokies 0
Halter–Neck Swagger–Flopsies 2
Whoopsadaisies 1
Bossom–Hearties 3
Log–Warmers 16
Boleros 2
Bobby–Knickers 0
Varsity–Roasters 0
Wraprascals 4
Bunny–Lariats 1
Todgerellos 16
Billows 7
Bufflers 2
Bung–Nasties 12
Ossops 6
Otter Tops 5
Hair Shirts 0
Sarongs 4
Squeamishes 9

Undersqueamishes 8
Squirters 14
Dinner Dirndls 1
Nightpanties 7
Club–Dorises 2
Slip–Goslings (Fur) 1
Slip–Goslings (Tweed) 0
Blouses 52
Chemises 14
Chive–Clamps 8
Hug–Bunters 2
Dress–Nancies 128
Swallow–Breasted Portscathos 1
Scugs 50
Scrotles 10
Nipple–Loops 2
Neckerchiefs 1, 761
Bullwinkles (Leather) 0
Handkerchiefs 89
Handbags 7
Handberties 2
Cuffs 144
Collars 144
Socks 432,507
Twinsets 0
Dress Jackets 18
Dress Shirts 20
Shirt Dresses 4
Shirts 28
Dresses 3
Smoking Jackets 1
Swimming Kilts 0
Matinee Plumes 0
Mess Petticoats 6

Breakfast Tabards 1

Stockings (Woollen) 30

Stockings (Silk) 12

Hunting Stocks 8

Fishing Spats 0

Spurs 12

Bustles 2

Rumpscallions 14

False Lillians 1

Dirty Bernards 0

Finger-Drearies 18

Bossops 6

Frullets 6

Fun-Clooties 1

Noot Pouches 20

Horaces (Winter) 6

Horaces (Summer) 0

Vests 38

Pinafores 9

Cummerbunds 11

Waffle Stompers 0

Whippet-Saddles 10

Rain-Wazzocks 0

Shuttlecockalorums 1

Hunting-Buns 60

Longjohns 0

Longjacquelines 3

Wispies 4

Jolly Jillies 5

Hussy-Bangles 12

Arse-Corks 0

Foltroons 906

Regimentals 42

Continentals 16

Incidentals 0

Oilskins 0

Sardine-Kirtles 0

Muzzies 81

Doublets 3

Stirrup-Pantaloons 19

Soup-Bibs 21

Popsocks 4

Brummells 2

Thrummels 2

Huffers 6

Grussets 86

Wendy-Cuffs 150

Farthingales 3

Stoat-Gauntlets 0

Toe-Cosies 0

Glossop-Aprons 8

Todger-Nauticals 0

Fishblusters 16

Dilly-Ribbons 2,204

Londonderries 1

Pull-on Rumpsters 1

Suits (Double-Breasted) 0

Suits (Single-Breasted) 0

Suits (Armour) 0

Suits (Cat) 1

Earmuffs 0

Ovengloves 0

Aprons (Pheasant) 1

Aprons (Salmon) 2

Aprons (Stag) 1

Aprons (Frilly) 16

Croquet Waistcoats (Brocade) 0

Croquet Waistcoats (Satin) 7

Croquet Waistcoats (Corduroy) 0

Huggies 2

Bibblers 11

Wind Binkies 8

Busbies 12

Nurses Outfits 2

Hose (Silk) 88

Hose (Garden) 0

Pantigirdles 0

Feather Boas 2

Boob Tubes 1

Basques 0

Leotards 16

Wolf Costume 1

Sense and Senility

SCENE ONE: THE KITCHEN

Baldrick is polishing shoes. Blackadder enters and adjusts his best neck tie – he is dressed more smartly than usual.

Baldrick
You look smart, Mr Blackadder. Going somewhere nice?

Blackadder
No. I'm off to the theatre.

Baldrick
Don't you like it then?

Blackadder
No, I don't! A load of stupid actors, strutting around shouting with their chests thrust out so far you'd think their nipples were attached to a pair of charging elephants. And the worst thing about it is having to go with Prince Minibrain.

Baldrick
Doesn't he like it either?

Blackadder
Oh, no – he loves it. The problem is he doesn't realize it's made up. Last year, when Brutus was about to kill Julius Caesar, the prince yelled 'Look Behind You, Mr Caesar.'

Baldrick
I don't see the point of theatre. All that sex and violence. I get enough of that at home. Well, apart from the sex, of course.

Blackadder
And while we're out, Baldrick, I want you to give the palace a good clean. It's so dirty, it would be unacceptable to a dung-beetle that had lost interest in its career and really let itself go.

The prince calls from outside.

Prince George
Come along, Blackadder! We'll miss the first act.

Blackadder
Coming, sir. Fast as I can.

He sits down with his legs up.

Stick the kettle on, Baldrick.

SCENE TWO: THE THEATRE

*Two actors are on stage in Egyptian garb,
fighting with sword and knife. Quite a lot
of over-acting involved.*

Keanrick
Now, sir, I give this advice to thee.

Never, never, never trust thine enemy.

*Keanrick draws his sword and stabs
Mossop very unrealistically through the
armpit. Prince George is horror-struck.
Mossop sinks to the floor.*

Thy life is forfeit, sir . . .

Mossop
Aaaagh!

*Keanrick kicks Mossop – he is supposed to
be dead – and begins his closing speech
once more.*

Keanrick
Thy life is forfeit, sir, and at an end. Like
our poor play . . .

*He turns to the audience with a grand
flourish.*

We hope we pleased you, friends.

Prince George answers from the box.

Prince George
Certainly not, you murdering rotter.
Guards – arrest that man!

Blackadder
Your Highness – it's only a play.

Prince George
That's all very well but what about the
poor fellow who's dead? Saying 'it's only a
play' won't feed and clothe the little ones
he leaves behind. Call the militia!

Blackadder
But he's not dead: see, he stands, awaiting

your applause.

As indeed he does.

Prince George
Oh I say, that's very clever! I thought he
was really dead. Bravo! Bravo!

*The prince's applause sets off the whole
audience clapping. On stage, Keanrick
and Mossop are taking a bow. Keanrick
whispers to Mossop.*

Keanrick
Blast! The prince likes it.

Mossop
Shit! We'll close tonight.

*Suddenly, a wild-eyed anarchist jumps up
on stage. He shouts at the royal box.*

Anarchist
Work for the weavers! Smash the Spinning
Jenny! Burn the Rolling Rosalind! Destroy
the Going-Up-and-Down-and-Then-
Moving-Along-a-Bit Gertrude! And death
to the stupid prince who grows fat on the
profits!

*He hurls a fizzing bomb into the box and
jumps offstage. Prince George catches the
bomb in very high spirits.*

Prince George
I say, how exciting! The play's getting better and better. Bravo!

*Blackadder is sensibly hiding behind the
curtains.*

Blackadder
It's not a play any more, sir. Just put the
bomb down and make your way quietly to
the exit.

Prince George
Oh, Blackadder – you silly old thing –
your problem is you can't tell when something's real and when it's not!

There is a very big explosion.

SCENE THREE: PRINCE GEORGE'S CHAMBERS

Prince George is on the chaise longue bandaged up and eating heartily. Blackadder is attending him.

Prince George
I must say, Blackadder, that was a close shave. Why on earth should an anarchist *possibly* want to kill you?

Blackadder
I think it might have been you he was after, sir.

Prince George
Oh, hogwash – what on earth makes you say that?

Blackadder
Well, sir, my suspicions were first aroused by his use of the words 'Death to the Stupid Prince.'

Prince George
That *was* a bit rude, wasn't it?

Blackadder
These are volatile times, your Highness, the American Revolution lost your royal father the colonies, the French Revolution murdered brave King Louis, and there have been tremendous rumblings in Prussia, although that might be something to do with the sausages. The whole world cries out, 'Peace, freedom and a few less fat bastards eating all the pie.'

Prince George muses thoughtfully on the pie in his hand.

Prince George
Well, yes quite. Something must be done. Any ideas?

Blackadder
Yes, sir. Next week it is your royal father's birthday celebrations – I suggest that I write a brilliant speech for you to recite, to show the oppressed masses how unusually sensitive you are.

Blackadder holds some smelling salts under the prince's nose to help him in his fragile state.

Prince George
Euch! But tell me more about these oppressed masses – what are they so worked up about?

Blackadder
They are worked up, sir, because they are so poor they're forced to have children simply to provide a cheap alternative to turkey at Christmas. Disease and deprivation stalk our land like two giant stalking things and the working man is poised to overthrow us.

Baldrick enters, holding a bucket and broom. Prince George jumps up and tries to hide in front of the fireplace.

Prince George
Oh, my God – and here he is!!

Blackadder
Don't be silly, that's Baldrick, my dogsbody.

Prince George
What's silly about that? He looks like an oppressed mass to me. Get him out of here at once.

Blackadder
Shoo, Baldrick. Carry on with your cleaning elsewhere. By the end of the night, I want the dining table so clean I could eat my dinner off it.

Baldrick exits with resignation.

Prince George
Crikey, Blackadder. I'm dicing with death here. The sooner I show how unusually sensitive I am, the better. (*He burps*) Oh! And I've just had another brilliant thought!

Blackadder
Another one, your Highness?

Prince George
Yes, actually, another one. Remember the

one I had about wearing underwear on the outside to save on laundry bills? Well this time I'm thinking – 'hello, why don't we ask those two actor chappies we saw tonight to teach me how to recite your speech.' Brilliant, eh?

Blackadder
No your highness. Feeble.

Prince George
What?

Blackadder
I would advise against it. It's a feeble idea.

Prince George
Well tish and pish to your advice Blackadder. Get them here at once. Dammit, I'm fed up with you treating me as if I'm some kind of a thicky! It's not me that's thick – it's you, and you know why? Because I'm a bloody Prince, and you're only a butler! Now, go and get those actors this minute, Mr Thicky Black Thicky Adder Thicky.

~

SCENE FOUR: MRS MIGGINS'S COFFEE SHOP

Mrs Miggins is behind the counter. Blackadder enters the shop.

Blackadder
Mrs Miggins. I'm looking for a couple of actors.

Mrs Miggins
Well, you've come to the right place, Mr B. There's more Shakespearian dialogue in here than there are buns. All my lovely actors pop in on their way to rehearsals for a little cup of coffee and a big dollop of inspiration.

She hands Blackadder a coffee.

Blackadder
You mean they actually rehearse? I thought they just got drunk, stuck on silly hats and trusted to luck.

Mrs Miggins
Oooh, no – there's ever so much hard work goes into the wonderful magic that is theatre today. Still, I don't expect you'd know much about that, being only a little butler.

She chucks him on his cheek. He's getting annoyed.

Blackadder
They do say, Mrs M, that verbal insults hurt more than physical pain. They are, of course, wrong as you will soon discover when I stick this toasting fork in your head.

The door flies open – there is a bellow from outside.

Keanrick
Ladies and gentlemen, would you please welcome Mr David Keanrick.

Mossop
And the fabulous Mr Enoch Mossop.

They enter grandly to general cheers. Blackadder is not impressed.

Keanrick
Settle down, settle down.

Mossop
No autographs, please.

Keanrick
My usual, Mrs M.

Mrs Miggins
Coming up, my lovie.

Blackadder
If I can squeeze through the admiring rabble here (*No one actually*), gentlemen, I've come with a proposition.

Mossop
How dare you, sir! You think just because we're actors we sleep with everyone.

Blackadder
I think being actors you're lucky to sleep

with anyone. I come here on behalf of my employer to ask for some elocution lessons.

Keanrick
I fear, sir, that is quite impossible. We are in the middle of rehearsing our new play – we could not possibly betray our beloved audience by taking time off.

Mossop
Oh, no – never upset the punters. Bums on seats, laddie, bums on seats.

Blackadder
And what play is this?

Mossop
It is a piece we penned ourselves, called *The Bloody Murder of the Foul Prince Romero and His Enormously Bosomed Wife.*

Blackadder
A philosophical work, then?

Keanrick
Indeed, yes. The violence of the murder and the vastness of the bosom are entirely justified artistically.

Blackadder
Right – well I'll tell the prince you can't make it.

Blackadder stands to go, now he has their total attention.

Keanrick
The prince?

Blackadder
Oh, yes, didn't I mention that? Yes, it's

the Prince Regent. Shame you can't make it. Still.

Mossop pushes Keanrick off his chair and propels Blackadder into it.

Mossop
Sir, wait, wait. I think perhaps we could find . . . a little time. Don't you think, Mr Keanrick?

Keanrick
Definitely, Mr Mossop.

Blackadder
No, no, you've got your beloved audience to think about.

Keanrick
Sod the proles, sir. We'll come.

Mossop
Yes. Worthless bastards to a man.

Blackadder
It's nice to see artistic integrity thriving so strongly in the acting community. This afternoon at four then, at the palace.

SCENE FIVE: PRINCE GEORGE'S CHAMBERS

Blackadder knocks and enters. Prince George's face is made up like the actors were earlier – ridiculous red cheeks and huge moustache. He is also wearing a toga.

Prince George
Well. What do you think?

Blackadder
Are you ill or something?

Prince George
No, I was simply trying to look more like an actor.

Blackadder
Well, I'm sure you don't need the false moustache, sir.

Prince George
No?

Blackadder grabs the moustache and yanks it viciously. The prince screams with pain, then goes to a cupboard to put the moustache away. When he opens the door, he finds Baldrick inside.

Egads! It's that oppressed mass again!

The prince drags Baldrick out of the cupboard and starts to strangle him.

Blackadder
No – that is Baldrick spring-cleaning.

Prince George
Oh, yes, so it is.

Blackadder
Finish the job later, Baldrick.

Baldrick
Certainly, sir. The cleaning or the being strangled?

Blackadder
Either suits me.

Prince George
Look, Blackadder. This is all getting a bit hairy, isn't it? I mean, are you sure we can even trust these acting fellows. The last time we went to the theatre, three of them murdered Julius Caesar – and one of them was his best friend, Brutus.

Blackadder
As I've told you about eight times – the man playing Julius Caesar was an actor called Kemp.

Prince George
Really?

Blackadder
Yes.

Prince George
Thundering gherkins! Brutus must have been pretty miffed when he found out.

Blackadder
What?

Prince George
Well, that he hadn't killed Caesar after

all, but just some poxy actor called Kemp.

This elicits a very exasperated look from Blackadder.

What do you think he did, go round to Caesar's place after the play and kill him then?

Blackadder
(*Not very under his breath*) Oh, God, it's pathetic.

~

SCENE SIX: THE KITCHEN

Baldrick is cleaning silver at the table. There is a loud sound of knocking above. He vaguely looks up. Even more knocking. Blackadder enters.

Baldrick
Is that the door?

Blackadder
Yes. But don't worry, it's only the actors.

Blackadder helps himself to some tea and sits down. The knocking continues.

Baldrick
My uncle Baldrick was in a play once.

Blackadder
Really?

Baldrick
Yes. It was called *Macbeth*.

More knocking.

Blackadder
And what did he play?

Baldrick
Second codpiece. Macbeth wore him in the fight scenes.

Even more knocking and even more ignoring of it.

Blackadder
So he was a stunt codpiece.

Baldrick
Yes, that's right.

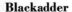

Blackadder
Did he have a large part?

Baldrick
Depends who was playing Macbeth.

Blackadder
Incidentally, Baldrick, actors are very superstitious so on no account mention the word 'Macbeth' this evening.

Baldrick
Why not?

Blackadder
Because it brings them bad luck and makes them very unhappy.

Baldrick
So you won't be mentioning it either?

Blackadder
No. Well, not very often, anyway.

~

SCENE SEVEN: THE VESTIBULE AND PRINCE GEORGE'S CHAMBERS

Keanrick and Mossop enter and brush past Blackadder.

Blackadder
You should have knocked.

Keanrick
Our knocks, you impertinent butler, were loud enough to wake the hounds of hell.

They throw their hats at Blackadder who catches them . . . and throws them straight out the front door. The actors go into the chambers and Blackadder follows.

Lead on, Macduff.

Mossop
I shall – lest you continue in your quotation and speak the name of the Scottish play.

Keanrick
Oho! Never fear, I shan't do that.

Blackadder
By the Scottish play, I suppose you mean *Macbeth*.

A moment of utter horror from the two actors, followed by a violent and stupid superstitious routine.

What was that?

Keanrick
Exorcizing evil spirits. Being only a butler you will know not of the great theatre tradition that one does never speak the name of the Scottish play.

Blackadder
What, *Macbeth*?

They do the superstitious stupidity again.

Good Lord, you mean you have to do that every time I say 'Macbeth'?

And they do it again.

Mossop
Will you please stop saying that. Always call it 'the Scottish play'.

Blackadder
So you want me to say 'the Scottish play'?

Both
Yes.

Blackadder
Rather than *Macbeth*?

They do it again. Prince George enters from his bedroom.

Prince George
For heaven's sake. What is all this hullabaloo out here, shouting and screaming and yelling blue murder?

Mossop and Keanrick bow.

Why, it's like that play we saw the other day, what was it called . . . ?

Blackadder
Macbeth, sir.

And once again the actors do their routine.

Prince George
No, it wasn't – it was called *Julius Caesar*.

Blackadder
Of course. It was *Julius Caesar* . . . not *Macbeth*.

The poor actors go through the ritual once more.

Are you sure you want these people to stay?

Prince George
Of course – I asked them, didn't I, Mr Thicky Butler?

Keanrick
Your Highness, may we say what an honour it is to be invited here?

Prince George
Why certainly.

Keanrick
Thank you. What a great honour it is to be invited here, to make merry in the halls of our king's loins' most glorious outpouring.

Prince George screws up his face in disgust at these words.

Mossop
Now, your Highness, shall we begin straight away?

Prince George
Certainly.

Mossop
Before we inspect the script, let us have a look at stance.

Prince George
Right, yes.

Keanrick
The ordinary fellow stands like this . . . as you do now.

He stands casually.

Mossop
But the hero – stands . . . thus!

Both actors spread their legs a good three feet and strike heroic poses.

Prince George
Ah. So more like . . . this.

He makes a very feeble attempt.

Keanrick
Excellent, sire, but even more.

Prince George
Like . . . this.

All three stand with legs ridiculously apart. There is a creak.

What was that noise?

Mossop
It wasn't me. We're used to standing in this position.

Prince George
It came from . . .

He flings open a chest Baldrick is polishing. Prince George is terrified.

Anarchist!

Baldrick
Cleaner!

Prince George
All right, so you've had a wash. That's no excuse.

Blackadder enters calmly. Prince George starts to strangle Baldrick again.

Die, traitor!

Blackadder
That's Baldrick, your Highness, still spring-cleaning.

Prince George
Rubbish, look – he's got a bomb.

Blackadder
It's not a bomb, sir, it's a sponge.

Prince George
So it is. Well, get out of here at once before it explodes.

Baldrick exits.

Now then, stance. I really think we had something there.

All three spread their legs even further.

Keanrick
Bravo. Your very posture tells me, 'Here is a man of true greatness.'

Blackadder
Either that or, 'Here are my genitals, please kick them.'

Mossop
Sir, I really must ask that this ill-educated oaf be removed from the room.

Keanrick
Yes – get out, sir. Your presence here is as useful as fine bone china at a tea party for drunken elephants.

Prince George
Is that right? Well then, yes, hang it all! Get out, Blackadder, and stop corking our juices.

Blackadder
Very well, your Highness – I'll leave you to dribble on in private.

Blackadder exits, and he is annoyed.

SCENE EIGHT: THE KITCHEN

Blackadder enters with an annoyed grunt. Baldrick is cleaning the floor.

Baldrick
Something wrong, Mr Blackadder?

Blackadder
Yup. I've had it just about up to here with the prince. One more insult and I'll be handing in my notice.

Baldrick
Does that mean I'll be the butler?

Blackadder
Not unless a kindly passing surgeon cuts your head open with a spade and sticks a new brain in it.

Baldrick
Oh, fine.

Blackadder
I don't know why I put up with it, I really don't. Every year at the Guild of Butlers Christmas Party, I'm the one who has to wear the red nose and the pointy hat for winning the 'Who's Got The Stupidest Master' competition. All I can say is, he'd better watch out. One more foot wrong, and the contract between us will be as broken as this milk jug.

He picks up a milk jug.

Baldrick
But that jug isn't broken.

Blackadder
You really do walk into these things, don't you, Baldrick?

He smashes the jug over Baldrick's head, picks up a tray and walks out.

SCENE NINE: PRINCE GEORGE'S CHAMBERS

Prince George is standing as before, legs spectacularly apart, and wearing the most contorted of grins. The actors are lounging.

Mossop
Excellent. And now, sir, at last – the speech.

Prince George
Right. (*Little cough*) 'Th . . .'

Keanrick
No, no – your Royal Highness – what have you forgotten?

Prince George
Look, if I stand any more heroically than this I'm in danger of seriously disappointing my future queen.

Keanrick
Not the stance – the roar.

Prince George
You want me to roar?

Mossop
Well, of course we wish you to roar. All great orators roar before commencing their speeches. It is the way of things. Mr Keanrick, from your *Hamlet* . . .

Keanrick takes a stance, then . . .

Keanrick
'Oooooooooo, to be or not to be . . .'

Definitely a roar.

Mossop
From your *Julius Caesar* . . .

Keanrick
'Oooooo, friends, Romans, countrymen . . .'

Mossop
From your leading character in a play connected with Scotland . . .

Blackadder enters casually.

Blackadder
That's *Macbeth*, isn't it?

The actors do the ritual once more.

Mossop
So, let's roar, shall we? One, two, three . . .

They all roar, Prince George loudest of all.

Keanrick
Excellent, your Highness. Now, shall we try putting it all together?

Prince George does the stance, the facial

expression, gives the loudest roar of all and says very blandly:

Prince George
'Unaccustomed as I am . . .'

Keanrick
No, sire. Alas, you mew it like a frightened tree. May I . . . see the speech?

He takes it and he and Mossop form a huddle. They read it and start sniggering.

Keanrick and Mossop
No, no, no. Dear me.

Keanrick
Who wrote this drivel?

Blackadder
Is there a problem with the speech?

Keanrick and Mossop
Problem?

They both laugh.

Prince George
Yes, there is a problem – the problem is that you wrote it, Mr Hopelessly-Drivelo-Can't-Write-For-Toffee-Crappy-Butler-Weed.

Blackadder drops his tray.

Blackadder
Whoops!

He exits. Perhaps for the last time.

SCENE TEN: THE KITCHEN

Blackadder enters. Baldrick is scrubbing the steps.

Baldrick
Shall I get their supper, sir?

Blackadder
Yes. Preferably something that has first passed through the digestive system of the cat. And you'll have to take it up yourself.

Baldrick
Why?

Blackadder
Because I'm leaving, Baldrick. I am about to enter the job market. Let's see.

He picks up a newspaper and settles for a good read.

Situations Vacant: Mr and Mrs Pitt are looking for a baby minder to take Pitt the Younger to parliament. Some fellow called Stephenson has invented a moving kettle – wants someone to help with the marketing. And there's a foreign opportunity here. 'Treacherous, malicious, unprincipled cad, preferably non-smoker, wanted to be King of Sardinia. No time-wasters please. Apply to: Napoleon Bonaparte, PO Box 1, Paris.' Right. We're on our way.

SCENE ELEVEN: THE DINING ROOM

Prince George and the actors are at supper.

Mossop
Sir, about costume. Any thoughts?

Prince George
Well, enormous trousers certainly. Then I thought perhaps an admiral's uniform, because we know what all the nice girls love, don't we? Tell you what – why don't I go and try them on for you?

Mossop
What a super idea.

Prince George
Help yourselves to wine – you'll need a stiff drink when you see the size of these damn trousers.

Prince George leaves.

Keanrick
My dear, what a ghastly evening.

Mossop
You're so right, love.

Keanrick
While he's gone, let's have a quick read through of *The Bloody Murder of the Foul Prince Romero and His Enormously Bosomed Wife*.

Mossop
Act one, Scene one.
'Spring is come with all its gentle showers, Methinks 'tis time to hack the prince to death . . .'

SCENE TWELVE: THE KITCHEN

Blackadder is all packed and ready to go, with hat and cape on.

Blackadder
Baldrick, I would like to say how much I will miss your honest, friendly companionship.

Baldrick
Thank you, Mr B.

Blackadder
But, as we both know, it would be an utter lie. I will therefore confine myself to saying simply, 'Sod off and if I ever meet you again, it will be twenty billion years too soon.'

The Prince Regent's Butler with something
revolting on his left shoulder

And he leaves, for ever . . .

Baldrick
Goodbye, you lazy, big-nosed, rubber-faced bastard.

Or not. Blackadder reappears in the doorway.

Blackadder
I fear, Baldrick, you'll soon be eating those badly chosen words. I wouldn't bet a single groat that you could survive five minutes here without me.

Baldrick
Oh, come on, Mr B – it's not as if we're going to be murdered or anything the minute you leave, is it?

Blackadder
Hope springs eternal, Baldrick.

And he leaves again. The bell rings.

Baldrick
Coming!

SCENE THIRTEEN: CORRIDOR AND DINING ROOM

Baldrick walks along the corridor towards the dining room. He is about to knock but he hears the actors talking very loudly. They don't notice him.

Mossop
Let's kill the prince.

Keanrick
Who shall strike first?

Mossop
Let me – and let this dagger's point prick his soft eyeball and sup with glee on its exquisite jelly.

Baldrick is terrified at what he has heard.

Keanrick
Have you the stomach?

Mossop
I haven't killed him yet, sir,
But when I do,
I shall have the stomach
And the liver too,
And the floppily doppilies in their horrid gloo.

Keanrick
What if a servant should hear us in our plotting?

Mossop
Ha ha! Then we shall have servant sausages for tea,
And servant rissoles shall our supper be.

Baldrick runs for it.

SCENE FOURTEEN: PRINCE GEORGE'S CHAMBERS

Prince George is trying on his big trousers. Baldrick charges in, terrified and yelling.

Baldrick
Murder! Murder! The revolution's started.

Prince George
What!

He draws his sword and gets Baldrick by the throat.

Baldrick
A plot, sir, a plot to kill you.

Prince George
Ah ha – so you've come clean at last, have you, you bloody little poor person.

Baldrick
No, not me – it's the actors downstairs – they're anarchists.

Prince George
Anarchists?

Baldrick
I heard them plotting, sir. They are going

to poke out your liver and turn me into a rissole. And then suck on your exquisite floppily doppilies.

Prince George
What are we going to do?

Baldrick
Well, Mr Blackadder always says, when the going gets tough, the tough hide under the table.

Prince George
Blackadder! Of course! Where is he?

Baldrick
He's in Sardinia.

Prince George
What? Why!

Baldrick
Well, you were rude to him. So he left.

Prince George
Oh, no! What a mad blundering, incredibly handsome young nincompoop I've been! Oh, God! What can we do? If we go downstairs, they'll chop us up and eat us alive. Oh, God – we're doomed, doomed, doomed!

They hear footsteps in the distance, getting closer. They both cower. Blackadder enters.

Blackadder
Good evening, your Highness. (*He consults his watch*) Four minutes and 22 seconds, Baldrick. You owe me a groat.

Prince George
Thank God you're here. We desperately need you.

Blackadder
Who, me, sir? Mr Thicky Black Thicky Adder Thicky.

Prince George
Doh! Tish! Nonsense!

Blackadder
Mr Hopelessly-Drivelo-Can't-Write–For-Toffee-Crappy-Butler-Weed?

Prince George
Yes, well . . .

Blackadder
Mr Brilliantly-Undervalued-Butler-Who-Hasn't-Had-a-Raise-For-a-Fortnight?

Prince George
Take an extra thousand . . .

Blackadder inspects his nails casually.

. . . guineas . . . per month?

Blackadder
All right – what's the problem?

Prince George
The actors have turned out to be vicious anarchists.

Blackadder is a touch sceptical.

They intend to kill us all.

Blackadder
What are they going to do – bore us to death?

Prince George
No – stab us. Baldrick overheard them.

Baldrick
I did.

Blackadder
Are you sure they meant it?

Prince George
Oh, quite sure. Baldrick, how far apart were their legs?

Baldrick demonstrates.

Their nipples?

Baldrick demonstrates.

They meant it all right.

Blackadder
Very well, sire, I'll see what I can do.

~

SCENE FIFTEEN: CORRIDOR AND DINING ROOM

Blackadder reaches the door to the dining room and listens.

Mossop
To torture him I lust
And singe his hair and up his nostrils
Hot bananas thrust.

Blackadder enters blithely.

Blackadder
Rehearsals going well, gentlemen?

Mossop
Be gone – a mere butler with the intellectual capacity of a squashed apricot can be of no help to us.

Keanrick
Exactly, sir – your participation is as irritating as a potted cactus in a monkey's pyjamas.

Blackadder responds very politely.

Blackadder
Oh, well, in that case I won't interrupt you any longer. Sorry to disturb, gentlemen.

~

SCENE SIXTEEN: PRINCE GEORGE'S CHAMBERS

Prince George and Baldrick are hiding under the table. Blackadder enters.

Prince George
Blackadder – thank God you're safe. What happened?

Blackadder
Sire – there was no need for you to panic. It was all perfectly straightforward.

Prince George
Well?

Blackadder
They're traitors, sir, and must be arrested, brutally tortured and then executed forthwith.

Prince George
Bravo!

~

SCENE SEVENTEEN: THE DINING ROOM

Two soldiers have Mossop and Keanrick bound. Blackadder, Baldrick and Prince George look on.

Mossop
But, your Highness, there's been a terrible mistake.

Blackadder
That's what they were bound to say, sir.

Keanrick
It was a play. A play! Look sire, all the words you heard written down on paper.

Blackadder
Text book stuff again. The criminals' vanity always makes them make one tiny but fatal mistake. Theirs was to have their entire conspiracy printed and published in play manuscript form. Take them away.

The actors are led out, bound – and bound for certain death.

Keanrick
Alas, sir, alas. We beg for mercy.

Blackadder
I've only one thing to say to you . . . 'Macbeth'.

They react accordingly and are dragged away.

Prince George
Well done, Bladders. What can I do to thank you?

Blackadder
You could start by not calling me Bladders, sir.

He shouts into the hall.

Macbeth!

Prince George
Of course, Bladders – no sooner said than done. And no hard feelings?

Blackadder
Absolutely none, sir. I'm glad to be back in the saddle – did I say 'saddle'? I meant harness.

Prince George
Bravo! So, we're the best of friends as ever we were?

Blackadder
Absolutely, sir.

Prince George
Hurrah!

Blackadder
In fact, sir, now that the anarchists Keanrick and Mossop have got their comeuppance, Drury Lane is free tonight and I thought we might celebrate by staging a little play that I've written.

Prince George
Well, what an excellent idea. And with my new-found skills, might there be a part in it for me?

Blackadder
I was hoping that you might play the title role, sir.

Prince George
What a roaringly good idea. What's the play called?

Blackadder
Thick Jack Clot Sits in the Stocks and Gets Pelted with Rancid Tomatoes.

Prince George
Excellent!!

Amy and Amiability

SCENE ONE: THE KITCHEN

Blackadder sits at breakfast and is over-whelmed by unfriendly mail.

Blackadder
Oh, God, bills, bills, bills. One is born, one runs up bills, one dies. And what have I got to show for it? Nothing! A butler's uniform and a slightly effeminate hairdo. Honestly, Baldrick, sometimes I feel like a pelican – whichever way I turn, I've still got an enormous bill in front of me. Pass the biscuit barrel. Let's see what's in the kitty, shall we? (*He empties it*) Nine pence. Oh, God, what are we going to do?

Baldrick
Don't worry, Mr B. I have a cunning plan to solve the problem.

Blackadder
Yes, Baldrick. Let us not forget, you tried to solve the problem of your mother's low ceiling by cutting off her head.

Baldrick
No, but this is a really good one. You

become a dashing highwayman. Then you can pay your bills and, on top of that, everyone will want to sleep with you.

Blackadder
Baldrick, I could become a prostitute and pay my bills and everyone would want to sleep with me, but I do consider certain professions beneath me. Besides which, I fail to see why a common thief should be idolized just because he has a horse between his legs.

Baldrick
My favourite is the Shadow. What a man. They say he's half way to being a new Robin Hood.

Blackadder
Why only half way?

Baldrick
Well, he steals from the rich, but he hasn't got round to giving it to the poor. Look! I've got a poster of him.

He produces a poster of a man in hat and kerchief. It reads:

Wanted for Hanging The Shadow Reward: £1,000

Blackadder
I've no desire to get hung for wearing a silly hat. If I want to get rich quick all I need to do is to go upstairs and ask Prince Fathead for a rise . . .

A ring on the bell.

Ah! The bank's open.

~

SCENE TWO: PRINCE GEORGE'S CHAMBERS

Prince George is sitting at his desk – it is also a mess of papers.

Blackadder
Good morning, sir. May I say how immensely rich you're looking. Now, was there anything you wanted, sir. Anything at all? Absolutely anything.

Prince George
Well, yes, old fellow, I was wondering if you could possibly lend me a bit of cash.

Blackadder
But of course, sir, I . . . cash?

Prince George
Yes, I'm rotten stinking stony broke.

Blackadder
But, sir – what about the £5,000 Parliament voted to give you to drink yourself to death with?

Prince George
All gone, I'm afraid – you see, I've discovered this terrifically fun new game – it's

called 'cards'. What happens is, you sit round a table with all your friends, deal out five 'cards' and then the object of the game is to give all your money away as quickly as possible. Do you know it?

Blackadder
Vaguely, sir, yes.

Prince George
All the chaps say I'm terrific at it.

Blackadder
I seem to remember I was very bad at it. I always seemed to end up with more money than I started with.

Prince George
Ah, yes, it's all down to practice – I'm a natural apparently. The only drawback, of course, is that it's pretty damn expensive. So basically, I was wondering if you could just lend me a couple of hundred.

Blackadder
I'm afraid that's impossible, sir. I'm as poor as a church mouse, that's just had an enormous tax bill on the very day his wife ran off with another mouse, taking all the cheese.

Prince George
What am I going to do?

Blackadder
Yes, it's a difficult one. Well, let's see now, you can't borrow money. You're not going to inherit money and obviously you can't earn money. Sir, drastic situations call for drastic measures. If you can't make money, you'll have to marry it.

Prince George
Marry! Never! I'm a gay bachelor, Blackadder. I'm a roarer, a rogerer, a gorger and a puker! I can't marry, I'm young, I'm firm buttocked, I'm . . .

Blackadder
Broke.

Prince George
Well, yes, I suppose so.

Blackadder
And don't forget, sir, that the modern church smiles upon roaring and gorging within wedlock and, indeed, rogering is keenly encouraged.

Prince George
And the puking?

Blackadder
I believe still very much down to the conscience of the individual churchgoer.

Prince George
Oh, well, tally-ho. Blackadder, fix it up. You know the kind of girls I like. They've got to be lovers, laughers, dancers . . .

Blackadder
And bonkers.

Prince George
Well, that goes without saying.

~

SCENE THREE: THE KITCHEN

Blackadder is consulting a large tome. Baldrick is gutting a chicken. Blackadder slams the book shut.

Blackadder
Oh, God!

Baldrick
Something wrong, Mr B?

Blackadder
Yes. I can't find a single person suitable to marry the prince.

Baldrick
Oh, please keep trying – I love a royal wedding, the excitement, the crowds, the souvenir mugs. The worrying about whether the bride has lost weight . . .

Blackadder
Unlikely with this lot, I'm afraid, if the prince had stipulated 'must weigh a quarter of a ton', we'd be laughing. Of the 262 princesses in Europe, 165 are over 80 – they're out – 47 are under 10 – they're out – and 39 are mad.

Baldrick
They sound ideal.

Blackadder
They would be if they hadn't all got married last week in Munich to the same horse. Which leaves us with two.

Baldrick
Well, what about them?

Blackadder
Well, there's Grand Duchess Sophia of Turin – we'll never get her to marry him.

Baldrick
Why not?

Blackadder
Because she's met him.

Baldrick
Which leaves . . .

Blackadder
Princesss Caroline of Brunswick as the only available princess in Europe.

Baldrick
And what's wrong with her?

Blackadder
(*Suddenly shouting*) Get more coffee! It's horrid, change it! Take me roughly from behind! No, not like that, like this! Trousers off, tackle out! Walk the dog! Where's my present?

Baldrick is very, very shaken by this outburst.

Baldrick
All right! Which one do you want me to do first?

Blackadder
No – that's what Caroline's like. She is famous for having the worst personality in Germany and, as you can imagine, that's up against some pretty stiff competition.

Baldrick
So you're stuck then.

Blackadder
Yes, I'm afraid I am. Unless . . . unless.

Pass me the paper, Baldrick, quick . . .

Baldrick gets the paper. It looks shredded.

Baldrick, why has half of the front page been cut out?

Baldrick
I don't know.

Blackadder
You do know, don't you?

Baldrick
Yes.

Blackadder
You've been cutting out the cuttings about the elusive Shadow to put in your high-wayman scrap book, haven't you?

Baldrick
Oh, I can't help it, Mr B! His life is so dark and shadowy and full of fear and trepidation!

Blackadder
So's going to the toilet in the middle of the night but you don't keep a scrap book on it.

Baldrick
Yes, I do.

Blackadder
Now, let me see . . . the society pages. You see, Baldrick, it needn't *necessarily* be a princess. All the prince wants is someone pretty and rich.

Baldrick
Oh dear – that rules me out then.

Blackadder
Now, let's see – 'Beau Brummel in purple pants probe', 'King talks to tree. Phew! What a Loony'. God, *The Times* has really gone downhill recently. Ahaa! Listen to

this: 'Mysterious Northern beauty, Miss Amy Hardwood, comes to London and spends flipping great wodges of cash.' Aha! That's our baby.

~

SCENE FOUR: PRINCE GEORGE'S CHAMBERS

Blackadder is brushing down Prince George's coat.

Prince George
Honestly, Blackadder, I don't know why I'm bothering to get dressed – the moment I get to the Naughty Hell Fire Club I'll be de-bagged and radished for non-payment of debts.

Blackadder
Radished, sir?

Prince George
Yes. They take your britches down, and then push a large radish up your . . .

Blackadder
Yes, yes, it's all right, sir. There's no need to hammer it home.

Prince George
Well, as a matter of fact, they do often . . .

Blackadder
No, no, no! Your money worries are over, sir.

Prince George
Well, hurrah for that.

Blackadder
I've found you a bride. Her name is Amy, daughter of the noted industrialist, Mr Hardwood.

Prince George
Oh, dammit Blackadder. You know I

loathe industrialists! Sad balding little proles in their damn-yer-eyes weskits. All puffed up just because they know where to put the legs on a pair of trousers.

Blackadder
Believe me, sir, these people are the future. This man probably owns half of Lancashire. His family's got more mills than you've got brain cells.

Prince George
How many mills?

Blackadder
Seven, sir.

Prince George
Quite a lot of mills.

Blackadder
Yes – he has patented a machine called the Ravelling Nancy.

Prince George
What does it do?

Blackadder
It ravels cotton, sir.

Prince George
What for?

Blackadder
That, I cannot say, sir. I'm one of those people who are quite happy to wear cotton but have no idea how it works.

He changes the subject.

She is also a beauty, sire.

Prince George
If she's going to be my bird, she'd better be. Right, so what's the plan?

Blackadder
Well, I thought I could take her a short note expressing your honourable intentions.

Prince George
Yes, I think so too. All right then, take this down . . . 'From His Royal Highness the Prince of Wales to Miss Amy Hardwood. Tally ho, my fine saucy young

trollop, your luck's in. Trip along here with all your cash and some naughty night attire, and you'll be staring at my bedroom ceiling from now till Christmas, you lucky tart! Yours with deepest respect, etc., signed George. PS Woof! Woof!' Well, what do you think?

Blackadder
It's very moving, sir. Would you mind if I change just one tiny aspect?

Prince George
Which one?

Blackadder
The words, sir.

Prince George
Well, I'll leave the details to you, Blackadder – just make sure she knows I'm all man, with a bit of animal thrown in. Worrr!

Blackadder
Certainly, sir.

~

SCENE FIVE: AMY HARDWOOD'S ROOM

The room is very fluffy and pretty. Blackadder is reading to Amy, who is a total drip. It is not quite the same letter.

Blackadder
'From His Royal Highness the Prince of Wales to Miss Amy Hardwood.

The upturned tilt of your tiny wee nosey,
Smells as sweet as a great big posy.'
Fanciful stuff of course, madam, but from
the heart.

Amy
He says my nosey is tiny?

Blackadder
And wee, madam.

Amy
Well, I must say, he must be a clever clogs
because you see my nosey *is* tiny and so wee
that I sometimes think the pixies gave it me.

She gives a tiny tinkling laugh.
Blackadder is stony-faced. Not really his
type of woman.

Blackadder
He continues . . . 'Oh, Lady Amy, queen
of all your sex' . . . I apologize for the
word, madam, but Prince George is a man
of passion.

Amy
Oh, don't worry – I can get pretty cross
myself sometimes. Tell me, Mr
Blackadder, I've heard a teensy rumour
that the prince has the manners of a boy
cow's dingle dangle – what do you have to
say to that?

Blackadder
Oh, that is a lie, madam. The Prince
Regent is shy and pretends to be bluff and
crass and unbelievably thick and gittish.
Whilst deep down he is a soft little marsh-
mallowy piglet type of creature.

Amy
Oh, I am so glad. You see, I am a delicate
tiny thing myself, weak and silly and like a
little fluffy rabbit. So I could never marry
a horrible heffalump or I might get
squished. When can I meet the lovely
prince?

Blackadder
You want to meet him?

Amy
If we're going to get married, I think I

probably ought to. I know, tell him to
come and serenade me, tonight – I'll be on
my balcony in my jim jams.

Blackadder
Certainly, madam.

He is about to go when Mr Hardwood
enters. A definitively bluff Northerner.

Hardwood
Eh up . . . who's this big girl's blouse?

Amy
Father, this is Mr Blackadder. He's come
a-wooing from the prince.

Blackadder
You have a beautiful and charming daughter, sir.

Hardwood
Indeed I do – I love her more than any
pig, and that's saying summat.

Blackadder
It certainly is.

Hardwood
But, let me tell you, I would no more place
her in the hands of an unworthy man than
I'd place my John Thomas in the hands of
a lunatic with a pair of scissors.

Blackadder
An attitude that does you credit, sir.

Hardwood
I'd rather take all my clothes off and paint
my bottom blue than give her to a man
who didn't love her.

Blackadder
What self-respecting father could do
more?

Hardwood
On the other hand, if it's the prince, he
can have her for ten bob and a pickled
egg.

Blackadder
I can see where your daughter gets her
ready wit, sir.

Hardwood
I thank you.

Blackadder
Although where she gets her good looks
and charm is perhaps more of a mystery.

Hardwood
No one ever made money out of good looks
and charm.

Blackadder
You obviously haven't met Lady
Hamilton, sir.

SCENE SIX: THE KITCHEN

*Baldrick is stuffing a chicken whilst
Blackadder wanders around the room
behind him.*

Blackadder
I'll tell you, Baldrick, I'm not looking
forward to this evening, trying to serenade
a light, fluffy, bunny of a girl in the
company of an arrogant, half-German yob
with a mad dad.

Baldrick
He *is* the Prince of Wales.

Blackadder
Have you ever *been* to Wales, Baldrick?

Baldrick
No, but I've often thought I'd like to.

Blackadder
Well, don't. It's a ghastly place, huge
gangs of tough, sinewy men roam the
valleys terrifying people with their close-
harmony singing. You need half a pint of
phlegm in your throat just to pronounce
the place names. Never ask for directions
in Wales, Baldrick – you'll be washing spit
out of your hair for a fortnight.

Baldrick
So being prince of it isn't considered a
plus?

Blackadder
I fear not. No – the crucial thing is that
they must never be left alone together
before the marriage.

Baldrick
Isn't that a bit unfair on her?

Blackadder
It's not particularly fair on him either –
the girl is wetter than a haddock's bathing
costume. But you know, Baldrick – the
world isn't fair. If it was, things like this
wouldn't happen, would they?

He hits Baldrick.

**SCENE SEVEN: THE HARDWOODS'
BALCONY**

*Blackadder and the prince are under the
balcony, whispering.*

Prince George
Right, so what's the plan again? Shin up
the drain and ask if she'll take delivery of
a consignment of German sausage?

Blackadder
No, sir. As we rehearsed, poetry first –
sausage later.

Prince George
Oh, all right. Do you think 'Harold the
Horny Hunter' should do the trick?

Blackadder
Er, remind me of it, sir.

Prince George
'Harold the Horny Hunter,

Had an enormous Horn . . . '

*He'd love to finish this delicate master-
piece, but Blackadder corrects him . . .*

Blackadder
Yes. It is absolutely excellent, sir.
However, might I suggest an alternative?

*Blackadder takes the lyrics from his pock-
et and hands them to Prince George.*

Prince George
'Lovely little dumpling,
How in love I am.
Let me be your shepherdkins,
And you can be my lamb.'

Well, I think we'll be very lucky if she doesn't just come out on to the balcony and vomit over us, but still. Let's give it a whirl.

Blackadder
Right. Just stand right here, sir. Call for her romantically.

Prince George
Righto. (*Steadies himself – then with huge and hideous volume*) OH, COME ON OUT, YOU ROLLICKING TROLLOPING SAUCE BOTTLE. WOOF! WOOF!

Blackadder clamps his hand over Prince George's mouth and pushes him behind a stone plant pot. Amy comes out on to the balcony.

Amy
George?

Prince George
Woof! Woof!

Amy
Is that you?

Blackadder feels he has to intercede.

Blackadder
Yes, yes, 'tis I, your gorgeous little love-bundle.

Amy
Oh, George, I think you must be the snuggly wuggliest lambkin in the whole of toy land!

Prince George
Yucch!

Amy
What was that?

Blackadder
Nothing, nothing. Just a little fly in my throaty. (*Coughs*) Yucch, yucch.

Amy
Do you want a hanky wanky to gob the phlegmy wemmy woo woo into?

Amy takes a hanky from her bosom.

Prince George
Phwoorrr! Crikey!

Amy
Is there someone else down there with you?

Blackadder
No, it's just the wind whistling through the trees and making a noise that sounded like 'Phwoorrr! Crikeeeee!'

Amy
Oh, joy. Then come, Prince Cuddly Kitten, climb up my ivy.

Prince George stands up and strides towards the balcony.

Prince George
Sausage time!

Amy
There *is* someone down there with you.

Blackadder
Oh, my God, yes, so there is – a filthy intruder, spying on our love.

Amy
Oh, hit him, George – hit him!

Blackadder
Very well. (*To Prince George*) Would you mind screaming your Highness? Take that. And that! And that!

He actually hits Prince George.

Prince George
Ah!

Blackadder
And that.

He hits him again. Prince George falls to the ground.

Amy
Oooh, you're so brave. And I'm so worn out with the excitement I'd better go sleepie bobos or I'll be all cross in the

morning – nighty night, Georgy Porgy.

Blackadder
Nighty, wighty, Amy Wamy.

She goes in. Blackadder helps the prince up.

I think it worked, sir. Tomorrow morning I'll go in and ask her father. You go out and start spending his money. I can't stand meanness when it comes to wedding presents. And well done, sir, you were brilliant.

Prince George
Was I?

Blackadder
Yes, sir.

Prince George
But I'm in agony.

Blackadder
Well, that's love for you.

~

SCENE EIGHT: AMY HARDWOOD'S ROOM

Blackadder stands before Mr Hardwood.

Blackadder
Sir, I come as emissary of the Prince Regent with the most splendid news. He wants your daughter Amy for his wife.

Hardwood
Well, his wife can't have her. Outrageous, sir, to come here with such a suggestion. Mind, sir, or I shall take off my belt and, by thunder, my trousers will fall down.

Blackadder
No, sir, you misunderstand, he wants to marry your lovely daughter.

Hardwood
(*Thrilled*) Oh. Can it possibly be true? Surely love has never crossed such boundaries of class.

Amy
What about you and Mum?

Hardwood
Well, yes, I grant thee – when I first met her, I was the farmer's son, and she was just the lass who ate the dung. But that was an exception.

Amy
And Aunty Dot and Uncle Ted?

Hardwood
Yes, all right – he was a pig poker and she was the Duchess of Argyll, but . . .

Amy
And Aunty Ruth and Uncle Isaiah. She was a milkmaid and he was . . .

Hardwood
The pope. Yes, all right, lass, don't argue. Suffice it to say, if you marry we need never be poor or hungry again. Sir, we accept.

Blackadder
Good, so obviously you'll be wanting an enormous ceremony . . . What did you say?

Hardwood
Well, obviously now we're marrying quality . . . we'll never be poor or hungry again.

Blackadder
Meaning . . . that you're poor and hungry at the moment?

Hardwood
Oh, yes – we've been living off lard butties for five years now. I'm so poor I use my underpants for drying dishes.

Blackadder
So you're skint?

Hardwood
Aye.

Blackadder
In that case, the wedding's off, good day.

Amy
But what about George's lovey wovey poems that won my hearty wearty?

Blackadder
All writteny witteny by me-ee we-ee, I'm afraidy waidy. Goodbye.

He exits with callous abruptness.

Amy
Aaaahhh!

She beats the door in love-lorn despair.

~

SCENE NINE: PRINCE GEORGE'S CHAMBERS

Blackadder enters, worried.

Blackadder
Sir. You know I told you to go out and spend a lot of money on presents, well apparent . . .

Blackadder looks around – the entire room is utterly full of golden clutter. The prince is idly inspecting a golden candlestick.

Prince George
Yes?

Blackadder
Nothing, sir – nothing.

~

SCENE TEN: THE KITCHEN

Blackadder storms in, throwing on his cape.

Blackadder
Crisis, Baldrick, crisis – no marriage, no money, more bills. I have decided for the first time in my life to follow a suggestion of yours. Saddle Prince George's horse.

Baldrick
Oh, sir, you're not going to become a highwayman, are you?

Blackadder
No I'm auditioning for the part of Arnold the Bat in Sheridan's new comedy.

Baldrick
Oh, that's all right then.

Blackadder
Baldrick, have you no idea what irony is?

Baldrick
Yes, it's like goldy and bronzy only it's made out of iron.

Blackadder picks up a tricornered hat and puts it on.

Blackadder
Never mind. Never mind. Just saddle the prince's horse.

He takes two pistols out of a box.

Baldrick
That'll be difficult, sir – he wrapped her round that gas lamp in the Strand last night.

Blackadder
Well, saddle my horse then.

Baldrick
What do you think you've been eating this last two months?

Blackadder
Well, go out into the street and hire me a horse.

Baldrick
Hire you a horse? For ninepence? On Jewish New Year? In the rain? A bare fortnight after the dreaded Horse Plague of Old London Town with the blacksmiths' strike in its fifteenth week and the Dorset Horse-Fetishists Fair tomorrow?

Blackadder
Right.

He chucks bit and blinkers at Baldrick.

Well get this lot on. It looks as though you could do with some exercise.

~

SCENE ELEVEN: A STAGECOACH

A dark and stormy night on a remote highway. The Duke of Cheapside and his daughter Sally are inside the stagecoach.

Sally
Honestly, Papa – since mother died you've tried to stop me growing up. I'm not a little girl, I'm a grown woman. In fact, I might as well tell you now, Papa, I'm preg-

nant. And I'm an opium fiend, and I'm in love with a poet called Shelley, who's a famous whoopsy. And mother didn't die, I killed her.

Cheapside
Oh, well, never mind.

There is a shot.

Blackadder
Stand and deliver!

Cheapside
Oh, no – disaster. It's the Shadow – we're doomed, doomed.

Blackadder's head appears at the window of the coach.

Blackadder
Good evening, Duke, and the lovely Miss Cheapside. Your cash bags, please.

And he duly takes them.

Cheapside
You'll never get away with this, you scoundrel. You'll be caught and damn well hung!

Sally
(*Flirtily*) I think he looks . . .

Blackadder
Madam, please, not the jest about me looking pretty well hung already, we have no time.

Sally
Pity.

Blackadder
Now, sir, turn out your pockets.

Cheapside
Never! A man's pockets are his own private kingdom. I shall protect them with my life!

Blackadder
I see, got something embarrassing in there, have you? Perhaps, a particularly repulsive handkerchief, hmmmm? One of those

fellows who has a really big blow and then doesn't change it for a week? Let's look, shall we?

He pulls out some jewels.

Aha!

Sally
Highwayman, I also have a jewel. I fear, however, that I have placed it here, beneath my petticoat, for protection.

Blackadder
Well, in that case, madam . . . I think I shall leave it – I'm not sure I fancy the thought of a jewel that's been in someone's pants. A single kiss of those soft lips is all I require.

Cheapside
Never, sir! A man's soft lips are his own private kingdom. I shall defend them with my life!

Blackadder
I'm not talking to you, grandad.

He kisses Sally.

Sally
Oh, I am overcome. Take me with you to live the life of the wild rogue – cuddling under haystacks and making love in the branches of tall trees.

Blackadder
Madam, sadly I must decline. I fear my horse would collapse with you on top of him as well as me.

Baldrick's head appears from below the window of the stagecoach.

Baldrick
I could try.

Blackadder
No, Quicksilver, you couldn't.

Baldrick
That just isn't fair then. I carry you on my back for ten miles, and I haven't even got a kiss out of it.

Blackadder
Oh, all right, very well then . . .

Sally looks worried, but Blackadder kisses Baldrick.

There, all fair now?

Baldrick
Not really, no.

Blackadder
Chh, no pleasing some horses. Hi ho, Quicksilver.

They disappear.

Sally
Papa, you did nothing to defend my honour.

Cheapside
Oh, shut your face, you pregnant junkie fag hag.

SCENE TWELVE: A LEAFY COPSE

Blackadder and Baldrick sit down to count the loot in a convenient copse.

Blackadder
Well, Baldrick, a good night's work. I think it is time to divide the loot. And I think it is only fair that we should share it equally.

Baldrick
Which I presume is highwayman talk for you get the cash, I get the snotty hanky.

Blackadder
No, no. We did the robbery together so you get half the cash . . .

He hands over one of the bags.

Baldrick
Thank you.

Blackadder
This robbery, on the other hand, I am doing alone.

He points the gun at Baldrick.

Hand it over, your money or your life.

Baldrick hands the bag back.

There you are, you see, all fair and above board.

Baldrick
Fair enough. As long as I haven't been cheated, I don't mind.

At which point, suddenly out of the blue, another highwayman enters. It is the Shadow.

Shadow
Hands up, I am the Shadow, and I never miss.

Blackadder
(*Very depressed*) Oh, no.

Shadow
You, the one that looks like a pig.

Blackadder
He's talking to you, Baldrick.

Shadow
Skedaddle!

He fires at Baldrick's feet as he scuttles off.

So, who have we here?

He tears off Blackadder's mask.

Well! A well set-up fellow indeed. Sir, a kiss.

Blackadder
Sorry! I'm not sure I heard that correctly.

Shadow
Oh, dear. (*He puts the gun to Blackadder's head*) Maybe your ears need unblocking.

Blackadder
Oh, a kiss! Of course, of course, of course. And then perhaps a little light supper, some dancing, who knows where it will lead.

So, a big kiss it is, during which the Shadow pulls off his hat. Long hair cascades down. He is a she, and she is Amy. At the end of kiss, she removes her mask.

Good Lord. It's you.

Shadow
Of course.

Blackadder
But your voice?

Shadow
Clever, isn't it?

Blackadder
Does your father know you're out?

Shadow
He had to go.

Blackadder
You mean, he's dead?

Shadow
Yes. Dead as that squirrel.

Blackadder
Which squirrel?

She shoots at a tree, there is a little squeak, followed by a little thud.

Oh, *that* squirrel. Of course! You killed your father for ruining your chances of a marriage to Prince George.

Shadow
Ha! I despise the prince. Don't you know it's you I want? I want a real man. A man who can sew on a button. A man who knows where the towels are kept.

Blackadder smiles bashfully.

And *yes* – I crave your fabulous sinewy body.

Blackadder
Well, you're only human.

Shadow
Here's the plan, Brown Eyes: you rob the prince of everything he's got, right down to the clothes he's standing in. I'll get my

stash and meet you here. Then we'll run away to the West Indies.

Blackadder
Well, I don't know, I'll have to think about it. (*No pause*) I've thought about it, it's a brilliant idea. See you here tomorrow

~

SCENE THIRTEEN: THE KITCHEN

Blackadder is packing pictures and silver on to a cart.

Blackadder
Right, I'm off.

Baldrick
Oh, sir, but what about the danger? Look, the reward is going up day by day.

He reveals the poster, which now says:

The Shadow
Wanted for
Hanging
Reward: £5,000

Blackadder
Ha – I laugh at danger and drop ice cubes down the vest of fear. Things couldn't be better. She'll get me abroad and make me rich. Then I'll probably drop her and get 200 concubines to share my bed.

Baldrick
Won't they be rather prickly?

Blackadder
Concubines, Baldrick, not porcupines.

Baldrick
Oh. I still can't believe you're leaving me behind.

Blackadder
Don't worry, Baldrick – when we're established on our plantation in Barbados, I'll send for you. No more sad little London for you, Balders, from now on you will stand out as an individual.

Baldrick
Will I?

Blackadder
Of course you will, all the other slaves will be black.

Blackadder turns to the door and bumps straight into Mrs Miggins.

Mrs Miggins
Oh, Mr Blackadder, what's all this I hear about you buying a bathing costume and forty gallons of coconut oil. Are you going abroad then, sir?

Blackadder
Yes, I'm off.

Mrs Miggins
Oh, sir – what a tragic end to all my dreams! And I'd always hoped you might settle down and marry me and that together we might await the slither of tiny Adders.

She catches hold of him and sobs into his waistcoat.

Blackadder
Mrs M, if we were the last three humans on earth, I would be trying to start a family with Baldrick.

That cruel remark breaks her heart.

SCENE FOURTEEN: THE LEAFY COPSE

It is dawn at the same leafy location as the night before. Blackadder wheels his cart in front of him.

Blackadder
Well, here I am, all packed and ready to go.

Shadow
Oh, darling, I'm so pleased to see you. And I've got a little surprise. Close your eyes and open your mouth.

Blackadder does and she puts her gun in it.

Hand over the loot, goat brains.

Blackadder
Ha ha! I always say the bedrock of a good relationship is being able to laugh together. Good. Well done. Now, which way to Barbados?

Shadow
You're not going to Barbados. Now, get away from the cart, Mr Slimy, or I'll fill you so full of lead we could sharpen your head and call you a pencil.

Blackadder
This is turning into a really rotten evening.

Shadow
(*Beginning to tie him up*) Well, you'd better make the most of it – it's your last. And it's a pity because it's normally against my principles to shoot dumb animals.

Blackadder
Except squirrels?

Shadow
Yes. Bastards!

She looks wildly about her.

I hate them with their long tails and their stupid twitchy noses!

She fires randomly and hits some squirrels.

I shall return at midnight to collect the loot – when I'll fill you so full of holes I could market you as a new English cheese.

She exits, laughing.

Blackadder
Oh, God, what a way to die. Shot by a transvestite on an unrealistic grassy knoll.

Blackadder has hours ahead of him – he cannot escape. At which moment of total despair . . . enter Baldrick.

Baldrick
Morning, Mr B.

Blackadder
Baldrick! Thank you for introducing me to a genuinely new experience.

Baldrick
What experience is that?

Blackadder
Being pleased to see you. What are you doing here, you revolting animal?

Baldrick
I've come for the Shadow's autograph. You know, I'm a great fan of the Shadow's.

Blackadder
Yes. Just untie me, Baldrick. Come on.

Baldrick
(*Untying Blackadder*) Has he gone? Oh, what a pity. I wanted him to autograph my new poster. Look, his reward's gone up to £10,000.

Blackadder
Good Lord, £10,000. That gives me an idea. Baldrick, take this cartload of loot

back to the palace, and meet me back here at midnight with ten soldiers, a restless lynch mob and a small portable gallows.

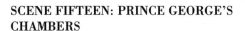

SCENE FIFTEEN: PRINCE GEORGE'S CHAMBERS

Blackadder enters with a breakfast tray. Prince George is reading a paper.

Prince George
Ha ha! Brekkers! I could eat fourteen trays of it this morning and still have room for a dolphin on toast.

Blackadder
Any particular reason for this gluttonous levity, sir?

Prince George
Well, what do you think? I'm in love. I'm in love, I'm in love, I'm in love. Oh, Amy, Amy, bless all ten of your tiny pinkies. Now, let's see, what's in the paper? Oh, my God!!! She's been arrested and hanged!

Blackadder
Oh, really!

Prince George
It turns out she was a highwayman.

Blackadder
Tsk. These modern girls.

Prince George
Yes, apparently someone tipped off the authorities and collected the £10,000 reward. What a greasy sneak. If only I could get my hands on him.

Blackadder
Tsk. You can't trust anyone these days, sir.

Prince George
It says here she had an accomplice.

Blackadder drops the tray.

But they don't know who it was.

The tray jumps back into Blackadder's hands.

Oh, Amy, Amy, I shall never forget you! Never, ever, never, ever! Now, what's for breakfast?

He's forgotten her.

Blackadder
Kedgeree.

Prince George
Great. Actually, come to think of it, I don't need to marry anyway. I've got pots of money.

Blackadder
Really?

Prince George
Yes. The most extraordinary thing happened. I was peckish in the night and nipped downstairs to the biscuit barrel.

A cold chill grips Blackadder.

Blackadder
The biscuit barrel.

George
And do you know what I found inside? Ten thousand pounds I never knew I had.

Blackadder
Ah!

Prince George
In fact, I've got so much money I don't know what to do with it.

Blackadder
How about a game of cards, sir?

Prince George
Excellent idea!

Duel and Duality

SCENE ONE: THE KITCHEN

Blackadder walks in and goes straight to his corner, ignoring Baldrick.

Baldrick
Ooh, Mr Blackadder!

Blackadder
Leave me alone, Baldrick. If I'd wanted to talk to a vegetable I would have bought one at the market.

Baldrick
So, you don't want this message?

He holds up a piece of paper.

Blackadder
No, thank you. God, I'm wasted here.

He flops into his chair. Life is just not worth the living.

It's no life for a man of noble blood, servant to a master with all the intellect of a jugged walrus and all the social graces of a potty.

Baldrick
I'm wasted too. I've been thinking about

bettering myself.

Blackadder
Oh, really – how?

Baldrick
Well, I applied for the job of village idiot of Kensington.

Blackadder
Get anywhere?

Baldrick
I got down to the last two, but I failed the final interview.

Blackadder
What went wrong?

Baldrick
I turned up. The other bloke was such an idiot he forgot to.

Blackadder
Yes. Well, I'm afraid my ambitions stretch slightly further than professional idiocy in West London. I want to be remembered when I'm dead. I want books written about me. I want songs sung about me. And then, hundreds of years from now, I

want episodes from my life to be played out weekly at 9.30 by some great heroic actor of the age.

Baldrick
Yes. And I could be played by some tiny tit in a beard.

Blackadder
Quite. Now, what's this message?

Baldrick
I thought you didn't want it.

Blackadder
Well, I may do – it depends what it is.

Baldrick
So you do want it?

Blackadder
Well, I don't know, do I? It depends on what it is.

Baldrick
(*Getting panicky*) Well I can't tell you what it is unless you want to know, and you said you didn't want to know, and now I'm so confused I don't know where I live or what my name is!

Blackadder
Your name is of no importance and you live in the pipe in the upstairs water closet.

He gets up and snatches the letter from the kitchen table.

Oh, no. Was the man who gave you this by any chance a red-headed lunatic with a kilt and a claymore?

Baldrick
Yes, and the funny thing is, he looks exactly like you.

Blackadder
Oh, God, my mad cousin MacAdder, the most dangerous man ever to wear a skirt in Europe.

Baldrick
Yeh – he came in here playing the bagpipes, then made a haggis, sang 'Auld Lang Syne' and punched me in the face.

Blackadder
Why?

Baldrick
Because I called him a knock-kneed Scottish pillock.

Blackadder
An unwise action, Balders, since Mad MacAdder is a homicidal maniac.

Baldrick
My mother told me to stand up to homicidal maniacs.

Blackadder
Yes, Baldrick, if this is the same mother who confidently claims that you are a tall handsome stallion of a man, I should treat her opinions with extreme caution.

Baldrick
I love my mum.

Blackadder
I love chops and sauce but I don't seek their advice. (*Looks at the letter*) Oh, God, I hate it when MacAdder turns up – he's such a frog-eyed, beetle-browed, basket case.

Baldrick
He's the spitting image of you.

Blackadder
(*Rattled*) No, he is not. We're about as similar as two completely dissimilar things in a pod. Now what's the old tartan throwback banging on about this time? (*Skimming letter*) 'Have come south for rebellion' . . . oh, God, surprise surprise. 'Staying with Miggins . . . the time has come . . . best sword in Scotland . . . Insurrection . . . blood . . . large bowl of porridge . . . rightful claim to throne' . . . (*Screws up letter*) He's mad! He's mad. He's madder than Mad Jack McMad, the winner of this year's Mr Madman competition.

The bell rings.

Ah! The walrus awakes.

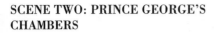

~

SCENE TWO: PRINCE GEORGE'S CHAMBERS

Blackadder enters, carrying the breakfast tray, which he sets down on the table in the living room.

Prince George
Ah, Blackadder. Notice anything unusual?

Blackadder
Yes, sir, it's 11.30 in the morning and you're moving about. Is the bed on fire?

Prince George
Well, I wouldn't know. I've been out all night. Guess what I've been doing? Gorrrr!

Blackadder
Beagling, sir?

Prince George
Better even than that, Blackadder. Sink me, Blackadder, if I haven't just had the most wonderful evening of my life.

Blackadder could not be less enthusiastic.

Blackadder
Tell me all, sir.

He takes off the prince's cloak.

Prince George
Well, as you know, when I set out I looked divine. At the party, as I passed, all eyes turned.

Blackadder
(*Flatteringly*) And I dare say, quite a few stomachs.

Prince George
Well, that's right – but then these two ravishing beauties came over to me and whispered in my ear that they loved me.

He leans provocatively against the door, and then wanders into the bedroom.

Blackadder
And what happened after you woke up, sir?

The prince throws himself luxuriously onto the bed.

Prince George
This was no dream, Blackadder. Five minutes later I was in a coach flying through the London night bound for the ladies' home.

Blackadder
Which ladies' home is this – a home for the elderly or a home for the mentally disadvantaged?

Prince George
No. It was Apsley House – do you know it?

Blackadder
(*Worried*) Yes, sir, it is the seat of the Duke of Wellington. Those ladies I fancy would be his nieces.

Prince George
So you fancy them too. Don't blame you. Bravo! I spent a night of ecstasy with a pair of Wellingtons and I loved it.

Blackadder
Yes. It might interest you to know, sir, that the Iron Duke has always let it be known that he will kill in cold blood anyone who

takes sexual advantage of any of his relatives.

Prince George
Oh, yes, but Big Nose Wellington is in Spain fighting the French – he'll never know.

Blackadder
On the contrary, sir. Wellington triumphed six months ago.

Prince George
I'm dead.

Blackadder
It would seem so, sir.

Prince George
I haven't got a prayer, have I, Blackadder?

Blackadder
Against throat-slasher Wellington, the finest blade his Majesty commands? Not really, no.

He gets up – his life now at stake.

Prince George
Then I shall flee. How's your French, Blackadder?

Blackadder
Parfait, monsieur, but I fear France is not far enough.

Prince George
How's your Mongolian?

Blackadder
Chang-ha-tang, matso moto. But I fear Wellington is a close personal friend of the chief Mongol. They were at Eton together.

Prince George
I'm doomed, doomed as the dodo!

There is a knock on the door.

Oh, my God, he's here. Wellington's here already.

Baldrick enters. Prince George throws himself at Baldrick's feet.

Forgive me, your Grace, forgive. I didn't know what I was doing – I was a mad, mad, sexually over-active fool.

Blackadder
Sir, it's Baldrick. You are perfectly safe.

Prince George
Hurrah!

Blackadder has taken Baldrick's message.

Blackadder
Until six o'clock tonight.

Prince George
(*Subdued*) Hurooo.

Which is the opposite of hurrah!

Blackadder
From the Supreme Commander, Allied Forces, Europe. 'Sir, prince or pauper, when a man soils a Wellington, he puts his foot in it. Open brackets, this is not a joke, I do not find my name remotely funny and people who do end up dead, close brackets. I challenge you to a duel tonight in which you will die. Yours, with sincere apologies for your impending violent slaughter, Arthur Wellesley, Duke of Wellington.'

Baldrick
Sounds a nice, polite sort of bloke.

Prince George starts to cry.

Blackadder
Don't worry, sir, please just consider that life is a valley of woe filled with pain, misery, hunger and despair.

Prince George
Not for me it bloody isn't. As far as I'm concerned, life is a big palace full of food, drink and comfy sofas.

Baldrick has been lurking at the door. He has an idea.

Baldrick
May I speak, sir?

Blackadder
Certainly not, Baldrick. The prince is about to die – the last thing he wants is to spend his final moments exchanging pleasantries with a certified plum duff.

Prince George
Easy, Blackadder – let's hear him out.

Blackadder
Very well, Baldrick, we shall hear you out, then throw you out. Speak.

Baldrick
Well, your Majesty, there is a cunning plan by which you could get out of this problem.

Blackadder
Don't listen to him, sir. It's a cruel proletarian trick to raise your hopes – I shall have him shot the moment he's finished clearing away your breakfast.

Prince George
Wait, Blackadder. Perhaps this disgusting, degraded creature may be a blessing in disguise.

Blackadder
If he is, it's a very good disguise.

Prince George
After all, did not Our Lord send a lowly earthworm to comfort Moses in his torment?

Blackadder
No.

Prince George
Hmm, well it's the sort of thing he might have done. Come on, Mr Spotty, speak.

Baldrick
Very well, your Majesty – I just thought, this Wellington bloke's been in Europe for years. You don't know what he looks like, he don't know what you looks like. So why don't you get someone else to fight the duel instead of you.

Prince George
But I'm the Prince Regent! My portrait hangs on every wall.

Blackadder
Answer that, Baldrick.

Baldrick
Well, my cousin Bert Baldrick, Mr Gainsborough's butler's dogsbody, says he heard that all portraits look the same these days, since they are painted to a romantic ideal, rather than as a true depiction of the idiosyncratic facial qualities of the person in question.

Blackadder
Your cousin Bert obviously has a larger vocabulary than you do, Baldrick.

Prince George
(*Excited*) But he's right, damn him! Anybody could fight the duel – Wellers would never know.

Blackadder
All the same, sir, Baldrick's plan seems to hinge on finding someone willing to commit suicide on your behalf.

Prince George
Oh, yes, yes, yes, but he would be fabulously rewarded! Money, titles, a castle . . .

Baldrick
That's right. I thought maybe Mr Blackadder himself would fancy the job.

Prince George
What a splendid idea!

Blackadder
Excuse me, your Highness, trouble with the staff.

~

SCENE THREE: THE VESTIBULE

Blackadder enters with Baldrick held firmly by the scruff of the neck.

Blackadder
Baldrick, does it have to be this way? Our valued friendship ending with me cutting you up into strips and telling the prince that you walked over a very sharp cattle grid in an extremely heavy hat?

Baldrick
But Mr Blackadder, you were only saying in the kitchen how you want to rise again, and here the prince is, offering the lot.

Blackadder
But tiny, tiny brain, the Iron Duke would kill me! To even think about taking him on you'd have to be some kind of homicidal maniac who was fantastic at fighting, like my cousin MacAdder.

And into his head pops a cunning plan.

MacAdder! MacAdder can fight the duel for me.

~

SCENE FOUR: PRINCE GEORGE'S CHAMBERS

Blackadder re-enters.

Blackadder
My apologies, sir. I was just having a word with my insurance people and obviously I would be delighted to die on your behalf.

Prince George
God's toenails, Blackadder, I'm most damnably grateful. You won't regret this, you know.

Blackadder
Excellent, sir. Just one point sir, re: the suicide policy. There is a duelling clause that requires the policy holder to wear a big red wig and affect a Scottish accent in the combat zone.

Prince George
Small print, eh?

~

SCENE FIVE: MRS MIGGINS'S COFFEE SHOP

It is in chaos – full of tartans and swords, and Mrs Miggins is lying against the bar as Blackadder enters.

Blackadder
Ah, Miggins – am I to assume by your look of pie-eyed exhaustion and the globules of porridge hanging off the walls that my cousin MacAdder has presented his credentials?

Mrs Miggins
Ooh! He has indeed, sir! You've just missed him.

Blackadder
I hope he's been practising with his claymore.

Mrs Miggins
I should say so. I'm as weary as a dog with no legs that's just climbed Ben Nevis.

Blackadder
A claymore is a sword, Mrs Miggins.

Mrs Miggins points to a wood carving which is just behind her up on the bar.

Mrs Miggins
See this intricate wood carving of the Infant Samuel at prayer? He whittled that with the tip of his mighty weapon with his eyes closed.

Blackadder
(*Unimpressed*) Exquisite.

Mrs Miggins
He bid me bite on a plank, there was a whirlwind of steel and within a minute three men lay dead and I had a lovely new set of gnashers.

Blackadder
Really. Well, just tell him to meet me here at five o'clock to discuss an extremely cunning plan. If all goes well, tomorrow the clan of MacAdder will be marching on the highroad back to glory!

Mrs Miggins
Oooh, that's lovely. I'll do you a nice packed lunch.

~

SCENE SIX: PRINCE GEORGE'S CHAMBERS

Blackadder enters.

Blackadder
Good news, your Highness. By evening, I shall have carved the duke into an attractive piece of furniture with some excellent dental work.

He then realizes Prince George isn't about.

Your Highness?

He suddenly notices Prince George behind the bedroom door with his fingers in his ears.

Your Highness?

Prince George
Oh, thank God it's you, Blackadder. I've just had word from Wellington. He's on his way here now.

Blackadder
That's awkward. The duke must believe that I am you from the very start.

Prince George
Any ideas?

Blackadder
There's no alternative, sir, we must swap clothes.

Prince George
Oh, yes – fantastic!! Dressing up – I love it! It's just like that story – 'The Prince and the Porpoise'.

Blackadder
And the Pauper.

Prince George
Oh, yes – 'The Prince and the Porpoise and the Pauper'. Jolly good stuff.

~

SCENE SEVEN: PRINCE GEORGE'S CHAMBERS

Blackadder is now wearing the prince's coat.

Prince George
Excellent, excellent – why, my own father wouldn't recognize me!

Blackadder
Your own father never can, he's mad.

Prince George
Oh, yes.

Blackadder
Unfortunately, sir, you do realize that I shall have to treat you like a servant.

Prince George
Oh, I think I can cope with that, Blackadder.

Blackadder
And you'll have to get used to calling me 'your Highness', your Highness.

Prince George
'Your Highness, your Highness.'

Blackadder
No, just 'your Highness', your Highness.

Prince George
That's what I said – 'your Highness, your Highness', your Highness, your Highness.

Blackadder
Yes, let's just leave that for now, shall we? Complicated stuff obviously.

Baldrick rushes in.

Baldrick
Big Nose is here.

He is totally flummoxed by the cunning switch of identities.

But what? Who? Where? How?

Blackadder
Don't even try to work it out, Baldrick. Two people you know well have exchanged coats, and now you don't know which is which.

Prince George
I must say I'm pretty confused myself. Which one of us is Wellington?

Blackadder
Wellington is the man at the door.

Prince George
Oh. And the porpoise . . . ?

Blackadder
Hasn't arrived yet. We'll just have to fill in as best we can without him. Sir, if you would let the duke in.

Prince George goes to the door.

Prince George
Certainly, your Highness, your Highness.

Blackadder
Right – and you better get out too, Baldrick.

Baldrick
Yes, your Highness, your Highness.

Blackadder
Oh, God. If only they had a brain cell between them.

Enter the Duke of Wellington, a tall, red-faced, arrogant-looking soldier. Prince George announces him.

Prince George
The Duke of Wellington.

Wellington
(*Bowing to Blackadder*) Have I the hon-our of addressing the Prince Regent, sir?

Blackadder
You do.

Wellington
Congratulations, Highness, your bearing is far nobler than I had been informed. (*To Prince George*) Take my coat at once, sir, lest you wish to feel my boot in your throat, and be quicker about it than you were with the door.

Prince George
Yes, my lord.

Wellington clips him for luck.

Wellington
I'm a duke, not a lord! Where were you trained? A dago's dancing class? Shall I have my people thrash him for you, your Highness?

Blackadder pauses. Prince George is getting very worried.

Blackadder
Umm, no, he's very new. At the moment I'm sparing the rod.

Wellington
Fatal error, sir. Give 'em an inch and before you know it they've got a foot – much more of that and you don't have a leg to stand on! Get out!

He whacks Prince George again.

Now then, sir, to business. I am informed that your royal father grows ever more eccentric and at present he believes himself to be (*reads from a paper he is holding*) 'a small village in Lincolnshire commanding spectacular views of the Nene Valley'. I therefore pass my full account of the war on to you, the Prince of Wales.

He hands over a heavy saddle bag. Blackadder takes out a very small piece of paper and reads . . .

Blackadder
Ah, that's excellent, thank you. 'We won.

Signed Wellington.' Right, well that seems to sum things up. Anything else?

Wellington
Two other trifling affairs, sir. The men had a whip round and got you this. Well, what I mean is, I had the men roundly whipped until they got you this. A cigarillo case, engraved with the regimental crest of two crossed dead Frenchmen emblazoned over a mound of dead Frenchmen motif.

Blackadder
Thank you very much. And the other trifling thing?

Wellington
Your impending death, Highness.

Blackadder
Oh, yes, of course. Mind like a sieve.

Wellington
I cannot deny, I am looking forward to it. Britain has the finest trade, the finest army, the finest navy in the world. And what have we for royalty? A mad Kraut sausage-sucker and a son who can't keep his sausage to himself. The sooner you're dead the better.

Blackadder
You're very kind.

Wellington
Now then, no doubt you are anxious to catch up with the latest news of the war. I have here the most recent briefs from my generals in the field.

Blackadder
Yes, well, if you could just pop them in the laundry basket on the way out.

He gets up, rings the bell, and they both sit down at the table, where Wellington is spreading out a map.

Tea?

Wellington
Yes, immediately. Now let's turn to the second front, my lord.

Blackadder
As I understand it, Napoleon is in North Africa. And Nelson is stationed in . . . ?

Wellington
Alaska, your Highness. In case Boney should trick us by coming via the North Pole.

Blackadder
Hmmm. Perhaps a preferable stratagem might be to harry him amid-ships as he leaves the Mediterranean. Let's see – ahm, Trafalgar might be quite a good spot.

He points on the map.

Wellington
(*Rather taken aback*) Trafalgar? Well, I'll mention it to Nelson. I must say I'm beginning to regret the necessity of killing you, your Highness. I'd been told by everybody that the prince was a confounded moron.

Blackadder
Oh, no, no, no.

Enter Prince George whistling. He puts the tea tray down on the map.

Wellington
Hell and buckshot! It's that tiresome servant again!

Prince George sits down next to Blackadder casually.

Prince George
Ooh, budge up, budge up!

Wellington
How dare you sit in the presence of your betters!

Prince George
Oh, cripes, yes, I forgot.

Wellington really smacks him.

Wellington
You speak when you're spoken to and not before, sir! Or perhaps you'd prefer to be flayed across a gun carriage. Well!

He hits him again. Prince George can

scarcely believe it. He comes and stands next to Blackadder, hoping for protection.

Blackadder
Sir, I fear you have been too long a soldier. We no longer treat servants that way in London society.

Wellington
Why, I hardly touched the man!

Blackadder
I fear that you hit him very hard.

Wellington
Nonsense – *that* would have been a hard hit.

He hits Prince George hard.

I just hit him like this.

He hits him again, quite hard actually.

Blackadder
No, sir. A soft hit would be like this (*soft hit*), and you hit him like this (*very, very hard hit*).

Prince George falls over, and picks himself up again.

Prince George
I wonder if I might be excused, your Highness, your Highness?

Blackadder
Yes, certainly.*(He whispers to Prince George)* Sorry about that, sir, but one has to keep up the pretence.

Prince George
(*Whispering*) Of course, quite understand, keep up the good work.

Blackadder
Very good, sir.

Blackadder punches him on the nose. Prince George tries to leave.

Wellington
Hang on, this is bloody coffee, I ordered tea.

He hauls Prince George back from the doorway by the ear.

You really are a most confounded fool. I had heard everywhere that the prince was the imbecile but his servant Blackadder was respected about the town. Now I discover the truth, I am disposed to beat you to death . . . Tea!

Prince George picks up the tray and scuttles out, almost crying. Wellington kicks his retreating backside.

Blackadder
Tell me, do you ever stop bullying and shouting at the lower orders?

Wellington
(*Bellowing*) Never! There's only one way to run a campaign – shout, shout and shout again!

Blackadder
You don't think then that inspired leadership and tactical ability has anything to do with it?

Wellington
No, it's all down to shouting! Baaah!

A mighty roar!

Blackadder
I hear that conditions in your army are appalling.

Wellington
Well, I'm sorry but those are my conditions and you'll just have to accept them. At least until this evening, when I shall kill you.

Blackadder
Who knows, maybe I'll kill you.

Wellington
Nonsense! I have never been so much as scratched – my skin is as smooth as a baby's bottom. Which is more than you can say for my bottom.

Blackadder
Just one point, sir. I should perhaps warn you that while duelling, I tend to put on my lucky wig and regimental accent.

Wellington
Well, that won't help you. It would take a homicidal maniac in a claymore and a kilt to get the better of me.

Blackadder
Oh, that's handy.

~

SCENE EIGHT: THE KITCHEN

Prince George is behaving like a temperamental diva.

Prince George
I tell you, Baldrick, I'm not leaving the kitchen until that man is out of the house.

A knock at the door.

Baldrick
All right, your Majesty. Don't worry. I'll deal with this.

Enter Mrs Miggins.

Mrs Miggins
Hello, Baldrick, I've brought your buns. Where's Mr Blackadder? Not upstairs again running about for that port-swilling, tadpole-brained smelly boots?

Prince George slides out of sight behind the door.

Baldrick
I don't know who you mean.

Mrs Miggins
Prince George, Baldrick. His boots smell so bad a man would need to have his nose

amputated before taking them off. That's what Mr Blackadder says.

Baldrick
(*Very worried*) As a joke.

Mrs Miggins
Didn't you write a little poem about him last week?

Baldrick
No, I didn't.

Mrs Miggins
Oh, you did. 'In the winter it's cool,
In the summer it's hot,
But all the year round,
Prince George is a clot.'

Baldrick
Prince George is a *lovely*. I said Prince George is a *lovely*.

Mrs Miggins
Well, I'd better be off. Tell Mr Blackadder to expect that Mr MacAdder at five o'clock.

She gets ready to leave.

As soon as that fat Prussian truffle pig's got his snout wedged into a bucket of tea cakes.

She makes a snorting noise and leaves.

Baldrick
I think it must be next door you're wanting, Strange-Woman-Who-I've-Never-Seen-Before, Mrs Miggins.

The prince reappears.

Prince George
Baldrick!

Baldrick
Your Highness?

Prince George
(*Very moved*) Is it true? Did you really write a poem about how lovely I am?

Baldrick
Yes. And Mr Blackadder loves you too.

He also slaps Prince George.

Wellington
Or China?

He kicks Prince George, who crashes into the table with his tray.

Don't bother to show me out, I don't want to die of old age before I reach the front door.

And he exits. It's not been a good day for the prince.

~

SCENE TEN: MRS MIGGINS'S COFFEE SHOP

Blackadder enters.

Blackadder
Ah, Miggins, where's MacAdder? I thought he was going to be here at five o'clock?

Mrs Miggins
Yes, I'm sorry – he's just popped out. You look ever so similar to each other, you know. It's quite eerie.

Blackadder
Look, did you tell him to be here or not?

Mrs Miggins
I did, I did! You just seem to keep missing each other – I can't imagine why.

MacAdder appears at the door – red-haired, wild and kilted. They really are astonishingly similar. If it wasn't physically impossible, a person would swear they were the same person in slightly different wigs – one of whom is putting on a rather unconvincing Scottish accent.

MacAdder
I'll tell you why – it's because no coffee shop in England is big enough for two Blackadders.

Blackadder
Ah – good day cousin MacAdder. I trust you are well.

Prince George
Well, I must say I find that very touching.

The bell goes. Prince George jumps to it.

I wish they wouldn't go on doing that.

SCENE NINE: PRINCE GEORGE'S CHAMBERS

Wellington and Blackadder are standing by the door. Wellington shakes Blackadder's hand.

Wellington
Goodbye, sir. May the best man win, sir, i.e. me.

Enter Prince George with tea tray.

Prince George
Your tea, sir.

Wellington
You're late! Where have you been for it – India?

He slaps Prince George.

Blackadder
Or Ceylon?

MacAdder
Aye, well enough.

Blackadder
And dear Morag?

MacAdder
She bides fine.

Blackadder
And how stands that mighty army, the Clan MacAdder?

MacAdder
They're both well.

Blackadder
I've always thought Jamie and Angus were such fine boys.

MacAdder
Angus is a girl.

Blackadder
Of course.

MacAdder
So tell me, cousin, I hear you have a cunning plan.

Blackadder
I do, I do. I want you to take the place of the Prince Regent and kill the Duke of Wellington in a duel.

MacAdder
Aye, and what's in it for me?

Blackadder
Enough cash to buy the Outer Hebrides. What do you think?

MacAdder
Fourteen shillings and six pence? Well, it's tempting but I've got a better plan. Why don't I pretend to be the Duke of Wellington and kill the Prince of Wales in a duel? Then I shall be the king and be crowned with the ancient stone bonnet of MacAdder.

Mrs Miggins
(*Clasping MacAdder's arm*) And I shall wear the granite gown and limestone bodice of MacMiggins, Queen of all the Herds.

Blackadder
Oh, for God's sake, MacAdder, you're not Rob Roy. You're a top kipper salesman with a reputable firm of Aberdeen fishmongers. Don't throw it all away. If you kill the prince, they'll just send the bailiffs round to arrest you.

MacAdder
Oh, blast. I forgot the bailiffs.

Blackadder
So we can return to our original plan then?

MacAdder
No, I'm not interested. I'd sooner go to bed with the Loch Lomond Monster and, besides, I have to be back in the office on Friday – I promised Mr McNulty I'd shift a particularly difficult bloater for him. Forget the whole thing – I'm off home with Miggsie.

Mrs Miggins
Yes, yes, show me the glen where the kipper roams free. Forget Morag for ever.

MacAdder
Never. We must do right by Morag. We must return to Scotland and you shall have to fight her for me in the old Highland way – bare-breasted and each carrying an eight-pound baby.

Mrs Miggins
I shall do it. I love babies.

MacAdder
You are a woman of spirit. I look forward to burying you in the old Highland manner. Blackadder – farewell, you spineless goon.

And they are gone.

Blackadder
Oh, God. Fortune vomits on my eiderdown once more.

SCENE ELEVEN: PRINCE GEORGE'S CHAMBERS

Enter Blackadder. The prince is deep in thought.

Prince George
Ah, Blackadder. It has been a wild afternoon full of strange omens. I dreamt that a large eagle circled the room three times and then got into bed with me and took all the blankets. And then I saw that it wasn't an eagle but a large black snake. Also, Duncan's horses did turn and eat each other – as usual. Good portents for your duel, do you think?

Blackadder
Not very good, sir. I'm afraid the duel is off.

Prince George
Off?

Blackadder
As in 'sod'. I'm not doing it.

Prince George
By thunder, here's a pretty game! You will stay, sir, and do duty by your prince, or . . . !

Blackadder
(*Suddenly annoyed*) Or what, you port-brained twerp? I've looked after you all my life. Even when we were babies I had to show you which bit of your mother was serving the drinks.

Prince George
(*Falling to his knees*) Oh please, please, please, you've got to help me! I don't want to die! I've got so much to give. I want more time!

Blackadder
A poignant plea, sir, enough to melt the stoniest of hearts, but the answer, I'm afraid, must remain 'You're going to die, fat pig.'

He goes to the door. Prince George leaps to his feet.

Prince George
Wait, wait, wait! I'll give you everything!

Blackadder
Everything?

This does rather stop Blackadder in his tracks. He shuts the door.

Prince George
Everything.

Blackadder
The money, the castles, the jewellery?

Prince George
Yes!

Blackadder
The highly artistic but also highly illegal set of French lithographs?

Prince George
Everything!

Blackadder
The amusing clock where the little man comes out and drops his trousers every half hour?

Prince George
Yes, yes, yes! All right.

Blackadder
All right, I accept. A man may fight for many things, his country, his friends, his principles, the glistening tear on the cheek of a golden child. But personally, I'd mud-wrestle my own mother for a ton of cash, an amusing clock and a sack of French porn. You're on.

Prince George
Hurrah!

~

SCENE TWELVE: A COLONNADE

Blackadder, still wearing the prince's wig and coat, and Baldrick are first to arrive for the duel. It is a misty morning, the kind of weather in which momentous deeds are done.

Blackadder
Right, Baldrick, here's the plan. When he offers me the swords, I kick him in the nuts and you set fire to the building. In the confusion we claim a draw. All right?

At which moment the Duke of Wellington enters.

Wellington
Your Highness. *(Bows to Blackadder)* Let us be about our business.

Blackadder takes Baldrick aside.

Blackadder
Don't forget, Balders, you . . . (*mimes lighting a match*) when I . . . (*mimes knee jerk*)

Wellington
Then, sir, choose your stoker.

He holds out a box. Blackadder takes out one of the furry plungers.

Blackadder
What! Are we going to tickle each other to death?

Wellington
No, sir. We fight with cannon!

Blackadder notices two small cannon at each end of the half-assembled colonnade.

Blackadder
But I thought we were fighting with swords?

Wellington
Swords! What do you think this is, the Middle Ages? Only girls fight with swords these days. Stand by your gun, sir. Hup two three, hup two three hup!

Blackadder
Wait a minute.

Wellington
Stand by cannon for loading procedure!

He shouts out bewildering technical lingo with movements like the Royal Tournament and with bits of metal snap-

ping into place.

Muzzle! Stoke! Crank the staunch pedal! Ready priming paper! Pull tinder!

Blackadder is not keeping up at all. He reads from the cannon's manual.

Blackadder
'Congratulations on choosing the Armstrong Whitworth four-pounder cannonette. Please read instructions carefully and it should give you years of trouble-free maiming.'

Wellington
Check elevation! Chart trajectory!

Blackadder doesn't know where to start. Meantime, Wellington is kneeling by a perfect little cannon, pointed at Blackadder, three feet away. He lights it with a taper at arm's length.

Prime fuse! Aim!

Blackadder
Now look, just wait a moment.

Wellington
Fire!

Huge cannon shot, Blackadder is blown over. When the smoke clears he lies with his head in Baldrick's lap, distinctly dying. Sad music wafts through the still air.

Baldrick
Mr B, oh, Mr B! (*Calling out*) Help me get his coat off.

Blackadder
Leave it, Baldrick, it doesn't matter.

Baldrick
It does, sir, blood's hell to shift. I want to get it in to soak.

Wellington kneels on one knee beside the heroic and doomed figure.

Wellington
You die like a man, sir, in combat.

Blackadder
You think so? Dammit, we must build a

better world. When will the killing end?

Wellington
You don't think that I too dream of peace? You don't think that I despise this damn dirty job they call soldiering?

Blackadder
Frankly, no. My final wish upon this earth is that Baldrick be sold to provide funds for a Blackadder foundation to promote peace and do research into the possibility of an automatic machine for cleaning shoes. Also, I charge that . . .

He dies. Woe upon woe.

Wellington
His Highness is dead.

The music jerks to a sudden stop.

Blackadder
Actually, I'm not sure I am . . .

Miracle upon miracle, he springs to his feet.

Fortunately that cigarillo box you gave me was placed exactly at the point the cannon ball struck. I've always said smoking was good for you.

Wellington rises.

Wellington
Honour is satisfied. God clearly preserves you for greatness. His Highness is saved. Hurrah!

And he drops to one knee again. At which point, Prince George enters, in Blackadder's wig and coat.

Prince George
Umm no, actually, it's me. I'm his Highness. Well done Bladders. Glad you made it.

Wellington is red with fury.

Wellington
What in the name of a Bonaparte's balls is this fellow about now?

Prince George
No, I really am the prince. It was all just larks, and uncommon fine larks at that, I thought.

Wellington
I have never, in all my campaigns, encountered such insolence! Your master survives a duel of honour and you cheek him like a French whoopsy. I can contain myself no longer.

He shoots Prince George cursorily. Sad music starts up again. Prince George lies in the laps of Blackadder and Baldrick.

Prince George
I die. I hope men will say of me that I did duty by my country.

Blackadder
I'm thinking that's pretty unlikely, sir. If I were you I'd try something a bit more realistic.

Prince George
Like what?

Blackadder
Uhm, you hope that men will think of you as a bit of a thicky.

Prince George
All right, I'll hope that. Toodle-oo, don't ye know, and all that.

Prince George dies.

There is a fanfare of trumpets, and a shout, 'Kneel for his Majesty, the King of England.' Enter the king, a big mad German carrying a plant. They all kneel.

King
Someone said my son was here. I want him to marry this rosebush, and want to make the wedding arrangements.

A short meaningful pause.

Blackadder
Here I am, Daddy. This is the Iron Duke Wellington, commander of all your Majesty's armed forces.

King
Yes, I recognize the enormous conk.

Wellington puts his arm around Blackadder as they face the king. He is very complimentary of Blackadder, who laps it up.

Wellington
A hero. A man of taste and wit and discretion.

King
Well, bravo! You know, son, for the first time in my life, I have a real fatherly feeling about you. I know people think I'm stark raving mad, and say the word 'Penguin' at the end of every sentence, but I believe we too can make Britain great – with you as prince regent and I as King Penguin.

Blackadder
Let's hope, eh? My Lord Wellington – will you come and dine with us at the palace? My family have a lot to thank you for.

Wellington
With pleasure. Your father may be as mad as a balloon but you have the makings of a fine king.

Blackadder
Oh, and Baldrick, clear away that dead butler, will you.

They leave. Baldrick is left alone with Prince George. He kneels beside him, full of sorrow.

Baldrick
A new star in heaven tonight, a new freckle on the nose of the giant pixie . . .

Prince George suddenly opens his eyes and sits up.

Prince George
No, actually, Baldrick, I'm not dead! You see, I had a cigarillo box too!

He searches for it in his pocket, but to no avail.

Oh damn, I must have left it on the dresser.

And he falls back down dead again. It is very much the end.

lad
A young boy or stable-hand

lady
A female gentleman

lea
That part of a sauce which is not a perrins

leak
Everyone knows what one of these is

lean-to
A kind of shed with a strange name

leapfrog
Any frog born on 29 February

lee
A small word with several 'e's in it

leech
A small black creature, a bit like a burnt sausage, used for sucking the blood out of people, they make attractive pets as they are easy to care for, and when placed on cushions next to one's host's cat, serve to make a very amusing practical joke

leek
A long, thin Welsh tomato

left behind
Part of the sitting apparatus of a personage

leg
Binary pedipalp of person, animal or arthropodic used for perambulation or unambulatory standation

legend
That part of a leg not in the middle

legendary
Don't know

legumifery
No idea

lull
A lull

me
A harmless lexicographical fellow

melt
A way of serving tuna fish

mitonchondria
Part of a horse's leg (probably)

mob
Last word on this page, phew, I'm off to the coffee house

BALDRICK'S

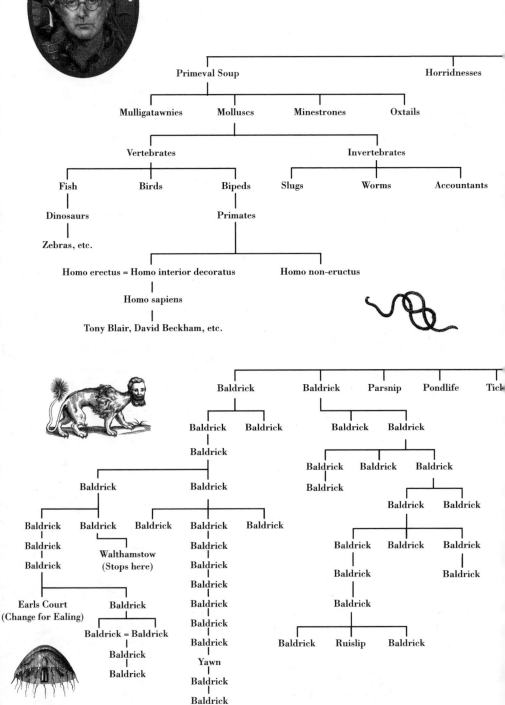

Primeval Soup

Horridnesses

Mulligatawnies   Molluscs   Minestrones   Oxtails

Vertebrates   Invertebrates

Fish   Birds   Bipeds   Slugs   Worms   Accountants

Dinosaurs   Primates

Zebras, etc.

Homo erectus = Homo interior decoratus   Homo non-eructus

Homo sapiens

Tony Blair, David Beckham, etc.

Baldrick   Baldrick   Parsnip   Pondlife   Tick

Baldrick   Baldrick   Baldrick   Baldrick

Baldrick   Baldrick   Baldrick   Baldrick

Baldrick   Baldrick

Baldrick   Baldrick   Baldrick   Baldrick

Baldrick   Baldrick   Baldrick   Baldrick   Baldrick   Baldrick   Baldrick   Baldrick

Baldrick   Baldrick   Baldrick   Baldrick   Baldrick

Baldrick   Walthamstow   Baldrick   Baldrick   Baldrick

           (Stops here)   Baldrick

Earls Court   Baldrick   Baldrick   Baldrick

(Change for Ealing)   Baldrick

Baldrick = Baldrick   Baldrick   Baldrick   Ruislip   Baldrick

Baldrick   Yawn

Baldrick   Baldrick

Baldrick

FAMILY TREE

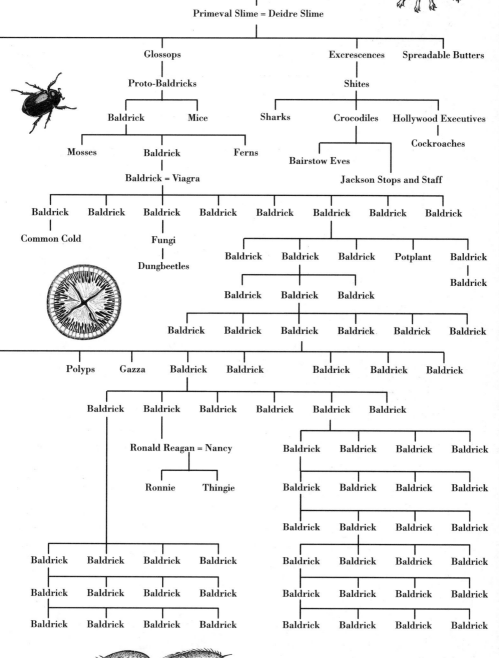

Volcanic Gloop

Primeval Slime = Deidre Slime

Glossops

Excrescences   Spreadable Butters

Proto-Baldricks

Shites

Baldrick   Mice

Sharks   Crocodiles   Hollywood Executives

Cockroaches

Mosses   Baldrick   Ferns

Bairstow Eves

Baldrick = Viagra

Jackson Stops and Staff

Baldrick   Baldrick   Baldrick   Baldrick   Baldrick   Baldrick   Baldrick   Baldrick

Common Cold

Fungi

Baldrick   Baldrick   Baldrick   Potplant   Baldrick

Dungbeetles

Baldrick

Baldrick   Baldrick   Baldrick

Baldrick   Baldrick   Baldrick   Baldrick   Baldrick   Baldrick

Polyps   Gazza   Baldrick   Baldrick   Baldrick   Baldrick   Baldrick

Baldrick   Baldrick   Baldrick   Baldrick   Baldrick   Baldrick

Ronald Reagan = Nancy   Baldrick   Baldrick   Baldrick   Baldrick

Ronnie   Thingie   Baldrick   Baldrick   Baldrick   Baldrick

Baldrick   Baldrick   Baldrick   Baldrick

Baldrick   Baldrick   Baldrick   Baldrick   Baldrick   Baldrick   Baldrick   Baldrick

Baldrick   Baldrick   Baldrick   Baldrick   Baldrick   Baldrick   Baldrick   Baldrick

Baldrick   Baldrick   Baldrick   Baldrick   Baldrick   Baldrick   Baldrick   Baldrick

The Blackadder Chronicles

PART FOUR:
INDUSTRY AND EMPIRE – 1815-1914

O n the death of George III in 1820, history tells us, George, Prince Regent, succeeded to the throne. We, of course, know better. It was Edmund Blackadder, the former butler, who ruled England as 'George IV'.

Not being a mad German, Blackadder proved to be a surprisingly effective king. He started the British Museum, the National Gallery, the Police Force and the world's first railway between Stockton and Darlington. He legalized trade unions and made it possible for Catholics to become MPs, as well as finding time to sleep with the Countess of Jersey, the Marchioness of Hertford, Lady Melbourne and the Marchioness of Conyngham, and have Baldrick transported to Australia for stealing a turd.

Surprisingly, Baldrick rather flourished in Australia. After a brief period working as a koala in Melbourne Zoo, he branched out into kangaroo farming, a venture that proved rather less than successful when he tried to economize on fencing and settled for a lovely, very cheap, foot-high post-and-rail arrangement.

Hearing of the Industrial Revolution which was now sweeping Europe, Baldrick became inspired to start sweeping Australia. It was a long and completely futile job, which he abandoned a third of the way along the south coast of Tasmania. Instead he settled down to enjoy the fruits of his greatest technological triumph, the Spinning Baldrick. This innovative idea – you put some wool on a table and Baldrick spun it for you – was a huge success in a country that was crammed to the rafters with sheep but populated exclusively by a bunch of idle Aussies who couldn't be arsed to get off their fat behinds by the pool and do any actual work.

Back in civilization, Queen Victoria came to the throne. Now began a prudish, prurient era when piano legs were covered to avoid exciting the lower orders and it was illegal to be caught in possession of genitalia after dark. This was a bad and boring time for the Blackadders, many of whom left to seek their fortune in the empire. One of them, Lt. Edmund Blackadder, VC, of the 21st/34th Lancers, is recorded as trying to negotiate the surrender of Rorke's Drift, with the immortal last words: 'Oh, just keep the bloody place then!'

At home, it was the first great age of popular entertainment. 'Elegant Eddie' Blackadder was the toast of the Music Halls with his roaringly hilarious numbers 'A Can Can Ain't A Can Can If You Keep Your Bloomers On (I Want My Money Back, You French Tart)' and the hugely patriotic 'Let's Shove, Shove, Shove (A Bayonet Up A Frenchman)'.

Meanwhile, science and technology made enormous strides in all directions. In engineering, Isambard Kingdom Blackadder invented a method of making virtually anything out of iron: steamships, bridges, benches, statues, tunnels, funnels, gloves and, of course, irons. In biology, Charles Darwin's famous 'Origin of Species' came to him suddenly one afternoon in Melbourne Zoological Gardens.

Idly chatting with a rather ugly koala, he guessed with a brilliant flash of intuition that Baldrick's brain must bear an uncanny resemblance to a mollusc. The Theory of Evolution was born.

In physics, scientists were beginning to discover the ultimate building blocks of matter. Towards the turn of the century the great physicist J. J. Thompson (later Lord Kelvin) discovered the tiny electron, and the not-so-great physicist E. E. Blackadder (later E. E. Blackadder, deceased) discovered the miniature hole in the side of his Biro. In medicine, it was widely put about by a certain Dr Blackadder that he had in fact invented penicillin the Wednesday before it was discovered by Sir Alexander Fleming, but had thrown it away because he didn't think the name was catchy enough.

Queen Victoria finally died in 1901, a Dr Blackadder by her side, and she was followed by a string of kings who all looked like Captain Haddock in *Tintin* and were all about as intelligent. Nothing very much happened for the next eight years, until in 1909 Captain Blackadder of the Antarctic claimed to have reached the South Pole – not only before Scott of the Antarctic, but even before Roald Amundsen, the famous explorer and writer of children's books. He was there when the others arrived, he maintained, but wasn't spotted because he was wearing a lightweight, cream-coloured summer suit. It was, after all, July.

And so we reach the last recorded scion of the dynasty. Edmund Blackadder had joined the British army in the 1888, at a time when it was less a modern fighting force and more a kind of exclusive travel agency for gentlemen who enjoyed hunting, shooting and sleeping with exotic races less well-armed and more naked above the waist than their own. Winning the Military Medal at the Battle of Mboto Gorge for his selfless action in blowing up a heavily defended mango dump when under fire by a hail of wortleberries, Captain Blackadder was promoted and drafted to France. Relaxing one morning over a small Turkish coffee and a medium-sized French postmistress, he glanced up and saw to his dismay that the horizon was blotted out by approximately 500,000 very large, very German Germans ...

BLACKADDER GOES FORTH

Front-line news from our Special Correspondents in the field, Richard Curtis and Ben Elton

CAPTAIN COOK
When General Haig unveils his new strategy to move his drinks cabinet six inches closer to Berlin, Blackadder volunteers to be Official War Artist.

CORPORAL PUNISHMENT
Orders for Operation Insanity arrive and Blackadder breaches regulations by eating the messenger. Can the Flanders Pigeon Murderer avoid the firing squad?

MAJOR STAR
The Russian Revolution produces two more appalling results: an offensive by Germany and a really offensive Charlie Chaplin impression by Baldrick.

PRIVATE PLANE
German machine-guns in front, British firing squads behind – the only way out is up tiddly up-up.

GENERAL HOSPITAL
The secret of the Great Plan is out. Ordered to find a spy in the hospital, Blackadder spots a man with a strong German accent, a beautiful nurse and a chance for three weeks in bed.

GOODBYEEE
Millions have died but the troops have advanced no further than an asthmatic ant with some heavy shopping. Now, at last, the final big push looms ...

The Cast

Captain Edmund Blackadder	Rowan Atkinson
Private S. Baldrick	Tony Robinson
General Sir Anthony Cecil Hogmanay Melchett	Stephen Fry
Lieutenant The Honourable George Colthurst St Barleigh	Hugh Laurie
Captain Kevin Darling	Tim McInnerny
Corporal Perkins	Jeremy Hardy
Sergeant Jones	Stephen Frost
Private Fraser	Lee Cornes
Private Robinson	Paul Mark Elliott
Private Tipplewick	Jeremy Gittins
Driver Parkhurst	Gabrielle Glaister
Squadron Commander Lord Flashheart	Rik Mayall
Baron von Richthoven	Adrian Edmondson
Lieutenant von Gerhardt	Hugo E. Blick
Nurse Mary Turnsouttobeaspyattheend	Miranda Richardson
Brigadier Smith	Bill Wallis

Captain Cook

SCENE ONE: THE DUG-OUT

A dug-out in a trench in the middle of the Great War. There is a general atmosphere of mud. It contains table, chair, bed, Captain Blackadder and Private Baldrick. 'Pomp and Circumstance' plays on the gramophone.

Blackadder is reading, but there is a tiny annoying scratching sound. He shifts slightly, trying to ignore it but finally, can't . . . He lifts the needle on the gramophone, but the scratch continues . . .

Blackadder
Baldrick, what are you doing out there?.

Baldrick
I'm carving something on this bullet, sir.

That's the scratching noise.

Blackadder
What are you carving?

Baldrick
I'm carving 'Baldrick', sir.

Blackadder
Why?

Baldrick
It's a cunning plan, actually.

Blackadder
Of course it is.

Baldrick
You know they say that somewhere there's a bullet with your name on it?

Blackadder
Yes.

Baldrick
Well, I thought if I owned the bullet with my name on it, then I'll never get hit by it. Because I won't ever shoot myself.

Blackadder
Shame.

Baldrick
And the chances of there being two bullets with my name on them are very small indeed.

Blackadder
Yes, it's not the only thing round here
that's very small indeed. Your brain's so
minute, Baldrick, that if a hungry
cannibal cracked your head open, there
wouldn't be enough to cover a small water
biscuit . . .

*George enters, with a nice new revolver
and a magazine. He is a very enthusiastic, bright-eyed and bubble-headed young
officer.*

George
Tally-ho, pip pip and Bernard's Your
Uncle.

Blackadder
In English we say 'Good morning'.

George
(*Excited*) Look what I've got for you, sir!

Blackadder
What?

Baldrick goes outside into the trench.

George
The latest issue of *King and Country*.
Damn inspiring stuff. 'The magazine that
tells the Tommies the truth about the war.'

Blackadder
Or, alternatively, the greatest work of fic-
tion since vows of fidelity were included in
the French marriage service.

George
Come, come, sir, you can't deny that this
fine newspaper is good for the morale of
the men.

Blackadder
Certainly not. I just feel that more could
be achieved by giving them some real toilet
paper.

George
Not with you at all, sir. What could any
patriotic chap have against this magnificent mag?

Blackadder
Apart from his bottom?

George
Yes.

Blackadder
Well look at it. This stuff is about as con-
vincing as Dr Crippen's defence lawyer!
The British Tommies are all portrayed as
six foot six with biceps the size of
Bournemouth.

George
Exactly – thoroughly inspiring stuff. Oh,
and look, sir, this also arrived for you this
morning.

*George holds out a gun wrapped in a
brown paper bag. Blackadder unwraps it
and handles it thoughtfully.*

Blackadder
Do you know what this is, Lieutenant?

George
It's a good old service revolver.

Blackadder
Wrong – it's a brand *new* service revolver,
which I've suspiciously been sent without
asking for it. I smell something fishy and
I'm not talking about the contents of
Baldrick's apple crumble.

George
It's funny, we didn't ask for those new
trench-climbing ladders either . . .

Blackadder
New ladders?

George
Yes, sir. Came yesterday. I issued them to
the men and they were absolutely thrilled.

He shouts out to the trench.

Isn't that right, men?

*Baldrick appears at the door to the duf-
out.*

Baldrick
Yes, sir. First solid fuel we've had since we
burnt the cat.

Blackadder goes out to the trench, fol-

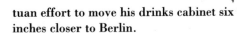

Blackadder
Mmm – something's going on, and I think I can make an educated guess what it is – something which you, George, would find hard to do.

George
True. When I was at school, education could go hang. As long as a boy could hit a six, sing the school song very loud and take a hot crumpet from behind without blubbing.

Blackadder
Yes, I, on the other hand, am a fully-rounded human being – a degree from the University of Life, a diploma from the school of hard knocks and three gold stars from the kindergarten of getting the shit kicked out of me. And my instincts lead me to deduce that we are at last about to go . . . over the top.

George
Great Scott, sir, you don't think the moment's finally arrived to give Harry Hun a darn good British-style thrashing, six o' the best, trousers down?!

Blackadder
If you mean are we all going to get killed, the answer is 'yes'. Clearly Field Marshal Haig is about to make yet another gargan-

tuan effort to move his drinks cabinet six inches closer to Berlin.

George
Bravo-issimo! Let's make a start, eh – up and over to glory! Last one in Berlin's a rotten egg!

He makes a move to charge up and over the trench walls.

Blackadder
Give me your helmet, Lieutenant.

George gives Blackadder his hat. He throws it up in the air. Massive machine-gun fire is heard. The hat descends totally perforated with bullet holes.

George
Yes, some clever hat camouflage might be in order.

He heads off sparkily.

Baldrick
Permission to speak, sir.

Blackadder
Granted – with a due sense of exhaustion and dread.

Baldrick
I have a cunning plan to get us out of getting killed, sir.

Blackadder
Oh, yes. What is it?

Baldrick
Cooking.

Blackadder
I see.

Baldrick
You see, sir, Staff HQ are always on the look-out for good cooks. Well, we go over, and we cook something and get out of the trenches that way.

Blackadder
Baldrick, it's a brilliant plan.

Baldrick
It is?

Blackadder
Yes, it's superb.

Baldrick
Permission to write home immediately, sir – this is the first brilliant plan a Baldrick has ever had. For centuries we've tried, and they've always turned out to be total pigswill. My mother will be as pleased as Punch.

Blackadder
If she were as good-looking as Punch, we'd all be a lot happier. There is, however, one slight flaw in the plan, Baldrick.

Baldrick
Ah.

Blackadder
You're the worst cook in the entire world.

Baldrick
Oh, yes, that's right.

Blackadder
There are amoeba on Saturn who can boil a better egg than you. Your filets mignons in sauce béarnaise look like dog turds in glue . . .

Baldrick
That's because they are . . .

Blackadder
Your plum duff tastes like a molehill decorated with rabbit droppings . . .

Baldrick
I thought you wouldn't notice . . .

Blackadder
And your cream custard has the texture of cat's vomit . . .

Baldrick
Again, it . . .

Blackadder
If you were to serve up one of your meals in Staff HQ, you would be arrested for the greatest mass poisoning since Lucretia Borgia invited 500 of her close friends round for a wine and anthrax party. No,

we'll have to think up a slightly better plan than that.

Baldrick
Right, how about a nice meal while you chew it over?

Blackadder
What's on the menu?

Baldrick produces a rat as if a bottle of wine.

Baldrick
Rat – sautéed or fricassee.

Blackadder puts on glasses.

Blackadder
Oh – the agony of choice. And sautéed involves?

Baldrick
Well you take the freshly shaved rat, and you marinate it in a puddle for a while.

Blackadder
Mhm, for how long?

Baldrick
Until it's drowned. After that you stretch it out under a hot light bulb, then you get within dashing distance of a latrine and you scoff it right down.

Blackadder
I see. so that's sautéeing, and fricasseeing?

Baldrick
Exactly the same. Just a *slightly* bigger rat.

Blackadder
Well, call me Old Mr Unadventurous, but I think I'll give it a miss this once . . .

Baldrick
Fair enough – more for the rest of us, eh, sir?

George
Absolutely, Private, tally ho, barf, barf!

George has just popped back in. The hat on his head is camouflaged by a coil of barbed wire wrapped round it. The field

telephone rings. Blackadder answers.

Blackadder
Hello, the Savoy Grill. Oh, it's you – yes, I'll be over there in forty minutes.

He puts the phone down.

Baldrick
Who was that, sir?

Blackadder
Strangely enough, Baldrick, that was his Holiness Pope Gregory IX inviting me to join him for drinks aboard his steam yacht *Saucy Sue* currently wintering in Montego Bay with the England cricket team and the Balinese Goddess of Plenty.

Baldrick
Really?

Blackadder
No, not really. I've been ordered to HQ – no doubt means that idiot General Melchett is about to offer me an attractive new opportunity to have my brains blown out for Britain.

He puts on his greatcoat.

SCENE TWO: STAFF HQ

It is a grand room, clearly purloined from a French mayor. There is a grand marble fireplace and a grand desk, at which Darling is sitting and writing. Maps cover the wall, filing cabinets and charts are off to one side. Blackadder enters.

Blackadder
What do you want, Darling?

Darling
It's Captain Darling to you. General Melchett wants to see you about a highly important secret mission.

General Melchett enters.

Melchett
What's going on, Darling?

Darling jumps up immediately from behind Melchett's desk.

Darling
Captain Blackadder to see you, sir.

Melchett
Ah, excellent – short back and sides today, I think, please.

Darling
No, sir – that's Corporal Black. Sir – Captain Blackadder is here about the other matter, sir. The 'secret' matter.

Melchett
Oh, yes, of course. The special mission. At ease, Blackadder. Now what I am about to tell you is absolutely tip-top secret, is that clear?

Blackadder
It is, sir.

Melchett
I've compiled a list of those with security clearance. Have you got it, Darling?

Darling
Yes, sir.

Melchett
Read it, please.

Darling
It's top security – I think that's all the captain needs to know.

Melchett
Nonsense – let's hear the list in full!

General Melchett takes the salute on behalf of Lord Haig, Lady Haig
and their tortoise, Alan

Darling

Very well, sir. (*Reading*) List of personnel cleared for Mission Gainsborough, as dictated by General C. H. Melchett: you and me, Darling, obviously, Field Marshal Haig, Field Marshal Haig's wife, all Field Marshal Haig's wife's friends, their families, their families' servants, their families' servants' tennis partners and some chap I bumped into in the mess the other day called Bernard.

Melchett

So it's maximum security. Is that clear?

Blackadder

Quite clear, sir. Only myself and the rest of the English-speaking world is to know.

Melchett

Good man!

Melchett now leads Blackadder across to the map table.

Now Field Marshal Haig has formulated a brilliant tactical plan to ensure final victory in the field.

Blackadder

Would this brilliant plan involve us climbing over the top of our trenches and walking slowly towards the enemy?

Darling

How did you know that, Blackadder? It's classified information.

Blackadder

It's the same plan that we used last time, sir. And the seventeen times before that.

They all move over to the desk.

Melchett

E-e-exactly! And that's what's so brilliant about it. It will catch the watchful Hun totally off guard. Doing exactly what we've done eighteen times before will be the last thing they'll expect us to do this time. There is, however, one problem.

Blackadder

That everyone always gets slaughtered in the first ten seconds?

Melchett

Exactly. Field Marshal Haig is concerned that this may be depressing the men a tadge, so he's looking for a way to cheer the men up.

Blackadder

His resignation and suicide seem the obvious answer.

Melchett

Interesting thought. Note it, Darling.

Darling

(*Uneasy*) Sir.

But Melchett has another thought. He reaches into a drawer.

Melchett

Take a look at this – I'm sure you know it. *King and Country*.

Blackadder

Yes, sir – without question my favourite magazine. It's soft, it's strong and thoroughly absorbent.

Melchett

Top hole, Blackadder. I thought it would be right up your alley. And Field Marshal Haig's plan is this: to commission a man to do an especially stirring painting for the cover of the next issue to inspire the men for the secret push. So what I want you to do, Blackadder, is labour night and day to find us a first-rate artist amongst your men.

Blackadder

Impossible. I know from long experience all my men have the artistic talent of a cluster of colour-blind hedgehogs in a bag.

Melchett

That's a bit of a blow. We needed a man to leave the trenches immediately.

Blackadder

Leave the trenches? I wonder if you have enjoyed, as I have, sir, the marvellous

painting in the National Portrait Gallery – *Bag Interior* by the Colour-Blind Hedgehog Workshop of Siena.

Darling
I'm sorry, are you saying you *can* find this man?

Blackadder moves over to the map on the wall.

Blackadder
I think I can, and might I suggest, sir, that having left the trenches it might be a good idea to have our man posted to Paris (*he points nonchalantly at Paris on the map*) to soak up a little artistic atmosphere there – perhaps even Tahiti (*gesticulating airily at another map*) so as to produce a real masterpiece.

Darling is alarmed.

Melchett
Yes, yes! But can you find the man?

Blackadder
Now I *know* I can, sir. Before you can say 'Sunflowers', I'll have Vincent van Gogh standing before you.

SCENE THREE: THE TRENCH

The trench has been turned into an informal artists' commune. Blackadder has an easel and Baldrick a drawing board. George is looking over Blackadder's shoulder, um-ing and ah-ing over the painting. Finally Blackadder stops, turns round and looks at him in annoyance.

George
No no, don't stop, it's coming, sir, it's definitely coming. I-hmm. I, I just wonder whether two socks and a hand-grenade are really the sort of inspiring stuff that covers of *King and Country* are made of.

Blackadder
They will be when I've painted them

shoved up the Kaiser's backside.

George
Ah, now this is interesting.

Blackadder
What is?

George
Private Baldrick is obviously a bit of an impressionist.

Blackadder
The only decent impression he can do is of a man with no talent. What's it actually called, Baldrick? *The Vomiting Cavalier?*

George
No, sir, that's not supposed to be vomit. It's dabs of light.

Baldrick
No, it's vomit.

George
Ah, now why did you choose that?

Baldrick
You told me to, sir.

George
Did I?

Baldrick
Yes, sir. You told me to paint whatever comes from within . . . so I did my breakfast. Look there's a little tomato.

Blackadder
Really, this is hopeless – if only I'd paid attention in nursery art classes instead of spending my entire time manufacturing huge papier mâché willies to frighten Sarah Wallis.

George
Funny – painting was the only thing I was ever any good at.

Blackadder
Well, it's a pity you didn't keep it up.

George goes into the dug-out, waffling apologetically.

George
Well, as a matter of fact I *did* actually. I

mean normally of course I wouldn't *show* them to anyone, because they're just embarrassing daubs really – but they give me pleasure – embarrassed to show them to you now, really – well, for what they're worth, should have my hands cut off . . .

He takes out a stack of drawings from under his bed. They're very good.

Blackadder
These are brilliant, George. Why didn't you mention these before?

George
Well, you know, one doesn't like to blow one's own trumpet.

Blackadder
No, but you might at least have told us you had a trumpet. These paintings could spell my way out of the trenches.

George
Yours?

Blackadder
That's right, ours. All you have to do is paint something heroic to appeal to the simple-minded Tommy. Over to you, Baldrick.

Baldrick
What about a Noble Tommy standing with a look of horror and disgust over the murdered body of a nun, brutally done over by a nasty German?

George
Excellent – I can see it now – the Nun and the Hun!

Blackadder
Splendid – no time to lose. George – set up your easel, Baldrick and I will pose. This

is art's greatest moment since Mona Lisa sat down and told Leonardo da Vinci she was in a slightly odd mood. Baldrick, you lie down and be the nun.

Baldrick
I'm not lying down there – it's all wet!

Blackadder
Let me put it this way – you can either lie down and get all wet or you can be knocked down and get a broken nose.

Baldrick
Actually, it's not that wet is it?

Blackadder
No.

He flicks Baldrick to the ground. There is a squelch of huge wetness. Baldrick looks up, his face covered in mud.

Baldrick
And who are you going to be then, sir . . . the noble Tommy?

Blackadder
Precisely, standing over the body of the ravaged nun.

Baldrick
I want a wimple.

Blackadder
Well, you should have gone before we started the picture.

Baldrick
You know, the funny thing is – my father was a nun.

Blackadder
No, he wasn't.

Baldrick
He was so, I know because whenever he

was in court and the judge used to say
'Occupation', he'd say 'Nun'.

*George has been in the dug-out, changing.
He returns in a big shirt and a beret,
transformed as best he can into an artist.*

Blackadder
Right, you ready?

George
Yes, if you'd just like to pop your clothes
on a stool.

Blackadder
I'm sorry?

George
Just pop your clothes on the stool over
there.

Blackadder
You mean . . . you want me . . . tackle
out?

George
Well, I would have thought so, yes.

Blackadder
If I can remind you of the realities of battle, George, one of the first things everyone notices is that all the protagonists
keep their clothes on. Neither we nor the
Hun favour fighting our battles *au
naturel* . . .

George
It's artistic licence, sir . . . it's the willing
suspension of disbelief.

Blackadder
Yes, well, I'm not having anyone staring in
disbelief at my willy suspension. Just get
on and paint the bloody thing, sharpish.

Blackadder poses for picture.

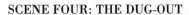

SCENE FOUR: THE DUG-OUT

*An hour later. Blackadder, George and
Baldrick are inspecting the painting.*

Blackadder
Brilliant, George – it's a masterpiece. The
wimple suits you, Baldrick.

Baldrick
But it completely covers my face!

Blackadder
Exactly. Now men, General Melchett will
be here any moment. When he arrives,
leave the talking to me, all right. I like to
keep an informal trench, but today, you
may only speak with my express permission. Is that clear?

They don't reply.

Is that clear?

*Still no reply. Their eyes are bulging.
Then at last Blackadder twigs.*

Permission to speak.

George and Baldrick
Yes, sir. All clear, sir.

*From the trench a loud cry is heard:
'Ten Shun!' Melchett and Darling enter.*

Darling
Dug-out – ten-shun!

Melchett
Excellent. At ease. Afternoon,
Blackadder. Where would you like me to
sit? I thought just a little trim of the moustache, nothing drastic.

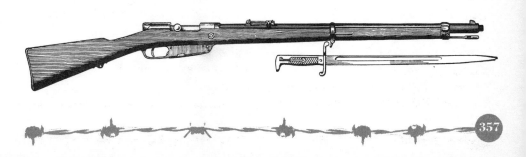

Darling
No, sir – we're here about the paintings.

Melchett
Oh, yes! Good Lord! George, how are you, my boy?

George remains silent

I said, how are you?

Blackadder, not having been concentrating, suddenly realizes that George isn't speaking.

Blackadder
Oh yes – permission to speak.

George
Thank you. I'm absolutely top-hole, sir, with a ying and a yang and yippideedoo.

Melchett
Splendid – your Uncle Bertie sends his regards: I told him you could have a week off in April – don't want you to miss the Boat Race, do we?

George looks questioningly at Blackadder – Blackadder suddenly clicks, and nods.

Blackadder
Permission to speak.

George
Certainly not, sir. Permission to sing boisterously, sir.

Blackadder
If you must.

George
(*Sings*) Row, row, row your punt!

Melchett and George
Gently down the stream,
Belts off, trousers down!
Isn't life a scream!
Oi!

All this is done with a little accompanying dance ending on a pelvic thrusting movement. Darling applauds enthusiastically and Blackadder claps drily.

Blackadder
Fabulous. University education – you can't beat it, can you?

Melchett
Bravo . . . What have we here? Name?!

Baldrick looks at Blackadder.

Blackadder
Permission to speak.

Baldrick
Baldrick, sir.

Melchett
Ha ha! Tally ho! Yippidee dap and zing zang spillett. Looking forward to the final chukker?

Baldrick says nothing. Blackadder wishes he'd never started this.

Blackadder
Permission to speak.

Baldrick still says nothing.

Answer the general, Baldrick.

Baldrick
I can't answer him, sir, I don't know what he's talking about, sir.

Melchett decides to speak to him like an intelligent foreigner.

Melchett
Are-you-looking-forward-to-the-big-push?

He pinches his cheek indulgently.

Baldrick
(*Answers the same way, and pinches the general's cheek back*) No-sir-I'm-absolutely-terrified.

Melchett
Mnmm! The healthy humour of the honest Tommy! And if you should falter my boy, always remember that Captain Darling and I are behind you.

Blackadder
About thirty-five miles behind you.

Darling, rather annoyed by this, twitches a little.

Melchett
Now then, stand by your beds, let's have a look at this artist of yours, Blackadder. Next to me, Darling.

Darling
Thank you, sir.

Melchett
Found someone for me, have you, Blackadder?

Blackadder
General, I think I have – none other than young George here.

George looks suitably modest.

Melchett
Bravo! Well, let's have a shufti then, shall we?

Blackadder takes out the picture he himself painted earlier.

Blackadder
It's simply called *War!*

The painting is not good.

Melchett
Damn silly title, George. Looks more like a couple of socks and a stick of pineapple to me.

George
Permission to speak, sir.

Blackadder
Ahm . . . I think *not* actually, Lieutenant.

Melchett
Quite right. If what happens when you open your mouth is anything like what happens when you open your paint box, we'll all be drenched in phlegm. This isn't what we're looking for at all, is it, Darling?

Darling
No, sir.

Melchett
No, sir.

Next Blackadder takes out Baldrick's painting.

Blackadder
There is this, sir – it's Private Baldrick's. He's called it *My Family and Other Animals*.

Melchett
Oh, good Lord, no.

Blackadder
Oh, dear, well, I'm afraid that's really it, apart from this little thing.

He takes out George's painting.

Melchett
Ah, yes, now that's more like it.

Darling
Who did this, Captain Blackadder?

Blackadder
Well, actually, it was me.

George
Permission to speak really quite urgently, sir!

Melchett
Blast and damn your goggly eyes – stop interrupting, George! Now this is excellent. Congratulations, man. It's totally inspiring – makes me want to jump over the top and yell, Boo Sucks to you, Fritzy!

Blackadder
Thank you, sir.

Darling
Are you sure you did this, Blackadder?

Blackadder
Of course I'm sure.

Darling
I'm afraid I don't believe you.

Blackadder
How dare you, Darling! General, I can't let that slur pass. What possible low, suspicious slanderous reason could this *office boy* have for thinking I didn't paint the picture?

Darling
Well, three reasons as a matter of fact. Firstly, you're in it.

Blackadder
It's a self-portrait.

Darling
Secondly, you told us you couldn't paint.

Blackadder
Well, one doesn't like to blow one's own trumpet.

George
Perm . . .

Blackadder
Denied.

Darling
Thirdly, it's signed . . . 'George'.

Blackadder moves casually over to the painting and looks at it.

Blackadder
Well spotted. But not *signed* George – ahm – dedicated to George, King George. Gentlemen, the King!

All
The King!

Baldrick
Where?

Melchett
Bravo, Blackadder! I have absolutely no hesitation appointing you our official regiment's artist. You're a damn good man – not a pen-pushing, desk-sucking, blotter-jotter like Darling, here, eh, Darling!

Darling
No, sir.

Melchett
No, sir. Accompany us back to HQ immediately.

Blackadder gets his suitcase, which is already packed.

Darling
Ten-shun!

George and Baldrick stand to attention as they leave.

George
Permission to jolly well speak right now, sir, otherwise I might just burst like a bally balloon!

Blackadder
Later, George, much later.

SCENE FIVE: STAFF HQ

Melchett
Congratulations on your new appointment, Blackadder.

Blackadder
Thank you, sir.

Darling
May I say, Blackadder, I am particularly pleased about it.

Blackadder
Are you?

Darling
Oh, yes.

But there is something very sinister about him.

Melchett
Now that you are our official war artist, we can give you the full briefing. The thing is, Blackadder, the *King and Country* cover story was just a cover story. We want you, as our top painting bod, to leave the trenches.

Melchett
We want you to come back with accurate drawings of enemy positions.

Blackadder
You want me to sit in No Man's Land painting pictures of the Germans?

Melchett
Precisely. Good man!

Blackadder starts to put his coat back on.

Blackadder
It's a very attractive proposition, gentlemen, but unfortunately not practical. You see my medium is light – it'll be pitch dark. I won't be able to see anything.

Melchett
Good point – we'll send up a couple of flares! You'll be lit up like a Christmas tree for miles around.

Blackadder
Excellent, excellent – glad I checked.

SCENE SIX: NO MAN'S LAND

Blackadder, George and Baldrick are crawling through very dangerous-looking terrain.

Blackadder
All right – total and utter quiet, do you understand? So, for instance, if any of us crawl over barbed wire they must on no account go (*screams*) Aaahhhhaaahh! (*Regaining himself*)

Baldrick
Did you just crawl over some barbed wire, sir?

Blackadder
No, Baldrick, I've put my elbow in a blob of ice-cream.

Baldrick
Ah!

Blackadder
Yes, good.

Melchett
Tonight.

Blackadder
Suits me.

Melchett
And go out into No Man's Land.

Blackadder
No Man's Land?

Melchett
Yes . . .

Blackadder
Not Paris?

Darling
No.

Blackadder
Now, where the hell are we?

George consults his map.

George
We-e-ell, it's a bit difficult to say. We've crawled into an area marked with little mushrooms . . .

Blackadder
Yes, and what do these symbols denote?

George
Uhm . . . that we're in a field of mush-rooms?

Blackadder
Lieutenant, that is a military map. It is unlikely to list interesting flora and fungi. Look in the key and I think you'll find those mushrooms aren't for picking.

George
Ah, yes, you're right, sir – it says 'mine' – so these mushrooms must belong to the man who made the map.

Blackadder
Either that or we're in the middle of a *mine* field.

Baldrick
Oh, dear!

George
So, he owns the field as well.

A star shell bursts and bathes them in light. Immediately the sound of machine-gun fire is heard.

They're firing, sir! They're firing!

Blackadder
Thank you, George . . . if they hit me, you'll be sure to point it out, won't you? Now get on with your drawing and let's get out of here.

George
Oughtn't we to wait for the flare, sir? You see, my medium is light . . .

Blackadder
Use your *imagination*, for heaven's sake.

(*Sudden revelation*) Wait a minute – that's the answer.

Baldrick
What?

Blackadder
I can't believe I've been so stupid.

Baldrick
Yes, that is unusual, because I'm usually the stupid one.

George
Yes, and I'm not over-furnished in the brain department.

Blackadder
Well, this time I've been the stupidest of all.

George
Oh, now, sir – I won't have that. Baldrick and I will always be more stupid than you. Isn't that right, Baldrick? Stupid, stupid, stupid?

Baldrick
Oh, yes – stupidy, stupidy, stupidy.

George
We're the stupidest stupids in the history of stupiditiness.

Machine-gun fire. They drop to the ground.

Blackadder
Finished? The obvious point is this: we'll go straight back to the dug-out and do the painting from there. You do the most exciting possible drawing of German defences from your imagination.

George
Oh, that *is* a challenge!

Blackadder
Well quite – whatever – come on, let's get out of here.

They start away.

George
Oh, one thing, sir. If we should happen to tread on a mine, what do we do?

Blackadder
Well, normal procedure is to jump 200
feet into the air and scatter yourself over a
wide area.

George
Thank you, sir.

~

SCENE SEVEN: STAFF HQ

*George and Blackadder stand at atten-
tion. Melchett and Darling are inspecting
the map. Now the entire German army is
massed opposite Blackadder's trench.*

Darling
Are you sure this is what you saw,
Blackadder?

Blackadder
Absolutely. I mean there may have been a
few more armament factories and not
quite as many elephants, but . . .

Melchett
Mmm. You know what this means?

Darling
If it's true – we'll have to cancel the push.

Melchett
Exactly . . .

George
Oh, damn.

Blackadder
What a nuisance.

Melchett
Exactly . . . what the enemy would expect
us to do, and therefore exactly what we
won't do.

Blackadder
(*High pitched*) Ah, now . . .

Melchett
If we attack them where their line is
strongest, Fritz will think our reconnais-
sance is a total shambles. This will lull him
into a false sense of security, and then

next week, we can attack where the line is
actually badly defended, and win the
greatest victory since the Winchester
flower-arranging team beat Harrow by 12
sore bottoms to one.

Blackadder
Tell me, have you ever visited the planet
Earth, sir?

Melchett
So best fighting trousers on, Blackadder.

George
Permission to yell 'Bravo' at an annoying-
ly loud volume, sir.

Melchett
Permission granted.

George
BRAVO!

Melchett
That's the spirit, Lieutenant. Just your
kind of caper, eh, Blackadder?

Blackadder
Yes.

Darling
Good luck against those elephants.

~

SCENE EIGHT: THE DUG-OUT

*Blackadder and George enter. Baldrick
has been cooking.*

Blackadder
Get me a chisel and some marble, will you,
Baldrick?

George
Taking up sculpture now, sir?

Blackadder
No, I thought I'd get my headstone done.

George
Really? What are you going to put on it?

Blackadder
'Here lies Edmund Blackadder – and he's
bloody annoyed.'

Baldrick
Are we going over, then?

Blackadder:
Yes, we are, unless I can think of some brilliant plan.

Baldrick
How about some rat au vin to help you think?

Blackadder
Rat au vin?

Baldrick
Yeah, it's rat that's been . . .

Baldrick and Blackadder
Run over by a van.

Blackadder
No, thank you, Baldrick. But that gives me an idea. Telephone, please.

SCENE NINE: STAFF HQ

A candle-lit table is set with crystal goblets and salt and pepper, with china dishes and silver serving dishes.

Darling and Melchett are finishing their main course and the pudding waits on a giant silver salver.

Darling
I suppose Blackadder and his boys will have gone over by now.

Melchett
Yes – I'd give anything to be out there with them, dodging the bullets instead of sitting here drinking Château Lafite and eating these filets mignons with sauce béarnaise.

Darling
My thoughts exactly, sir. Damn this Château Lafite!

He takes a nice big satisfied sip.

Melchett
He's a very brave man, Blackadder – and of course that Lieutenant of his – George – Cambridge man, you know. His uncle and I used to break wind for our college.

He takes a bite.

Unusual taste this sauce béarnaise.

Darling
Yes. (*His face shows it tastes vile*) And to be quite frank, these mignons are a little, well . . .

Melchett
What?

Darling
Well, dungy . . .

Melchett
What on earth's wrong with the cook?

Darling
Well, it's a rather strange story, sir.

Melchett
Well, tell, tell.

Darling
I received a phone call this afternoon from

Pope Gregory IX telling me that our cook has been selected for the English Cricket Team and must sail to the West Indies immediately.

Melchett
Really?

Darling
A moment later the phone rang again. It was a trio of wandering Italian chefs who happened to be in the area offering their services, so I had the quarter-master take them on at once.

Melchett seems satisfied at this, and takes a bite of his pudding.

Melchett
Jumping Jupiters! Are you sure these are raisins on the Plum Duff?

Darling
I'm sure they are, sir. Everything'll be all right when the cream custard arrives.

SCENE TEN: THE DUG-OUT

Enter Blackadder, George and Baldrick with false moustaches and chefs' coats on after their night of catering at HQ.

George
Well, that was all jolly good fun, sir, but dash it all, we seemed to have missed the big push.

Blackadder
Oh, damn, so we have. One thing puzzles me, Baldrick. How did you manage to get so much custard out of such a small cat?

Corporal
Punishment

SCENE ONE: THE DUG-OUT

*It is morning. Blackadder is on the phone.
George is listening keenly.*

Blackadder
You'd like to book a table for three by the
window for 9.30 p.m. – not too near the
band – in the name of Ober Leutnant von
Genschler? Yes, I think you might have
the wrong number. Yes. That's all right.

He hangs up.

George
Another crossed line, eh, sir? This phone
system's an absolute shambles. No wonder
we haven't had any orders.

Blackadder
On the contrary, George, we've had plenty
of orders – we've had orders for six
metres of Hungarian crushed velvet curtain material, four rock salmon and a
ha'p'orth of chips, and a cab for a Mr
Redgrave picking up from No 14 Arnos

Grove, ring top bell.

George
We don't want those kind of orders! We
want orders to death or glory. When are
we going to give Fritz a taste of our British
spunk?

Blackadder
George, please. No one is more anxious to
advance than I am, but until I get these
communication problems sorted out, I'm
afraid we're stuck.

The phone rings again.

Captain Blackadder speaking. No, I'm
afraid the line's very xxxxsahh.

*He makes a very strange, dysfunctional
phone sound. Darling is on the other end
of the line in Melchett's HQ.*

Darling
Hullo, hullo, Captain Blackadder? Hullo,
hullo?

Blackadder rustles a newspaper into the

phone and bangs it against the receiver.

Blackadder
Schnell! Schnell! Kartoffelkopf.

Darling
I said there's a terrible line my end! You are to advance on the enemy at once!

Now Blackadder starts blowing raspberries into the phone and then begins to sing.

Blackadder
Ppppft ppppft pfffffft. A wandering minstrel I, a thing of . . . beeoooolerum . . . gale force eight imminent.

And hangs up.

George
Oh, so come on, sir, what's the message? Do tell. I'm on tenterhooks!

Blackadder
As far as I can tell, the message was he's got a terrible lion up his end so there's an advantage to an enema at once.

George
Oh, damn.

Baldrick enters.

Baldrick
Message from HQ, sir.

He hands George a telegram and then exits.

George
Ah – this will be it – a telegram ordering an advance.

Blackadder
Mmm. I'm afraid not, George. It *is* a telegram, it *is* ordering an advance – but unfortunately it seems to be addressed to someone called Catpain Blackudder. Do you know a Catpain Blackudder, George?

George
Rings a bell, sir, but no.

Blackadder
No, me neither.

He screws up the telegram and throws it away.

Don't worry, George – I'm sure if they really want to contact us they'll find a way.

Baldrick rushes in, shouting.

Baldrick
Pigeon, sir! Pigeon! There's a pigeon in our trench.

He exits again.

George
Ah, now, this'll be it.

They leave the dug-out and see a large pigeon at the top of the trench.

Bravo – it's one of the King's Carrier Pigeons!

Baldrick
No it isn't – that pigeon couldn't carry the king. It hasn't got a tray or anything.

Blackadder
Lieutenant, revolver, please.

Blackadder takes George's gun.

George
Oh, no, sir – you really shouldn't do this, you know.

Blackadder
Oh, come on. With 50,000 men getting killed a week, who's going to miss a pigeon?

Blackadder shoots the pigeon. Feathers fly.

George
Well, not you, obviously, sir.

Blackadder
In any case, it's scarcely a court-martial offence. Get plucking, Baldrick.

Baldrick
All right, sir. Oh look, there's a little ring round its leg. There's a novelty.

George
Oh, really? Has it got a paper hat as well?

Baldrick
No, but there's a joke; read it out, sir.

George
Well, it's a bit charred but . . . 'something, something at once. P.S. Due to communication crisis – the shooting of pigeons is now a court-martial offence.' I don't see what's funny about that, sir.

Blackadder
It's not funny, it's deadly serious. We're in trouble – so I shall eat the evidence for lunch. And if anyone asks you any questions at all, we didn't receive any messages, and we definitely did not shoot this delicious plump-breasted pigeon.

SCENE TWO: THE DUG-OUT

Blackadder has just finished eating the pigeon.

Blackadder
Mmm. Delicious.

Suddenly from outside . . .

Melchett
Blackadder!

Darling
Ten Shun!

Blackadder and Baldrick stand to attention. Melchett and Darling sweep in.

Melchett
And why, Captain, are you not advancing across No Man's Land?

Blackadder
Ah, well, General – call me a bluff old traditionalist, but I was always taught to wait for the order to attack before attacking.

Melchett
You mean you haven't had your orders to advance? What the hell are you playing at, Darling?

Darling
This is a blatant lie, sir. I spoke to

Captain Blackadder less than an hour ago.

Blackadder
Yes, you did. To tell me some gobbledegook about having a lion up your bottom.

Melchett
Hmmmmm. As I thought, it's the old communications problem again. Stand easy. Action on this is imperative. Take that down, Darling.

Darling unwillingly takes it down in his notebook.

Darling
Yes, sir.

Melchett
And make a note of that word 'gobbledegook' – I like it. I want to use it more often in conversation.

Darling
Yes, sir. I must say, sir, I find all this very unlikely. Not only did I telephone Captain Blackadder, but, as you'll recall, we sent him a telegram and a carrier pigeon.

Blackadder
(*Amazed*) Did you?

Darling
Are you telling us you haven't had a pigeon, Blackadder?

Blackadder eyes his plate nervously.

Blackadder
Er ...

He deftly pulls a napkin over the carcass.

Melchett
You must have done. I sent our top bird: Speckled Jim. My own true love, who's been with me since I was a nipper.

He swiftly returns to business matters . . .

To business. I'm giving you your orders to advance now. Synchronize watches, gentlemen. Private, what time is it?

Baldrick
We didn't receive any messages, and

Captain Blackadder definitely did not shoot this delicious plump-breasted pigeon, sir.

Melchett roars back at him.

Melchett
What?

Blackadder
Do you want to be cremated, Baldrick, or buried at sea?

Baldrick
Ummmmmmm . . .

At which moment George enters, humming.

Darling
Ah, Lieutenant – do you mind answering a couple of questions?

George
Not at all, sir. (*Reciting*) We didn't receive any messages and Captain Blackadder definitely did not shoot this delicious plump-breasted pigeon.

Blackadder
Thanks, George.

Darling
And look, pigeon feathers! White feathers – very apt, eh, Blackadder?

Melchett takes the feathers Darling has found and examines them.

Melchett
White feathers?

Baldrick
Oh, no, sir, that's gobble a duke! Well, they're not white – they're sort of speckly.

Melchett
Speckly! Ahhhhh! You shot my Speckled Jim?

Darling
You're for it now, Blackadder. (*To Melchett*) Quite frankly I've suspected this for some time, sir. Captain Blackadder has clearly been disobeying orders with a

breathtaking impertinence.

Melchett
I don't care if he's been rogering the Duke of York with a prize-winning leek. He shot my pigeon! Ahh! Ahh! Ahh!

Darling holds back Melchett, who has gone mad and is trying to whip Blackadder.

Darling
Easy, sir, easy. I think we should do this by the book, sir.

Melchett
Yes, you're right. I'm sorry.

Darling
Dug-out, Ten Shun! Captain Blackadder, as of this moment you are to consider yourself under arrest. Do you know what the penalty for disobeying orders is?

Blackadder
Court martial, followed by immediate cessation of chocolate rations?

Darling
No – court martial, followed by immediate death by firing squad.

Blackadder
Oh, so I got it half right.

SCENE THREE: A CELL IN A MILITARY PRISON

A small cell, bars on the window. Blackadder sits reading. Perkins the

jailer enters. He is a really friendly love.

Perkins
All settled in and happy, are we then, sir?
Written all our goodbyes?

Blackadder
Oh, no need for that, Perkins. I've just
dashed off a couple of notes, one asking
for a sponge bag and the other sending for
my lawyer.

Perkins
Oh, your lawyer – don't you think that
might be a bit of a waste of money, sir?

Blackadder
Not when he's the finest mind in English
legal history. Ever heard of Bob
Massingbird?

Perkins
Oh, yes, indeed, sir. He's a very gifted
gentleman.

Blackadder
Well quite. I remember Massingbird's
most famous case – the Case of the Bloody
Knife. A man was found next to a murdered body. He had the knife in his hand,
thirteen witnesses had seen him stab the
victim and when the police picked him up
he said to them, 'I'm glad I killed the bastard.' Massingbird not only got him
acquitted he got him knighted in the New
Year's Honour's list and the relatives of
the victim had to pay to have the blood
washed out of his jacket.

Perkins
I hear he's a dab hand at prosecution as
well.

Blackadder
Quite. Look what he did to Oscar Wilde.

Perkins
Old 'Butch' Oscar.

Blackadder
Exactly – big, bearded, bonking, butch
Oscar, the terror of the ladies. A hundred
and fourteen illegitimate children, world
heavyweight boxing champion and author
of the bestselling pamphlet 'Why I Like to
Do It with Girls' – and Massingbird had
him sent down for being a whoopsy.

*There is a knock at the door – Perkins
goes to answer. Baldrick enters and
Perkins leaves.*

Baldrick, anything from Bob Massingbird
yet?

Baldrick
Yes, sir, just arrived, sir.

Blackadder
What is it?

Baldrick
A sponge bag.

Blackadder
A sponge bag?

Baldrick
Yes, sir.

Blackadder
Baldrick, I gave you two notes. You sent
the note asking for a sponge bag to the
finest mind in English history?

Baldrick
Certainly did, sir.

Blackadder
And you sent the note requesting legal rep-
resentation to . . . ?

George enters.

George
Well, tally ho! With a bing and a bong and a buzz buzz buzz!

Blackadder
Oh, God.

George
May I say first of all, sir, that I am deeply, deeply honoured.

Blackadder
Baldrick, I'll deal with you later. Am I to understand, George, that you are going to represent me at the court martial?

Baldrick leaves before this important briefing.

George
Absolutely, family tradition actually. My uncle's a lawyer, you know.

Blackadder
Your uncle's a lawyer . . . but you're not?

George
Oh good Lord, no! I'm a complete duffer at this sort of thing. In the School Debating Society I was voted 'boy least likely to complete a coherent . . .' erm . . .

Blackadder
Sentence?

George
Yes. Anyway, my dear old friend – it's an honour to serve.

Blackadder
George, I'm in deep trouble here. I need to construct a case that's as water-tight as a mermaid's brassiere. I'm not sure your particular brand of mindless optimism will contribute much to the proceedings.

George
Oh . . . that's a shame, sir, because I was hoping to play the mindless optimism card pretty strongly during the trial.

Blackadder
I beg your pardon?

George
Yes, I've already planned my closing address based on that very theme . . . (*He takes out paper and grandly prepares to read*) 'Oh go on let him off, go on please, your honour. After all, it's a lovely day, pretty clouds, trees, birds etc. I rest my case.'

Blackadder
So, Counsel, with that summing up in mind, what are my chances, do you think?

George
Well, not good I'm afraid. As far as I can see from the evidence, you're as guilty as a puppy sitting beside a pile of poo.

Blackadder
Charming.

~

SCENE FOUR: MELCHETT'S HQ

Melchett's chamber has been transformed into a court of law. A clerk of the court is getting the judge's papers ready. Blackadder is standing between two guards. George charges in after him, in a wig and gown. He rushes forward to speak.

George
Crikey, *so* sorry I'm late, m'lord. Anyway, let me open my defence straight away by saying I've known this man for three years, he's an absolutely corking chap . . .

Blackadder
George.

George
Yes.

Blackadder
That's the clerk of the court.

George
Is it?

Blackadder
We haven't started yet.

George
Ah.

Darling enters.

Darling
Good luck, Blackadder.

Blackadder
Thank you, Darling. What's your big job today? Straightening chairs?

Darling
No – in fact, I'm appearing for the prosecution. (*He puts on a wig*) I wouldn't raise your hopes – you're guilty as hell. You haven't got a chance.

Blackadder
Why, thank you, Darling, and I hope your mother dies in a freak yachting accident.

Darling
Just doing my job, Blackadder, obeying orders. And, of course, having *enormous fun* into the bargain.

Blackadder
I wouldn't be too confident if I were you – any reasonable impartial judge is bound to let me off.

Darling
Well, absolutely.

Blackadder
Who is the judge by the way?

Melchett's familiar 'barp' sounds from outside.

I'm dead.

And Melchett enters, judge and jury.

Melchett
Come on. Get this over with in five minutes, and we can have a spot of lunch. The court is now in session, Sir Anthony Cecil Hogmanay Melchett in the chair. The case before us is that of the Crown versus Captain Edmund Blackadder, alias the Flanders Pigeon Murderer. Oh, and hand me the black cap, will you – I'll be needing that.

Blackadder
I love a fair trial.

Melchett
Anything to say before we kick off, Captain Darling?

Darling
May it please the court, there is. As this is an open and shut case, I beg leave to bring a private prosecution against the defence counsel for wasting the court's time.

Melchett
Granted! The defence counsel is fined £50 for turning up.

George
(*To Blackadder*) This is fun! Just like a real court.

Melchett
Let the trial begin. The charge before us is that the Flanders Pigeon Murderer did deliberately, callously and with beastliness aforethought murder a lovely innocent pigeon . . . and disobeyed some orders as well – is that true?

George springs to his feet.

George
Perfectly true, sir – I was there.

Blackadder
Thanks, George.

He suddenly realizes his mistake.

George
Damn! Dammit!

Melchett
Right. Counsel for the defence, get on with it.

George gets up hurriedly.

George
Ah. Oh. Yes, right. I'd like to call my first witness. Captain Darling.

Melchett
You wish to call the counsel for the prosecution as a defence witness?

George
That's right. (*He whispers to Blackadder*) Don't worry, sir – I've got it all under control.

Blackadder is sceptical. Darling takes the stand.

You are Captain Darling of the General Staff?

Darling
I am.

George makes a thumbs-up gesture to Blackadder – so far, so good!

George
Captain – leaving aside the incident in question, would you think of Captain Blackadder as the sort of man who would *usually* ignore orders?

Darling
Yes, I would.

George
Ah. (*Pause*) Are you sure? I was rather banking on you saying no there.

Darling
I'm sure. I've actually got a list of other occasions he disobeyed orders, if it would be useful. (*He pulls out a notebook*) May 16th, 9.15 a.m., 10.23 a.m., 10.24 a.m., 11.17 a.m.

George
(*Reading the list with him*) You've missed one out there.

Darling
10.30 a.m. Thank you. 11.46 a.m. . . .

Blackadder
George.

George
Ah, oh, yes. Thank you, Captain, no further questions.

Darling leaves the stand.

Blackadder
Well done, George, you really had him on the ropes there.

George
Yes, but don't worry old man, I have a last, and I think you will find decisive, witness. Call Private Baldrick.

Guard
Call Private Baldrick.

Enter Baldrick. Blackadder is not hopeful and whispers to him as he passes.

Blackadder
Deny everything, Baldrick.

Baldrick goes into the dock.

George
Are you Private Baldrick?

Baldrick
No.

George
But you are Captain Blackadder's batman?

Baldrick
No.

Blackadder is now in despair. He bangs his head on the desk in front.

George
Oh, come on, Baldrick – be a bit more helpful, it's me.

Baldrick
No, it isn't.

Darling
Sir, I must protest.

Melchett
Quite right. We don't want your kind here, get out. George, sum up please.

George
Ahmm, yes. (*He gathers himself for the grand summary*) Sir. Ahmm . . . ahmm . . .

Blackadder hands him a piece of paper. George begins to read it.

Sir. You have heard all the evidence presented before you today, but in the end, it is up to the conscience of your hearts to decide. And I firmly believe that, like me, you will conclude that Captain Blackadder is, in fact, totally and utterly guilty.

He sits down pleased with himself. Blackadder politely turns over the piece of paper to show George the other side. George stands up again.

. . . of nothing more than trying to do his duty under difficult circumstances.

Melchett
Nonsense. He's a hound and a rotter and he's going to be shot. However, before I proceed to the formality of sentencing the deceased – I mean, defendant (*he laughs at this excellent joke*) – I think we'll enjoy hearing the case for the prosecution . . . Captain Darling, if you please.

Darling clears his throat.

Darling
Sir – my case is very simple. I call my first witness. General Sir Anthony Cecil Hogmanay Melchett.

Melchett
Ah, excellent.

George
(*Thrilled*) Clever! Clever!

Darling
General – did you own a lovely, plump, speckly pigeon called Speckled Jim which you hand-reared from a chick and which was your only childhood friend?

Melchett, now in the witness stand, is very moved.

Melchett
Yes! Yes, I did.

Darling
Did Captain Blackadder shoot the afore-mentioned pigeon?

Melchett is very moved and very angry.

Melchett
Yes! He did.

Darling
Can you see Captain Blackadder in this courtroom?

Melchett
Yes! Yes! That's him. That's the man there! Ahh!

He screams and points.

Darling
No further questions, sir.

Melchett recovers instantly and goes back to his judicial seat.

Melchett
Splendid. First class. Very good. I therefore have absolutely no hesitation in announcing that the sentence of this court is that you, Captain Edmund Blackadder, be taken from this place and suffer death by shooting at dawn. Do you have anything to say?

Pause.

Blackadder
Yes, could I have an alarm call, please?

SCENE FIVE: THE CELL

Blackadder is lying on his bed. Perkins, the guard, enters.

Perkins
Chappy to see you, Captain.

Blackadder
What does he look like?

Perkins
Short, ugly . . .

Blackadder
Hullo, Baldrick.

Baldrick enters just after Blackadder says his name. He is carrying a sack. He is also talking in a rather odd, staccato manner.

Baldrick
I've brought you some food, sir: for your final breakfast tomorrow.

Blackadder
You're not putting much hope on a last-minute reprieve then?

Baldrick
No, sir, you're as dead as some doo-doos.

Blackadder
The expression, Baldrick, is 'as a dodo'. Dead as a dodo.

Perkins
I'll leave you to it then, shall I?

Perkins leaves.

Baldrick
Do not despair, sir. All my talk of food was only a dead herring. In fact, I have a cunning plan. (*He holds up the bag*) This is not food! It's an escape kit!

Blackadder
Good lord. With a saw, a hammer, a chisel, a gun, a change of clothes, a Swiss passport and a huge false moustache, I may just stand a chance.

This throws Baldrick slightly.

Baldrick
Ah.

Blackadder
Now, let's see. What have we here?

He reaches into the bag and takes out a little object.

A small painted wooden duck.

Baldrick
Yes – I thought if you get caught near water, you could balance it on the top of your head as a brilliant disguise.

Blackadder
Yes, I would, of course, have to escape first. (*He reaches into the bag*) Ah, unless I'm much mistaken, a hammer and chisel?

Baldrick
You are much mistaken.

Blackadder takes out two more objects from the bag.

Blackadder
A pencil and a miniature trumpet?

Baldrick
That's right. A pencil so you can drop me a postcard saying how the break-out went and then a small, little, miniature, tiny trumpet in case during your escape you have to win favour with a difficult child.

Blackadder
Baldrick, I'm not going to waste my last few precious hours rummaging through this feeble collection of stocking fillers. Let me ask you some simple questions. Is there a saw in this bag?

Baldrick
No.

Blackadder
A hammer?

Baldrick
No.

Blackadder
A chisel?

Baldrick
No.

Blackadder
A gun?

Private 4th Class S. Baldrick is refused entry to the Royal Flying Corps for carrying too much hand luggage

Baldrick
No.

Blackadder
A false passport?

Baldrick
(*Thinks for a second*) No.

Blackadder
A change of clothing?

Baldrick
Yes, sir, of course, I wouldn't forget a change of clothes.

Blackadder
Ah, well, that's something. Let's have a look.

Blackadder takes out a little hat and a toy bow and arrow.

A Robin Hood costume?

Baldrick
Yes – I put in a French peasant's outfit first, but then I thought – what if you arrive in a French peasant village and they're in the middle of a fancy-dress party?

Blackadder
And what if I arrive in a French peasant village dressed in a Robin Hood costume and there isn't a fancy-dress party?

Baldrick
To be quite frank, sir, I didn't consider that eventuality, 'cause if you did, you'd stick out like a . . .

Blackadder
. . . a man standing in a lake with a small, painted, wooden duck on his head?

Baldrick
Exactly.

Perkins enters.

Perkins
Excuse me, sir.

Blackadder
All right, thank you, Baldrick, we'll finish this picnic later.

Baldrick
Yum, yum.

He leaves.

Perkins
Mind if I disturb you for a moment, sir?

Blackadder
No, no – go ahead – my diary's pretty empty this week. 'Thursday morning – get shot.' That's just about it actually.

Perkins
Oh, good – there's a few fellows out here would like a bit of a chin wag.

Blackadder
Oh, lovely – always keen to meet new people.

Perkins brings in a miscellaneous bunch of pleasant-looking Tommies.

Perkins
This is Sergeant Jones, and Privates Robinson, Fraser and Tipplewick.

Blackadder shakes hands with them all.

Blackadder
Ah. Nice of you to drop by. (*Pause*) And what do you do?

Sergeant Jones
We're your firing squad, sir.

Blackadder
Of course you are.

Private Robinson
Good size chest.

He's inspecting Blackadder professionally.

Sergeant Jones
Shut up, lad.

Private Robinson
Sir.

Sergeant Jones
You see, us firing squads are like taxmen really. Everybody hates us, but we're just doing our job, aren't we, lads?

Blackadder
My heart bleeds for you.

Private Robinson
Well sir, we *aim* to please. (*They all laugh*) Just a little firing squad joke there, sir.

Sergeant Jones
You see, sir, we take pride in the terminatory service we supply, so is there any particular area you'd like us to go for? We can aim anywhere.

Blackadder
Well, in that case, just above my head might be a good spot.

They all roar with laughter.

Sergeant Jones
Ha ha! You see, a laugh and a smile and all of a sudden the job doesn't seem quite so bad, does it?

Private Tipplewick
(*Pointing*) Lovely roomy forehead.

Private Robinson
Yes, good pulsing jugular there as well.

They touch Blackadder, who swats them away.

Blackadder
Look, I'm sorry – I know you mean to be friendly, but I hope you won't take it amiss if I ask you to sod off and die.

Squad
Ooooh!

They're actually rather hurt.

Sergeant Jones
Now, now, fair enough. Of course not, sir. No one likes being shot first thing in the morning, do they, lads?

Squad
True. Course not. No.

Sergeant Jones
Look forward to seeing you again tomorrow. You'll have the blindfold on, but you'll recognize me. I'm the one who says, 'Ready, Aim, Fire!'

Blackadder
Could I ask you to leave a pause just before the word 'aim' and the word 'fire' – thirty or forty years perhaps?

The lads fall about laughing again.

Sergeant Jones
Ooh, I just wish I could pause, I really wish I could, sir, but I can't. I'm a gabbler, me . . . (*He says quickly*) 'Ready-aim-fire!' No style, no finesse, but it gets the job done, eh, boys? Come along, boys, let's go.

On the way out they are heard talking between themselves.

Private Tipplewick
Whoever gets closest to the mole gets to keep his gold teeth.

Private Robinson
Sleep well, sir.

Blackadder is left alone.

Blackadder
Goodnight. Perfect! I wonder if anything on earth could depress me more?

Re-enter Baldrick.

Baldrick
Excuse me, sir.

Blackadder
And of course it could.

Baldrick
Sorry – I forgot to give you this letter from Lieutenant George, sir.

Blackadder
Oh, joy. What wise words then from the world's greatest defence counsel? 'Dear Mother . . . thanks for the case of scotch' . . . hmmm, unusual start. You've excelled yourself, Baldrick – the wrong letter again.

Baldrick
Come to think of it, he did write two.

Blackadder

Yes – his mother is about to receive a note telling her he's sorry she's going to be shot in the morning: and I have to read this drivel. (*He reads on*) 'Hope that Celia thrives in the Pony Club Trials and Freddy scores a century for the first eleven.' You can't deny it's a riveting read . . . 'And send my love to Uncle Rupert – who'd have thought it? Mad Uncle Rupe – Minister of War with power of life and death over every bally soldier in the army.' That's it! All George has to do is send him a telegram and he'll get me off. Baldrick, I love you! I want to kiss your cherry lips and nibble your shell-like ears. I'm free!

Baldrick puckers up. He's game.

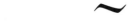

SCENE SIX: THE DUG-OUT

George is in a very quiet mood.

George

Oh, I'm useless, useless.

Baldrick enters.

Baldrick

Sir, sir!

George

Ah, hullo, Baldrick. How is the . . . captain?

Baldrick

Oh, he's absolutely fine, sir, but . . .

George

You're just trying to cheer me up, Baldrick, but I know the truth. He hates me because I completely arsed up his defence.

Baldrick

Yes, sir, but . . .

George

I'm thick. I'm as thick as the big print version of the Complete Works of Charles Dickens.

Baldrick

I know, sir, but . . .

George

If only I could have saved him, if only . . .

Baldrick

But you can, sir!

George

What? How?

Baldrick

You send a telegram!

George

Yes of course! I send a telegram! Who to?

Baldrick

The person who was in your letter.

George

What letter?

Baldrick

To your mother.

George

I send a telegram to my mother!

Baldrick

No.

George

No!

Baldrick

You send a telegram to the person in the letter to your mother.

George
Who was in the letter to my mother?

Baldrick
I can't remember, sir.

George
Well think, think.

Baldrick
No, you think think!

George
Celia! The Pony Club Trials! Yes! Celia could leap over the walls of the prison and get the captain out.

Baldrick
No, no, no.

George
No, no, no. (*He spots a cricket bat*) Cricket! Yes! Cousin Freddie! Of course! He could knock out the firing squad with his cricket bat!

Baldrick
No, no, no, someone else.

George
Who?

Baldrick
I don't know.

George
Neither do I.

Baldrick
Think, think.

George
You think!

Baldrick
You think, sir.

George
I'm stuck, I'm stuck.

Baldrick hits George over the head with the cricket bat.

No, that hasn't helped.

Baldrick has a sudden revelation ...

Baldrick
Yes, it has, sir, your Uncle Rupert who has just been made Minister of War.

George
Of course, Uncle Rupert who has just been made Minister of War! I'll send him the telegram. He'll pull strings, scratch backs, fiddle with knobs and get the captain off.

Baldrick
Hurray, sir.

George
Well, we got there in the end.

Baldrick
We did, sir.

George
I think this calls for a celebration. What about some Old Moorhead's Shredded Sporran that Mumsie's just sent me.

He gets a whisky bottle out and pours them both a drink.

A toast to Captain Blackadder and freedom.

George and Baldrick
Captain Blackadder and freedom!

~

SCENE SEVEN: THE COURTYARD

The firing squad are loading up. Enter Blackadder and Perkins. Blackadder walks on to the top step. He's very chipper indeed.

Blackadder
Morning!

Squad
Morning, sir.

Perkins
I must say, Captain, I've got to admire your balls.

Blackadder
Perhaps later.

He moves down to the squad.

So, boys? How you doing?

Private Fraser
Very well, thank you, Captain.

Blackadder
Excellent. Robinson, good to see ya.

He does a little mime of pointing a gun at him – all very jovial.

Private Robinson
Good to see you too, sir.

Blackadder
And Corporal – how's the voice?

Sergeant Jones
Excellent, sir. Ready! Aim! . . . Fire!

The squad snatch up their guns at his command.

Wait for it! Wait for it!

Blackadder
The phone is on the hook, isn't it, Perkins?

Perkins
Oh, yes, sir.

Blackadder
Splendid. So where do you want me?

Sergeant Jones
Well, up against the wall is traditional.

Blackadder
Course it is. This side or the other side?

They all laugh – what a jolly day.

No messengers waiting, Perkins?

Perkins
Oh, I'm afraid not, sir.

Blackadder
Fair enough, fair enough.

Blackadder is starting to worry.

Sergeant Jones
All right, lads, line up.

The squad is ready.

Blackadder
Now, look – I think there might have been a bit of a misunderstanding here. You see, I was expecting a telegram.

Sergeant Jones
Ten shun!

Blackadder
Quite an important one actually.

Sergeant
Take aim!

They point their guns at him.

Perkins
Stop!

Blackadder
I think that's what they call the nick of time.

Perkins
It's a message for you, Captain.

Blackadder
Of course it is. Read it please.

Perkins
'Here's looking at you – love from all the boys in the firing squad.'

Sergeant Jones
You soft bastards, you!

Private Robinson
I saw the card – I couldn't resist it!

They are all giggling – very pleased with themselves.

Blackadder
How thoughtful.

Sergeant Jones
Ten shun!

Blackadder
Yes. Something's gone spectacularly badly wrong.

Sergeant Jones
Take aim.

Blackadder
Baldrick – you're mince-meat.

Sergeant Jones
F …

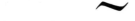

SCENE EIGHT: THE DUG-OUT

Baldrick and George are waking up where they passed out. They were clearly deeply, deeply drunk.

George
(*Groaning*) My head . . . oh, my *head* . . . feels like the time I was initiated into the Silly Buggers Society at Cambridge. I misheard the rules and tried to push a whole aubergine up my earhole.

Baldrick
Permission to die, sir.

George
Now, what started us drinking . . . ? Oh yes, we were celebrating getting Captain Blackadder off scot free . . . Oh, my sainted trousers! We forgot!

He jumps up.

Baldrick
Oh, whoops.

George
I shall never forgive myself, he's dead dead dead because of us, because we're a pair of dirty rotten selfish so and sos. Oh,

my God – I could just put a rope round my neck and bally well hang myself till it really hurt.

Blackadder enters, bright, breezy and casual, looking the room over.

Blackadder
Morning, George, Morning, Baldrick . . .

They gape, open-mouthed in surprise, not quite believing that Blackadder is alive.

Still the striking resemblance to guppy fish at feeding time. Yup. It arrived in the nick of time.

He waves the telegram.

George
(*Uncomprehending*) Oh, excellent.

Blackadder
Ah. See you've got the scotch out anyway.

George
Oh, not at all. Of course, sir, we wanted to lay on a bit of a celebration for your safe return.

Blackadder helps himself to whisky, noting there's very little left.

Blackadder
There was a second telegram which arrived, George, addressed to you personally from your uncle …

George
Oh, thank you.

George reaches for it, but Blackadder casually opens it, and reads.

Blackadder
'George, my boy . . . Outraged to read in dispatches how that arse Melchett made a complete pig's ear of your chum Blackadder's court martial. Have reversed the decision forthwith. Surprised you didn't ask me to do it yourself, actually.'

He looks up at George and Baldrick. They know they're in trouble.

Now. This is interesting, isn't it?

George
Yes . . . well . . . the thing is, sir . . .

Blackadder
You two got whammed last night, didn't you?

George
Well, not whammed . . . a little tiddly, perhaps . . .

Blackadder
And forgot the telegram to your uncle?

George
Well . . . no! No – not completely – I mean, partial . . . ahm. Yes. Yes – entirely.

Baldrick
I think I can explain, sir.

Blackadder
Can you, Baldrick?

Baldrick
No.

Blackadder
As I suspected. I'm not a religious man, as you know, but henceforth I shall pray nightly to the God who killed Cain and squashed Samson that he comes out of retirement and gets back into practice with the pair of you.

The field phone rings. Blackadder snatches it up.

Blackadder. Ah, Captain Darling. Well, you know, some of us just have friends in high places, I suppose. No, I can hear you perfectly. You want what? You want two volunteers for a mission into No Man's Land. Codename – Operation Certain Death. Yes I think I have just the fellows.

He hangs up and looks at them.

God is *very quick* these days.

MAJOR STAR

SCENE ONE: THE DUG-OUT

George is sitting on the table oiling a cricket bat and whistling irritatingly. Blackadder is lying on his bed getting irritated. Blackadder does a big sigh.

George
Are you a little bit cheesed off, sir?

Blackadder
George, the day this war began I was cheesed off. Within ten minutes of you turning up, I had finished the cheese and moved on to the coffee and cigars, and at this late stage I am in a cab with two lady companions on my way to the Pink Pussycat in Lower Regent Street.

George
Because if you *are* cheesed off, sir, you know what'd cheer you up? A Charlie Chaplin film! Oh, I love old Chappers, don't you, Cap?

Blackadder
Unfortunately, no, I don't. I find his films about as funny as getting an arrow through the neck and then discovering there's a gas bill tied to it.

George
Oh, beg pardon, sir, but come *off*! His films are ball-bouncingly funny.

Blackadder
Rubbish.

George
All right, well – let's consult the men for a casting vote, shall we? Baldrick!

Baldrick enters.

Baldrick
Sir?

George
Charlie Chaplin, Baldrick. What do you make of him?

Baldrick
Oh, sir, he's as funny as a vegetable that has grown into a rude and amusing shape, sir.

Blackadder
So you agree with me – not at all funny.

George
Oh, come on skipper, play fair. In that last film of his, when he kicked that fellow

 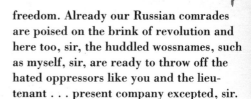

in the backside, I thought I'd die.

Blackadder
Well, if that's your idea of comedy, we can provide our own without expending a ha'penny for the privilege.

He chucks Baldrick's cap to the ground. As Baldrick bends to pick it up, Blackadder kicks Baldrick in the pants.

There, did you find that funny?

George
Well, of course not, sir. You see, Chaplin is a genius.

Blackadder
He certainly is a genius, George. He invented a way of getting paid a million dollars a year for wearing a pair of stupid trousers. Did you find that funny, Baldrick?

Baldrick
What funny, sir?

Blackadder chucks Baldrick's hat on the floor again. Baldrick bends and Blackadder kicks him.

Blackadder
That funny.

Baldrick
No, sir. And you mustn't do that to me, sir. Because that is a bourgeois act of repression, sir.

Now this is something new.

Blackadder
What?

Baldrick
Haven't you smelt it, sir? There's something afoot in the wind. The huddled masses yearning to be free.

Blackadder
Baldrick, have you been at the diesel oil again?

Baldrick
No, sir, I have been supping the milk of freedom. Already our Russian comrades are poised on the brink of revolution and here too, sir, the huddled wossnames, such as myself, sir, are ready to throw off the hated oppressors like you and the lieutenant . . . present company excepted, sir.

Blackadder
Go and clean out the latrines.

Baldrick
Yes, sir, right away, sir.

Baldrick exits.

George
The reason why Chaplin is funny is because he's part of the great British music-hall tradition.

Blackadder
Ah, yes. The great British music-hall tradition. Two men with incredibly unconvincing Cockney accents going: 'What's up with you then? What's up with me then? Yeh, what's up with you then? What's up with me then? I'll tell you what's up with me then. I'm right browned off, that's what's up with me. Right browned off? Yes, right browned off.' *Get on with it!*

George
Now, sir, that was funny. You should go on the boards yourself.

Blackadder
Thank you, George, but if you don't mind, I'd rather have my tongue beaten wafer-thin with a steak-tenderizer and then stapled to the floor with a croquet hoop.

From the trenches outside comes a loud cheer. Baldrick enters with a bucket and newspaper.

Baldrick
Sir, sir, it's all over the trenches.

Blackadder
Well mop it up then.

Baldrick
No, sir.

He gives the newspaper to Blackadder, who sits on the bed to read it.

The news. The Russian Revolution has started. The masses have risen up and shot all their nobs.

George
Oh, hurrah!

Blackadder is engrossed in the paper.

Blackadder
Oh, no, the bloody Russians have pulled out of the war.

George
Well, we soon saw them off, didn't we, sir? Miserable, slant-eyed, sausage eating swine.

Blackadder
The Russians are on our side, George.

George
Oh, are they, sir?

Blackadder
And they have abandoned the Eastern front.

Baldrick is heading back to the celebrations.

Baldrick
And they've overthrown Nicholas the Second who used to be bizarre.

Blackadder
Who used to be the *Czar*, Baldrick. The point is that now the Russians have made peace with the Kaiser, at this very moment over three-quarters of a million Germans are leaving the Russian Front and coming over here with the express purpose of using my nipples for target practice. There's only one thing for it, I'm going to have to desert. And I'm going to do it right now.

Blackadder reaches for his coat and is about to exit as Melchett comes through the door.

Melchett
Leaving us, Blackadder?

Blackadder
No, sir.

Melchett
Well, I'm relieved to hear it because I need you to help me shoot some deserters later on. There have been subversive mutterings amongst the men. You'll recall the French army last year at Verdun, where the top echelons suffered horrendous uprisings from the bottom?

Blackadder
Yes, sir, but surely that was traced to a shipment of garlic éclairs?

Melchett
Nonsense, Blackadder, it was bolshiness, plain bolshiness, and now that the Ruskies have followed suit, I'm damned if I'm going to let the same thing happen here.

Blackadder
And what are you going to do about it, sir?

Melchett
We're going to have a concert party to boost the men's morale.

George
A concert party! Well, hurrah!

Melchett
You fancy an evening at a concert party, Blackadder?

Blackadder
Well, frankly, sir, I'd rather spend an evening on top of a stepladder in No Man's Land smoking endless cigarettes through a luminous balaclava.

Melchett
Didn't think it would be quite your cup of tea, but I do need someone to help me organize it, you know. Obviously not a tough, grizzled soldier like yourself but

some kind of damp-eyed nancy-boy who'd be prepared to spend the rest of the war in the London Palladium.

Blackadder
Oh, the show's going to the London Palladium, sir?

Melchett
Yes, of course. It's no good crushing the revolution over here only to get back home to Blighty and find that everybody's wearing overalls and breaking wind in the palaces of the mighty.

Blackadder
Good point, sir.

Melchett
Now, the thing is, Blackadder, finding a man to organize a concert party is going to be damn difficult. So, I've come up with a rather cunning set of questions with which to test a candidate's suitability for the job.

Blackadder
And what sort of questions would these be, sir?

Melchett
Well, the first question is: do you like Charlie Chaplin?

Blackadder turns to George.

Blackadder
Dismissed, Lieutenant.

George salutes and leaves.

Do you like Charlie Chaplin? Yes, that is a good question for a candidate. To which my answer would, of course, be, yes, I love him. Love him, sir. Particularly the amusing kicks.

George
(*At door*) That's funny, sir, because I thought you said . . .

Blackadder
Goodbye, George.

Melchett
And the second question is: do you like music hall?

Blackadder
Ah, yes, another good question, sir. Again my answer would have to be, yes, absolutely love it.

He grabs hold of his lapels and starts to sing.

'Oops, Mr Rothschild,
'ows yer apples and pears!'

Melchett
Well, you see, it's my view, Blackadder, that the kind of person who answered yes to both of those questions would be ideal for the job . . . wait a minute!

Blackadder
(*Smugly*) What, sir?

Melchett laughs.

Melchett
Why – without knowing it, Blackadder, you've inadvertently shown me that you could do the job.

Blackadder
Have I, sir?

Melchett
Yes, sir! You have, sir! And I want you to start work straight away. A couple of shows over the weekend and, if all goes well, we'll start you off in London, well, next Monday.

Blackadder
Oh, damn.

Melchett
Now, in case you need any help fetching and carrying backstage and so on, I'll lend you my driver, if you like. (*He calls out*) Bob!

Enter Bob, a pert and efficient young lass. She stands to attention and salutes. There is something pleasantly familiar about her.

Bob
Driver Parkhurst reporting for duty, sir.

Melchett
All right, at ease, Bob, stand easy.

Captain Blackadder, this is Bob.

Blackadder
Bob.

Bob
Good morning, sir.

Blackadder
Unusual name for a girl.

Melchett
Well, yes, it would be an unusual name for a girl. But it's a perfectly straightforward name for a young chap like you, eh, Bob? Now, Bob, I want you to bunk up with Captain Blackadder for a couple of days, all right?

Bob
Yes, sir.

Melchett
I think you'll find Bob's just the man for this job, Blackadder. He has a splendid sense of humour.

Blackadder
He, sir? He? He?

Melchett
You see, you're laughing already. Well now, Bob, I'll leave you two together. Why don't you get to know each other – play a game of cribbage, have a smoke, something like that. They tell me that Captain Blackadder has rather a good line in rough shag. I'm sure he'd be happy to fill your pipe. Carry on.

Melchett leaves, satisfied with a job well done.

Blackadder
So, you're a chap, are you, Bob?

Bob
Oh, yes, sir. Yo ho ho. Grrr, grrr.

Blackadder
You wouldn't say you're a girl at all?

Bob
Definitely not, sir. I understand cricket, I fart in bed and everything.

Blackadder
Well, let me put it another way, Bob. You *are* a girl. And you're a girl with as much talent for disguise as a giraffe in dark glasses trying to get into a polar-bears-only golf club.

Bob
Oh, sir, please don't give me away, sir. I just wanted to be like my brothers and join up. I want to see how a war is fought *so badly*.

Blackadder
Well, you've come to the right place, Bob. A war hasn't been fought this badly since Olaf the Hairy, High Chief of all the Vikings, accidentally ordered 80,000 battle helmets with the horns on the inside.

Bob
I want to do my bit for the boys, sir.

Blackadder
Oh, really.

Bob
I'll do anything, sir.

Blackadder
Yes, I'd keep that to yourself if I was you, Bob.

SCENE TWO: THE DUG-OUT

The next day. Blackadder and Bob are sitting at the table with Baldrick standing by. Blackadder hangs up the phone. Bob has a clipboard and is taking notes.

Blackadder
So, Bob, the second half starts with Corporals Smith and Johnson as the Three Silly Twerps.

Bob
Right, sir.

Blackadder
The big joke being there's only two of them . . .

Baldrick

I love that, that always cracks me up, sir.

Blackadder

To be followed by Baldrick's impersonation of Charlie Chaplin . . .

*Baldrick puts on a bowler hat and pulls a
Chaplin face.*

Bob, take a telegram.

Bob

Yes, sir.

Blackadder

Mr C. Chaplin, Sennett Studios,
Hollywood, California. 'Congrats. Stop.
Have discovered only person in world less
funny than you. Stop. Name – Baldrick.
Stop. Yours E. Blackadder.' Stop. Oh, put
a PS . . . 'Please please please – stop.'
And then after that we also have, ladies
and gentlemen, the highlight of our show.

Baldrick

Da daaa!

George emerges in full drag.

George

I feel *fantastic.*

Blackadder

Gorgeous Georgina. The traditional soldiers' drag act.

Baldrick

You look absolutely lovely, sir.

Blackadder

Baldrick, you are either lying, blind or
mad. The lieutenant looks as all soldiers
look on these occasions – about as femi-
nine as W. G. Grace. What are you going
to give 'em, George?

George

Well, I thought one or two cheeky gags followed by 'She was only the ironmonger's
daughter, but she knew a surprising
amount about fish as well'.

Blackadder

Inspired. At least you've made an effort
with the dress.

*George goes over to Blackadder's bed and
sits.*

Yes, what about your costume, Baldrick?

Baldrick

I'm in it, sir.

Blackadder

I see, so your Charlie Chaplin costume
consists of that hat?

Baldrick

Yes, sir, except that in this box I have a
dead slug as a brilliant false moustache.

He takes it out of the box.

Blackadder

Hmmm, yes, only *quite* brilliant, I fear.
How, for instance, are you to attach it to
your face?

Baldrick

Well, I was hoping I could persuade the
slug to cling on.

Blackadder

Baldrick, the slug is dead. If it failed to
cling on to life then I see no reason why it
should wish to cling on to your upper lip.

*Blackadder loses interest and gets on with
his work. George beckons Baldrick over
to him.*

George

Baldrick, Baldrick, slugs are always a problem. What you've got to do is screw your face up like this, you see, and then you can clamp it between your nose and your upper lip.

Baldrick

What, like this? . . .

Baldrick leans back and attempts this complex manoeuvre with the slug.

George

Yes, that's it, that's it, splendid. Sir, sir, there's a visitor to see you.

Blackadder looks up.

Blackadder

Good Lord – Mr Chaplin! This is indeed an honour. Why, it calls for some sort of celebration. Baldrick! Baldrick!

George is doubled over with laughter.

George

Sir, that's extraordinary! Because, you see, this isn't Chaplin at all. This *is* Baldrick.

Baldrick removes the slug and stands up straight.

Baldrick

Yes – it's me, sir!

Blackadder

I know, I know – I was, in fact, being sarcastic.

George

Oh, I see.

Blackadder

Everything goes over your head, doesn't it, George. You should go to Jamaica and become a limbo dancer.

~

SCENE THREE: WINGS OF THE THEATRE

George is taking a bow on stage, with an armful of flowers. There is a roar of wild applause. More flowers are thrown at George. Blackadder, Bob and Baldrick are backstage.

Bob

They love him, sir – we're a hit!

Blackadder

Yes – in one short evening, I have become the most successful impresario since the manager of the Roman Colosseum put the Christians and the lions on the same bill.

Baldrick

Sir, some people seem to think I was best – would you agree?

Blackadder

Baldrick – in the Amazonian rain forests there are tribes of Indians as yet untouched by civilization who have developed more convincing Charlie Chaplin impressions than yours.

Baldrick

Oh, thank you very much, sir.

Bob

He's coming off.

The stage curtains open and George backs through them. They are drawn in front of him. The audience are still cheering.

George

What do you think, Bob? One more? God, I love the theatre.

Bob opens the curtains once more and George takes another bow before stepping backstage once more.

It's in my blood and in my soul. Baldrick, put those in some water, would you?

George throws flowers at Baldrick.

Baldrick

Yes, sir.

Baldrick puts the flowers upside down in the fire bucket hanging on the wall.

George

I need that applause in just the same way

that an ostler needs his . . . ostle.

Bob
Well done, sir.

George
Oh, no – really, I was hopeless, wasn't I?
Tell me honestly, sir, because I was, wasn't
I? Out with it, sir, I was hopeless. Now,
you're trying to be nice, and that's very
sweet of you, sir, but, please, come on, I
can take it, I was hopeless.

Blackadder
George, you were bloody awful.

George immediately bursts into tears.

But you can't argue with the box office.
Personally I thought you were the least
convincing female impressionist since
Tarzan went through Jane's handbag and
ate her lipstick, but I'm clearly in a
minority. Look out London. Here we
come.

SCENE FOUR: MELCHETT'S HQ

*Same night, immediately after the show.
Darling is at his desk.*

Blackadder
Ah, Captain Darling.

Darling
Ah, Captain Blackadder. I must say I had
an absolutely splendid evening.

Blackadder
Oh, glad you enjoyed the show.

Darling
The show – I didn't go to the show, I had
some important regimental business.

Blackadder
A lorry load of paperclips arrive?

Darling
Two lorry loads actually.

General Melchett enters.

Melchett
Ah, welcome to the great director,
Maestro!

Blackadder
You enjoyed it, sir?

Melchett
Well, it was mostly awful but I enjoyed the
slug-balancer.

Blackadder
Private Baldrick, sir.

Melchett
That's right. Slug fell off a couple of times
but you can't have everything, can you? I
just suggest a bit more practice and perhaps a little sparkly costume for the slug.

Blackadder
I'll pass that on, sir.

Melchett
But I do have certain other reasons for
believing the show to be nothing but a triumph. Captain Darling has your travel
arrangements: ticket to Dover, rooms at
the Ritz and so forth.

Blackadder
Thank you, sir.

*Blackadder confidently reaches out for
the travel folder that Darling holds.*

Melchett
However, there is one small thing you
might do for me.

Blackadder
Yes?

Melchett
Captain Blackadder, I should esteem it a
signal honour if you would allow me to
escort your leading lady to the Regimental
Ball this evening.

Blackadder
My leading lady?

Melchett
The fair Georgina.

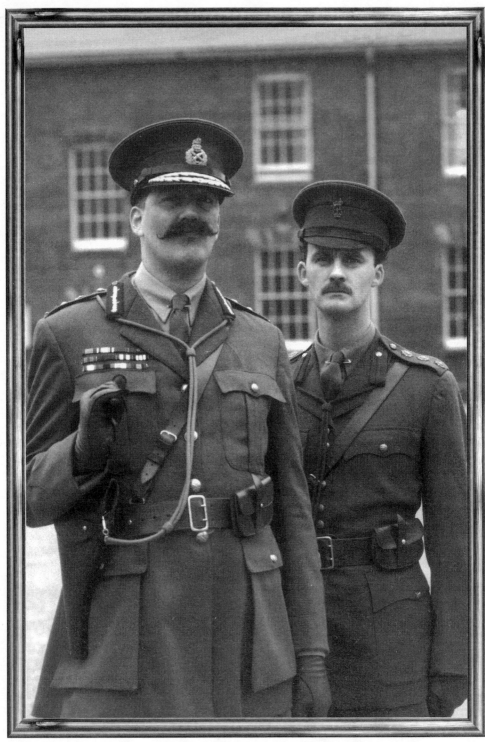

General Sir Anthony Cecil Hogmanay Melchett and a member of the Women's Royal Balloon Corps (showing regulation moustache)

Blackadder
Ah, very amusing!

Melchett
Do you think she'll laugh in my face – I'm too old, too crusty?

Blackadder has to accept it. This is no joke. Melchett is in love with George.

Blackadder
No, no, it's just that as her director, I'm afraid I could not allow it.

Melchett
We can always find another director who would allow it.

Blackadder
Quite. Well, I'll see what I can do. But I must insist that she be home by midnight and there be no hanky-panky, sir, whatsoever.

Melchett
I shall, of course, respect your wishes Blackadder, although I'm not sure you need to be quite so protective. I'm sure she's a girl with a great deal more spunk than most women you find.

Blackadder
Oh, dear me.

~

SCENE FIVE: THE DUG-OUT

Later that night. George and Blackadder are standing face to face. George is still in the dress.

George
Absolutely not, sir! It's profoundly immoral and utterly wrong. I will not do it.

Blackadder
We can always find another leading lady.

George
Well . . . the dress will need a clean.

Blackadder
Excellent! Now the important thing is that Melchett should, under no circumstances, realize that you're a man.

George
Yes, yes, understand that.

Blackadder
In order to ensure this, there are three basic rules. One – never, I repeat never, remove your wig.

George
(*Concentrating hard*) All right.

Blackadder
Second – never say anything. I'll tell him at the beginning of the evening that you're saving your voice for the opening night in London.

George
Excellent, sir. And what is the third?

Blackadder
The third is most important – don't get drunk and let him shag you on the verandah.

~

SCENE SIX: MELCHETT'S HQ

The atmosphere is romantic. Darling is helping Melchett get ready; he is dressed to the nines. The candles are lit, it is a sparkly, perfect night for a ball.

Melchett
How do I look, Darling?

Darling
Girl bait, sir. Pure bloody girl bait.

Melchett
Moustache . . . bushy enough?

Darling
Like a privet hedge, sir.

Melchett
Good, because I want to catch a very beautiful creature in this bush tonight.

Darling
I'm sure you'll be combing women out of your moustache for weeks, sir.

Melchett
God, it's a spankingly beautiful world and tonight's *my* night . . . I know exactly what I'll say to her – 'Darling . . .'

Darling leaps to attention at the mention of his name.

Darling
Yes, sir?

Melchett
What?

Darling
. . . Uhm . . . I don't know, sir.

Melchett
Well, don't butt in.

Darling
(*Confused*) Sorry, sir.

Melchett
'I want to make you happy, darling.'

Darling
(*Slightly embarrassed*) Well . . . that's very kind of you, sir . . .

Melchett
Will you kindly stop interrupting! If you don't listen, how can you tell me what you think? . . .

He composes himself.

'I want to make you happy, darling, I want to build a nest for your ten tiny toes. (*Darling is becoming very uncomfortable indeed*) I want to cover every inch of your gorgeous body in pepper and then sneeze all over you . . .'

Darling can take no more.

Darling
Really sir! I must protest!

Melchett
What is the matter with you, Darling?

Darling
Well . . . it's just all so sudden, sir . . . I mean, the nest bit is fine but the pepper business is definitely out.

Melchett
How dare you tell me how I may or may not treat my beloved Georgina.

Darling
Georgina?

Melchett
Yes, I'm working on what I'm going to say to her this evening.

At last the penny drops. He is not the object of Melchett's desire.

Darling
Oh, yes, of course, thank God.

Melchett
All right?

Darling
Yes, sir, I'm listening, sir.

Melchett
Honestly, Darling, you really are the most graceless dim-witted bumpkin I've ever met.

Darling
Oh, I don't think you should say that to her, sir.

Melchett shakes his head in exasperation at Darling's stupidity. It is no use explaining anything to him.

Melchett
(*Annoyed*) Ohhh . . .

SCENE SEVEN: THE DUG-OUT

Blackadder and Baldrick are in the dug-out. It's very late indeed.

Blackadder
Where the hell is George? It's three o'clock in the morning. He should be careful wandering around the trench at night with nothing to protect his honour but a cricket box.

Enter George, in his dress, carrying a bunch of roses.

George
Hullo, Captain.

Blackadder
About time. Where the hell have you been?

George
Oh, I don't know . . . it's all been like a dream, my very first ball! The music, the dancing, the champagne, my mind's a mad whirl of half-whispered conversations with the promise of indiscretion ever hanging in the air.

Blackadder
Oh – did that old stoat Melchett try for a snog behind the fruit cup?

George
Certainly not. The general behaved like a perfect gentleman. We tired the moon with our talking about everything and nothing; the war, marriage, the proposed changes to the LBW rule . . .

Blackadder
Melchett isn't married, is he?

George
No, no, all his life he's been waiting to meet the perfect woman . . . and then, at last, tonight, he did.

Blackadder
Some poor unfortunate had old walrus face dribbling in her ear all evening, did she?

George
Oh yes, as a matter of fact in the end I did have to drape a napkin on my shoulder.

Blackadder
George, are you trying to tell me that *you* are the general's perfect woman?

George
Well, yes, I . . . rather think I am.

Blackadder
Well, thank God the horny old blighter didn't ask you to marry him.

George flutters coyly behind the roses he is holding.

He did?

George looks coy again.

Well, how did you get out of that one?

George
Well, to be honest, sir, I'm not absolutely cert that I did.

Blackadder
What?!

George
You can't understand what it was like, sir – the candles, the music, the huge moustache – I don't know what came over me.

Blackadder
You said yes?

Yes, he did.

George
Well, after all, sir, he *is* a general, I didn't really feel I could refuse . . . he might have had me court-martialled.

Blackadder
Whereas on the other hand, of course, he's going to give you the Victoria Cross when he lifts up your frock on the wedding night and finds himself looking at the last turkey in the shop?

George
Oh, God, sir, I know it's a mess, but he got me squiffy and then when he looked

into my eyes, and said, 'Chipmunk, I love you', I just . . .

Blackadder
Chipmunk?

George
It's his special name for me, you see, he said my nose looks just like a chipmunk's.

Blackadder
Oh, God. We are in serious, serious trouble here. If the general ever finds out gorgeous Georgina is a strapping six-footer from the rough end of the trench, it could precipitate the fastest execution since someone said 'This Guy Fawkes bloke, do we let him off, or what?'

The phone goes.

Hullo. Yes, sir. Straight away, sir.

He hangs up and looks at George.

That was your fiancée . . . Chipmunk. He wants to see me at once. If I should die, think only this of me – I'll be back to get you.

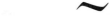

SCENE EIGHT: MELCHETT'S HQ

Blackadder enters. Melchett is sitting at his desk with Darling standing close by. They are still in ball attire.

Blackadder
Sir, I can explain everything.

Melchett
Can you, Blackadder, can you?!

Blackadder
Well, no, sir, not really.

Melchett
I thought not. I thought not. Who *can* explain the mysteries of love? I'm in love with Georgina, Blackadder. I'm going to marry her on Saturday and I want you to be my best man.

Blackadder
I don't think that would be a very good idea, sir.

Melchett
Why not?

Blackadder
Because there's something wrong with your fiancée, sir.

Melchett
Oh, my God, she's not Welsh is she?

Blackadder
No, sir, it's a terrible story but true. Just a few minutes ago, Georgina arrived unexpectedly in my trench. She was literally dancing with joy, as though something wonderful had happened to her . . .

Melchett
Makes sense.

Blackadder
Unfortunately, she was in such a daze, she danced straight through the trench and out into No Man's Land. I tried to stop her, but before I could say 'Don't tread on a mine', she trod on a mine.

Melchett's heart snaps.

Melchett
(*Distraught*) Oh! No!

Blackadder
Well, I say a mine, it was more a cluster of mines and she was blown to smithereens, and as she rocketed up into the air, she

said something that I couldn't quite catch, sir – totally incomprehensible to me – something like 'Tell him his little Chipmunk will love him for ever.'

Melchett
Oh, howl, howl, howl.

It is a deep and tragic sound.

Darling
That's heartbreaking, sir.

Blackadder
Oh, I am sorry, sir.

From which Melchett swiftly recovers.

Melchett
(*Completely back to normal*) Can't be helped. Can't be helped.

Darling
Jolly bad luck, sir.

Melchett
Hey ho.

Darling
Of course, on top of everything else, without your leading lady, you won't be able to put on the show, so no show, no London Palladium.

Blackadder
Ah . . . on the contrary – I was simply intending to rename it 'The Georgina/Melchett Memorial Show'.

Melchett
Oh, no – Georgina was the only thing that made the show come alive. Apart from her it was all awful.

Darling
Awful.

Melchett
Yes, you'll never find another girl like Georgina by tomorrow.

Blackadder
Well, it's funny you should say that, sir, because I think I already have.

Darling
Who is she?

Melchett
Who is she?

There is a pause as pregnant as a mother of quadruplets a week after her due date.

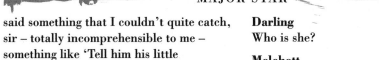

SCENE NINE: THE DUG-OUT

Blackadder and George are sitting at the table deep in conversation.

George
So, come on, sir, who is she?

Blackadder
Well, that's the problem, isn't it! I haven't a bloody clue. The only attractive woman round here is carved out of stone, called Venus and is standing in a fountain in the middle of the town square with water coming out of her armpits.

George
So, we're a bit stuck?

Bob walks in.

Bob
Morning, chaps.

George and Blackadder
Morning, Bob.

Blackadder
You can say that again, George. We're in the stickiest situation since Sticky the Stick Insect got stuck on a sticky bun. We are in trouble.

Baldrick enters. He has on a hat, shawl and dress. The closest he can get to womanhood – which is not close.

Baldrick
Not any longer, sir . . . May I present my cunning plan.

Blackadder
Don't be ridiculous, Baldrick. Can you

sing? Can you dance? Or are you offering to be sawn in half?

Baldrick
Oh, I don't think those things are important in a modern marriage, sir – I offer simple home-cooking.

Blackadder
Baldrick, our plan is to find a new leading lady for our show. What is your plan?

Baldrick
My plan is that I will marry General Melchett. I am the other woman.

George
Ah, well, congratulations, Baldrick. I hope you'll be very happy.

Baldrick
I will be, sir, because when I get back from honeymoon I'll be a member of the aristocracy, and you will have to call me 'Milady'.

Blackadder
What happened to your revolutionary principles, Baldrick? I thought you hated the aristocracy.

Baldrick
I'm working to bring down the system from within, sir. I'm a sort of a frozen horse.

Blackadder
Trojan horse, Baldrick.

Baldrick
Anyway, I can't see what's so stupid about marrying into power and wealth and not having to sleep in a puddle.

Blackadder
Baldrick, no! It's the worst plan since Abraham Lincoln said, 'Oh, I'm sick of kicking around the house tonight, let's go take in a show.' For a start, General Melchett is in mourning for the woman of his dreams – he's unlikely to be in the mood to marry a two-legged badger wrapped in a curtain. Secondly, we are

looking for a great entertainer and you're the worst entertainer since St Paul the Evangelist toured Palestine with his trampoline act. No, we'll have to find somebody else.

George
What about Corporal Cartwright, sir?

Blackadder
Corporal Cartwright looks like an orangutan. I've heard of the bearded lady, but the all-over-body-hair lady frankly just isn't on.

George
Willis?

Blackadder
Too short.

George
Petheridge?

Blackadder
Too old.

George
Taplow?

Blackadder
Too dead. Oh, this is hopeless. There just isn't anyone.

Bob is heard singing.

Bob
'Goodbyeee, goodbyeee, wipe the tear baby dear from your eyeee.'

Blackadder
What am I doing?

He calls out.

Bob?

Bob enters, wearing nothing but a towel.

Bob
Sir?

George
Sir, what a brilliant idea. Bob, can you think of anyone who could be our leading lady?

SCENE TEN: WINGS OF THE THEATRE

Bob is taking curtsies on stage, blowing kisses and holding an armful of flowers. There is tumultuous applause.

George opens the stage curtains and Bob sweeps through them, still blowing kisses to the audience.

George
What do you think, Bob? One more?

Bob
No, George – always leave them hungry.

Blackadder
Congratulations, Bob. I have to admit, I thought you were bloody marvellous.

Bob
Thank you, sir. Permission to slip into something more uncomfortable, sir.

Blackadder
Permission granted.

Bob salutes and exits. Baldrick approaches holding a box.

Baldrick
Oh, sir – it's going to be wonderful. Not just for me but for my little partner, Graham, doing our Charlie Chaplin all round the world.

Baldrick takes the slug out of the box, leans back and places it under his nose.

Blackadder
Yes – from Shaftesbury Avenue to the Côte d'Azur they'll be saying, 'I like the little black one, but who's that berk he's sitting on?'

Baldrick
I'm not with you, sir.

Baldrick places the slug back into the box.

Blackadder
Of course not. But don't worry – we'll have years in luxury hotels for me to explain.

He takes the box from Baldrick.

Now you two, get packing, get packing. The boat-train leaves at six, and we're going to be on it.

Darling enters.

Darling
Blackadder!

Blackadder
Ah, Darling – everything all right?

Darling
Oh, yes.

Blackadder
Got the tickets?

Darling
Oh, yes.

Darling is about to hand Blackadder the tickets when Melchett is heard bellowing.

Melchett
Blackadder!

Melchett enters.

Blackadder
Oh, hi, General. Enjoy the show?

Melchett
(*Very angry*) Don't be ridiculous. The worst evening I've ever spent in my life.

Blackadder
I'm sorry?

He backs away in fear.

Melchett
Will you stand still when I'm talking to you! If by a man's works shall you know him, then you're a steaming pile of horse manure.

Blackadder
But surely, sir, the show was a triumph?

Melchett
A triumph? The Three Twerps were one twerp short *again*. The slug balancer seems now to be doing some feeble impression of Buster Keaton, and, worst of all, the crowning turd in the waterpipe, that revolting drag act at the end.

Blackadder
Drag act?

Melchett
Yes, poor Bob Parkhurst being made to look a total arse. With that thin reedy voice and the stupid effeminate dancing.

Blackadder
Ah.

Darling
(*Very smug*) So, the show's cancelled. (*He tears up the tickets*) Permanently.

Blackadder
But what about the men's morale, sir? With the Russians out of the war and everything . . .

Melchett
For goodness' sake, Blackadder! Have you been living in a cave? The *Americans* joined the war yesterday.

Blackadder
So how is that going to improve the men's morale, sir?

Melchett
Because, you jibbering imbecile, they've brought with them the largest collection of Charlie Chaplin films in existence! (*Blackadder is unimpressed*) Oh, I've lost patience with you. Fill him in, Darling.

Melchett exits.

Darling
Yes, sir. We received a telegram this morning from Mr Chaplin himself at Sennett Studios. (*He reads from it*) 'Twice nightly screening of my films in trenches – excellent idea. Stop. But must insist E. Blackadder be projectionist. Stop. PS Don't let him ever. Stop.'

Blackadder
Oh, great.

Darling
No hard feelings, eh, Blackadder?

Blackadder has a tiny thought – and offers Darling the box with the slug in it.

Blackadder
Not at all, Darling. Care for a liquorice allsort?

Darling
Oh, thank you.

He takes the slug and puts it in his mouth. His reaction to this particular taste experience is not recorded.

The Great War: A Graphic Illustration of the Front Line
December 1915 and June 1917

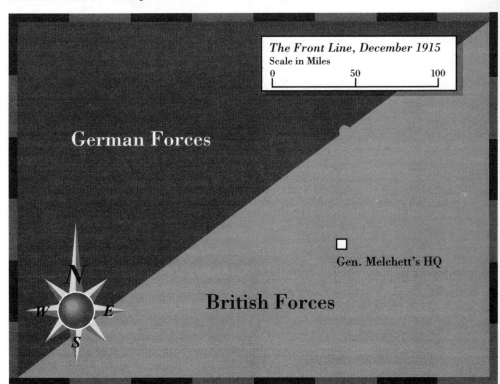

The Front Line, December 1915
Scale in Miles
0   50   100

German Forces

☐
Gen. Melchett's HQ

British Forces

N
W   E
S

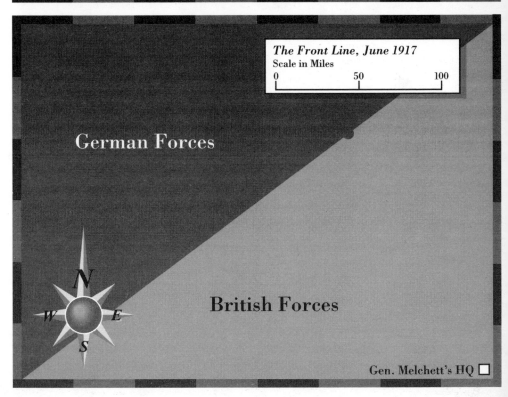

The Front Line, June 1917
Scale in Miles
0   50   100

German Forces

British Forces

N
W   E
S

Gen. Melchett's HQ ☐

PRIVATE PLANE

SCENE ONE: THE TRENCH AND DUG-OUT

It is early morning. There is a massive cannonade going on outside; it is drowning out the gramophone that Blackadder is listening to. He joins George outside in the trench.

Blackadder
Oh, God. Why do they bother?

George
It's to kill Jerry, isn't it, sir?

Blackadder
Yes, but Jerry is safe underground in concrete bunkers. We've shot off over a million cannon shells and what's the result? One dachshund with a slight limp.

He shouts out in the general direction of the shelling.

Shut up!

The shelling suddenly stops and the music on the gramophone is heard clearly.

Thank you. (*Then to George*) Right, I'm off to bed where I intend to sleep until my name changes to Rip Van Adder.

Blackadder goes back in and turns off the gramophone. There is a moment of beautiful peace. He sits on his bed, stretches and then lies down with a satisfying yawn. Instantly there is the huge noise of an aeroplane swooping overhead.

Oh, God, bloody Germans, they can't take a joke, can they? Just because we take a few pot-shots at them, they have to have an air raid to get their own back.

The noise continues, along with the rattle of machine-guns. Blackadder gets up and puts on his helmet.

Where are the air force? They're meant to defend us against this sort of thing.

There is another burst of dangerous gun-fire.

Right, that's it. (*He grabs the phone and dives under the table with it*) Hello? Yes, I'd like to leave a message for the Head of the Flying Corps, please! To Air Chief Marshal, Sir Hugh Massingbird-Massingbird, VC DFC and bar, message reads, 'Where are you, you bastard?'

Baldrick
Here I am, sir.

He is totally relaxed, despite the massive bombing outside.

Blackadder
Baldrick, for God's sake take cover.

Baldrick
Why's that, sir?

Blackadder
Because there's an air raid going on, and I don't want to have to write to your mother at London Zoo and tell her that her only human child is dead.

Baldrick
Oh, all right, sir. (*He joins him hiding under the table*) It's just that I didn't know that there was an air raid going on.

The air raid stops.

I couldn't hear anything above the noise of the terrific display by our wonderful boys of the Royal Flying Corps.

Blackadder
What?

George enters and hangs up his helmet.

George
I say! Those boys can't half thunder in their airborne steeds, can't they just!

He sees Blackadder and Baldrick under the table.

Oh, what's going on here – a game of hide and seek? Excellent! I'll go away and count to a hundred, no, better make it five actually.

Blackadder
George!

George
Oh, I see, it's sardines. Excellent. That's my favourite one.

Blackadder
George!

George
Yes, sir?

Blackadder gets out from under the table.

Blackadder
Shut up and never say anything again as long as you live.

George
Right you are, sir. (*Pause*) Crikey, but what a show it was, sir. Lord Flashheart's Flying Aces. How we cheered when they dived, how we shouted when they spun, how we applauded when one chap got sliced in half by his own propellor. It's all part of the joke for those magnificent men in their flying machines.

Blackadder
For 'magnificent men' read 'biggest show-offs since Lady Godiva entered the royal enclosure at Ascot claiming she had literally nothing to wear'. I don't care how many times they go up-diddly-up-up, they're still gits.

Baldrick
Oh – come on, sir. I'd love to be a flyer – up there where the air is clear.

Blackadder
The chances of the air being clear anywhere near you Baldrick are zero.

Baldrick
Oh, but, sir, it'd be great, swooping and diving . . . (*He flaps his hands by his head and makes an alarming noise*) Eeeeeeeeooowwww! Eeeeeooooow. Eeeow.

Blackadder
Baldrick, what are you doing?

Baldrick
I'm a Sopwith Camel.

Blackadder
Oh, it's a Sopwith Camel. I always get confused between the sound of a Sopwith Camel and the sound of a malodorous runt wasting everyone's time . . . Now, if you can do without me in the nursery for a while, I'm going to get some fresh air.

He picks up his pipe and goes out into the

trench. He is about to light the pipe when from behind him a glamorous, handsome man in flying gear suddenly attacks. It is Squadron Commander, the Lord Flashheart, and he throws Blackadder to the ground in a display of brilliant fighting. In an instant, his boot is on Blackadder's shoulder.

Flashheart
Ha! Eat knuckle Fritz! How disgusting – a Boche on the sole of my boot! I shall have to find a patch of grass to wipe it on. Probably get shunned in the officers' mess . . . 'Sorry about the pong, you fellows, trod on a Boche and just can't get rid of the whiff . . .'

He lets Blackadder get up but keeps his gun pointed at Blackadder's head.

Blackadder
Look, do you think we could dispense with the hilarious 'doggy doo' metaphor for a moment . . . I'm not a Boche. This is a British trench.

Flashheart
Is it? Oh, that's a bit of luck, thought I'd landed sausage-side. (*He puts his gun away*) Mind if I use your phone? If word gets out that I'm missing, 500 girls will kill themselves and I wouldn't want them on my conscience – not when they ought to be on my face!

He grabs the phone.

Hi, Flashheart here. Cancel the state funeral, tell the king to stop blubbing! Flash is *not dead*! I simply ran out of *juice* and before all the girls start saying, 'oh what's the point of living any more', I'm talking about *petrol*! Woof! Woof! I've dumped the kite down on the proles . . . so, send a car. General Melchett's driver will do, she hangs around with the big nobs, so she'll be used to a fellow like me! Woof! Woof!

Blackadder
Look, do you think you can make your

obscene phone call somewhere else?

Flash ignores him totally.

Flashheart
No, not in half an hour, you rubber desk johnny. Send the bitch with the wheels right now or I'll fly back to England and give your wife something to hang her towels on. (*He slams down the phone*) Okay, dig out your best booze and let's talk about me till the car comes! You must be pretty impressed, having Squadron Commander the Lord Flashheart drop in on your squalid bit of line!

Blackadder
Actually, no – I was more impressed by the contents of my handkerchief the last time I blew my nose.

Flashheart
Yeah? Like hell! You've probably got little piccies of me on the walls of your dug-out, haven't you? I bet you go all girly and giggly whenever you look at them.

Blackadder
Ah! I'm afraid not – unfortunately, most of the infantry think you're a prat. Ask them who they'd prefer to meet – Squadron Commander Flashheart or the man who cleans the public toilets in Aberdeen and they'd go for Wee Jock Poo-Pong McPlop every time.

Flashheart
Ha ha!

He biffs Blackadder on the nose and then enters the dug-out. Blackadder follows. Inside Baldrick and George are still discussing the display.

George
When that fellow looped the loop, I honestly thought I'd . . . (*He is stopped short, seeing Flash*) My God!

Flashheart
Yes, I suppose I am.

George
Lord Flashheart! This is the greatest hon-

our of my life! I hope I snuff it right now to preserve this moment for ever.

Blackadder
It could be arranged.

Baldrick is totally thrilled.

Baldrick
Lord Flashheart! I want to learn to write so I can send a letter home about this golden moment.

Flashheart
So all the fellows hate me, eh? (*Ruffling Baldrick's hair*) Not a bit of it. I'm your bloody hero, eh, old scout? Oh, Jesus!

He has got something extremely unpleasant on his hand gleaned from Baldrick's hair. He wipes it off on Blackadder.

Baldrick
My lord. I've got every cigarette card they ever printed of you. My whole family took up smoking just so that we could get the whole set. My grandmother smoked herself to death so we could afford the album.

Flashheart
Of course she did, of course she did, the poor love-crazed octogenarian. Well, all right, you fellows, let's sit down and yarn about how amazingly attractive I am.

Blackadder
Yes, yes, if you'll excuse me, I have urgent business. There's a bucket outside I have to be sick into . . .

He leaves. Flashheart makes a sarcastic hoity-toity noise.

Flashheart
Whoooooooooh! All right, you chaps – right, let's get comfy. (*To Baldrick*) You look a decent British bloke, I'll park the old booties on you, if that's all right?

Baldrick
It would be an honour, sir.

Baldrick kneels and Flashheart puts his feet up on Baldrick's back.

Flashheart
Of course it would. Have you any idea what it's like to have the wind rushing through your hair?

George
No, sir.

Flashheart breaks wind loudly.

Flashheart
(*Indicating Baldrick*) He has, lucky devil.

SCENE TWO: THE DUG-OUT

It is later. Baldrick is in the same position, as he and George listen in rapt attention to Flashheart. Blackadder ostentatiously reads a book and ignores them.

Flashheart
. . . so I flew straight through her bedroom window, popped a box of chocs on her dressing table, machine-gunned my telephone number into the wall and then shot off and shagged her sister . . .

George claps his hands and guffaws. Bob, the driver, appears. She clears her throat.

Bob
Driver Parkhurst reporting for duty, my lord . . .

Flashheart
Well, well, well, if it isn't little Bobby Parkhurst, saucier than a direct hit on a Heinz factory.

Bob
I've come to pick you up.

Flashheart
That's how I like my girls – direct and to my point! Woof!

He grabs her hand and pulls her on to his lap.

Bob
Woof!

They kiss very noisily.

George
Gosh.

Blackadder looks at his watch.

Flashheart
Tally-ho, then, back to the bar.

He sweeps Bob up – she is kissing his shoulder.

You know, you should join the Flying Corps, George . . . that's the way to fight the war – tasty tucker, soft beds and a uniform so smart it's got a PhD from Cambridge . . . You could even bring old breath-monster here. (*Breath-monster is Baldrick*) Anyone can be a navigator if they can tell their arse from their elbow.

Blackadder
Well, that's Baldrick out I fear.

Flashheart
We're always looking for talented types to join the Twenty Minuters.

Blackadder
And there goes George.

Flashheart
Tally-ho, Bobby! Hush, here comes a whiz bang, and I think you know what I'm talking about! Woof!

Bob
Woof!

Blackadder
God – it's like Crufts in here.

And Flash leaves, with Bob in his arms.

George
I say! What a splendid notion. The Twenty Minuters – soft tucker, tasty beds, fluffy uniforms! Not half!

Baldrick
Beggin' your permission, sir, but why do they call them the Twenty Minuters?

George
Now then, yes, this one's in my Brooke Bond Book of the Air, I think . . . you have to collect all the cards you see and stick them in this wonderful presentation booklet . . . (*He gets it out*) Ah, here we are: 'Twenty Minuters' – damn, I haven't got the card yet but the caption says, 'Twenty minutes is the average amount of time new pilots spend in the air.'

Blackadder
Twenty minutes?

George
That's right.

For the first time in his life, George has Blackadder's total attention.

Blackadder
I had a twenty-*hour* watch yesterday with four hours' overtime. In two feet of water.

George
Then for goodness' sake, sir! Why don't we join?!

Baldrick
Yeh, it would be better than just sitting around here all day on our elbows.

Blackadder
No, thank you. I've no desire to hang around with a bunch of upper-class delinquents, do twenty minutes' work and then spend the rest of the day loafing about in Paris drinking gallons of champagne and having dozens of moist, pink, highly experienced French peasant girls galloping up

and down my – hang on . . .

A very big thought occurs.

SCENE THREE: MELCHETT'S HQ

Darling is sitting at the desk. Blackadder knocks on the door.

Darling
Come.

Blackadder enters.

Ah, Captain Blackadder.

Blackadder
Good morning, Captain Darling.

Darling
What do you want?

Blackadder
You're looking so well.

Darling
I'm a busy man, Blackadder. Let's hear it, whatever it is.

Blackadder
You know, Darling, every man has a dream and when I was a small boy, I used to watch the marsh warblers swooping in my mother's undercroft and I remember thinking, 'Will men ever dare to do the same' . . . And you know . . .

Darling realizes what Blackadder wants. He stands up.

Darling
Oh, you want to join the Royal Flying Corps?

Blackadder
(*Casually*) That's a thought – could I?

Darling
(*Equally casually*) No, you couldn't. Goodbye.

He sits down and goes back to work.

Blackadder
Oh, come on, Darling. Just give me an application form.

Darling
It's out of the question. This is simply a ruse to waste five months in training after which you'll claim you can't fly after all because it makes your ears go 'pop'. Come on, I wasn't born yesterday, Blackadder.

Blackadder
More's the pity – we could start your personality from scratch. So, the training period is five months, is it?

Darling
It's no concern of yours if it's five years and comes with a free holiday in Tunisia, and contraceptives supplied. Besides, they wouldn't admit you – it's not easy getting transfers, you know.

He picks up his pencil and carries on writing.

Blackadder
Oh, you've tried it out yourself, have you?

Darling breaks his pencil lead. Blackadder has touched a nervy nerve.

Darling
No, I have not.

Blackadder
Trust you to skive off to some cushy option.

Darling
There is nothing cushy about life in the Women's Auxiliary Balloon Corps.

Blackadder looks; Darling realizes he's let something out by mistake. General Melchett enters with George, who is in the middle of telling a rude joke.

George
. . . so the Bishop said, 'I'm sorry, I didn't realize you meant an organist!'

Melchett laughs perfunctorily.

Melchett
Thank you, George. At ease, everybody, now! (*He dumps a pile of files on the map*) Where's my map?

Darling
Sir.

Darling hands it to him, and he unrolls it the wrong way round.

Melchett
God – it's a barren, featureless desert out there, isn't it?

Darling
Other side, sir.

Blackadder
Hullo, George – what are you doing here?

George
Me, sir? I've just popped in to join the Royal Flying Corps.

Melchett
Hullo, Blackadder. What are you doing here?

Blackadder
Me, sir? I've just popped in to join the Royal Flying Corps.

Darling
Of course, I said . . .

Melchett
'Bravo', I hope, Darling. You know sometimes I've had my doubts about you trenchy-type fellows, think there might be a touch of battle-dodging, nappy-wearing, 'I'd rather have a cup of tea than charge stark naked at Jerry' about you, but if you're willing to go up there with the Twenty Minuters, then you're all right by me, and welcome to marry my sister any day.

Darling
Sir, are you sure about this?

Melchett
Certainly. You should hear the noise she makes eating a boiled egg, I'd be glad to get her out of the house. So report back here 0900 hours for your basic training.

SCENE FOUR: A ROYAL FLYING CORPS LECTURE ROOM

Blackadder and George are present with one or two other new recruits. There is a blackboard with a picture of a plane on it.

George
Crikey, sir, I'm looking forward to today. Up diddly up, down diddly down, whoops, poop, twiddlydee – decent scrap with the fiendish Red Baron – bit of a jolly old crash landing behind enemy lines – capture, torture, escape, and then back home in time for tea and medals.

Blackadder
George, who is using the family brain cell at the moment? This is just the beginning of the training – the beginning of five long, lazy months of very clever, very dull men looking at machinery.

There is a sound of screaming girls outside, followed by a familiar voice. Blackadder is not overjoyed.

Flashheart
Hey, girls! Look at my machinery.

The girls scream even more and Flashheart enters.

Enter the man who has no underwear! Ask me why.

They all stand, enraptured.

All
Why do you have no underwear, Lord Flash?

Flashheart
Because the pants haven't been *built* yet that'll take the job on! *That's* the type of guy who's doing the training round here. Sit down. Well, well, if it isn't old Captain Slack Bladder.

Blackadder
Blackadder.

Flashheart
Couldn't resist it, eh, Slack Bladder? Told you, you thought I was great. Right let's do-o-o-o it! The first thing to remember is, always treat your kite like you treat a woman.

George
How d'you mean, sir? Do you mean take her home at the weekend to meet your mother?

Flashheart
No, I mean get inside her five times a day and take her to heaven and back.

Blackadder
I'm beginning to see why the Suffragette Movement want the vote.

Flashheart
Any bird who wants to chain herself to my railings and suffer a jet movement (*another subtle thrust of the hips*) gets my vote. Right, that's it! See you in ten minutes for take-off.

He makes to leave.

Blackadder
Hang on, hang on, what about the months of training?

Flashheart
Hey, wet pants, this isn't the Women's Auxiliary Balloon Corps, you're in the Twenty Minuters now!

Darling suddenly pops up at the back. He has an annoying smug look about him today.

Darling
Uh, sir, sir.

Flashheart
Yes, prat at the back.

Darling
I think we'd all be intrigued to know. Why are you called the Twenty Minuters?

George
Mr Thicko! Imagine not knowing that!

Flashheart
Simple, really – the average life expectancy of a new pilot is twenty minutes.

Darling
Aha.

Blackadder
(*Not happy*) Life expectancy of twenty minutes?

Flashheart
Right! Goggles on, chocks away – last one back's a homo. Hurray!

Flash goes. The other trainees follow him.

Blackadder
We take off in ten minutes, we're in the air for twenty minutes, which means we'll be dead by twenty-five to ten.

George
Hairy blighters! This is a turn-up for the plus fours.

Darling strolls over, delighted.

Darling
Oh, I shouldn't worry about it too much, Blackadder. Flying's all about navigation. As long as you've got a good navigator, you'll be fine.

He snorts and moves to the door. Baldrick enters in full flying gear – leather coat, flying goggles. Baldrick the navigator.

SCENE FIVE: THE SKIES OVER FRANCE

A flight of First World War planes soar through the skies. Blackadder's voice is heard in the cockpit of one of the planes.

Blackadder
Actually, they're right – this is a doddle.

The plane dips dramatically.

Whoops, a little wobble – but I'll get the hang of it. All right, Baldrick, time to take stock of our chances of survival – how many rounds have we got?

Baldrick
Five hundred, sir: cheese and tomato for you, rat for me.

George passes them in his plane.

George
Hello, sir. Tally bally ho!

Baldrick
What's this, sir?

The plane soars upwards at an incredibly steep angle. Baldrick has hoisted himself up out of his seat and is balancing precariously with his arms outstretched.

Blackadder
Baldrick, will you stop arsing about and get back in the cockpit?

Baldrick
Woohoo! Sir, I can see a pretty red plane from up here.

Baron von Richthoven
(*For it is he*) *Schnell*, ah ha, ha.

Blackadder
Oh, no. Watch out, Baldrick, it's stood right on our tail. Yes. This is developing into a distinctly boring situation. Luckily we're still on our side of the lines, so I'll crash land and claim my ears went 'pop' first time out.

Baldrick
Let's hope we fall on something soft.

Blackadder
Fine – I'll try and aim between General Melchett's ears.

The plane heads towards the earth then hits it with a terrible crash.

SCENE SIX: A SINISTER GERMAN CELL

Baldrick and Blackadder are much dishevelled and in captivity.

Blackadder
I don't believe it! A German prison cell! For two and a half years the Western Front's been as likely to move as a Frenchman who lives next door to a brothel. Then, last night the Germans advance a mile and we land on the wrong side!

Baldrick
Oh, dear, Captain B. My tummy's gone all squirty.

Blackadder
That's because you're scared, Baldrick, and you're not the only one. I couldn't be more petrified if a wild rhinoceros had just come home from a hard day at the swamp and found me wearing his pyjamas, smoking his cigars and in bed with his wife.

Baldrick
I've heard what these Germans do, sir, they'll have their wicked way with anything of woman born.

Blackadder
In which case, Baldrick, you're safe. However, the Teutonic reputation for brutality is well founded. Their operas last three or four days and they have no word for 'fluffy'.

Baldrick
I want my mum.

Blackadder
Hmm, yes, it would be good to see her. I should imagine a maternally outraged gorilla would be a pretty useful ally when it comes to the final scrap.

They hear footsteps both ominous and sinister.

Prepare to die like a man, Baldrick – or as close as you can get without actually shaving the palms of your hands . . .

The door bursts open. A German officer enters – he is tough and sinister and sly and nasty.

Von Gerhardt
Good evening – I am Ober Leutnant von Gerhardt and I have a message for you from Baron von Richthoven, the greatest living German.

Blackadder
Which, considering the competition consists almost entirely of very fat men in leather shorts burping to the tune of 'She'll Be Coming Round The Mountain', is no great achievement.

Von Gerhardt
Quiet!

He hits Baldrick.

Blackadder
And what is this message?

Von Gerhardt
It is 'Prepare for a fate vorse than death, English flyer fellow.'

Blackadder
Ah. So it's the traditional warm German welcome.

Von Gerhardt
Correct! Also he is saying – 'Do not try to escape, or you will suffer even vorse.'

Blackadder
A fate worse than a fate worse than death – that's pretty bad.

SCENE SEVEN: MELCHETT'S HQ

Darling and George are arguing over the desk. George is furious.

George
It's all very well for you sitting behind a comfy desk.

Darling
(*Also furious*) Don't take that tone with me, Lieutenant, or I'll have you on a charge for insubordination!

George
Well, I'd rather have a charge of insubordination than a charge of deserting a friend!

Darling
How dare you talk to me like that!

Melchett enters. He sees Darling and George arguing.

Melchett
Now then, now then, now then, now. Now then, then now, now then. What's going on?

Darling
That damn fool Blackadder crashed his plane behind enemy lines and this young idiot wants to try and rescue him. It's a total waste of men and equipment.

George
He's not a damn fool, sir, he's a bally hero.

Melchett
All right – I'll deal with this, Darling – delicate touch needed, I fancy.

He takes a very godfatherly attitude and puts his arm round George.

Now, George, do you remember when I came down to visit you when you were a nipper for your sixth birthday – you had a rabbit, beautiful little thing, do you remember?

George
Flossy.

Melchett
That's right – and do you remember what
happened to Flossy?

George
You shot him.

Melchett
That's right. It was the kindest thing to do,
after all he had been run over by that car.

George
By your car, sir.

Melchett
Yes, by my car, yes, but that too was an
act of mercy after you remember that dog
had been set on him.

George
Your dog, sir.

Melchett
Yes, yes, my dog. But what I'm trying to
say, George, is the state that young Flossy
was in after he'd been scraped off my
front tyre is very much the state young
Blackadder will be in now – if not very
nearly dead then very actually dead.

George is very upset indeed.

George
Permission for lip to wobble, sir.

Melchett
Permission granted.

George wobbles his lip.

Stout fellow.

George
Surely, sir, you must let me at least try to
save him.

Melchett
No, George, as pointless as trying to teach
a woman the importance of a good forward
defensive stroke. Besides, it would take a
superman to get him out of there – not the
kind of weed who blubs just because somebody gives him a slice of rabbit pie instead
of birthday cake.

George
I suppose you're right, sir.

Melchett
Course I am, sir. Now, let's talk about
something more jolly, eh? Look, this is the
amount of land we've recaptured since yesterday.

George
(*Totally distracted*) Oh, excellent.
*They lean over the large map, a mixture
of grass and earth.*

Melchett
What's the actual scale on the map,
Darling?

Darling
Uhm . . . one to one, sir.

Melchett
Come again?

Darling
Ahm – the map is actually life size, sir. It's
superbly detailed – look, there's a little
worm.

Melchett
Oh, yes. So, the actual amount of ground
retaken is . . . ?

Darling
Excuse me, sir.

He jumps forward to measure the map.

About seventeen square feet, sir.

Melchett
Well – excellent. You see, Blackadder didn't die horribly in vain after all.

George
If he did die, sir.

Melchett
That's the spirit, George! If nothing else works, a total pig-headed unwillingness to look facts in the face will see us through.

SCENE EIGHT: THE GERMAN CELL

Blackadder and Baldrick are asleep. There is a clunk as the door unlocks and there stands the greatest of Germans – blond and mighty.

Richthoven
Zo, I am the Red Baron von Richthoven. And you are der two English flyer aces responsible for the spilling of the precious German blood of many of my finest and my blondest friends. I have waited many months to do this.

He grabs Blackadder by the shoulders and then kisses him formally on both cheeks.

Blackadder
You may have been right, Balders – looks like we're going to get rogered to death after all.

Baldrick
Do you want me to go first, sir?

Richthoven
Ha! You English and your zense of humour. During your brief stay I look forward to learning more of your vit, your punning and your amusing jokes about the breaking of the vind.

Blackadder
Baldrick's the expert there.

Baldrick
Certainly am, sir.

Richthoven
Ha! Ha! How lucky you English are to find the toilet zo amusing, for us it is a mundane and functional item, for you it is the basis of an entire culture.

They all laugh – he hits Baldrick.

Silence! I must now tell you of the full horror of what avaits you.

Blackadder
You see, Baldrick, dress it up in any amount of pompous verbal diarrhoea, the message is square heads down for the big Boche gang bang.

Richthoven
As an officer and a gentleman you vill be looking forward to a qvick and noble death.

Blackadder
Well, obviously.

Richthoven
But instead an even vorse fate avaits you. So, tomorrow you vill be taken back to Germany . . .

Blackadder
Here it comes.

Richthoven
To a convent school outside Heidelberg, vhere you spend zhe rest of zhe var teaching the young girls Home Economics.

Blackadder
Umm . . .

Richthoven
For you, as a man of honour, the humiliation vill be unbearable!

Blackadder
I think you'll find we're tougher than you imagine.

Richthoven
I can tell how much you are suffering by your long faces.

Blackadder
Yes, but not suffering too much to say

thank you. Say thank you, Baldrick.

Baldrick
Thank you, Baldrick.

Richthoven
Ha, very amusing. But now – forgive me. I must take to the skies once again, the noble Lord Flashheart still eludes me!

Blackadder
I think you'll find he's overrated – bad breath and ahm, impotent, they say.

Richthoven
Ah, sexual innuendo. But enough of that – as you say in England – 'I must fly!' Ha ha! Perhaps I will master this humour after all!

Blackadder
I wouldn't be too optimistic.

Richthoven
And . . . (*At the door he stops coyly*) Uhm, the little fellow, if you get lonely in the night, I'm in the old Château . . . there's no pressure.

As he is leaving, he trips over the stairs, and turns around with delight.

Ha! Ha! A pratfall!

He exits.

Baldrick
Is it really true, sir? Is the war really over for us?

The question finds Blackadder in the best mood of his life.

Blackadder
Yup! Out of the war and teaching nuns how to boil eggs. For us, the Great War is finito, a war which would be a damn sight simpler if we just stayed in England and shot fifty thousand of our men a week! No more mud, death, rats, bombs, shrapnel, whiz bangs, barbed wire and bloody awful songs that have the word 'Whoops!' in the title. Damn, he's left the door open.

Baldrick
Oh, good, we can escape.

Blackadder
Are you mad, Baldrick? I'll go and find someone to lock it for us.

There is a knock on the door. Blackadder sweeps it open. It is George, also in flying gear.

George
Shhhh! Cave! Mum's the word! Not half or what!

Blackadder slams the door shut on him in horror.

Baldrick
Why did you slam the door on Lieutenant George?

Blackadder
I can't believe it. (*He calls out through the door*) Go away!

George
It's me – it's me!

He re-opens the door. There stands George, grinning.

Blackadder
What the hell are you doing here?

George
(*Very pleased with himself*) Oh, never mind the 'hows and whys'. And the 'do you mind if I don'ts'.

Blackadder
But it would take a superman to get in here.

George
Well, funny you should say that, because I did, in fact, have some help from a spiffing fellow. He's taken a break from some crucial top-level shagging.

Blackadder
Oh, God.

Flashheart swings in through the door on a rope.

Flashheart
It's me. Hurray!

Baldrick
Hurray!

Squadron Commander the Lord Flashheart pictured uncharacteristically alone
and fully clothed

Flashheart hits Baldrick.

Flashheart
God's potatoes, George! You said noble brother flyers were in the lurch. If I'd known it was only Slack Bladder and the mound of the hound of the Baskervilles, I'd have let them stew in their own juice. And let me tell you, if *I* ever tried that, I'd probably *drown*!

Baldrick is up again and laughing. Flashheart hits him again.

Still, since I'm here, I might as well doo-o-o it! As the bishop said to the net-ball team. Come on, chums!

They run away – then look back through the door. Blackadder has stayed behind. He sinks to the ground and starts moaning.

Come on.

Blackadder
Uhm, look, sorry, chaps, but I've splintered my pancreas and I've got this awful cough.

He coughs. The coughs sound suspiciously like:

Guards! Guards!

Flashheart
Wait a minute! I may be packing the kind of tackle you'd normally expect to find swinging about between the hind legs of a Grand National winner, but I'm not totally stupid – and I've got a feeling you'd rather we hadn't come.

Blackadder
No, no, no. I'm really grateful but I'd slow you up.

Flashheart
I think I'm beginning to understand.

Blackadder
Are you?

Flashheart
Just because I can give multiple orgasms to the furniture just by sitting on it doesn't mean I'm not sick of this damn war. The blood, the noise, the endless poetry.

Blackadder
Is that what you really think, Flashheart?

Flashheart gets out a gun and points it at Blackadder.

Flashheart
Of course . . . it's not what I think! Now get out that door before I redecorate this room in an exciting new colour called Hint of Brain.

Blackadder
Excellent – nice and clear. In that case, let's get back to that lovely war . . .

Flashheart
Woof!

George
Woof!

Baldrick
Bark!

But too late! Richthoven melodramatically appears at the doorway.

Richthoven
Not so fast, Blackadder!

Blackadder
(*With massive relief*) Damn – foiled again – what bad luck!

Richthoven
Ah, and Lord Flashheart, this is indeed an honour. Finally the two greatest gentlemen flyers in the world meet. Two men of honour who have jousted together in the cloud-strewn glory of the skies are face to face at last. How often have I rehearsed this moment of destiny in my dreams. The valour we two encapsulate, the unspoken nobility of our comradeship, the . . .

And Flashheart shoots him – 'bang'. He's dead now.

Flashheart
What a poof! Let's go!

All
Hurray!

SCENE NINE: MELCHETT'S HQ

Darling is polishing door knobs. Blackadder opens the door, which bangs him firmly on the nose.

Blackadder
Hullo, Darling.

Darling backs away. Blackadder advances towards him.

Darling
Good Lord – Captain Blackadder. I thought you were . . .

Blackadder
Playing tennis?

Darling
No, I mean . . .

Blackadder
Dead?

Darling
Yes, unfortunately.

Blackadder
No – I had a lucky escape. No thanks to you.

Flashheart is there standing on the desk.

This is a friend of mine.

Flashheart
Hi, creep.

Blackadder
Flash, this is Captain Darling.

Flashheart
Captain Darling! Funny name for a guy, isn't it? The last person I called 'darling' was pregnant twenty seconds later. I hear you couldn't be bothered to help old Slackie here.

Darling
Oh, well, er, it wasn't that at all – we weighed up the pros and cons, and it didn't seem a reasonable use of our time and resources.

Flashheart
Well, this isn't a reasonable use of my time and resources, but I'm going to do it anyway.

Darling
What?

Flashheart
This.

He head-butts the miserable pen-pusher.

All right, Slacky. I've got to fly. Two million chicks, only one Flashheart. And always remember – if you want something, take it. Bobby!

Enter Bob.

Bob
My lord?

Flashheart
I want something.

Bob
Take it.

She starts to undo her coat buttons, and exits smartly.

Flashheart
Woof!

He follows her out.

Blackadder
Git.

Enter Melchett.

Melchett
Ah, Blackadder! You escaped!

Blackadder
Yes, sir.

Melchett
Bravo!

He notices Darling lying unconscious across the table.

Don't slouch, Darling.

Blackadder
I was wondering whether, after being tortured by the most vicious sadist in the German army, I might be allowed a week's leave to recuperate.

Melchett
Excellent idea – your Commanding Officer would have to be stark raving mad to refuse you.

Blackadder
You are my Commanding Officer.

Melchett
Well?

Blackadder
Can I have a week's leave to recuperate, sir?

Melchett
Certainly not.

Blackadder
Thank you, sir.

Melchett
Baaah!

Mad, you see, stark raving mad.

THE FAGIN SCHOOL

ANNUAL REPORT MARTINMAS TERM, 1880

NAME OF PUPIL: S. Baldrick   **AGE**: 6.4 (approx)

CHIMNEY-SWEEPING

This boy (if indeed he be such, and not a chimpanzee!) is unusually stunted and was filthy from head to toe when he joined us so he had the advantage of his fellows. The hideous bruising to the base of the spine, bleeding grazes on knees and elbows, broken leg, asthma, etc. are a result of diet (too many good things, I suspect, at home!) and have nothing to do with his studies.   R.St.R.W.

MUDLARKING

Must put more effort into scampering charmingly, and his toothless grins show little genuine enthusiasm. Several of the tufty-faced old gentlemen on our London Bridge spectator panel confessed themselves left sexually cold after his performance. A disappointing term.

D.G.S.

LATIN

Forsan et hoec olin meminisse iuvabit!

J.H.W.L.

POSING FOR OLD SEPIA PHOTOGRAPHS

Satis.

F.R.deV.

CORPORAL PUNISHMENT

Good. Baldrick is more enjoyable to beat than many other boys because of the satisfying pigletty squeals he emits. We look forward to seeing more of him next term!

P.E.

NATURE TABLE

I am leaving at the end of term to join the Little Friars of St Norris at their monastery on the island of Gloy where I shall devote the rest of my life to distilling Fratello, their powerful Holy Liqueur. A year 'teaching' S. Baldrick has destroyed my faith in Darwin's Theory of Evolution, which I am now convinced is fatally flawed in some way. Also, I need a bloody great drink.   E.J.

DIVINITY

Baldrick finds it difficult to remember that God loves him, and I have had to beat this into him on numerous occasions. I have recommended detention during the Easter holiday. Three weeks on bread and water in the ditty-hole should do the trick, Headmaster!   GBH

HEADMASTER'S COMMENTS

Baldrick is a happy little chap, we wish him well, etc. etc.

E.A.B.-F.

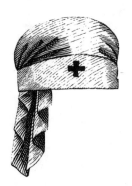

GENERAL HOSPITAL

SCENE ONE: THE DUG-OUT

The chaps are sitting around.

George
I spy with my little eye . . .

He looks at the table next to him. All that there is on it is one mug.

. . . something beginning with . . . 'm'.

Baldrick
Mmmm, mmmm, mmmm.

Baldrick is totally baffled. George waggles his head at the mug.

George
Mmmm. Mmm.

Baldrick
Mmmmm.

They continue like this, getting louder, until Blackadder snaps.

Blackadder
Mug!

George
Oh, well done, sir! Your turn.

Blackadder
Ahm, I spy with my bored little eye something beginning with . . . 't'.

Baldrick
Breakfast.

Blackadder
What?

Baldrick
My breakfast always begins with tea, then I have a little sausage. Then an egg with some little soldiers.

Blackadder
When I say it begins with 't', I meant a letter.

Baldrick
No, it never begins with a letter, the postman don't come until 10.30.

Blackadder
I can't go on with this. George, you take over.

George
All right, sir. I spy with my little eye something that begins with 'r'.

Baldrick
Army.

Blackadder
For God's sake, Baldrick – army starts with an 'a'. He's looking for something that starts with an 'r'. Rrrrrr. (*He rolls his 'r's*)

Baldrick
Motor bike.

Blackadder
What?

Baldrick
Motor bike starts with an 'r', rrrr, rrrrr.

He does his rolling 'r' motorbike impression.

Blackadder
Right, my turn again. What starts with 'Come here' and ends with 'Ow'?

Baldrick
Don't know, sir.

Blackadder
Right, come here!

He hits Baldrick.

Baldrick
Owwww!

George
No – ha, ha – I don't think you've quite got the hang of this game. Let's try another one. I hear with my little ear something beginning with 'b'.

Blackadder
What?

George
Bomb.

Blackadder
I can't hear a bomb.

George
Listen very carefully.

Blackadder listens. Then, casually . . .

Blackadder
Oh yes.

An enormous explosion outside sends debris everywhere.

SCENE TWO: THE FIELD HOSPITAL WARD

George is in bed. He has a bandaged arm. He is reading back a letter to lovely, sweet Nurse Mary, sitting beside him. They are very matey.

George
Finished!

Mary
Come on then.

George
All right and you can tell me what you think, but be honest now!

Mary
I will!

George
'Dear Uncle H, how are you?'

Mary laughs.

It's good, isn't it: 'It's beastly rotten luck being laid up here but everyone's very nice and at least now I can write to you every day.' Oh, er, then there's a silly bit, but it's nothing.

Mary
What?

George
No, no!

Mary
Oh, go on, you can tell me!

George is embarrassed, but pleased.

George
'And the nurse is an absolute peach.' Er, oh.

Mary smiles, pleased. She is soppily fond of, and gentle with him. George continues.

'Captain Blackadder was marvellous, he joked and joked, "You lucky lucky lucky bastard," he cried . . . and then he lay on his back, stuck his foot over the top of the trench and shouted, "Over here, Fritz! What about me!" . . .'

Mary
Captain Blackadder does indeed sound like a witty, courageous chap.

George
Yes, and he's very amusing and brave as well. Not to mention being as clever as a chap with three heads.

Mary ruffles George's hair and plumps up his pillows.

Gosh – well, thanks ever so much. You really are terribly kind and dashed pretty to boot.

Mary
Oh, I don't know – a fluffy pillow and a big cheery smile is the least my boysies deserve. Now you take a little trip to Dozyland. You've got visitors coming, and we don't want to be all tired and cross-patch, do we?

In the spirit of it all, George starts to suck his thumb.

George
Absolutely not. It'll be so jolly to see Baldrick and the Cap. They'll have been worried sick about me, you know.

Enter Baldrick and Blackadder through the swing doors.

Blackadder
All right, where is the malingering git?

George
Hallo, Cap! Pip pip, Balders! Here I lie!

Baldrick
Nice to see the lieutenant looking so well, sir.

Blackadder
Course he's looking well, there's nothing wrong with him.

George
Ha, ha! Didn't I tell you, the Captain was a super cove?

Mary
You did. Well, Captain, you're indeed fortunate to have a loyal friend like darling Georgie.

Blackadder
Mmm. I'm afraid you're under a slight misapprehension here, Nurse – I lost closer friends than 'darling Georgie' the last time I was deloused. Now, if you'll excuse me I've got better things to do than exchange pleasantries with a wet blanket. Would you get out?

Mary gasps.

We've got some important military business.

Mary
Well, ten minutes only then.

He points to the way out. She leaves. Blackadder sits down next to George.

Blackadder
Right, porkface, where's the grub?

George
Pardon?

Blackadder
Come on – the moment that collection of inbred mutants you call your relatives heard you were sick, they will have sent you a hamper the size of Westminster Abbey.

George
My family is not inbred!

Blackadder
Oh, come on – somewhere outside Saffron

Walden there's an uncle who is seven feet tall with no chin and an Adam's apple that makes him look as if he's constantly trying to swallow a ballcock.

George
I don't have any uncles like that! And anyway he lives in Walton-on-the-Naze.

Blackadder
Pay attention! Now where's the tuck?

George
Well, there were one or two things, yes . . . a potted turkey, a cow in jelly, three tinned sheep, and twelve hundred choco-lates, but in my weakened state . . .

Blackadder
Yes?

George
I . . . I ate them.

Blackadder
What?

George
Well, Nurse Mary nibbled a trotter or two . . . Oh Cap, she's such a wonderful girl – helps me with my letters because she can spell all the German names and is terribly good at punctuation . . .

Blackadder
I don't care if she can sing 'I May Be A Tiny Chimney Sweep, But I've Got An Enormous Brush'. Come on, Baldrick – the only thing we're going to get for free round here is dysentry.

Baldrick
(*Whispering*) I haven't given Lieutenant George my bunch of flowers yet.

Blackadder
All right, hurry up, hurry up.

Baldrick
Here you are, sir. I got you these.(*He holds out a bunch of dead stalks*) Unfortunately they've had their heads shot off.

Blackadder
Where others choose to say it with flowers, Baldrick says it with stalks.

Nurse Mary returns.

Mary
I'm afraid you'll have to leave us, Captain.

Blackadder
Oh, really?

Mary
Yes – you must report to General Melchett immediately.

Blackadder
Oh, great. Yet another tempting opportu-nity for suicide beckons.

George
Oh, gosh, I wish I was going with you, sir.

Mary
Oh no, you must stay here, my brave hero!

Blackadder
(*Exasperated*) Brave hero? Nurse, I was more wounded the last time I clipped my toenails.

Mary
Take no notice of him.

Blackadder
(*In a sarcastic baby voice*) Yes, pay no attention to the nasty man.

Mary
If I can't give my brave boys a kind word and a big smile, what can I give them?

Blackadder
Well, one or two ideas do suggest them-selves, but . . . you'd probably think they were unhygienic.

Mary
Oh!

She storms out. A bearded man with glasses, wearing a bandage on his head, limps through the doors.

Blackadder
Come on, Baldrick. (*He notices the man walking in*) Hullo, what's your name?

The man replies in a thick German accent.

Smith
My name iz Mr Smith.

Blackadder
Yes, well I'm sorry you've been landed opposite such a total git, Smith. Bad enough being wounded without having to share a ward with banana brain.

Smith
Oh, *danke schön. Ich bin ganz* comfortable, old fruit.

Blackadder looks at him doubtfully, and walks out.

SCENE THREE: MELCHETT'S HQ

Blackadder knocks on the door.

Melchett
Enter!

Blackadder enters but the room appears to be completely empty.

Blackadder
Hello? Hello!

He looks round, and wanders towards the board covered with maps. Someone is standing behind it. He pulls back a flap and sees Melchett's face. As he does so, Darling pounces on Blackadder, drags him over to the fireplace, and frisks him.

Darling
He's clean, sir.

Melchett
Baaah!

Blackadder
Can anyone tell me what's going on?

Melchett
Security, Blackadder.

Blackadder
Security?

Melchett
'Security' isn't a dirty word, Blackadder. 'Crevice' is a dirty word, 'security' isn't.

Blackadder
So, in the name of security, everyone who comes into the room has to have his bottom fondled by this drooling pervert?

Darling
Only doing my job, Blackadder.

Blackadder
Oh, how lucky you are then that your job is also your hobby.

Melchett
There's another dirty word – 'job'.

Blackadder
Sir, is there something the matter?

Melchett
You're damn right there's something the matter. Something sinister, and grotesque. And what's worse is that it's right here under my nose!

Blackadder
Oh, come now, sir, your moustache is lovely.

Darling
What the general means, Blackadder, is there is a leak.

Melchett
Now 'leak' is a positively disgusting word.

Darling
The Germans seem to be able to anticipate our every move. We send up an aeroplane, there's a Jerry squadron parked behind the nearest cloud. We move troops to Boulogne, the Germans have bought the entire town supply of lavatory paper. In short, a German spy is giving away every one of our battle plans.

Melchett
You look surprised, Blackadder.

Blackadder
I certainly am, sir. I didn't realize we had any battle plans.

Melchett
Of course we've got plans – how else do you think our battles are directed?

Blackadder
Our battles are directed, sir?

Melchett
Of course they are: directed according to the grand plan.

Blackadder
Oh, I see. And that would be the plan to continue with total slaughter until everybody's dead except Field Marshal Haig and Lady Haig and their tortoise Alan.

Melchett
(*Jumping up in alarm*) Great Scott! Even you know it! Bolt the doors! Hammer large bits of crooked wood against all the windows! This security leak is far worse than I'd imagined.

Darling
So you see, Blackadder, Field Marshal Haig is most anxious to eliminate all German spies.

Melchett
Filthy Hun weasels, fighting their dirty, underhand war!

Darling
And fortunately, one of our spies . . .

Melchett
Splendid fellows, brave heroes risking life and limb for Blighty . . .

Darling
. . . has discovered that the leak is coming from the field hospital.

Blackadder
You think there's a German spy in the field hospital? I think you might be right there.

Melchett
Good – and your job, Blackadder, is to root this spy out. How long do you think you'll need?

Blackadder checks his watch.

Blackadder
Ooh err . . .

Melchett
You'll have to be away from the trenches for some time.

Blackadder
Ooh, six months.

Darling
Too bad, Blackadder, you've got three weeks.

Melchett
Yes, three weeks, Blackadder, to smoke the bugger out. Use any method you see fit – I'd personally recommend you get hold of a cocker spaniel, tie the suspect to a chair with a potty on his head, pop his todger between two floury baps and shout, 'Dinner time, Fido!' If you're successful, I'll want you back here permanently to head up our new security network – Operation Winkle.

Blackadder
Winkle?

Melchett
Yes, to winkle out the spies.

Darling
You never mentioned this to me, sir!

Melchett
We have to have some secrets, don't we, Darling.

Blackadder
Right, I'll be back in three weeks.

Melchett
Excellent. And if you come back with the information, Captain Darling will pump you thoroughly in the debriefing room.

Blackadder
Not while I've got my strength he won't.

Blackadder exits.

Darling
Damnation, sir, his insolence makes my blood boil! And what's more, I don't trust Blackadder, sir. I think it would be best if I went to the hospital myself to keep an eye on him.

Melchett
What, spy on our own spy as he searches for their spy? Yes – why not? Sounds rather fun! Under cover, of course.

Darling
Definitely, sir.

Melchett
You'll have to have a convincing wound.

Darling
Naturally, sir.

Melchett points the gun at Darling's foot and shoots. Darling screams and falls to the floor.

Melchett
There – that looks quite convincing.

SCENE FOUR: THE DUG-OUT

Blackadder enters.

Blackadder
Baldrick, pack me a toothbrush. We're going on holiday.

Baldrick
Hurray! Where to?

Blackadder
Hospital.

Baldrick
Oh no, I hate hostipals! My grandad went into one and when he came out he was dead!

Blackadder
He was also dead when he went in – he'd been run over by a traction engine.

Baldrick
I don't like them doctors. If they start poking around inside me . . .

Blackadder
Baldrick, why would anyone wish to poke around inside you?

Baldrick
They might find me interesting.

Blackadder
Baldrick, I find the Great Northern and Metropolitan sewage system interesting, but that doesn't mean I want to put on some rubber gloves and pull things out of it with a pair of tweezers.

Baldrick
Still, tell you what, sir – you might have a chance to get to know that pretty nurse.

He makes what he hopes is a suggestive face. It is not.

Blackadder
No, thank you, Baldrick – she's as wet as a fish's wet bits. I'd rather get to know you.

Baldrick
I'm not available, sir. I'm waiting for Miss Right to come along and gather me up in her arms.

Blackadder
Yes – I wouldn't get too hopeful – we'd have to get her arms out of her strait-jacket first. Now, get packing!

SCENE FIVE: THE FIELD HOSPITAL WARD

George is reading back another letter, this time to Mary and Smith, who is still talking in a thick German accent.

Smith
Ach, ach, so very interesting. Please, do continue, old bean.

George
Right, then, I go on to say, the orders came through at 0800 for us to advance in a pincer movement.

Mary
Gosh, how exciting.

George
Yes, it was.

The doors swing open for Baldrick and Blackadder.

Blackadder
Afternoon, George.

George
Hullo, Cap.

Mary
Ah, Captain. I hope you're going to conduct yourself with a little more decorum this time.

Blackadder
No, I'm going to conduct myself with no decorum. Shove off!!

Mary
(*Outraged*) Oh!

Mary leaves. Blackadder motions for Smith to move away from the side of George's bed.

George
So, Cap, what's going on?

Blackadder
There's a German spy in the hospital and it's my job to find him.

George
A Ger . . . well, snakes alive! Exciting stuff, eh? Wait a minute! I think I've got a plan already.

Blackadder
What is it?

George
Well, look down the list of patients and see if there's anyone here whose name begins with 'von' – he's almost bound to be the bloke.

Blackadder
Yes – I think we may find he's using a false name actually, George.

George
Well, that's hardly fair, is it?

Baldrick
I too have a cunning plan to catch the spy, sir.

Blackadder
Do you, Baldrick, do you?

Baldrick
Yes. Go around the hostipal and you ask everyone, 'Are you a German spy?'

Blackadder
Yes, I must say, Baldrick, I appreciate your involvement on the creative side.

Baldrick
If it was me, I'd own up.

Blackadder
Of course you would, but sadly the enemy have not yet added to the German army entrance form the requirement 'must have intellectual capacity of a boiled potato'. Now, see that man over there?

He points to Smith, who is lying in bed watching them through binoculars.

Baldrick
Yes?

Blackadder
I want you to stick to him like a limpet

and make sure he doesn't leave the hospital.

Enter Darling, limping with a cane.

Hello, Darling, what are you doing here?

Darling
Bullet in the foot.

Blackadder
I can understand people up the front shooting themselves in the foot, but to do it when you're 35 miles behind the lines . . .

Darling
I did not shoot myself. The general did it.

Blackadder
Finally got fed up with you, did he?

Darling
No, it was a mistake.

Blackadder
Aiming for your head, was he?

Darling
He wasn't aiming for anything.

Blackadder
Oh, so going for between your legs then.

Darling
Very funny, Blackadder. You'll be laughing on the other side of your face if you don't find this spy.

Blackadder
Don't worry, Darling, I intend to start interviewing suspects immediately.

Blackadder
The first rule of counter-espionage is to suspect everyone. Believe me, I shall be asking myself some pretty searching questions later. Tell me – what is the colour of the Queen of England's favourite hat?

Darling
How the hell should I know?

Blackadder
(*Sinisterly*) I see. Then let me ask you another question. What is the name of the German Head of State?

Darling
Well, Kaiser Wilhelm, obviously!

Blackadder
So, you're on first-name terms with the Kaiser, are you?

Darling
Look, what did you expect me to say?

Blackadder
Darling, Darling. Ssh-ssh. Cigarette?

Suddenly, he's a nice cop.

Darling
Thank you.

Blackadder gets up, puts a cigarette in Darling's mouth, and lights it. After a few seconds he snatches it away.

Blackadder
(*Shouting*) All right you stinking piece of crap!

SCENE SIX: THE SURGERY ROOM IN THE HOSPITAL

Darling is tied to a hideous home-made torture chair, with a potty on his head. Blackadder is sitting behind a desk.

Darling
This is completely ridiculous, Blackadder, you can't suspect *me*! I've only just arrived!

And now, he's nasty.

Darling
I beg your pardon . . .

Blackadder
(*Really loud*) Shut your ugly cake hole, sonny! I know you! Tell me, von Darling, what was it finally won you over, eh? Was it the pumpernickel? Or was it the thought of hanging around with big men in leather shorts?

Darling
(*Really scared*) I'll have you court-martialled for this, Blackadder!

Blackadder
For carrying out a general's orders? That may be the way you do it in Munich, or should I say, München! – but not here, Werner. You are a filthy Hun spy, aren't you?! Baldrick, the cocker spaniel, please.

Darling
No, I'm not! I'm engaged, I was born in Croydon, I was educated at Ipplethorpe Primary School, I've got a girlfriend called Doris and I know the words of all three verses of 'God Save the King'.

Blackadder
Four verses.

Darling
Four verses! Four verses! For God's sake, I'm as British as Queen Victoria!

Blackadder
You mean your father's German, you're half German and you married a German.

Darling
No! No! For God's sake, I'm not a German spy!

Now Darling is crying. And suddenly Blackadder is totally quiet and casual and pleasant.

Blackadder
Good, thanks very much. Send in the next man, would you?

Mary bursts in.

Mary
What is all this noise about? Don't you realize this is a hospital!

Darling
You'll regret this, Blackadder! You'd better find the real spy or I'll make it very hard for you.

Blackadder
Please, Darling – there are ladies present.

Darling storms out still tied to the chair. There is a loud crash and a cry from outside.

Mary
Well, well, Captain Blackadder – this is an unexpected pleasure.

Mary is suddenly changed – practical and frank and not the slightest bit sissy.

Blackadder
What?

Mary
Nice to have you back with us. A spy catcher eh? That silly kid George was right. You *are* a bally hero.

Blackadder
Wait a minute. I thought you liked George.

Mary
No – it's just my bedside manner. What I call my fluffy bunny act.

Blackadder
So, you're not a drip after all?

Mary
Oh, no. So, Mr Spy Catcher, how's it going?

Blackadder
Well, not much luck so far. I think the spy might be as difficult to find as a piece of hay in a massive stackful of needles.

Mary
So, you're going to be around for a while then.

Blackadder
Yes – looks like it.

She undoes her cap.

Mary
Good. It can get pretty lonely round here, you know. God, it's nice to have someone *healthy* to talk to . . . cigarette?

This is flirting with a capital 'F'.

Blackadder
No, thank you. I only smoke cigarettes after making love. So, back in England I'm a 20-a-day man.

Mary lights her cigarette and blows it in Blackadder's face. He blinks.

Mary
A man should smoke. It acts as an expectorant and gives his voice a deep, gravelly, masculine tone.

Blackadder
God, I love nurses. They're so disgustingly clinical.

There's definitely something in the air.

Mary
Tell me, Captain Blackadder –

Blackadder
Edmund.

Mary
Edmund. When this war's over, do you think one day we might . . . get to know each other better?

Blackadder
Yes, why not? When this madness is finished, perhaps we could go cycling together – take a spin down to the Old Swan at Henley, go for a walk in the woods.

Mary
Yes. (*Pause*) Or we could just do it right now on the desk.

Blackadder is unfazed. He looks at the desk.

Blackadder
Yes, okay.

SCENE SEVEN: THE FIELD HOSPITAL WARD

A few days later. Smith enters, closely followed by Baldrick. George is writing.

George
Hello, Baldrick. Have you seen Nurse Mary? I need someone to post this letter.

Baldrick
She's in her office with the captain.

George
Poor girl. Tied to her desk day and night.

Enter Blackadder, breezy and confident.

Hello, Cap. I hear you've been seeing a lot of Nurse Mary.

Blackadder
Yes, almost all of her, in fact.

George
How is she, sir?

Blackadder
Unbelievable.

George
Cap, Cap, what I really want to know, sir, is are you any closer to the spy?

Blackadder
Oh. I think I'm getting there. Everything all right, Smith?

Smith is now in bed, with Baldrick sitting up next to him reading a magazine.

Smith
Excellent, *jawohl*, excellent.

Blackadder
Jolly good.

No sooner arrived, when he's off again.

George
Smithy, you haven't seen any suspicious-looking characters who might be German spies?

Smith
Nein.

George
(*Amazed*) Nine? The Cap's got his work cut out then.

SCENE EIGHT: THE SURGERY ROOM

Blackadder and Mary are lying together in the surgery bed, both smoking cigarettes.

Mary
Tell me, Edmund, do you have someone special in your life?

Blackadder
Well, yes, I do, as a matter of fact.

Mary
Who?

Blackadder
Me.

Mary
No, someone you love and cherish and want to keep safe from all the horror and the hurt?

Blackadder
Still me, really.

Mary
No, but back home in England, there must be someone waiting, some sweetheart?

Blackadder
Oh, a girl! Nah! You see, I've always been a soldier, married to the army – the book of King's Regulations is my mistress, possibly with a Harrods lingerie catalogue discreetly tucked between its pages.

Mary
And no casual girlfriends?

Blackadder
Skirt? Ha! If only. When I joined up we were still fighting colonial wars: if you saw someone in a skirt you shot him and nicked his country. What about you? Have you got a man? Some fine fellow in an English country village? A vicar maybe? Quiet, gentle, hung like a baboon.

Mary
There was a man, I cared for a little. Wonderful chap, strong, athletic.

Blackadder
And what happened to him?

Mary
He bought it.

Blackadder gets up and looks for his wallet.

Blackadder
I'm so sorry, I didn't realize that was the arrangement. What's it been – let's say twelve nights, and what, nine afternoons and a couple of mornings . . .

Mary
I mean, he died.

Blackadder
Oh, I'm sorry.

Mary
He was test driving one of those new tank contraptions and the bloody thing blew up. What a waste. God, I hope they've scrapped the lot.

Blackadder
Fat chance. They're going to use forty of them next week – whoops, sorry – I musn't talk about it. You never know who might be listening.

Mary
Oh, no, of course. Oh, God, I miss him so much – he was such a wonderful chap.

Blackadder
Clever too, I expect.

Mary
Yes, brilliant.

Blackadder
One of the great universities I suppose – Oxford, Cambridge, Hull.

Mary
Yes. But why are we making small talk when we could be making big love?

Blackadder
Good point. This could be the last time. My three weeks are up. I'm going back to Staff HQ tomorrow. Look, why don't you come and have supper or something?

Mary
How about something first, then supper?

Blackadder
Good idea.

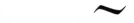

SCENE NINE: MELCHETT'S HQ

Blackadder and Mary are seated in front of the fire. Melchett enters.

Melchett
Ah, hullo, Blackadder.

Blackadder
Morning, sir. May I introduce Nurse Fletcher-Brown – she's been very support-ive during my work at the hospital.

Melchett
How do you do, young lady. Sit down. Tell me, Blackadder, any news about our spy yet?

Blackadder
Yes, sir.

Melchett
Excellent – the Germans seem to know every move we make. I had a letter from Jerry yesterday. It said 'isn't it about time you changed your shirt, Walrus-Face?' Tell me, have you got any ideas who it

might be, my dear?

Mary
Well, sir, I'm only a humble nurse, but I did think at one point that it might be Captain Darling.

Melchett
Well, bugger me with a fish-fork! Old Darling a Jerry morse-tapper! What made you suspect him?

Mary
Well, sir, he pooh-poohed the Captain here, sir, and said he'd never find the spy.

Melchett
Is this true, Blackadder? Did Darling pooh-pooh you?

Blackadder
Well, perhaps a little.

Melchett
Then dammit all – what more evidence do you need? The pooh-poohing alone is a court martial offence!

Blackadder
I assure you, sir, the pooh-pooh was pure-ly circumstantial.

Melchett
I hope so Blackadder – if there's one thing I've learnt in the army, it's never ignore a pooh-pooh! I knew a major got pooh-poohed, and made the mistake of ignoring the pooh-pooh. He pooh-poohed it! Fatal error! Because it turned out the soldier who'd pooh-poohed him had been pooh-poohing a lot of other officers who'd also pooh-poohed their pooh-poohs. In the end we had to disband the regiment – morale totally destroyed by pooh-pooh.

Blackadder
Yes, I think we're rather drifting slightly from the point here, sir, which is unfortunately, and to my lasting regret, Captain Darling is not the spy.

Melchett
Well, well, who the hell is it?

Mary
Well, sir, there is a man in the hospital with a pronounced limp and a very strong German accent. It must be him – it's obvious.

Blackadder
Obvious, but wrong, it's not him.

Melchett
And why not?

Blackadder
Because, sir, not even the Germans would be stupid enough to field a spy with a strong German accent.

Mary
Well, who is it then?

Blackadder
Well, it's perfectly simple. (*He turns to Mary*) It's you.

Mary leaps up and away from Blackadder.

Mary
Edmund!

Blackadder
Baldrick!

Baldrick enters and holds a rifle to Nurse Mary.

Melchett
Explain yourself, Blackadder – before I have you shot for being rude to a lady.

Blackadder
Well, sir, the first seeds of suspicion were sown when Lieutenant George unwittingly revealed that she spoke German . . . Do you deny Nurse Fletcher-Brown – or should I say Nurse Fleischer-Baum – that

you helped George out with the difficult German words in his letters?

Mary
No, I did, but . . .

Blackadder
My suspicions were confirmed when she probed me expertly about tank movements.

Mary
Edmund, how could you? After all we've been through!

Blackadder
And then the final irrefutable proof. Remember you mentioned a clever boyfriend.

Mary
Yes.

Blackadder
Well, I leapt on the opportunity to test you. I asked you whether he had been to one of the great universities, Oxford, Cambridge, Hull.

Mary
Well?

Blackadder
What you didn't spot is that only two of those are great universities.

Mary
You swine!

Melchett
That's right. Oxford's a complete dump!

Blackadder
Well, quite, no true Englishwoman would have fallen into that trap.

Mary
Oh, Edmund – I thought there was something beautiful between us – I thought you . . . loved me.

Pause. They stare and stare at each other and then . . .

Blackadder
Nah. Baldrick! Take her away!

Baldrick
Certainly, sir. *Raus! Raus!*

They exit, traitor and troglodyte.

Melchett
Good work, Blackadder. I'd better ring for a firing squad.

Blackadder stands by as Melchett sits down at the desk to use the phone when Smith enters and approaches Melchett, unseen. Then suddenly Darling enters behind Smith and pounces on him.

Darling
Watch out, sir!

He attacks Smith, who he thinks is about to assassinate the general. After a brief struggle:

Melchett
Darling! What on earth do you think you're doing?

Darling
I'll tell you exactly what I'm doing, sir – I'm doing what Blackadder should have done three weeks ago!

Melchett
What?

Darling points a gun at Smith.

Darling
This is the guilty man.

Melchett
Darling, you're getting hysterical.

Darling
I'm not, sir. Ask him outright. Are you a spy?

Smith
Jawohl, I em a spy.

Darling
You see, sir!

Melchett
Of course he's a spy, Darling. A British spy! He's Brigadier Sir Bernard Proudfoot-Smith – the finest spy in the British army.

Darling
But he can't be, sir. Listen to him, he doesn't even *sound* British.

Smith
Unfortunately, I hef been under cover in Chermany so long, I've picked up a teensy weensy bit of an accent.

Melchett
This, Darling, is the man who told us there was a German spy in the hospital in the first place. Well, that's that then – Blackadder.

Blackadder
Yes, sir?

Melchett
You are now Head of Operation Winkle.

Blackadder
Thank you, sir.

Melchett
Darling?

Darling
Yes, sir?

Melchett
You are a complete arse.

Darling
Thank you, sir.

Melchett
Come on, Bernard. Let's go and watch the firing squad.

Smith
Jawohl!

They exit just as George enters.

George
Sir, what the devil is going on? I've just seen the lovely Nurse Mary being led away to a firing squad.

Blackadder
Nurse Mary is the spy, George.

George
What? Impossible!

 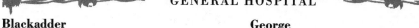
Blackadder
'Fraid so.

George
Well, cover me with eggs and flour and bake me for forty minutes. Who'd have thought it! Nurse Mary – a Boche nose poker inner? Still, pretty exciting stuff to put in my next letter to my Uncle Herman in Munich.

Blackadder
Sorry?

George
The letters I've been writing in hospital to my German uncle.

Blackadder looks worried.

Darling
New information, Blackadder?

George
Oh, I know there's a war on, but family is family . . . and old Uncle Hermie does so love to be kept abreast of what's going on. I even wrote and told him about old Walrus-Face Melchett and his smelly old shirts!

Darling
(*Very smugly*) Would you like me to tell this one to the general, Blackadder – or would you enjoy that very special moment?

Blackadder turns and runs out followed by Darling.

There is probably trouble in store. As for Nurse Mary, we can only hope the firing squad was stopped in time. Rumour has it that Baldrick was delegated to give them the message.

MOST SECRET

**APPLICATION FOR EMERGENCY TRANSFER TO SOMEWHERE MUCH SAFER
BY A SERVING OFFICER WHO IS A CLOSE RELATIVE, OLD SCHOOLFRIEND OR
MISTRESS OF A MINISTER OF THE CROWN OR MEMBER OF THE ROYAL FAMILY.**

ALL SECTIONS TO BE COMPLETED *IN TRIPLICATE* (BLOCK CAPITALS) AND *IN INK ONLY*. DO NOT USE PENCIL, BLOOD,
MUD, SWEAT, TEARS, URINE, ETC. SEND NO MONEY NOW. PLEASE ENCLOSE STAMPED ADDRESSED ENVELOPE
(HMSO ISSUE NO. 1471/A/765R6 (C)).

1. **DATE:** 17 October 1917

2. **NAME OF APPLICANT:** Darling, K.   3. **RANK:** Captain, General Staff

4. **DECORATIONS (IF ANY):** Silver Service Medal (Royal Military Catering College, Farnborough). One Length Swimming Certificate (Beckenham Tadpoles)

5. **CAREER AND EDUCATION:**

September 1884 – July 1892:

Ipplethorpe Primary School, Slimy Green, Kent: Milk Monitor, Teacher's Pet (Miss Ridgeway), Captain of Hopscotch, Alderman Williams Joined–Up Writing Prize.

September 1892 – July 1897:

King's School, Penge: Form Prefect, Vice–Captain of Caning, Lance Corporal and Senior Coward, Combined Cadet Force (Conscientious Objector Section). School Certificates: Grocery, English as a Foreign Language, Woodwork, Underarm Bowling (Distinction).

6 September 1897 – 23 September 1897:

Corpus Christi College Cambridge, Massachussets World Postal University: PO BOX 32, Sevenoaks Kent: M.A. (Hons) First Class: Theoretical Physics, Ancient Chinese Philosophy and Mountaineering.

October 1897 – June 1900:

Royal Military Catering College, Farnborough: Passed out 76th in class of 115. Qualified: Chef Petty Officer (Medieval and Modern Potato Management). Dissertation: (Mildly Commended) The Covert Use of the Parsnip Behind Enemy Lines in the Peninsular War (1808 – 1813) 12pp.

Army Career: September 1900: King's Own Royal Jersey Jacket Potatoes (Ipswich) Junior Butterman (Third Class); November 1906: Promoted Cheese Squad: Grater–Loader (Second Class); January 1911: Transferred 17th/23rd Lincolnshire Pastrycooks; August 1712: Promoted Iced Bunner (Rear); September 1913: Recommended by Commanding Officer for Commission (or Secondment to Pitcairn Island – whichever could be arranged sooner); October 1913: Entered Women's Royal Balloon Corps as 4th Lieutenant (responsible for blowing up the larg–er balloons for Royal Flying Corps parties); September 1914: Won Captaincy (to include honour of working for Gen. Melchett on front line) as 17th Prize in Officers' Mess Raffle.

6. HEIGHT: 5' 9 1/2")   **7. WEIGHT:*** 5st 4lbs

8. HOW DO YOU WISH TO TRAVEL?
❑ 1ST CLASS   ☑ 2ND CLASS   ❑ 3RD CLASS
❑ 4TH CLASS (IN COFFIN MARKED 'DANGER UNEXPLODED MINES')
❑ 5TH CLASS (NOT RECOMMENDED UNLESS APPLICANT IS OLD HARROVIAN)
❑ ANY OF THE ABOVE

9. IF TRAVELLING 4TH CLASS, STATE WHETHER WILLING TO SHARE BERTH WITH DECEASED BODY AND/OR GRAMMAR SCHOOL BOY OR WOG
❑ YES   ❑ NO   ❑ DEPENDS ON SEX AND CONDITION OF WOG

10. DO YOU REQUIRE BAGGAGE TO ACCOMPANY YOU? (STATE NUMBER OF ITEMS)
☑ DITTY-BAG(S) ☑ CABIN-TRUNK(S)
☑ FIRM-BREASTED FRENCH PEASANT GIRL(S)   ☑ LABRADOR
❑ REGIMENTAL WINE CELLAR   ❑ INCRIMINATING PAPERS
❑ SEVERED LIMBS OR OTHER EXTREMITIES
FORMERLY ATTACHED TO APPLICANT
❑ OTHER   ☑ MOTHER**

11. NAME OF RELEVANT MINISTER OR ROYAL PERSONAGE:
Jolybus, Arnold F.

12. POSITION: Undersecretary of State (Horses), Ministry of War Memorials

13. RELATIONSHIP TO MINISTER OR ROYAL PERSONAGE:
Fifth cousin, four times removed or a great uncle on my mother's side, whichever is the closer.

14. REASON FOR TRANSFER: Unable to Continue Duties at Division
Headquarters Due to Loss of All Pairs of Uniform Trousers and Underpants and Acute Highly Infectious Diarrorhechhroea (Squirty Kind)

15. ACTUAL REASON FOR TRANSFER: Oh please help help I don't want to die

16. PREFERRED DATE OF TRANSFER: Most Immediate

....

For Official Use Only   APPLICATION APPROVED   ❑

APPLICANT TO BE SHOT AT DAWN   ❑

APPLICANT TO BE WASHED AND SENT TO MY TENT   ❑

Signature of Authorizing Officer: AR3/8b

* NB. APPLICANTS CONSIDERED OVERWEIGHT MAY BE UNABLE TO TRAVEL BY AIR
** OR FIRM-BREASTED FRENCH PEASANT GIRL DISGUISED AS SAME.

GOODBYEEE

SCENE ONE: THE TRENCH AND DUG-OUT

It is night, it is pouring with rain and the shelling is constant. Blackadder and George have just inspected the troops in the trench. They are ankle-deep in mud.

George
Care for a smoke, sir?

Blackadder
No, thank you.

George offers Baldrick a cigarette.

George
Private?

Baldrick
Thank you, sir.

He eats it. Suddenly George gets emotional.

George
Oh, dash and blast all this hanging about, sir. I'm as bored as a pacifist's pistol.

When are we going to see some action?

Blackadder
Well, George, I strongly suspect your long wait for certain death is nearly at an end. Surely you must have noticed something in the air?

George
Well yes, of course, but I thought that was Private Baldrick.

Blackadder
Unless I'm much mistaken, soon we will at last be making the final big push, the one we've been *so* looking forward to all these years.

George
Hurrah with highly polished brass knobs on. About time!

The field phone rings: it is on Baldrick's back. Blackadder picks it up.

Blackadder
Hullo, Somme Public Baths. No running, shouting or piddling in the shallow end.

Oh, it's you, Darling. Tomorrow at dawn.
Oh, excellent. See you later then. Bye!

He hangs up.

Gentlemen – our long wait is nearly at an
end. Tomorrow morning, General
'Insanity' Melchett invites you to a mass
slaughter. We're going over the top.

George
Huzzah and hurrah! God Save the King,
Rule Britannia and boo sucks to Harry
Hun!

Blackadder
Or to put it more precisely, you're going
over the top, I'm going to get out of it.

*Blackadder and George move to the dug-
out.*

George
Oh, come on, Cap! May be a bit risky –
but it's sure as bloomin' 'ell worth it,
guv'nor.

*Blackadder undresses while George
resses for battle.*

Blackadder
How can it possibly be worth it? We've
been sitting here since Christmas 1914,
during which time millions of men have
died, and we've moved no further than an
asthmatic ant with heavy shopping.

George
No, but this time I'm pos we'll break
through – it's ice-cream in Berlin in fifteen
days.

Blackadder
Or ice-cold in No Man's Land in fifteen
seconds. No, the time has come to get out
of this madness once and for all.

George
What madness is that?

Blackadder
Oh, for God's sake, George, how long have
you been in the army?

George
What, me? Oh, I joined up straight away –

10 August 1914. What a day that was.
Myself and the fellows leap-frogging down
to the Cambridge recruiting office, then
playing tiddly-winks in the queue. We'd
hammered the hell out of Oxford's tiddly-
winkers only the week before and here we
were off to hammer the Boche. A
crashingly superb bunch of blokes, fine,
clean-limbed – even our acne had a strange
nobility about it.

Blackadder
Yes, and how are all the boys now?

George
Well, Jocko and the Badger bought it at
the first Ypres, unfortunately – quite a
shock that. I remember Bumfluff's house-
master wrote and told me that Sticky had
been out for a duck and the Gubber had
snitched a parcel sausage-end and gone
goose-over-stumps frog-side.

Blackadder
Meaning?

George
I don't know, sir, but I read in *The Times*
that they'd both been killed.

Blackadder
And Bumfluff himself?

George
Copped a packet at Gallipoli with the
Ozzies. So did Drippy and Strangely
Brown – I remember we heard on the first
morning of the Somme when Titch and Mr
Floppy got gassed back to Blighty.

Blackadder
Which leaves?

George
Gosh, yes – I suppose I'm the only one of
the Trinity's Tiddlers still alive. Cor blimey
– there's a thought, and not a jolly one.

Blackadder
My point exactly, George.

George
I might get a bit mis if it wasn't for the

thought of going over the top tomorrow. Permission to get weaving, sir.

Blackadder
Permission granted.

George exits to trench.

Baldrick.

Baldrick
Captain B?

Blackadder
This is a crisis, a large crisis. In fact, if you've got a moment, it is a twelve-storey crisis with a magnificent entrance hall, carpeted throughout; twenty-four-hour porterage and an enormous sign on the roof saying, 'This is a Large Crisis'. And a large crisis requires a large plan. Get me a ruler, two pencils and a pair of under-pants.

SCENE TWO: THE DUG-OUT

Later, inside the dug-out. Blackadder has pants on his head, and a pencil up each nostril. Baldrick is in attendance.

Blackadder
Now, Baldrick, this is an old trick I picked up in the Sudan. We tell HQ that I have gone insane and I will be invalided back to Blighty before you can say 'wibble', a poor gormless idiot.

Baldrick
But I'm a poor gormless idiot, sir, and I've never been invalided back to Blighty.

Blackadder
Yes, Baldrick – but you never said 'wibble'. Go on – ask me some simple questions.

Baldrick
What is your name?

Blackadder
Wibble.

Baldrick
What is two plus two?

Blackadder
A wibble.

Baldrick
Where do you live?

Blackadder
London.

Baldrick
Eh?

Blackadder
A small village on Mars, just outside the capital city, Wibble.

Enter George.

George
All present and correct, sir. Ready for the off, eh!

Blackadder
I'm afraid not, Lieutenant. I'm just off to Hartlepool to buy some exploding trousers.

George
Come again, sir! Have you gone barking mad?

Blackadder
Yes, George, I have – cluck cluck gibber gibber – my old man's a mushroom, etc. Go and send a runner to tell General Melchett your Captain has gone insane and must return to England at once.

George
But, sir – how utterly ghastly for you. I mean, you'll miss the whole of the war!

Blackadder
Yes – very bad luck. Beep.

George
Right . . .

Blackadder
Beep.

George
I'll be back as soon as I can.

Blackadder
Pap paa.

George
Whatever you do, don't excite him.

Blackadder
Fat chance.

George exits. Blackadder takes off some of his mad garb.

Now, all we have to do is wait.

He makes himself comfortable for a long night ahead.

Baldrick, fix us some coffee, will you . . . and try and make it taste slightly less like mud this time.

Baldrick
Not easy, I'm afraid, Captain.

Blackadder
And why is that?

Baldrick
Because it *is* mud. We ran out of coffee thirteen months ago.

Blackadder
So every time I've drunk your coffee since, I have in fact been drinking hot mud.

Baldrick
With sugar.

Blackadder
Which of course makes *all* the difference.

Baldrick
Well, it would do if we had any sugar. But we ran out New Year's Eve 1915, since when I've been using sugar substitute.

Blackadder
Which is?

Baldrick
Dandruff.

Blackadder
Brilliant.

Baldrick
Still, I could add some milk this time – well, saliva.

Blackadder
No, thanks, Baldrick. Call me Mr Picky, but I've decided to cancel the coffee.

Baldrick
That's probably because you're mad, sir.

Blackadder
Well, quite.

George rejoins them.

George
Didn't go down at all well, sir. Captain Darling said they'd be here directly – but you better be pretty damn doolally.

Blackadder
Don't worry, George, I am.

He does some mad actions.

When they get here, I'll show them what totally and utterly bonkerooni means. Fwaaaff. Till then, there's bugger-all to do except sit and wait.

George
Or we could have a jolly game of charades.

Baldrick
Oh, yes.

George
And a good sing-a-long of music hall hits like 'Birmingham Bertie' and 'Whoops, Mrs Miggins, You're Sitting on My Artichokes!'

Blackadder
Yes. I think bugger-all might be rather more fun.

A sense of genuine time totally on their hands.

Baldrick
Permission to ask a question, sir.

Blackadder
Permission granted Baldrick, as long as it isn't the one about where babies come from.

Baldrick
No. The thing is – the way I see it, these days there's a war on, right? And ages

ago, there wasn't a war on, right? So there must have been a moment when there not being a war went away, right, and there being a war came along, right? So what I want to know is, how did we get from the one case of affairs to the other case of affairs, right?

Blackadder
You mean, how did the war start?

Baldrick
Yes, sir.

George
(*Authoritatively*) The war started because of the vile Hun and his villainous empire-building.

Blackadder
George, the British empire at present covers a quarter of the globe while the German empire consists of a small sausage factory in Tanganyika. I hardly think we can be entirely absolved from blame on the imperialistic front.

George
Oh, no sir, absolutely not, sir.

He looks at Blackadder pityingly and taps the side of his head.

(*To Baldrick*) Mad as a bicycle.

Baldrick
I heard it started when some chap called Archie Duke shot an ostrich because he was hungry.

Blackadder
I think you mean it started when the Arch-Duke of Austro-Hungary got shot.

Baldrick
No – there was definitely an ostrich involved.

Blackadder
Well possibly. But the real reason for the whole thing was that it was just too much effort not to have a war.

George
By gum this *is* interesting. I always loved history – The Battle of Hastings, Henry VIII and his Six Knives.

Blackadder
Yes, you see, Baldrick, in order to prevent a war in Europe, two super blocs developed: us, the French and the Russians on one side, and the Germans and Austro-Hungary on the other. The idea was to have two vast opposing armies, each acting as the other's deterrent. That way there could never be a war.

Baldrick
Except, well, this is a sort of war, isn't it?

Blackadder
That's right, there was one tiny flaw in the plan.

George
Oh, what was that?

Blackadder
It was bollocks.

Baldrick
So the poor old ostrich died for nothing.

Darling
(*From outside*) Ten shun!

George
They're here, Baldrick. Keep him warm while I go and prepare the ground.

George goes out to meet Melchett and Darling in the trench.

Melchett
George, how's the patient?

George
Very much touch and go, sir – can't vouch for his behaviour at all. He's gone mad, you see, stir-fry crazy.

Melchett
I see. Is that genuinely mad? . . . Or has he just put his underpants on his head

and stuffed two pencils up his nose?

George
Ah, well . . .

Melchett
That's what they all used to do in the Sudan. I remember I once had to shoot a whole platoon for trying that.

George
Errr . . .

Melchett
Well, let's have a look at him.

Blackadder suddenly stands in front of Baldrick. He is still in his mad gear.

Blackadder
And the other thing they used to do in the Sudan was to get dressed up like this and pretend to be mad, but don't let me catch you trying that one, Baldrick, or I'll have you shot – dismissed. Oh, hello, General (*very smoothly*), didn't see you come in.

Melchett
Now then, Blackadder. They told me you've gone mad.

Blackadder
No, sir, must be a communication breakdown. Someone clearly heard I was 'mad' with excitement, waiting for the off.

Melchett
You see, Darling, I told you there'd be a perfectly good explanation. Come on then, George, have your chaps fall in.

Darling
Well, that's very odd, sir. The message was very clear: 'Captain Blackadder gone totally tonto – bring strait-jacket for immediate return to Blighty.'

Melchett
Don't be ridiculous, Darling. The hero of Mboto Gorge – mad? Look at him, he's as sane as I am. Baah.

Darling
Was that the Mboto Gorge when we massacred the peace-loving pigmies of the Upper Volta and stole all their fruit?

Blackadder
No – totally different Mboto Gorge.

He pauses.

Cup of coffee, Darling?

Darling
Oh, thank you.

Blackadder
Baldrick, do the honours.

Baldrick
Yes, sir. (*To Darling*) Sugar, sir?

Darling
Three lumps.

Blackadder
Can you manage three lumps, Baldrick?

Baldrick
I'll rummage around and see what I can find.

Baldrick exits.

Darling
Make it a milky one.

Baldrick
Coming up.

In the trench.

Melchett
So, George – looking forward to the big push?

George
Absolutely, sir – at last, our chance to show the Hun that it takes more than a pointy hat and bad breath to defeat the armies of King George.

Melchett
That's the spirit!

The sound of Baldrick spitting is heard.

Back in the dug-out. Baldrick hands Darling the coffee. He splutters in horror at its taste. Big smile from Blackadder.

Darling
Oh, cappuccino. Got any of that brown stuff you sprinkle on the top?

Baldrick
I'm sure I . . .

Blackadder
No. No.

Blackadder pushes Baldrick out of the way.

Darling
Ten shun!

All stand to attention.

Melchett
At ease. Fine body of men out there.

Blackadder
Yes, sir – shortly to become fine bodies of men.

Melchett
Oh, nonsense. You'll pull through. I remember when we thrashed the old Harrovians back in 1895, they all said we'd never get through their back line – but we ducked and we bobbed and we wove and we damn well won the game, 15–4.

Blackadder
Yes, sir – but the Harrow full back wasn't armed with a heavy machine-gun.

Melchett
No, that's a good point. Make a note, Darling: recommendation for the Harrow governors, heavy machine-guns for full backs. Excellent idea, Blackadder. Now then, Private – looking forward to giving those Frenchies a good licking?

Darling
No, sir, it's the Germans we'll be licking.

Melchett
Don't be revolting, Darling! I wouldn't lick a German if he was glazed in honey.

Darling
Sorry, sir.

Melchett
Now you, soldier, do you love your country, soldier?

Baldrick
Certainly do, sir.

Melchett
And do you love your king?

Baldrick
Certainly don't, sir.

Melchett
Why not?

Baldrick
My mum told me never to trust men with beards.

Melchett
Excellent native Cockney wit. (*He hits Baldrick*) Well, good luck to all of you. Sorry I can't be with you, but . . . obviously there's no place in the front line for an old general with a dicky heart and a wooden bladder.

He turns to go.

Oh, George, by the way, if you feel like coming back to HQ – hear the results as they come in tomorrow – there's a spare place in the car.

Blackadder looks at George.

George
Oh, no, thank you, sir. Wouldn't miss this for the world. I'm as excited as an excited person who's got a special reason to be excited.

Melchett
That's my boy! Must be going – tally-ho and pip pip all. I'll see you all in Berlin for coffee and cake.

Darling spits out coffee.

What is the matter with you today, Darling? I'm terribly sorry, Blackadder. Come on, Darling – we're going.

They exit. Blackadder sinks in despair.

George
By Jove, sir – I'm glad you're not barking any more.

Blackadder
Thank you, George – although it looks like you are. You were offered a way out and you didn't take it.

George
Absolutely not, sir, can't wait to get stuck into the Boche.

Blackadder
(*Exasperated*) You won't get time to get stuck into the Boche. We'll all be cut to pieces by machine-gun fire before we have time to yell 'Charge'.

George
So what shall we do now?

Baldrick
Shall I do my war poem, sir?

Blackadder
How hurt will you be if I give the honest answer, which is, 'No – I'd rather French-kiss a skunk'?

Baldrick
So would I, sir.

Blackadder
Good, fire away, Baldrick.

Baldrick
Hear the words I sing,

War's a horrid thing.
But still I sing, sing, sing
Ding a ling a ling.

George
(Clapping) Bravo!

Blackadder
It started badly, it tailed off a little in the middle and the less said about the end the better – but apart from that it was excellent.

Baldrick
Shall I do another one then, sir?

Blackadder
We wouldn't want to exhaust you.

Baldrick
Oh, don't worry, I could go on all night.

Blackadder
Not with a bayonet through the neck you couldn't.

Baldrick
This one's called 'The German Guns'.

George
Oh, spiffing! Let's hear that!

Blackadder puts his head in his hands.

Baldrick
Boom, boom, boom, boom,
Boom, boom, boom,
Boom boom boom boom.

Blackadder
Boom boom boom?

Baldrick
How did you guess?

George
Gosh! Spooky, eh?

Blackadder
(*Wildly*) I'm sorry, but I've just got to get out of here.

Baldrick
I have a cunning plan, sir.

Blackadder
All right, Baldrick, for old time's sake.

Baldrick
You phone Field Marshal Haig and ask him to get you out of here.

Blackadder
Baldrick, even by your standards, it's pathetic. I've only ever met Field Marshal Haig once and it was over twenty years ago – and my God, you've got it, you've got it!

He kisses Baldrick.

Baldrick
Well, if I've got it, you've got it too, now, sir.

Blackadder
I can't believe I've been so stupid! One phone call will do it – one phone call and I'll be free. Let's see – it's 3.30 – I'll call about quarter to six. Excellent, excellent! Ah! (*Huge satisfied sigh*) Now where were we? I must get packing.

Totally accessible and bonhomous, he starts to pack his case merrily.

George
You know, I won't half miss you chaps after the war.

Baldrick
Don't worry, Lieutenant, I'll come visit you.

George
Oh, will you really? Bravo, yes! Jump in the jalopy and come down to stay in the country. We can relive the old times.

Blackadder
What – dig a hole in the middle of the gar-den, fill it with water and get the game-keeper to shoot at us all day?

George
That's the one thing I don't understand, you know, Captain. You're a professional soldier, and yet sometimes you sound as if you bally well haven't enjoyed soldiering at all.

Blackadder
Well, you see, I did like it, George, back in the old days when the prerequisite of a British battle was that the enemy should, under no circumstances, carry guns . . . Even spears made us think twice. The kind of people we liked to fight most were two feet tall and armed with dry grass.

George
Oh, but come off it, sir. What about Mboto Gorge, for heaven's sake?

Blackadder
Yes, that was a nasty one. Ten thousand Watutsi warriors armed to the teeth with kiwi fruit and guava halves. After the battle, instead of taking prisoners, we simply made a huge fruit salad. When I joined up, I never imagined anything as awful as this war. Fifteen years of military experience perfecting the art of ordering a pink gin and saying, 'do you do it doggy doggy?' in Swahili, then suddenly four and a half million heavily armed Germans hove into view. It was a shock, I can tell you.

Baldrick
I thought it was going to be such fun too. We all did. Joining a local regiment and everything. The Turnip Street Workhouse Pals: I'll never forget. It was great – the first time I've ever really felt popular, everyone was cheering and throwing flowers, a girl actually came up and kissed me.

Blackadder
(*To George*) Poor woman – first casualty of the war.

Baldrick

I loved the training, all we had to do was bayonet sacks full of straw – even I could do it. I remember telling my mum, 'these sacks will be easy to outwit in a battle situation'.

Blackadder throws Baldrick a look and bangs his pipe on the post.

And then we all met up just before Christmas 1914 . . .

George

Yes, that's right. I'd just arrived and we had that wonderful Christmas truce . . . do you remember, sir? We could hear 'Silent Night' drifting across the still clear air of No Man's Land . . . And then they came, the Germans . . . emerging out of the freezing night mist, calling to us, and we clambered up over the top and went to meet them . . .

Blackadder

Both sides advanced further during one Christmas piss-up than we've managed in the next two and a half years.

Baldrick

Sir, sir, do you remember the football match, sir?

Blackadder

Remember it? How could I forget it. I was *never* off side, I could not *believe* that decision!

Baldrick

Since then we've been stuck here for three flipping years, we haven't moved! All my friends are dead: my pet spider, Sammy, Katie the worm, Bertie the bird – everyone except Neville the fat hamster.

Blackadder

(*Solemn*) I'm afraid Neville bought it too, Baldrick . . . I'm sorry.

Baldrick

Neville – gone, sir?

Blackadder

Actually, not quite gone, he's in the corner bunging up the sink.

Baldrick gets up and wanders across the room.

Baldrick

(*Upset*) But it didn't have to happen. If it wasn't for this terrible war Neville might still be alive today, sniffling his little nose and going 'eek'.

Blackadder

On the other hand, if he hadn't died I wouldn't have been able to insert a curtain rod in his bottom and use him as a dish mop.

Baldrick

Why can't we stop, sir? Why can't we just say, 'no more killing, let's all go home'? Why can't we pack it in? Why?

George

(*Leaping up*) Now, look here, you just stop that conchie talk right now, Private. It's absurd, it's bolshevism and wouldn't work anyway.

Baldrick

(*Innocently*) But why not, sir?

George

Why not? Erm, you mean, why, why wouldn't it work? Well, it wouldn't work, because . . . it wouldn't work because . . . get on with polishing your boots, Private – and less of that lip.

He turns to Blackadder.

It's all right, sir – I think I've crushed the mutiny. To think, in a few hours, at last we're going to be off! Not that I won't miss all this though – ha – we've had some times, haven't we? We've had some damnably good laughs, eh?

Pause.

Blackadder
Yes. Can't think of any specific ones myself.

SCENE THREE: MELCHETT'S HQ

The lights are on very low. Melchett comes in wearing a dressing gown and a beautiful hair-net over his moustache.

Darling has dozed off at the desk.

Melchett
Darling!

Darling jumps up at the sound of his voice.

Darling
Sir.

Melchett
Can't sleep either, eh?

Darling
No, sir. Thinking about the push, sir. Hoping the Boche'll forget to set their alarm clocks, oversleep and still be in their pyjamas when our boys turn up, sir.

Melchett
Yes, yes. I've been thinking, too. Darling . . .

Darling
Sir?

Melchett
You know – over these last years, I've come to think of you as a sort of son. Not a favourite son, of course – Lord no! – more a sort of illegitimate, backstairs sort of sprog. You know, the sort of spotty squit you never really like – but still fruit of my overactive loins.

Darling
Thank you, sir.

Melchett
And I want to do what's best for you,

Darling. So I've thought about it a great deal and I want you to have this . . .

He hands him a piece of paper.

Darling
(*Trying to look pleased*) A postal order for ten shillings.

Melchett
Ah – no – sorry. My godson's wedding present.

He hands over another piece of paper.

Darling
Ah, no, sir – this is a commission for the front line, sir.

He tries to hand it back.

Melchett
Yes. I've been awfully selfish keeping you back here instead of letting you join in all the fun and games. This will let you get to the front line immediately.

Darling
But, sir – I don't want to . . .

Melchett
To leave me? I appreciate that, Darling. But dammit – I'll just have to enter Berlin without someone to carry my special feathery hat.

Darling
No, sir – I mean, I don't want to go into battle . . .

Melchett won't let Darling finish his sentences.

Melchett
. . . without me? I know. But I'm too old. I'll just have to sit this one out on the touchline with the half-time oranges and the fat wheezy boys with a note from matron, while you young bloods link arms for the glorious final scrum down.

Darling stands up, and comes round next to General Melchett.

 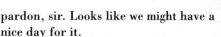

Darling
You're not listening, sir. I'm begging –
please, for the sake of all the times I've
helped you with your dickie bows and
your dicky bladder, please . . .

*He falls on his knees in front of the
General.*

. . . don't make me . . .

Melchett
(*Patting him reassuringly on the
head*). . . go through the farewell debag-
ging ceremony in the mess? No, I've
spared you that, you touchingly senti-
mental young booby. Look – no fuss, no
bother – the driver is already here.

*The door opens. Light floods in, shining
on Darling's face. A big shadow appears
at the door, and he turns round, still on
his knees, to face it.*

Darling
But . . .

Melchett
No, not a word. Believe me, Kevin. I
know what you want to say. I know.

Melchett stands.

Goodbye, Kevin Darling.

He salutes.

Darling
Goodbye, sir.

He salutes and walks sadly to the door.

SCENE FOUR: THE DUG-OUT/
THE TRENCH AND FIELD MARSHAL
HAIG'S STAFF HQ

*It's dawn and becoming a little lighter.
Blackadder has his coat and hat on, and
is ready to go. Baldrick is looking out of
the dug-out flap.*

Baldrick
It's stopped raining at last, begging your

pardon, sir. Looks like we might have a
nice day for it.

George goes to the dug-out entrance.

George
Yes, it's nearly morning . . .

Blackadder
Good Lord, so it is – time to make my
call. (*He dials breezily. It answers*) Hello,
Field Marshal Sir Douglas Haig, please.
Yes, it's urgent.

*Haig is standing in his very opulent
office, in front of a battle reconstruction,
with lots of tiny model soldiers.*

Haig
Haig.

Blackadder
Hello, Sir Douglas.

Haig
Who is this?

Blackadder
This is Captain Blackadder, sir.
Erstwhile of the 19/45th East African
Rifles.

Haig
Good Lord! Blackie!

*He knocks over one set of soldiers with a
deft sweep of the hand.*

Blackadder
Yes, sir.

Haig
(*Knocking over another set*) By heaven,
Blackie – I haven't seen you since . . .

Blackadder
'92, sir. Mboto Gorge.

Haig
By jingo, yes. We sure gave those pigmies
a good squashing.

Blackadder
Certainly did, sir. And do you
remember . . .

Haig

My God, yes – you saved my damn life that day, Blackie. If it weren't for you, that pigmy woman with the sharpened mango could have seriously . . .

Blackadder

Well, yes, sir. And do you remember you said then that if I was ever in real trouble, if I ever really needed a favour, I was to call you and you'd do anything you could to help me?

Haig

Yes, yes I do. And I stick by it. You know me, not a man to change my mind.

He starts sweeping up the toy soldiers with a dustpan and brush.

Blackadder

No, we've noticed that.

Haig

So, what do you want? Spit it out, man.

He chucks the dustpan's contents over his shoulder.

Blackadder

Well, sir, it's like this. I'll be blunt. It's the big push today and I'm not *all that* keen to go over the top.

Haig

(*Not happy*) Ah. Oh, I see. Well . . .

He sits down.

Blackadder

(*Casually*) It was a viciously sharp mango slice, wasn't it, sir . . .

Haig

Well, this is most irregular, but, all right. But if I fix it for you I never want to hear from you again, is that clear?

He picks up one of the toy soldiers he's knocked over and sets it upright.

Blackadder

Suits me, Duggie.

Haig

Very well, listen carefully, Blackadder, I won't repeat this. Right – first put your underpants on your head, and two pencils up your nose. They'll think you're crazy and send you home. Right, favour returned.

He hangs up. Blackadder is not amused.

Blackadder

I think the phrase rhymes with 'clucking bell'.

Baldrick

Does that mean that you're going to have to go over the top now?

Blackadder nods. Phone rings. Blackadder leaps on it.

Blackadder

Field Marshal!

Melchett

(*At his HQ*) Ha! Ha! No – not quite. Or not yet. Blackadder, wanted to let you know I've sent a little surprise over for you.

Darling appears framed in the door of the trench in fighting gear.

George

Sir.

Blackadder

Captain Darling.

He puts down the phone. They stare at each other knowing what it means for both of them.

Darling

Captain Blackadder.

Blackadder

Here to join us for the last waltz?

Darling

Ahm – yes, that's right – tired of folding the general's pyjamas.

George

Well, this is splendid comradely news!

Together we'll fight for king and country and be sucking sausages in Berlin by tea-time . . .

Blackadder
Yes. I hope the cafés are well stocked. Everyone seems determined to eat out the moment they arrive.

George
But really this is brave, splendid, and noble . . .

Blackadder doesn't react. Long pause as all four stand together.

Sir.

Blackadder
Yes, Lieutenant.

George
I'm scared, sir.

Baldrick
I'm scared too, sir.

George
I'm the last of the tiddly-winking leapfrog-gers from the golden summer of 1914. I don't want to die . . . I'm really not over keen on dying at all, sir.

Blackadder
How are you feeling, Darling?

Darling
Ahm – not all that good, Blackadder. Rather hoped I'd get through the whole show, go back to work at Pratt and Sons, keep wicket for the Croydon Gentlemen, marry Doris. Made a note in my diary on the way here. Simply says: 'Bugger'.

Blackadder
Well, quite.

Outside is heard the muffled faraway cry: 'Stand to, stand to, fix bayonets!'

Come on, come on, let's move.

They all move out. At the door, Blackadder turns to George.

Don't forget your stick, Lieutenant.

George
(*Picking up his stick*) Rather, sir. Wouldn't want to face a machine-gun without this.

They emerge in the misty trenches and all stand in a line, ready for the off. Then suddenly there is a silence. The machine-guns stop.

Darling
I say, listen – our guns have stopped.

George
You don't think . . .

Baldrick
Perhaps the war's over. Perhaps it's peace.

George
Hurrah! The big nobs have got round a table and yanked the iron out of the fire.

Darling
Thank God – we lived through it – The Great War, 1914 to 1917.

All Three
Hip hip hurray!!!

Blackadder
I'm afraid not. The guns have stopped because we are about to attack. Not even our generals are mad enough to shell their own men. They feel it's more sporting to let the Germans do it.

George
So, we are, in fact, going over. This is, as they say, it?

Blackadder
Yes, unless I can think of something very quickly.

A command is heard: 'Company, one pace forward.' They all take one step forward.

Baldrick
There's a nasty splinter on that ladder,

sir. A bloke could hurt himself on that.

A call: 'Stand ready.' They put their hands on the ladders, ready to climb over.

I have a plan, sir.

Blackadder
Really, Baldrick, a cunning and subtle one?

Baldrick
Yes, sir.

Blackadder
As cunning as a fox who's just been appointed Professor of Cunning at Oxford University?

Baldrick
Yes, sir.

Another call is heard: 'On the signal, Company will advance.'

Blackadder
Well, I'm afraid it's too late. Whatever it was, I'm sure it was better than my plan to get out of this by pretending to be mad. I mean, who would have noticed another madman round here?

A whistle goes. He looks at Baldrick.

Good luck, everyone.

Blackadder blows his whistle. There is a roar of voices – everyone leaps up the ladders. As they rise above the sandbags they are met by thunderous machine-gun fire.

Blackadder, Baldrick, George and Darling run on, brandishing their hand-guns. They will not get far.

Silence falls. Our soldiers fade away. No Man's Land turns slowly into a peaceful field of poppies. The only sound is that of a bird, singing sweetly.

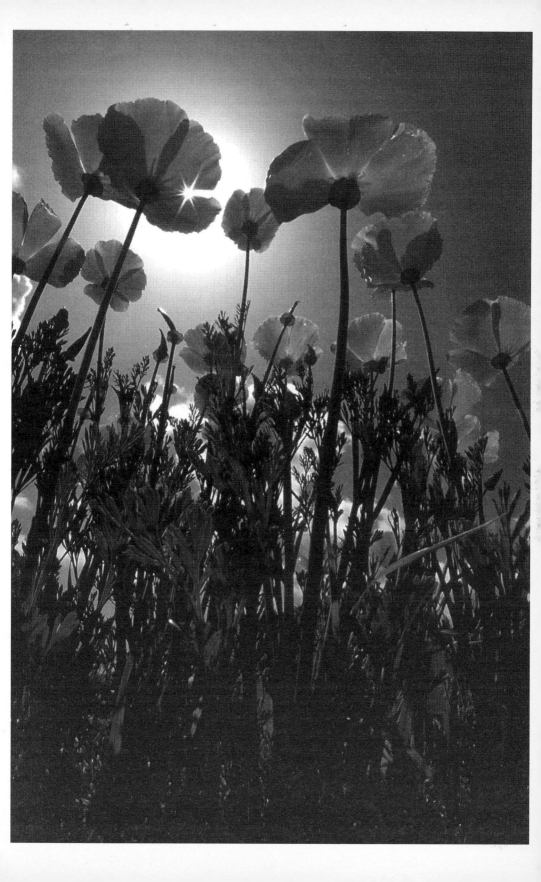

Index of
Blackadder's Finest Insults

Throughout his long and numerous lives, Blackadder found it hard to be nice about people, places and things. Here, for your delectation, is an alphabetical list of some of those things about which he felt most strongly. Feel free to use them at your will ...

acting:
I'd rather have my tongue beaten wafer-thin with a steak-tenderizer and then stapled to the floor with a croquet hoop. (385)

Baldrick:
God made man in his own image, and it would be a sad look out for Christians throughout the globe if God looked anything like you Baldrick. (131)

He looks like what he is, a dungball in a dress. (131)

Your services might be as useful as a barber's shop on the steps of the guillotine. (263–4)

Your brain's so minute, Baldrick, that if a hungry cannibal cracked your head open, there wouldn't be enough to cover a small water biscuit. (349)

Baldrick's acting:
Baldrick, in the Amazonian rain forests there are tribes of Indians as yet untouched by civilization who have developed more convincing Charlie Chaplin impressions than yours. (390)

You're the worst entertainer since St Paul the Evangelist toured Palestine with his trampoline act. (398)

The only decent impression he can do is of the man with no talent. (355)

Baldrick's kitchen:
O God! This place stinks like a pair of armoured trousers after the Hundred Years War. Baldrick, have you been eating dung again? (184)

Baldrick's plans:
I've a horrid suspicion that Baldrick's plan will be the stupidest thing we've heard since Lord Nelson's famous signal at the Battle of the Nile: 'England knows Lady Hamilton's a virgin, poke my eye out and cut off my arm if I'm wrong'. (263)

As cunning as a fox who's just been appointed Professor of Cunning at Oxford University. (452)

Bob:
You are a girl. And you're a girl with as much talent for disguise as a giraffe in dark glasses trying to get into a polar-bears-only golf club. (388)

Charlie Chaplin:
I find his films about as funny as getting an arrow through the neck and then discovering there's a gas bill tied to it. (384)

concert parties:
I'd rather spend an evening on top of a stepladder in No Man's Land smoking endless cigarettes through a luminous balaclava. (386)

the Flying Aces:
For 'magnificent men' read 'biggest show-offs since Lady Godiva entered the royal enclosure at Ascot claiming she had literally nothing to wear'. (403)

the French:
We hate the French! We fight wars against them! Did all those men die in vain on the field of Agincourt? Was the man who burnt

Joan of Arc simply wasting good matches? (275)

Lieutenant George:
I lost closer friends than 'darling Georgie' the last time I was deloused. (422)

Lieutenant George's acting:
You were the least convincing female impressionist since Tarzan went through Jane's handbag and ate her lipstick. (391)

Mrs Miggins:
Mrs M, if we were the last three humans on earth, I would be trying to start a family with Baldrick. (322)

the palace:
It's so dirty, it would be unacceptable to a dungbeetle that had lost interest in its career and really let itself go. (292)

Percy:
You are about as much use to me as a hole in the head, an affliction with which you must be familiar, never having had a brain. (61)

You would bore the leggings off a village idiot. (95)

You ride a horse rather less well than another horse would. (95)

Your brain would make a grain of sand look large and ungainly and the part of you that can't be mentioned I am reliably informed by women around the court wouldn't be worth mentioning even if it could be. (95)

You wouldn't know a joke if it got up and gave you a haircut. (95)

You look like a bird who's swallowed a plate. (138)

The eyes are open, the mouth moves, but Mr Brain has long since departed, hasn't he, Perce? (187)

Prime Minister Pitt:
He's about as effective as a cat flap in an elephant house. (237)

Prince George:
He's got a brain the size of a weasel's wedding tackle. (263)

A master with all the intellect of a jugged walrus and all the social graces of a potty. (324)

the Scarlet Pimpernel:
He's the most overrated human being since Judas Iscariot won the AD 31 Best Disciple Competition. (282)

Squadron Commander Flashheart:
Most of the infantry think you're a prat. Ask them who they'd prefer to meet – Squadron Commander Flashheart or the man who cleans the public toilets in Aberdeen and they'd go for Wee Jock Poo-Pong McPlop every time. (404)

the theatre:
A load of stupid actors, strutting around shouting, with their chests thrust out so far you'd think their nipples were attached to a pair of charging elephants. (292)

war:
A war hasn't been fought this badly since Olaf the Hairy, High Chief of all the Vikings, accidentally ordered 80,000 battle helmets with the horns on the inside. (388)

COMIC RELIEF

THE STORY SO FAR

In thirteen years of fundraising and grant-giving, Comic Relief has raised over £139 million. This has been used to help support some of the poorest and most disadvantaged people in the UK and Africa. Extraordinary things have happened in the name of Comic Relief.
Here are some of them ...

December 1985
Comic Relief is launched on Noel Edmonds' Late Late Breakfast Show with a live broadcast from a refugee camp in Sudan. The camp provides temporary shelter for many thousands of Ethiopian people escaping the dreadful impact of the 1984 famine, which gave rise to Band Aid and Sports Aid.

February 1986
'Livin' Doll' by Cliff Richard and the Young Ones is released. It spends four weeks at number one and raises over £250,000. This single demonstrates Comic Relief's commitment to having the maximum of fun while raising desperately needed cash.

March 1986
Comic Relief Live – three nights of comedy at the Shaftesbury Theatre that read like a 'Who's Who' of British comedy, from Ben Elton to Ronnie Corbett and from Rik Mayall to Billy Connolly. Frank Bruno teams up with Lenny Henry for a classic version of Romeo and Juliet, and one night the show doesn't end until 3.40 a.m. BBC1 showcases the event in a special edition of Omnibus.

December 1986
The Utterly, Utterly Merry Comic Relief Christmas Book featuring everyone from Adrian Mole to the Young Ones and from Terry Jones to Douglas Adams goes to number one and swells the Comic Relief coffers by more than £400,000.

February 1988
Comic Relief decides that, as many of its key supporters are leading TV personalities, now is the time to do big stuff on the box. The plan is to wrap this in lots of public fundraising – and Red Nose Day is born! The demand for Red Noses takes everybody by surprise, and the event raises an unprecedented £15 million. There's no going back now ...

March 1989
In an early attempt to test everyone's stamina and sanity, Comic Relief does 'back-to-back' Red Nose Days. This year sees the birth of the big red car nose, sales of which help the RND total on its way to a phenomenal £26.7 million.

March 1990
Follow your Nose is broadcast – four films on BBC1 that show how Red Nose money is being spent in the UK and Africa. The public gets the chance to see exactly what impact their cash can have in tackling poverty.

September 1990
Comic Relief's mission has always been to raise awareness as well as cash, so an education team is set up to reach out to UK schools. It starts its work with Video Relief – a national competition challenging young people to make their own videos about the work of Comic Relief, and Teacher Relief, an educational video pack for use with 8- to 13-year-olds in the classroom, making use of some of the best documentary footage screened on Red Nose Days 1 and 2.

March 1991
Red Nose Day 3 is called 'The Stonker'! This time around the nose has funny hands, Tom Jones defeats Theophilus P. Wildebeest in 'The Battle of the Sex Gods', Hale and Pace take 'The Stonk' to the top of the charts and a policeman sponsored to dress up as a burglar arrests someone breaking into a house. The madness continues ... to the tune of £21 million.

March 1992
Trying to get to the roots of why the work of Comic Relief is needed, Behind the Nose is broadcast. It's a two-hour show which includes 'The Totally and Utterly Sponditious Stab at Explaining Why So Many People in Africa Are So Damn Poor', and a look at the great work being done with Red Nose money in the UK. Reporting back to the public is a central part of Comic Relief's philosophy.

March 1993
Red Nose Day 4 goes by the catchy title of 'The Invasion Of The Comic Tomatoes'. The colour-changing T-shirt is a smash hit and the night of TV is as fantastic as ever, featuring Mr Bean on Blind Date and Victor Meldrew in the bath with only a rubber duck for company. The day raises over £18 million.

May 1994
Raiders of the Lost Nose is broadcast – a retrospective look at Comic Relief's fundraising achievements, including the best moments from RND 4. At the end of the show, Tony Robinson makes an appeal on behalf of the Disaster Emergency Committee for Rwanda, raising £200,000.

May 1994
In an effort to get the message across about inclusive education, Altogether Better is published – a video and booklet for teachers and governors promoting the idea of educating disabled children in mainstream schools.

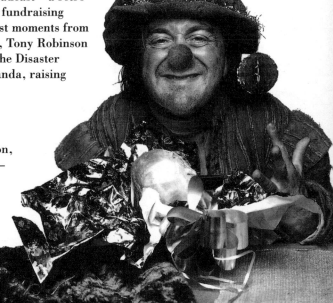

Comic Relief's Disability Grant-Making Programme has benefited from the support of the disability movement – this kind of collaboration is important and helps get their voices heard.

March 1995
Red Nose Day 1995 coincides with St Patrick's Day, so part of the evening is broadcast live from Northern Ireland. Comic Relief's on top of the charts again with the haunting 'Love Can Build A Bridge', performed by Cher, Neneh Cherry and Chrissie Hynde with Eric Clapton on guitar: 310,000 people buy the single, helping the fifth Red Nose Day to a grand total of £22 million.

August 1995
Victoria Wood's Dirty Weekend is broadcast on BBC1 – a half-hour documentary of Victoria's stay with the Masara family in Zimbabwe, where she sees how Comic Relief money is making a real difference.

March 1996
Comic Relief celebrates its tenth birthday. The celebrations include a one-hour Omnibus programme on BBC1 which charts much the same course as this potted history, and The Nose at 10 – six half-hour programmes comprising the best of Red Nose comedy.

March 1997
Red Nose Day '97 adopts the mantra 'Small Change – Big Difference'. This time the Red Nose Day action is on-line as well as on TV – the Red Web receives 4 million hits in just four weeks. The Spice Girls donate all the royalties from the massive-selling single 'Who Do You Think You Are?', team up with Comic Relief's 'Sugar Lumps' for the video, and perform live on the Night of TV. The nose goes furry and the public goes mad for it. Delia Smith's special Red Nose Collection raises over £1 million as chocolate mini-muffin mania sweeps the land. It all adds up to an amazing £27 million – the biggest total so far.

Christmas 1997
A second internet experience is had via Rudolph's Red Nose Website. Comic Relief is on the World Wide Web to stay.

Christmas 1998
Blackadder: The Whole Damn Dynasty is published – you buy it, give yourself a pat on the back, then read these pages and, with any luck, start making plans for Red Nose Day 1999: 12 March. The twenty-first century awaits Comic Relief's next cunning plan ... and cunning it will be.

Comic Relief
74 New Oxford Street
London
WC1A 1EF

Telephone: 0171-436 1122   Fax: 0171-436 1541   e-mail: red@comicrelief.org.uk
Registered Charity No. 326568